STUDIES

IN

THE LITERARY RELATIONS

OF

ENGLAND AND GERMANY

IN THE SIXTEENTH CENTURY

STUDIES

IN

THE LITERARY RELATIONS

OF

ENGLAND AND GERMANY

IN THE SIXTEENTH CENTURY

CHARLES E. HERFORD

Routledge
Taylor & Francis Group

LONDON AND NEW YORK

First published by Frank Cass & Co. Ltd.

First Edition   1886
New Impression   1966

Published 2005 by Routledge
2 Park Square, Milton Park, Abingdon, Oxfordshire OX14 4RN
711 Third Avenue, New York, NY 10017

First issued in paperback 2016

Routledge is an imprint of the Taylor and Francis Group, an informa business

ISBN 13: 978-1-138-98328-1 (pbk)
ISBN 13: 978-0-7146-2062-6 (hbk)

PREFACE.

THE researches embodied in the present volume were prosecuted during my tenure of one of the Berkeley fellowships of the Owens College; and I have, at the outset, to express my acknowledgments to the Council, not merely for thus enabling me to follow out a long-formed scheme of investigation, but for the extreme indulgence which I have enjoyed during its protracted execution.

An unusually explicit statement of literary obligations is one of the few ways in which those who venture to write books on unfamiliar subjects can acknowledge their indebtedness to those who read them. I should otherwise shrink from the egoism of saying that the present volume owes its original stimulus to a few lectures upon the German literature of the sixteenth century, by three masters in it, Professors Erich Schmidt, Geiger and Scherer, to which I had the privilege

of listening (in the last case as a casual visitor)
at Vienna and Berlin, in the summers of 1881
and 1882. I do not think that much of the
book in its present shape is directly due to them,
even where it deals most immediately with German
literature; but I owe to their luminous and vivid
exposition the sense for the peculiar power of
this remarkable literature, without which I should
hardly have attempted to trace its reflexions in our
own. Among other aids to the study of the German
branch of the subject I need scarcely refer to the
classical editions of particular books by Zarncke,
Adelbert v. Keller, Lappenberg, Hoffmann v. Fallersleben, Oesterley, Schade, the brilliant incidental
work done by Scherer and Erich Schmidt on the
Latin drama and the novel in scattered articles and
lectures, still less to the invaluable *Grundriss* of
Goedeke, nowhere so invaluable as for exactly this
period. In working out the English side, I owe
most to a somewhat old-fashioned school of anti-
quarians,—Thoms, Wright and Kemble, to various
publications of the Percy, Shakspeare, and New
Shakspere Societies, to the editorial work of Dyce,
Ward, Wagner, Oesterley, and, finally, to the two
admirable essays of Prof. K. Elze,—one of them
contained in the introduction to his edition of the
Alphonsus,—which, excepting perhaps the melancholy abortions of the late William Bell, are the
only previous attempts with which I am acquainted to carry out a design somewhat resembling that of the present volume. It remains to
refer to more personal obligations. I have to thank

the librarians of the Bodleian, of Queen's College, Oxford, and of the Royal Library at Berlin, for exceptional kindness in sending particulars of books in their possession; Mr F. Seebohm for making inquiries about Ralph Radcliff at Hitchin; and Prof. Ward, Dr H. Hager, Dr Furnivall, Dr J. Bolte of Berlin, and Mr A. H. Bullen for incidental help always willingly given. For more ordinary good offices I am indebted to the librarians of Lambeth, the Cambridge Public Library, the Free, Chetham and Owens College libraries in Manchester, and above all to the late and present superintendents of the Reading-room of the British Museum. Superfluous as it may seem, I cannot refrain from expressing the immensity of my debt to the last-named library, some idea of which will be conveyed by my notes. Not only has almost the entire work of research been done there, but a great part of it could have been done nowhere else. There alone, whether in Germany or in England, was it possible to draw upon a collection in which the original literatures of both countries were richly represented, where above all there was an unrivalled store of the German satires and pasquils of the Reformation. I have accordingly been enabled to attempt throughout a fairly high degree of minuteness in the matter of references. The infinite opportunities of error which this method brings with it I cannot indeed possibly hope to have escaped; and I am painfully conscious of needing in this respect as in others an indulgence which I have neither the right to ask, nor the critic, perhaps, to give. It may at least, however, be taken, where the contrary is not implied, that every book here referred to I have seen, and that every judgment passed is founded upon first-hand knowledge.

I have reserved to the close a special obligation. I have to thank Professor Ward both for the loan of books (for which I am also indebted to my friends Dr H. Hager, and Mr J. Finlayson) and for the great kindness with which, in the midst of multifarious work, he undertook to revise my proof-sheets. Almost all of them owe something to having passed under the eye of undoubtedly the most competent of living English scholars in the double field which I have attempted to traverse. It is now a considerable number of years since I derived from Prof. Ward the first impulse to literary study; I rejoice at the circumstances which have permitted me thus to resume under a new guise somewhat of the old forms, and to renew some of the old privileges, of studentship.

A book like the present is necessarily addressed mainly to two classes of literary specialists, not precisely identical in character. I have in general avoided dealing at length with matters thoroughly familiar to English as well as to German scholarship. In certain parts of the subject however it was necessary to be either obscure to the one or redundant to the other; and here my German critics will hardly blame me for having, in an English book, considered chiefly the English reader. The introductions, particularly, to the various chapters, and other portions dealing with German literature, though founded throughout on original study, pretend to no originality of result; but I am not without hope that they may be acceptable to the English student of a too much neglected epoch.

Portions of Chapter I. have already appeared in the *Academy*, of Chapter III. in the *Englische Studien*, and of Chapter VI. in the *Cornhill Magazine*. I have to thank Messrs Smith and Elder in the last case for permission to reprint.

LONDON, *April*, 1886.

CONTENTS.

CHAPTER III.

The Latin Drama (70—164).

PART II.

CHAPTER IV.

THE FAUSTUS CYCLE (165—241).

CHAPTER V.

THE ULENSPIEGEL CYCLE (242—322).

CHAPTER VI.

THE SHIP OF FOOLS (323—378).

CHAPTER VII.

GROBIANUS AND GROBIANISM (379—398).

INTRODUCTION.

THE present volume is an attempt to lessen the obscurity
of that tract of international literature in which Barclay's
Ship of Fools, Marlowe's *Faustus*, and Decker's *Gul's
Horn-booke* are luminous but isolated points. To these
isolated points I have endeavoured to supply in some
degree both the intervening detail and the continuous
background; in other words, to give a connected and
intelligible account of the phases of German literary
influence upon England in the sixteenth century. I
venture to emphasise the epithet in the last clause. It
is exclusively a *literary* influence with which I propose
to deal. With the transmission of doctrines or ideas, I
am concerned only so far as they coloured or inspired
literature imaginative or poetic in form. Protestantism,
the most colossal of all witnesses to 'German influence,'
is of interest here only as it took shape in hymns,
dialogues and dramas. Luther is, for us, solely the
author of *Ein feste Burg*, Melanchthon, the deviser of
the legend of Eve and her unlike children, immortalised
in drama by Birck and Sachs.

Whether, in this strict sense, Germany, in the sixteenth century, exercised any 'literary' influence at all,
is no doubt a 'question to be asked.' To all appearance,
no European people was less qualified for the work. To

the most strongly-marked literary tendency of the time it gave almost no response. Everywhere else the demand for elegance and harmony of literary form was being raised with continually greater insistence and authority; in Germany, outside the sphere of Humanists, it was a cry in the wilderness, which the most approved literary orthodoxy ignored with impunity. The old court-poetry of Thüringen and the Upper Rhine was as completely forgotten as that of Provence, and had left scarcely more palpable traces behind; nor did sixteenth-century Germany, like France and Spain, and even England, resume the broken continuity at a new point by the aid of Petrarch. No school of Italianate versifiers endangered the popularity of the *Narrenschiff*, or ruffled the industrious equanimity of Hans Sachs. To a degree unparalleled elsewhere in Europe, literature had become plebeian. The complete decay of the courts as centres of literary culture,—a decay against which only here and there a Mathilde of Würtemberg raised a forlorn protest,—had thrown literature into the hands of a bourgeois class not only itself lacking in the old courtly graciousness and refinement, but indisposed by a century of life and death feuds with the leagued nobility to revive its memory; and the antagonism was heightened by internal revolutions, which, with rare exceptions (as at Nürnberg), put every town in the hands of its least cultivated class. It was a literature of the workshop and the stall, a literature of men habitually familiar to brutality, plain-spoken to grossness, drastic in their ridicule, ferocious in their earnestness, not without sterling honesty, but wanting in the grace of good manners, in chivalry, in subtle and delicate intellect.

The repelling rudeness and roughness of this literature was, nevertheless, closely bound up with its distinctive power. The decay of the courts and of the courtly poetry was only the most palpable symptom of one of those epochs of general social disintegration in which few poets but many satirists are born. Never had the disruption of German society been more profound or appeared more helpless than in the closing decades of the fifteenth century. Moral debasement had proceeded step by step with political disruption ; the empire broken up by internal dissension, directly threatened by the Turk without, saw its former dependencies consolidating themselves in the shelter it provided ; the corruption of the Roman clergy, which Germany shared with the rest of Christendom, was there aggravated by the impotence of the secular government, and by the grossness of the laity. State and Church, noble and citizen, absorbed in private indulgence or in mutual feuds, appeared equally incapable of providing a medicine for the common malady. Of such a society satire was the natural speech. Its inexhaustible antagonisms were reflected in a literature of equally inexhaustible raillery and abuse. The fertile field of class antipathies and local jealousies produced a rich harvest of malicious jests. The sly peasant, the licentious priest and monk, the gluttonous Saxon, the naïve Swabian, were standing butts of ridicule. The vanities and perversities of women were laid bare with remorseless zest by the unruly subjects of the 'last knight of chivalry'; and the Carnival playwrights of Nürnberg founded whole plays on ridicule of the 'Fools of Love.' Often such special attacks were only the casual discharges of a general satiric animus, or a pessimism too profound to discriminate its objects. The triumph of lawless unreason, the frail tenure of all the ideal bonds of society, drove every quick and sensitive mind to find relief in derision and despair; and the most characteristic as well as most famous poem of the age was that in which Sebastian Brandt, resuming with a sterner bias the mediaeval 'satire upon all classes,' summoned the greater part of his contemporaries to the *Ship of Fools*.

With the first quarter of the sixteenth century this ground-tone of satire, the last bequest of mediaevalism, far from dying away, only grew more fierce and dominant under the influence of the double revolution which for northern Europe inaugurated the modern world. Neither Humanist nor Protestant dealt much in the hollow sarcasms of despair; but their positive enthusiasm, rich and buoyant as it was, habitually took a polemical form; their larger command of the resources of beauty and knowledge was employed chiefly in giving brilliance and keenness to their weapons. Precisely here, however, lay the advance. The savage scorn of fifteenth century satire rang still incessantly from the pages of Hutten and of Luther; but it had gained enormously in imaginative range, in moral depth, in tragic intensity. Its conventional scenery, its recurring stock-types were enriched by a Titanic fancy, caught from Lucian and Aristophanes, which played familiarly with gods and heroes, and ranged with easy step from heaven to hell; the vivid mythology of the Greek Hades and the mediaeval paradise, Pluto on his throne, St Peter at the gate, were called in to the aid of sublunary polemics. The political foe appears as an emissary of the lower world, or as its favoured *protégé;* infernal councils discuss his prospects and send him reinforcements and encouragement; or he is dragged after death before a higher tribunal, which listens with a deaf ear to his *apologia*, and exultingly dismisses him to endless tortures.

Applied theology of this sort was evidently capable

of much grim humour, of a kind likely to be made the most of by a generation of pamphleteers ; but to the more mystic side of the Protestant genius it also represented sober and terrible truth. The 'old savage enemy' had been transformed by Luther from a half-ludicrous legend to a threatening and imminent peril. The colossal institution of the Roman Church was become a palpable result of infernal councils, an all but triumphant effort of Pluto to rule the world. To the little band of reformers their own struggle was only a particular moment, near the close, of a sublime encounter of heaven and hell, the changing phases of which made up the greater part of what they understood by history. It was the most heroic and the most inspired moment of the new religion. For a few years the Protestant faith, on the whole so unkind a nurse to poetry, passed through one of those rare crises of exalted imagination which twice or thrice repeated have given it a fair title to figure in the history of *belles-lettres.* The age of Luther produced nothing artistically comparable to D'Aubigné, still less to Milton ; but its work, rude and rough as it was, was both in its kind unique and for its purpose extraordinarily effective. Luther's Spiritual Songs, with their trenchant simplicity, their bursts of fiery and heroic energy, their human and manly tenderness, were something more than adaptations of the hymn of the Catholic Church to a differing ritual and doctrine. And the mingled scorn and fervour of the Protestant genius never found more energetic expression than when Manuel drew the death-bed of the Sick Mass thronged with helpless counsellors and idle prescribers, or when Kirchmayer sketched in vague and colossal dramatic outline the league of pope and devil, capturing the church of Christ by an irresistible *coup d'état*, or aiding the most implacable enemy of the Reformation in his desperate struggle with his people.

In England the literary position of Protestantism was notoriously very different. As a political movement it produced convulsions hardly less violent and far-reaching than in Germany; as an intellectual movement it was from the first respectable if not eminent; but as a literary movement it was, from the first, insignificant. Its memorable names are those of statesmen, divines, martyrs, rather than of great writers; Tyndale and Coverdale, Cranmer and Latimer, Bale and Foxe, luminaries in the annals of Protestantism, are phantoms in the history of literature;—learned expounders, or heroic defenders, of a faith which they neither originated nor by any striking originality of thought or expression made their own. No one rivalled Luther's felicity in grafting abstract doctrine upon the native mother-wit of fable and proverb. No one uttered the wrath and ardour of English Protestantism in ringing verse like his. The fierce irony of Hutten, the sly laughter of Manuel, the sombre imagination of Kirch-mayer, were feebly reflected in the polemics of a revo-lution which of all others bears the deepest stamp of English character, the faintest and most fugitive of English genius.

It would have been strange nevertheless if a struggle admittedly inspired by Germany had been carried to the close without an effort to adopt her finer weapons. A series of such efforts was in fact made, which, partly from the incompetence of their authors, partly from the vicissitudes of Henry's theological taste, fell into an ob-scurity which to this day has only here and there been dissipated. The literary war of the Swiss and Alsatians with the 'sick' and 'dying' Mass, of which Manuel's dialogue was the most brilliant effort, was faintly continued by the two English refugees in Strassburg who devoted a well-known tract to the inquiry where it should be buried. It was first proscribed by the king, and then recanted by its converted author. A few years later Miles Coverdale essayed with his ungifted pen to translate the spiritual songs of Luther. Another royal proscription thrust his volume into an obscurity which permitted Sternhold and Hopkins to rule undisturbed over the infancy of the English Hymn. The trying last decade of Henry's reign saw the great papal drama of Kirchmayer acted at Christ's, translated and imitated by Bale; but the actors and the college incurred the formidable wrath of Gardiner, the translation has never been heard of, and the imitation—which I venture to detect in the *Kyng Johan*—was unknown but the other day. In lyric, in dialogue, in drama, the imaginative language which the genius of German Protestantism had shaped out for itself was caught up with fitful and momentary energy, and then as rapidly forgotten.

Thus Germany contributed merely a set of parentheses to the literature of the Reformation, itself a parenthesis in the national literature of England. It was in the wide region outside, of popular jest, of satire often serious, often steeped in theological ideas, but not primarily inspired by the war of Churches, that her work left more enduring traces. The *Ship of Fools*, translated in the first years of the century, helped essentially to accelerate the development of English satire; Rush and Ulenspiegel, translated at one of the keenest crises of the Reformation, became standing figures in English jest and legend. And the two generations which followed developed new points of contact which proved the most fruitful of all. The political triumph of Protestantism was no sooner assured than the literary tide began to ebb away with a

sustained and gathering force to which a far more brilliant
and vigorous literature must have succumbed. Court
and University sowed the seeds of a new Humanism still
less in sympathy than the old with the religion of Luther
which most of its disciples ostentatiously professed. The
work of a professional literary class, trained on Petrarch
and Ovid, Seneca and Boccaccio, Cinthio and Guevara,
cheapened the pious testimonies of citizen and divine
against the Roman Antichrist. A vigorous and brilliant
culture of literary form placed the most formidable ob-
stacle in the way of a return to the Egypt of Bale and
Coverdale. The monotonous ferocity, the vague and
tremulous drawing, of Protestant satire, gave way to a
quick and observant humour and a style touched with
the vividness and pungency of an etching. The Morality
was swept away before a drama which consciously strove
to hold up the mirror to nature, and not to a symbolic
substitute for it in the didactic mind.

The result of all these steps was, on a first glance,
completely to alienate literary England from literary
Germany. If she had imitated feebly and abortively,
while her course lay parallel, all imitation was now apparently put out of the question by her changed aims in
art. Nevertheless, it was precisely in this epoch of brilliant progress in the one country, of slow decay relieved
by uncertain symptoms of a yet remote recovery in the
other, that their literary intercourse bore the richest fruit
to the richer, as it notoriously did to the poorer of the
two. In literary form Germany could now less than ever
teach her rival; but the raw material of satire and tragedy
thrown out in three generations of revolution had capacities yet unexhausted, of which the Elizabethan genius,
though approaching by a quite different route, was qualified to make the most. The gross and drastic realism,

the bold and familiar play with the supernatural, the Grobianism and Titanism, in which Germany of the sixteenth century had uttered her cry of mock exultation or of tragic exasperation at her evil state, fell in with the literary fashions of the most brilliant and sanguine age of English history, and offered acceptable pabulum to a school of satire steadily developing a genius for close observation, and a school of tragedy persistently striving after thrilling effects. The indignant irony, the feverish fancy of the social reformer were taken at their æsthetic valuation. The energetic phrases in which character had uttered its protest against evil, found echo and applause where energetic phrases were keenly relished for their own sake. Dedekind's ironical exposure of the gross manners of his countrymen was reproduced in the *Gul's Horn-booke;* the *Ship of Fools,* reprinted after an interval of sixty years, was still an unexhausted model of satire. And a new source of dramatic effect, destined to create a prolonged attraction on the English stage, was discovered in the dealings of some specially audacious or specially favoured hero with supernatural Powers: Faustus, by his pact with the devil, Fortunatus by the gift of Fortune, careering with privileged security through a romantically uncritical world; or a whole convent of ascetics seduced into gluttonous riot by the dissimulated devilry of Friar Rush. Possibly we ought to add the Shaksperean Prospero, but the German origin of the *Tempest* is still at most a plausible guess. In this region of half-grandiose, half-humorous supernaturalism lay, beyond a doubt, the most important direction of German influence, as of German achievement, both in mass and in result. It was the line of cleavage at which the otherwise difficult barrier of national unlikeness yielded ready passage. Marlowe's *Faustus* was not only a play of immense popularity ; it was not only, as I hope to render probable, the starting-point of a series of related dramas, the *Fortunatus* among them, all more or less evidently coloured by its influence. It introduced a new class of situations into English drama, by substituting, as a tragic motive, for the ferocious murders and ill-omened love-intrigues of the Italian novel, for the family feuds and incests of Seneca, and the military casualties of the English chronicle, the exciting suspense of a diabolic pact.

To sum up in a single trait. If the extraordinarily gifted, yet relatively barbarous, Germany of the sixteenth century was, in pure literature, of any moment for its neighbours, it was chiefly in so far as it made literary capital of its barbarism. Its moods of ideal aspiration, its laborious efforts to honour virtue and nobility, its pictures of pure women and heroic patriots, counted for little. The endless Susannas and Josephs of its stage remained as unknown as Fischart's brilliant celebration of the peaceful league of Switzerland and Alsace, or Hans Sachs' quaint retelling of the most famous stories of all literature, or the unpretending beauties of the popular song. Even the Humanists of Germany, proficients though they were in the graces of Humanist style, commonly arrived at European fame, if at all, by some other channel. Had Horace, like Frischlin's Cicero, revisited the upper world, northern Europe could have shown him no Latin lyrics so graceful and sparkling as those of Celtes and Hessus ; but Celtes and Hessus remained provincial stars when Markolf and Ulenspiegel and the *Ship of Fools* had the ear of Europe ; and all the fascinating brilliancy of Hutten did not save him from being celebrated abroad chiefly as the advocate of an unedifying drug. It was not in her casual and fitful wooing of beauty that Germany caught the attention of the world, but when she grappled with ugliness, plunging breast-high in the slough and de-risively impaling its creeping population of foul things. Clowns and fools, rogues and necromancers, were, so far as most Englishmen knew, the staple literary product of the German people. They heard only the harsher and fiercer notes of its voice; in *Grobianus*, its ironical scoff at brutal manners; in the *Ship of Fools*, its harsh rebuke of presumption and of brutality in the name of sober self-concern and civil decorum; in Ulenspiegel, its robust effort to capitalise the humour of every conceivable offence against decency; in *Faustus*, its cry of blended horror and exultation at the boundless aspirations of emancipated intellect.

I need hardly add a word upon the plan of the present volume. The two parts are devoted to the two wholly distinct regions of literary intercourse which I have in-dicated. The first three chapters attempt to follow out in detail the brief and, on the whole, abortive literary influence of German Protestant art, in its several branches,—the hymn, the dialogue, the drama. The second part deals with the more fruitful influence of secular literature,—roughly grouped under four heads,—which for the purpose of international intercourse are fairly adequate,—the literature of sorcerers, of jesters, of 'fools' and of Grobians.

ADDENDA ET CORRIGENDA.

p. 3, n. *for* Oegier *read* Oeglin.

p. 8, l. 11. for *Goostly Psalmes and Spiritual songs* read *Goostly Songs and Spiritual Psalmes.*

p. 9, l. 14. *for* Masculus *read* Musculus.

p. 9, l. 15. *for* Hubert *read* Huber.

p. 17, l. 16. *for* Kolrose *read* Kolross.

p. 32. (English polemical dialogues). A reference should here have been added to the grammarian Lily's *Anti-borricon* against Whittington.

p. 44, n. *for* Enser *read* Emser.

p. 63, n. *for* Shraxton *read* Shaxton.

p. 88, l. 2. *For* it belongs quite to the type of the.. *Acolastus.* *read* it was drawn not less than the...*Acolastus.*

p. 93, *marg. Dele* 1.

p. 95, l. 7. *for* ille *read* illi.

p. 97, l. 2. *for* Birch *read* Birck.

p. 97, l. 25. *for* Caleminus *read* Calaminus.

p. 113 n. Radcliff's work, like the Oxford play, was doubtless based on A. Guarna's *Grammaticale Bellum, Nominis et Verbi Regum de principalitate orationis inter se contendentium* (Argent. et Lips. 1512). It was translated into English 1569, (2nd edition 1576).

p. 167 n. *for* yon...yon *read* you...you.

ib. for Becarus *read* Becanus.

p. 173. ('News-sheets from Germany'). This paragraph is well illustrated by a passage in Earle's description of the 'pot-poet': 'His frequentest works go out in single sheets, and are chanted from market to market to a vile tune and a worse throat; whilst the poor country-wench melts like her own butter to hear them. And these are the stories of some men of Tyburn, or *a strange monster out of Germany.*'

p. 179 n. I am glad to learn that the latter part of this note is no longer in point, a new edition of Prof. Ward's *Faustus and Friar Bacon* being in the press.

p. 243. (Bebel and Pauli). A reference should here be introduced to Ottomar Luscinius' *Joci et Sales*, 1524.

p. 264 n. 2. *for* 1574 *read* 1474.

PART I.

CHAPTER I.

LYRICS.

IN introducing the first printed edition of Wyatt and Surrey to his readers, the publisher, Tottell, thought it necessary to dwell with some emphasis on the strange fashion of the new poetry. ' If perhappes some mislike the statelinesse of stile removed from the rude skill of common eares,......I exhort the unlearned, by reading to learne to be more skilfull, and to purge that swine-like grossenesse that maketh the swete maierome not to smell to their delight[1].' And in a great degree the implied judgment was true. If Wyatt and Surrey did not found the English lyric, as popular criticism is apt to assume, they undeniably gave it a new development very sharply distinguished from the old.

German and English lyric literature. c. 1535.

No such definite turning-point can be found in the course of the contemporary lyric literature of Germany. The tide was no doubt setting gradually in the same direction; and the growing cultivation of music at the courts told entirely in favour of a more refined and artificial lyric style. But courtly Humanists like Surrey, or Ronsard, did not yet write in German ; Conrad Celtis,

---

[1] Tottell's *Miscellany*, ed. Arber.

perhaps the nearest parallel to Surrey among the German
Humanists, was only the first of Latin poets, and Ronsard
had nearly a century to wait for the doubtful honour of
inspiring Opitz[1].

The superiority of England is less clear when we
compare the unreformed songs from which Tottell strove
to wean his readers, with the abundant stores of contemporary Germany. It is true that Tottell was far
too contemptuous; in his zeal to commend the dainty
refinement of the new songs, he was a little blind to
the genuinely lyrical quality of many of the old. There
are quite enough vivacious carols[2], tender and graceful
love-songs[3], spiritual-songs[4], lays of summer and spring[5],
to vindicate the often nameless poets of the 15th and
early 16th century from the charge of complete barbarism.
But such a charge would be still more out of the question
as applied to the lyrics currently familiar among Tottell's
contemporaries in Germany. It may even be said that
if there was one branch of literature in which, in the
first quarter of the century, England might distinctly
have learnt from Germany, it was that of the popular
lyrics,—those *Volkslieder* which are, after all, among the
chief glories of German poetry. In range of subject,
in variety of emotion, in beauty and vigour of line, in

---

[1] Cf. his *Buch der deutschen Poeterey.*

[2] Cf. Wright, *Songs and Carols of the 15th century.* Ritson,
Ancient Songs and Ballads: e.g. No. 6 (Syr Christenmasse).

[3] E.g. 'My hart, my mynde and my hole powre,' with music by
Taverner, in the unique 'Boke' of 1530 (Br. Mus.), which deserves
to be reprinted entire. Some quotations are made by Ritson, u.s.
and Chappell *Music of the O. T.*

[4] E.g. the beautiful 'In youth and age in welth and woo
Auxilium meum in domino,'—in the above *Boke.* Cf. also Wright,
Songs and Carols of the 15th century.

[5] E.g. 'Pleasure yt ys To here I wys' in the *Boke.*

sure, instinctive acquaintance with the inexhaustible wells
of lyric inspiration, very little that existed in England
at the same time can compare with the treasure of songs
first collected on a large scale by Georg Forster[1]. They
are the result of natural lyric faculty working in the
presence of a very rich literary tradition, now wholly
independent of it, now involuntarily catching its likeness.
They are unsurpassed in that artless utterance of simple
feelings which goes so far towards lyric pathos,—the
mere 'Ach Got wie weh thut scheiden!' or brief snatches
of verse such as this, which, for simple intensity, could
not easily be paralleled in the English lyrics of the time,

> Ach Elslein, lieber bule,
> wie gern wär ich bei dir;
> so fliessen zwei tiefe wasser
> wol zwischen mir und dir[2].

But this natural lyric style is enriched at a number
of points by traits caught from that *Minne*-cult which in
England was at most an exotic and short-lived growth.
The writers of these lyrics were certainly not a race of
laborious epigoni like the Meistersänger, but something of
the quality of the extinct *Minnelied* reappears in not a
little of their verse, its union of refined artifice of form
with artless unreserve of expression, its singing and
lilting lines, its unsought distinction of manner, its gracious
and noble passion. They continually recal the beautiful

---

[1] Ein auszug guter alter un newer Teutscher liedlein...Nürn-
berg, 1539. The first extant printed collection is Oegier's, 1512
(Goedeke § 110). I have used Uhland's great collection (*Die
deutschen Volkslieder*) and Tittmann's excellent *Liederbuch des 16ten
J.* The well-known *Des Knaben Wunderhorn* of Arnim and
Brentano is of course more comprehensive than the latter, but
useless for critical study.

[2] Forster's *Samlung*, 1540, pt. II., Tittmann *Ldbch* I. 84.

but half conventional symbolism of the *Minnelied*, by
which the red rose, the nightingale, the daisy, the falling
leaf served to interpret the play of love.   Classic situations
of the *Minnelied*—such as that of the *Tageweise* or *Aubade*
the parting song of lovers at dawn, upon the *wächter's*
cry,—are transferred from the feudal society to which
they naturally belong into close company with peasant
courtships by the spring or the *Fensterle* still familiar in
Tyrol.

Meisterge-sang, 'His-torisches Lied.' And, apart from such suggestions of a past which
in England had scarcely existed, the lyric of the 15th
and 16th centuries underwent peculiar developments of
its own.   Nothing in English society quite resembled
two institutions which first took definite shape in the age
of Maximilian I., and each of which set its stamp upon
the national lyric.   The poetic gilds, of which the Meistersänger were the highest rank, carried it into a scholastic
region in which all sense of the true value of form was lost
in excessive elaboration of it, and the elaborate metrical
machinery of the canzone applied unconcernedly to the
homeliest bit of *genre*[1].   On the other hand, no small
number of the 'historic songs' of Germany proceeded
from the very different school of the *Landsknechte*[2].
Wholly careless of niceties of style, often barely satisfying
the simplest laws of verse, writing hastily in the intervals
of action[3], their strength lay in literal narrative, in the

---

[1] E.g. *Von einem Freiheit und von Cunz Zwergen* (Leipzig 1521),
and *Von einem Schneider und Schuhmacher* (o. O. u. J.) (repr.
Tittmann, *Liederbuch*, pp. 363, 374);—the one relates a grotesque
village incident, the other a neighbours' quarrel, in stanzas of fourteen lines.

[2] The *Historische Lieder* are collected in the great work of
Liliencron.

[3] Cf. e.g. the French account of the siege of Metz, where the
author, a lansquenet who had taken part in it, describes himself as

eloquence of bare facts. Instead of the business-like
assiduity of the *Meister*, their cultivation of poetry was
a casual and perfunctory service, of which the reward was
a style rugged and graceless enough, but natural, and
with all its dryness, not incapable of a certain stern
pathos.

The germs of the Meistersänger school no doubt
existed in the annual performances of Mysteries by the
English Gilds, and perhaps nothing in Middle English
literature is so like the normal *Meistergesang* as the occasional strophic passages in the Towneley plays. But the
germ did not develope; the culture of poetry never
passed, among the English craftsmen, from an extraordinary and ceremonial effort into a systematic occupation. The analogy of the English political ballads to
those of Germany is no doubt closer. But, apart from
the vastly greater mass of the latter, the fundamental
social differences of the two countries are in themselves
a ground of contrast. The enormous complexity of
German politics, the divisions of states, the open feuds
of city, noble, peasant, knight, the predominance in war
of personal loyalty and class-feeling over patriotism, make
German historic song a genus apart, with an atmosphere,
scenery, and motives almost wholly strange to that of
England.

And, finally, with still less of precise analogy to any *Geistliches*
literary growth yet known in England, was the Spiritual *Lied.*
Song, as renewed and recreated by Luther, which must
be discussed more at large.

Reserving for a moment the class last mentioned, *German*
scarcely a stray ballad or two, out of this immense harvest *lyrics in*
of songs, can be shown to have crossed the sea. Douce *England.*

writing beside the town fountain, over a dish of bacon. (Leroux de
Lincy, *Chants historiques*, II.).

was inclined to connect the famous *Nut-brown Maid*
with the equally famous 'ich stund an einem morgen an'
translated by Bebel in his *Facetiae* (' *Vulgaris cantio*');
the resemblance is however as he says only general, and
appears to me quite inconclusive. The 'ich stund' is
an ordinary lovers' parting in dialogue, differing from the
ordinary *Aubade* chiefly in the 'fräulein's' eagerness to fly
with her 'knabe': the essence of the *Nut-brown Maid* is
that the parting is only feigned. A more certain, though
less important, instance has I believe never been noticed.
The Stationers' Register, under 14 Sep. 1593, gives the
mutilated titles of two German 'bookes,' in the following
form :

[1.]   John Wolf. Entred for his Copie under thandes
of Master Harwell and Master Woodcoke a booke intituled
Warer erhaltenen underlang ten victori, so undter der furst,
&c.[1]

[2.]   Thos. Creede.   Entred for his Copie under
thandes of Master Harwell and Master Woodcoke a
descripcon intituled *Marhastige gluckliche Reittung aufs
Crabaten, von Dem Sigder Christen,* &c.[2]

In the margin of (2), where the name of 'John Wolf'
has been crossed out, is a note stating that 'this ballad
of the overthrowe of the Turke' is turned over to Creede,
with Wolf's consent.

We have then clearly the trace of a German ballad,
itself apparently not known[3].

About its subject however there is no doubt. In
September 1593 'the overthrowe of the Turks' could only
refer to the great rout before Siseg the same summer. It

[1] I.e., probably ' Warer [Bericht einer] erhaltenen und erlangten
victorie, so unter dem furst ' &c.
[2] Warhaftige [? Beschreibung einer glücklichen] &c.
[3] It is not to be found in Liliencron.

was still fresh in memory when Knolles wrote, and he has described it at length[1]. Hassan the 'Bassa of Bosna' came with an army of 20,000 men to attack the convent of Siseg in Croatia which was at the same time a fortress. Auersberg, governor of Carolstadt, collected forces from Carinthia, Croatia and Silesia, marched upon Siseg, and, after a momentary check, succeeded in putting the Turks to flight, with a computed loss of 18,000 of their number, as well as rich treasure and arms.

I turn to consider more specially the Spiritual Song[2]. *Geistliches* The phrase itself happily expresses the close kinship *Lied.* with the 'Song' to which almost every good Hymn bears witness, and the literature of Spiritual Songs, to which Luther gave the most vigorous impulse, reflected almost every feature of the secular lyric. At a national crisis like the Reformation lyric inspiration of a certain order was indeed not difficult to catch, and it is not surprising that even when it takes the form of a mere statement of doctrine, as in the Creeds, the Hymn resembled rather a war-song of the Protestant host than a piece of prescribed ritual. But there was also, as in Catholic times, a systematic imitation of the secular song. Not only their rhythms, not only their favourite situations, but even their special phraseology were adopted. There were spiritual Hunting and Drinking songs[3], spiritual *Reuterslieder*, and even spiritual *Aubades*, where the Christian soul described its pursuits, its thirsts, its conflicts in the

---

[1] *History of the Turks*, p. 1020 f. (ed. 1621).

[2] Philip Wackernagel, *Das deutsche Kirchenlied*, 5 Bde. Bd. III. contains the Hymns of Luther and his followers. Cf. also Hoffmann v. Fallersleben, *Das geistl. Lied vor Luther.*

[3] The most notorious example is the 'Den liebsten buhlen den ich han,' where the Muskateller in the Wirthskeller is replaced by the Deity on his throne.

world, and its awakening at the call of the Christian watchman[1]. And where imitation was not carried out to this tasteless extent, the spirit and manner of the *Volkslied*, in all its flexible variety, influenced unconsciously the writers of the Spiritual Song, and gave it a measure of the same many-sided power. It was thus not a mere subdivision of the lyric literature of Germany, but in some sense a résumé of it, which would meet the English fugitive as he turned over the pages of the Lutheran Enchiridion.

Coverdale.   Such a fugitive was Miles Coverdale, whose *Goostly Psalmes and Spiritual Songs* are among the most sincere and laborious monuments to Luther in the English language[2].

Lutheran Hymn-ology 1524 -31.   To put the result in one word, it may be said that Coverdale had a very full knowledge of the first period of Lutheran Hymnology, from 1524 to 1531, and of that period exclusively. It is the period of Luther's complete predominance among Protestant hymn-writers; his round score of Songs and Psalms are still the staple of every collection. Fellow-workers were already abundant, but the field was not yet crowded by the legion of medio-crities who later excited his indignant warning against 'sham masters[3].' The productions of the little Wittenberg

---

[1] Sachs: *Eine geistliche Tageweise,* 1525 (Tittmann, *Ldbuch des 16. J.,* II. No. 34). Cf. the version of ' Ich stund an einem morgen an' (ib. No. 38).

[2] The relation of Coverdale's Hymns to Luther's was first pointed out by Prof. A. Mitchell (*The Wedderburns,* Edinb. 1868). My own results were obtained independently and published in the *Academy* of 31 May, 1884. A letter by Prof. Mitchell appeared in *Acad.* 28 June, 1884, supplementing them. The following account contains some criticism of his supplemental results.—Wedderburn, as a Scotsman, lay outside my plan.

[3] Tittmann, *Liederbuch,* p. 185.

circle formed from the first a modest appendix to his own. Paul Speratus, and Elizabeth Creuziger, the faithful Justus Jonas, and the ex-monk Styffel, figure in the earliest *Enchiridia* of Erfurt and Wittenberg. Nürnberg, the stronghold of the Reformation in Franken, almost instantly followed, with Councillor Lazarus Spengler, one of the earliest of Luther's adherents there, and Master Hans Sachs. Somewhat apart, even in hymn-writing, from the main Lutheran movement, stood Strassburg. Few of the Strassburg hymns ever appeared in the Saxon and Bavarian Enchiridia ; yet no city possessed so long a list of noted poets[1]. The preachers, Capito and Symphorian Pollio (Althiesser), the painter Vogtherr, the musicians, Dachstein and Greitter, the ex-monk Oeler, and Butzer's friends and helpers, Wolfgang Masculus and Conrad Hubert, were each the author of one or more hymns, of which, however, through the doctrinal isolation of the city, only three appear to have gained a vogue[2].

Beyond this area, the early Hymns were relatively few, and dialect interposed a more serious barrier to their rapid diffusion. Switzerland in the south and the vast region of Plattdeutsch in the north, number many names of note,—Ambrose Blaurer at Constanz, Nicolaus Hövesch at Brunswick, Johann Agricola, the early folklorist, at Eisleben and the dramatist Burkard Waldis at remote Riga ; but though often translated and collected at a later time, they contributed almost nothing to the early and classical *Enchiridia*.

The early Lutheran Hymnology was thus drawn from a somewhat broad local basis. Each district moreover had certain individualities of manner or of subject; its

---

[1] O. Lorenz u. W. Scherer : *Geschichte des Elsasses*, S. 182 f.

[2] Dachstein's *An Wasserflüthen Babylon's*, and two of Greitter's. Scherer, u. s.

characteristic trait of style, its favourite rhythms and keys of feeling. Each had in some sort a lyric school of its own. Wittenberg was under the immediate influence of the manner of Luther; and Luther's manner bore in the highest degree the stamp of his mind. Whether he re-wrote Catholic hymns, or versified psalms, or found good words for some of the 'good tunes' which 'the devil' had hitherto monopolised, he is always bold, energetic, simple, disdainful of mere flowers of language as of mere prettinesses of rhythm, but with bursts of rugged harmony, and often defying the conventions of modern hymn-writing by drastic picturesqueness of phrase [1].

At Nürnberg, on the other hand, the literary atmosphere was coloured not by one dominating personality but by a vigorous popular tradition. Nürnberg was the focus of the Meistergesang, and the Nürnberg hymns are full of its manner and method. The busy production that went on among the craftsmen of the poetic gild entered too largely into the intellectual life of the city to be without influence; and moreover the most distinguished of Nürnberg hymn-writers was, as has been said, the master of Master Singers Hans Sachs. Sachs and Spengler, as well as Paul Speratus who, though he wrote at Wittenberg, had spent most of his eventful life in Bavaria, all show in various degrees the characteristic effort of the Meistersinger to combine a style full of caprice and surprise in detail with elaborate symmetry

---

[1] In rhythm he had a noticeable fondness for the *unsymmetrical.* E.g. the striking five-syllabled lines which open the *Abgesang* of *Ein feste Burg:* '*Der alt böse Feind, Mit ernst er's jtzt meint,*' &c., which later versions softened into iambics. In regard to stanza, Luther decidedly favoured those more unsymmetrical forms of it in which the number of lines is not a multiple of the couplet,—seven or nine lines rather than six or eight. He loved too the single unrhymed line at the close.

in large masses. The mixture of long and short lines, the internal rhymes, and the complex stanzas, which secured this in a fashion for the secular lyric, are freely adopted in several of the Spiritual Songs of Sachs; and Speratus, after his stormy and adventurous life, retained sufficient relish for the most recherché virtuosities of the school, to lavish them in ample measure upon his version of the *Credo.*

The Strassburg work, finally, was marked by the influence neither of a commanding master, nor yet with the mannerisms of a school. The most important writers, the only ones whose voice found any echo beyond Alsace, —were musicians, with the musician's love of simple and regular rhythms; and the rhythms of many of the Strassburg hymns are simple and regular to the verge of insipidity [1]. The short lines for instance, and the internal rhyme, are as unfamiliar to them as the less melodious unevennesses of the Wittenberg school.

Of the Lutheran hymnology of 1524—31, Coverdale's *Coverdale's* ' *Goostly Songs* ' is, as has been said, a fair selection. The *Goostly Songs.* majority of his originals first appeared in one or other of the *Enchiridia* of 1524—5; the latest of them in 1531 [2].

---

[1] E. g. Greitter's *aabbccddeeffg, aabccbddeffe;* or Dachstein's *ababccdeed.*

[2] Prof. A. Mitchell, who assigns a comparatively late date to the 'Goostly Songs,' says that they contain an imitation of a hymn which first appeared in 1540. In his own list of the supposed originals, are only two to which he can possibly refer, (1) Coverdale's ' Hymn to the Holy Ghost,' which he assigns, though doubtfully, to a certain : Ein Gesang vor anfang der kinder predigt (Wackernagel III. 674), 1537. It is difficult to say what resemblance, beyond a slight one in the stanza, Dr Mitchell can have found here. The Hymn is not even addressed to the 'Holy Ghost' at all. In the second case, Coverdale's *Gloria in excelsis* is probably not independent of the hymn of Hövesch, ' Allein Gott in der Höhe sei ehr'; the

Wittenberg, Nürnberg, Strassburg are all represented in
his collection, and by their best writers: Luther, Jonas,
Creutziger, Hegenwalt, Speratus; Sachs and Spengler;
Dachstein and Greitter[1].   Lower Germany by J. Agri-
cola and probably N. Hövesch.   Upper Saxony claims
Moibanus, the author of a *Patrem* certainly followed by
Coverdale, and probably the anonymous author of another
Patrem, the original of Coverdale's second 'Pater noster,'
published at Erfurt, 1527[2].

A few examples will show the nature and degree of
Coverdale's imitation.   Here, for instance, is the first
stanza of his version of *Ein feste Burg*.   It is intended,
like the original, to be sung to Luther's melody, which is
printed above the words.

> Oure God is a defence and towre
> A good armour and good weapen,
> He hath ben ever oure helpe and sucoure
> In all the troubles that we have ben in.
> Therefore wyl we never drede
> For any wonderous dede

High German forms of which first appeared in 1540. The Low
German original was however already famous, and had appeared
originally in 1526, ·and repeatedly afterwards (Rostock, 1531,
Magdeburg, 1534).

[1] Mitchell would add Symphorian Pollio, on the ground of his
Magnificat ('Mein seel erhebt') 1524; but Coverdale's Magnificat is
much nearer to the original than to Pollio. He also adds Conrad
Huber, Coverdale's friend and correspondent between 1540—8: but
the resemblance to his version of Psalm 133 (printed 1545) is of the
vaguest.

[2] Mitchell would add Johann Kolross of Basel, on account of
his *ad te levavi oculos*. But there is no definite correspondence, and
Kolross's version is not known to have been published before 1550.
By an apparent misunderstanding of Wackernagel's language,
Mitchell states the *Patrem* to be also by Moibanus, for which there
is no evidence.

By water or by londe
In hilles or the sea-sonde.
Our God hath them al i his hond.

Here the first quatrain is tolerably literal, the remainder deserts Luther to follow the psalm. One feels that Coverdale has on the whole been more concerned to adopt Luther's music than his words, and in the other stanzas this is still more clear. He loses too the peculiar refinement of the measure, the mingling of abrupt trochaic and flowing iambic lines; the original can be detected, but is scarcely recalled. I add, further, a specimen of the most elaborately articulated metre in the volume, the *Credo* of Paul Speratus:—

P. SPERATUS.	COVERDALE.
In Got | gelaub ich, dz er hat	In God I trust | for so I must,
Aus nicht | geschaffen hyml und erden,	He hath made heaven and earth also;
Kein not | mag mir zu fugen spott,	My father is he, his chylde am I;
Er sycht | das er mein bschutzer werde.	My comfort he is, I have no mo:
Zu aller frist | almechtig ist	In all my rede, he maketh me spede;
Sein gwalt muss man bekennen	His power is with me always,
Läst sych eyn vater nennen.	To kepe me every daye.
Trotz wer mir thue	There is no evill can have his wyll,
Der ist mein rwe	Agaynst my health nor yet my wealth,
Todt sund und hel	But it must come to my furtherance.
Kein ungefel	He is my kynge that ruleth all thynge,
Widder dysen Gott kan bryngen	The devill can make no hynderaunce.
O herre Got	
Vor frewd mein hertz muss auffspringen.	

This is a fair specimen of Coverdale's way of adapting. It is clear that while he displays anything but a servile deference to the meaning, he follows the rhythm of his

original rather closely but with characteristic simplifica-
tions. For the rest the correspondence is slight enough.
The two 'Credes' are constructed on different lines:
Coverdale's in three stanzas, deals successively with the
three persons of the Trinity; Speratus', like the Nicene
creed, with the successive incidents in the life of Christ.

Finally, we may take an instance from the most
famous and beautiful of the Strassburg hymns, Dachstein's
version of Psalm 137.

An wasserflüssen Babilon	At the rivers of Babilon
Da sassen wir mit schmerzen,	There sat we downe ryght hevely;
Als wir gedachten an Sion,	Even whan we thought upon Sion,
Da weinten wir von herzen;	We wepte together sorrofully.
Wir hingen uff mit schwerem mut	For we were in soch hevynes, That we forgat al our merynes,
Die orglen und die harpffen gut,	And lefte of all oure sporte and playe.
An yere böum der weyden,	On the willye trees that were thereby
Die drinnen sind in irem land;	We hanged up oure harpes truly,
Da musten wir vil schmach und schand	And morned sore both nyght and daye.
Teglich von inen leyden.	

Novel metres. It will be seen from these examples, among other
things, that Coverdale was in some degree a metrical
innovator. Unskilful and timid as his imitation is, he
still preserves some rude likeness of the original rhythms,
—as indeed, since he mostly borrowed their melodies,
was inevitable, and many of these if not unknown were
certainly unfamiliar in England. The habitual psalm-
stanza of the Lutheran poets is that of seven lines of
four feet ($ababcc_d^b$). Seven-line stanzas were in any
case rare among the English poets for verse of this length,
and when they occur their rhyme is, like that of the
'rime royal,' *ababbcc*. It is more important that Coverdale's treatment of the longer stanza in three divisions is

thoroughly foreign. In England it tended usually to the form in which two symmetrical parts (the *Stollen*) are followed by a third sharply distinguished from them, the *Abgesang:* Coverdale frequently (as in the two latter examples above) substitutes the symmetry of the first and third, with a contrasted passage interposed.

Coverdale was a sincere, fervent, homely man, who *Conclu-* wrote what he felt as he felt it; and whose chief merit as *sion.* a writer of hymns is that his uncouth amble never for an instant recals the false gallop of Sternhold and Hopkins. The style of such men is rarely very sensitive to new influences, it does not easily take the impression of a different mind and manner. Almost devoid of lyric faculty, his verse limps laboriously after the stirring measures of Luther. His lines never ring. When for a moment he catches an effective rhythm, he seems to owe more to the happy accident which brings the right words together than to any sensitiveness of ear; and the effect is immediately lost in some line of deadly flatness, or one of the prosaic tags of which, like most contemporary English rhymers of the older school, he has an abundant store.

One hardly looks then in Coverdale for vivid repro-duction of what is most characteristic in his originals. He has not the good translator's sensitiveness and elasticity of style. Yet his very sincerity and simplicity often do the work of refined taste. He is never rhetorical or frigid; he never dresses up a plain phrase or dilutes a strong one. 'Wake up, wake up, ye Christen men!' he cries, with Hans Sachs, and the lusty call of the *Wächter* in the old Daybreak songs to the sleeping lovers rings out in the English as in the German verse[1].

---

[1] This is evidently the origin of the ' Wach auf, wach auf,' not infrequent in the opening of Hymns. Cf. e.g. Nicolai's 'Wachet auf

Moreover what was from a literary point of view an accident, led to an extensive adoption of the German metres.   Hence it happens that at least the rhythmical peculiarities of German schools of hymn-writing are roughly reproduced in this book of English hymns.   For the first and only time, the rich traditions of German lyric poetry produced a faint echo beyond the sea; for the first and only time, the finer sense of melody, the command of 'striking and piquant effects, the variety of rhythmical movement which were the fruit of a prolonged and often extravagant study of the formal side of verse, were dimly reflected in a literature which, with all its abundance of natural song, had hitherto borne far less considerable traces of the cultivation of lyric art.   Had Coverdale been the man to introduce a new school of lyric writing in England, the opportunity and the means were ready to his hand.   But he was not the man, and at the very time of his abortive attempt, the two who were had achieved the work in another fashion and yoked English verse for a generation to the car of Petrarch.

ruft uns die Stimme Der wächter,' &c. (Tittmann, No. 23), and Sachs' 'Wach auf meins herzen schöne' (ib. 34).

TABLE OF COVERDALE'S HYMNS.

I ADD by way of summary a complete table of Coverdale's Hymns, and their established correspondences with the German Kirchenlied. Those marked * are due to Prof. Mitchell (Acad. 28 June, 1884); several correspondences there suggested by him which seem to me untenable are marked †. The sign = does not imply literal translation, but only some degree of deliberate adaptation, however slight.

I. Original hymns (or translations direct from Latin).

†1. 'To the Holy Ghost.' M. suggests Wack. III. 674.

†22. Magnificat. M. suggests Pollio's ' Meyn seel erhebt,' but C. follows the original far more closely.

†25. Psalm II. M. suggests Aberlin's ' Ihr heiden was tobt.'

†34. Psalm XXIV. M. suggests Kolrose's ' Herr ich erheb mein seel zu dir'; there is no resemblance, and this is not known to have appeared before 1550 (Froschover's Gesangbuch).

38. Psalm CXXXIII. M. suggests Huber's 'Nun sieh wie fein' (1545). Huber's version contains four stanzas, Coverdale's only two.

41. 'Let go the whore of Babylon.' M. suggests, though doubtfully, a piece (Wack. *ed.* 1840, No. 816) which bears the slightest possible resemblance to it.

II. Founded upon the German.

A. *Wittenberg circle.*

(*a*) Luther.

*2. ' Another to the [Holy Ghost]'=' Komm heiliger geist' (*Erfurt Enchir.* 1524. *Walther'sches Gesangbuch,* 1524).

*3. 'Another to the same'='Nu bitten wir den heiligen geist' (*Walther'sches Gesangbuch*, 1524).

4. 'Unto the Trinitie' = 'Gott der Vater won uns bey (W. G. B.).

5. 'The Ten Commandments' = 'Die zehen gebot' (E. E. and W. G. B.).

6. 'Another of the same'='Die zehn gebot auffs kurtzte' (W. G. B.).

7. 'The Creede' = 'das deutsche Patrem' (W. G. B.).

11. 'Be glad now all ye Christian men' = 'Nun freut euch lieben christen gmein' (E. E. and W. G. B.).

14. 'Media vita' = 'Mitten wir im leben sind' (E. E. and W. G. B.).

18. 'Of the birth of Christ' = 'Gelobet seist du' (E. E. and W. G. B.).

20. 'Of the resurrection' (2) = 'Christ lag in todes banden' (E. E. and W. G. B.).

*23. 'Nunc dimittis' = 'Mit frid und freud' (W. G. B.).

24. Psalm XI. = 'Ach Gott vom himel sieh darein' (E. E. and W. G. B.).

26. Psalm XLVI. = 'Ein feste Burg' (Nürnberg, 1529).

?27. Psalm CXXIV. = 'Wär gott nicht bei uns' (W. G. B.).

29.   = 'Wol dem der in Gottes' (E. E. and W. G. B.).

33. Psalm CXXIX. = 'aus tiefer not' (W. G. B.).

35. Psalm LXVII. ='es wolt uns Got genedig sein' (E. E. and W. G. B.).

36. Psalm XIII. = 'es spricht der unweisen mund wol' (E. E. and W. G. B.).

(β) 'E. Creuziger.'

13. 'Christ is the only son of God' = 'Herr Christ der eynig gottes son' (W. G. B.).

(γ) Speratus.

12. 'Now is our health' = 'Es ist das heil' (E. E.).

*8. 'Credo' = 'In Gott gelaub ich' (E. E.).

(δ) Erhart Hegenwalt.

32. Psalm L = 'Erbarm dich mein O herre Got' (W. G. B.).

(ε) Joh. Agricola.

17. 'I call on thee' = 'ich ruff zu dir' (1531).

(ζ) Moibanus (?)

*9. Pater noster = 'Ach Vater unser' (1526).

(η) Anon.

*10. Pater noster = 'Vater unser' (Erfurt, 1527). [M. wrongly says 'Moibanus'].

*40. = 'O Herre Gott' (Erfurt, 1527).

B. *Nürnberg.*

(α) Sachs.

16. 'Wake up, wake up' = 'Wach auff in Gottes namen' (Etliche geistliche Lieder, Nürnb. 1525).

(β) Spengler.

15. 'Through Adam's Fall' = 'Durch Adams Fall' (W. G. B.).

(γ) Anon.

*30. = 'Wol dem der des Herren' (*Nürnb. Enchir.* 1527).

C. *Strassburg.*

(α) Dachstein, W.

28. Psalm CXXXVII. = 'An Wasserflüssen Babilon' (*Psalmen u. Lieder*, 1530).

(β) Greitter.

31. Psalm LI. = 'O herre Gott begnade mich' (*Teutsch Kirchenampt*, 1525).

D. *Low Germany.*

(α) Nicolaus Hövesch (Decius).

*21. 'Gloria in Excelsis' = 'Allein Gott in der Hohe sei ehr' (Eyn gantz schone nutte ghesanck, 1526)[1].

---

[1] G. Milchsack (*Archiv f. Litt. gesch.* 12, 312 ff.) has attempted to show that the first stanza of this hymn is borrowed from the *Primus chorus angelorum* in the Eger Spiel; the resemblance appears to me rather shadowy.

*37.　Psalm CXLVI. = 'Hierusalem des loven stadt' (1526).

(β)　Anon.

*39.　'Christe qui lux' = 'Christe du bist licht' (Rigi'sche Kirchenordnung, 1530).　(M. wrongly says 'Decius.')

I have not included in the list a hymn founded upon one of the older Easter hymns—familiar in *Faust :*

19.　Resurrection = 'Christ ist erstanden.'

CHAPTER II.

POLEMICAL DIALOGUES.

THE dialogues of the early sixteenth century are *The dia-*
among the classics of modern pamphleteering. Extremely *the six-*
various in form, ranging from the Attic vivacity of *teenth cen-*
Erasmus to the unassuming but admirable prose of Hans *tury.*
Sachs, they presented, at their best, a degree of combined literary distinction and popular persuasiveness
to which the Dialogue had not attained since Lucian.
Though only in part a direct product of Humanism,
there is no better illustration of the characteristic genius
of the German Humanists, of the union of literary culture
with moral and religious fervour, by which in their hands
literature became a fine art without losing hold of church
and market-place, and, in acquiring academic refinement,
only pressed closer to the heart of national life.

The history of these remarkable works has never, to
my knowledge, been written. They had suffered the
fate to which a hybrid *genre* is always liable but which it
does not invariably merit, of being neglected by both the
classes to whom it partially appeals. Lying between the
purely dogmatic treatise, on the one hand, and the
professed drama on the other, they have proved too doctrinal for the men of literature, too literary for the men
of doctrine. Even in Germany, where the choicest
specimens were produced, they have been relatively

neglected; and in England while every vestige of the
drama has been laboriously exhumed, the numerous dialogues which slumber on the shelves of Lambeth and
the Bodleian have for the most part ministered only to
the brief curiosity of the bibliographer. I accordingly
make no apology for offering, in the present chapter,
not certainly a history of the Dialogue, but some contributions to such a history somewhat more extensive than
my immediate subject demanded.

Mediaeval   The dialogue form had of course been familiar
Dialogues. throughout the middle ages, but only in a few conventional applications, and with a very narrow conception
of its powers.   With rare exceptions it never passed the
limits of a single type, that of a simple debate between
two opponents—a type kept prominent and alive by
several characteristic mediaeval institutions, by the scholastic disputation, the poetic wit-contest, and even by
the pseudo-debate of master and scholar in examination
and catechism, and finally, by the current interpretation
of the word, shown by the spelling *Dyalogus*, as a ' discussion between *two* [1].' Nearly all the professed dialogue
literature of the middle ages would in fact fall into one
of three groups, between which it is difficult to draw an
absolute line, and all following the manner of a disputation.   On the one hand there were the purely didactic
treatises, of the type of the *Lucidaria*, where the dialogue
form is simply a pedagogic device for commending
instruction, a graphic way of presenting necessary know-

---

[1] The same view is of course implied in Wiclif's neologism for
a dialogue of three—*Trialogus ;* it is explicitly asserted at the outset of the Renaissance by the German translation of Pope Gregory's
dialogues with his deacon:—' haisset das buch in latein liber dyalo-
gorum *das ist zu teütsch so vil als buch der zwayer red mit ainander.*'
Ed. 1473 n. l.

ledge. There is no discussion, no contrast of parts, the conversation is a variety of monologue, a literary *hendia-dys*. In the immense class of 'Debates,' on the other hand, we touch the opposite pole of literature. The dialogue form is here essential, and the matter nothing; the effect depends wholly on the dramatic qualities of the situation, on antagonism of character or piquancy of reply. For the most part therefore the speakers were direct antagonists, and, as usual, the most satisfying degree of antagonism was found in pitting against one another personified abstractions or types,—Summer and Winter, Wine and Water, Pride and Lowliness, Body and Soul, Pain and Reason[1], Owl and Nightingale, Flower and Leaf, Ivy and Holly, etc. The very sharpness and abstractness of their contrasts, however, made the higher dramatic qualities of dialogue difficult to attain; while it encouraged the stiff symmetry of form, the nicely-balanced antithesis of plea and counter-plea, which is most opposed to the free movement of colloquial discussion. Between these, and drawing something from both, lies the polemical dialogue, touching on the one side the didactic treatise, with its charge of serious thought, and on the other the debates, with their genuine discussion, a mediator between the formality of the school and the dramatic vivacity of popular art. It is true that the vivacity never went very far. Very ancient precedent had made the dialogue a favourite method of Christian polemics in almost every age of the Church. The dispute of Justin with the Jew Tryphon was a type

---

[1] Petrarch's beautiful and original dialogue, translated by Niklas von Wyle under the title *Tröstung in Widerwärtigkeit*, was one of the most familiar to the generation of Germans immediately preceding Erasmus and Hutten. It is reprinted in *Stuttgart Lit. Verein Bibl.* with Wyle's other translations.

on which even more elaborate treatises than his were
built. Imaginary opponents array their objections in
severely systematic order, and are confuted through
chapter after chapter, and book after book. For the
most part, though introduced expressly because, as Wiclif
puts it, 'locutio ad personam multis plus complacet quam
locutio generalis''—for the sake of popular interest,—
the debaters are little more than personified attractions—
suggestions of personality annexed to antithetic stages
of the argument, delivering themselves at the proper
moment of their quantum of objection or reply, but
almost without a hint of the play of emotion and character, the enthusiastic *entrain*, the ironical humility,
which humanise the dialectic of the great master of
polemical dialogue[2].

Erasmus
and
Hutten.

From these limitations the polemical dialogue was
first decisively released, in northern Europe, by two

[1] *Trialogus*, Prol.

[2] To refer only to books which in some sort coloured English
tradition, Wiclif's *Trialogus*, where Alithia, Pseustis and Phronesis
are the names of three intellectual figments, of whom the first always
maintains, the second objects, and the third decides. In Henry
Parker's long and elaborate *Dives et Pauper*, the two speakers are
shadowy types of wealth and poverty, and their argument follows a
pedantically elaborate scheme, one book being devoted to each of
the Ten Commandments. The *Dives et Pauper* was printed by
Berthelet in 1536. Even in Ockham's little dialogue *Clericus et
Miles*, better known in Germany than in England till far on in the
sixteenth century, the close reasoning is scarcely relieved by one
dramatic touch. This interesting dialogue may, at the same time,
well have had more literary influence upon the German dialogues
of the Reformation than has been hitherto allowed it. The early
editions of it printed in Germany are very numerous. A South-
German dialogue '*zwischen ainem Priester unn Ritter von ainer
steuer über die gaistlichen etwan in Franckreich angelegt, gehalten*'
(Goedeke, § 140, No. 53) is, I presume, a translation of it. It was
translated into English about 1550.

men : Erasmus and Hutten.   From the somewhat confined, scholastic air in which it had hitherto breathed,
they brought it into the stir of public life ; they substituted at the same time the easy informal movement of
classic dialogue for the pedantic symmetry which had
habitually regulated the arrangement of the speeches or
of the topics : they replaced the shadowy and abstract
types by real figures drawn not seldom with the pencil of
Holbein, and of every grade of society ; and lastly, they
called into the service of serious polemics, hitherto waged
mostly with heavy bludgeons, the rapier point of the
refined satirist, now in airy raillery, and now in the scathing and implacable laughter of Aristophanes and Lucian,
which as little resembles the merriment of the carnival as
the seriousness of the pulpit.

Erasmus, the riper scholar of the two, understood
the capacities of his instrument probably better than
Hutten; his dialogues have a wider range of subject
and produce their effect with less obtrusive directness of
expression ; graphic pictures of social life, as in the *Deversoria ;* serious and meditative discussions of literature
and theology, as in the Convivia; satires, now explicit,
now veiled and ironical, upon the abuses of the day,—
the ignorant monks, the alchemists, the beggars.   Hutten's
method is less leisurely, less elaborately witty, less 'familiar',
less penetrated with the refined indolence of the scholar ;
the polemical aim is more obtrusive, the style more mus-
cular, vehement, full-blooded.   He carries on the war
begun in the *Epistolae Obscurorum Virorum*, against the
monks, the corruptions of the Church, the venality of the
Roman court, the unscrupulous cunning of the 'pale,
passionate Italian,' the gross manners of the guileless
Teuton.   He loves, like his model Lucian, to play with
mythology, and to put his satire in the mouths of gods

and heroes. He makes Phalaris rise from the dead to give counsel to his disciple the duke of Würtemberg, and the Sun discourse with Phaethon on the character of the German people[1]. He revels in a Shelleyan vastness of contour and proportion, and paints with broad and careless sweeps of the brush. He knows as little of the confined scenery of *genre* painting as of its minute touch. His characters move about on a vast open-air stage, and the impression is somehow conveyed that the entire universe is looking on. The Titanic energy of his own nature begot a boyish delight in Titanic imagery, as Erasmus' infirmities made him prefer as an artist the scenery in which he most congenially moved,—the re-fined interior, the scholarly banquet, the subtle jest over the good wine. Erasmus, even when directly dealing in satire, struck at individual foes only under the effigy of general types : Hutten, with a fearless audacity which his friends often reproved, attacked the general type in the guise of the individual enemy, and founded the literature of personal invective in which the Reformation was so profuse and at times so great. His victim, the new ' Phalaris,' Ulrich of Würtemberg, is the precursor of Luther's victim, ' arger Heinz' of Brunswick.

German Dialogues, 1521-   The series of Hutten's dialogues opened in 1517 with the *Phalarismus.* In 1521 it closed with the *Bulla*, the *Monitor* and the *Praedones.* But his example had already begun to inspire before it was withdrawn. The year in which the last appeared is marked by a host of dialogues from other hands. For the next five years the torrent of production flowed steadily without a check, and inter-mittently for at least another generation[2].

[1] *Inspicientes*, 1520.
[2] Comparatively few of these are as yet collected. O. Schade, *Pasquillen u. Satiren aus der Reformationszeit* contains several ;

As a whole they cannot be described as directly Humanist productions. They rather testify to the extraordinary vitality which mediaeval tradition retained in the palmy days of Humanism. In the majority the outlines of the mediaeval 'dyalogus' are clearly perceptible. But they tend to break away from this model in three directions, which may be concisely summarised as picturesque scenery, range of character, and dramatic action. One small but brilliant group of dialogues follows directly in the path of Hutten; the debate, lively and piquant in itself, owes half its effect to the imaginary background on which it is thrown. An *Apologia* for the life of Franz von Sickingen is conveyed in a spirited debate at the gate of heaven between St Peter and the 'old soldier come for his pay,' and clinched by his triumphant entrance[1]; while the embarrassments of departed enemies in the same circumstances furnished the motive for the scathing dialogues upon 'Heinz' of Brunswick[2],—a sixteenth-century way of 'adding a new terror to death,' which Byron borrowed three centuries later to pillory the still living Southey[3].

but for the most part I have used the original editions in the British Museum specified below. Uhland, in his Tübingen lectures (*Schriften*, ed. Holland II. 499 ff.), notices several in a rather perfunctory manner.

[1] *Dialogus von Franz von Sickingen vor des Himels Pforten mit S. Peter...gehalten* (O. Schade, *Pasquillen der Reformationszeit*, II.).

[2] 1541. This, which in scale and pretensions is a small tragedy in three acts, is printed with several other dialogues on 'Lycaon' in Schade *u. s.*

[3] These are an insignificant portion of the extraordinarily rich *Himmel-pforte* literature. The somewhat similar dialogue on Julius II. (*Quomodo Julius II. papa post-mortem coeli pulsando ab janitore illo S. Petro intromitti nequiverit*), once attributed to

In a much larger number no attempt is made at imaginative colouring of this sort. They are meant for solid and fruitful discussion, and the scenery, such as it is, apparently serves merely to provide it with a starting-point. Nothing can be simpler than the action becomes where this point of view prevails. The problem is reduced to that of bringing the adversary into a situation in which he will consent to discussion instead of abuse or retreat. But this meagreness of scenery is atoned for by a remarkable freedom in the choice of characters; who moreover are no longer abstract types but real persons. All classes of society are represented. Not merely the 'rich' and the 'poor,' the priest and knight, the 'Lutheran' and 'Catholic,' but peasants, scholars, nobles, monks, clerks, courtiers, beggars, fools, pedlars, innkeepers, weavers, tailors, Wurst-buben, women and children, young and old, pious and froward, pass across the stage; and though deliberate character drawing was an art quite outside the scope of these writers, yet many graphic traits escape as it were incidentally from their pens. The champion of Reform is commonly a peasant, an artizan, a citizen, a schoolmaster; that of the Church most often a priest or monk. A priest and a *Schultheiss* meet in a tavern[1]; a peasant at work in his garden sees his priest pass by and questions him 'ettlicher Artikel halben'[2]; a shoemaker, bringing a pair of shoes home to

Hutten, was probably not of German authorship. Unlike the German dialogues it became at once a European classic, was translated into French and English as well as into German, and was quite familiar to well-read Englishmen in the middle of the century It is alluded to, for example, by Turner, *Examination of the Hunter*, and by Bale, *Catalogus* &c., sub nom. *Julius II*.

[1] *Ein schöner Dialogus*, &c. 1521 (B. Mus.).
[2] *Ein schön Frag*...&c. by Veltin Sendler (B. Mus.).

his precentor, is drawn into theological disputation[1]; a weaver and a priest fall in together on the road towards Augsburg, and engage in amicable altercation[2]; a monk lies starving at the roadside, because the old supply of wine and cheese once so willingly given by the peasantry is now cut off, a peasant passing by takes pity on him, brings him to his house, seats him at his table and seasons breakfast with the inevitable argument[3]. The tone of the dispute is by no means always bitter: it ranges from the fiercest railing to friendly and even genial argument. At times even the form of *disputation* is wholly lost: two Protestant peasants, for instance, meet and discuss the last Reformation news, or criticise with erudition μείζων ἢ κατ' ἀγροίκους the last production of Erasmus[4].

In a third group, finally, this simplicity of structure wholly disappears. A more ambitious art, or perhaps a more limited faith in the persuasiveness of arbitrary argument, carried the *Gespräch* into a higher stage. The canvass was extended, famous men were introduced, subordinate figures appeared in the background; and with the extension of the *personnel*, the action naturally grew more complex and fell into more or less detached scenes. We find in short the dialogue turning into what is perhaps best called the *drama of debate*. The Swiss taste for a crowded stage was partly responsible for the notable dialogues of the Zurich pastor Utz Eckstein and his more gifted contemporary in Berne, the poet painter Niklas Manuel; the *Concilium*[5], where a

---

[1] *Disputation zwischen ainem Chorherren u. Schuchmacher*, &c. by Hans Sachs, 1524.

[2] *Ain hübsch Gesprechbüchlein*, &c. by Utz Rychsner, Weber, 1524.

[3] *Ain schöner Dialogus wie ein bawr mit aim...münch redt*, &c. (B. Mus.).

[4] '*Cünz und der Fritz, die brauchent wenig witz*' (B. Mus.).

[5] *Concilium. Hie in dem buch wirt disputirt Das puren lang zyt hat verfürt*, &c....(B. Mus.).

body of champions from the two ecclesiastical parties
hold a formal discussion; the *Rychstag*[1], where the
peasants' delegate in the same way pleads their case
with the nobles; and the most interesting of all,
Manuel's *Barbali*[2], where a young girl, whom her mother
desires to place in a nunnery, convinces herself by prolonged midnight study of a gospel, bought with her
earnings, that the Apostles knew nothing of nunneries,
and not only resists her mother's pressure, but holds her
ground victoriously against the combined resources of
the local clergy.   Either the *Rychstag* or the *Barbali*
might be divided into at least five distinct scenes, covering
in the latter case more than a year of time[3].   A somewhat less elaborate example of the same type is the
dialogue called *Maria*[4], certainly among the earliest
of the Protestant dialogues.   A Pfarrer of Lutheran sympathies devotes a sermon to a castigation, under well-
chosen figures of speech, of the monks; a 'Monk' in
the audience resents his freedom, but an 'Old woman'

[1] *Rychsztag der Edlen und Pauren bricht und Klag*, &c....(B.
Mus.).
[2] *Barbali. Ein Gespräch. Kurtzwylig wie ein muoter wolt Dz
ir tochter in ein kloster solt*...(B. Mus.).   Reprinted with notes in
Baechthold's admirable edition of Manuel.
[3] To show more clearly how far such dialogues as this approach
drama, and how far they fall short of it, I add a brief analysis.
Scene 1. Barbali and Mother. The latter complains of their want,
and urges B. to enter a nunnery. B. begs for a year's grace, that she
may have leisure to buy and examine a New Testament. 2. After
the year is over, the mother renews her appeal, but B. having found
no biblical authority, refuses more firmly than before. 3. Mother
consults Herr Hiltprand Stulgang, pfarrer zu Bild. He severely
blames her for suffering B. to look at the N.T. 4. Dispute between B. and Stulgang. 5. S.'s failing forces are supplemented by
a company of allies, who after a long argument are likewise igno-
miniously beaten.
[4] *Eyn schoner Dialogus von den vier grosten beschwernuss eins
jeglichen Pfarrers*...(B. Mus.).

(*Vetula*) applauds, and a young nobleman, led by the persuasive conversations of the Pfarrer, warmly takes his side.   The Monk appeals to his superiors, but the Pfarrer after examination by the 'Vicarius' is acquitted in triumph, and the Monk dismissed in ignominy.

The masterpiece of these semidramatic 'dialogues' is however the *Drei lustige Gespreche* already mentioned in another connexion; where Henry of Brunswick comes to take his trial before his old ally Pluto, in an under-world drama, the scenery in which is drawn essentially from the Vergilian Hades, borrowing at certain points, however, a more lurid colouring from the Christian Hell.   A crowd of figures pass before us, distinguished with no contemptible art : the Furies Megaera and Tisiphone, the ferryman Charon, the judges Minos and Rhadamanthus, the would-be merciful Pluto, the implacable and indignant 'Genius' who descends from heaven to be the representative of God and Protestantism; lastly the duke himself, of stature tall, splendidly habited, eloquent, but of deadly pallor and 'cheeks that droop like a blood-hound's.' The trial is carried out and sentence pronounced with all ceremony, and the duke, who had arrived elate in the confidence that the powers of darkness whom he had served would not desert him in his need, is dragged away to his unexpected doom,—a genuine tragic motive handled with at least the elements of tragic power.

No such epoch of prolific and feverish production *The Dialogue in England.* marks the annals of Dialogue in England.   It was not here the chosen vehicle for half a decade of some of the fiercest class and sect hatred and not a little of the most drastic satire known to history.   Good and even brilliant examples are certainly scattered through the literature of the century, but they occur at intervals, in isolation, and clearly for the most part owe their peculiarities of form at least as much to deliberate or even arbitrary choice, as to the contagion of any literary vogue. They present indeed a variety almost beyond classification. They range from the Ciceronian type, in which the form of dialogue is merely a device to facilitate monologue, a group which includes, for instance, both the *Utopia* and the *Toxophilus*[1]—to little dramas alive with many-sided character and picturesque scenery, like the masterly *Dialogue* of William Bullen[2]. Prescriptions of health, spiritual as well as physical, were still conveyed by the time-honoured method of question and answer[3]. John Heywood still represented for England, as Hans Sachs did for mediaeval Germany, the mediaeval disputation of abstractions[4], though, if it is rightly assigned to him, he also produced a more characteristic piece of genuine human conversation in the *Gentylnes*

[1] Though it contains much serious debate, W. Starkey's elaborate dialogue between Cardinal Pole and Lupset, Professor of Law at Oxford (ed. Herrtage and Cowper, E. E. T. S.), belongs to this type. It is a *quaestio* rather than a debate, a formal inquiry into the conditions of a sound polity.

[2] A distinguished namesake and descendant of his to whose learning and critical acuteness the dramatists of the century already owe not a little, has recently undertaken an edition of this *chef-d'œuvre* of one who, without serious error, might be classed among them.

[3] W. Bullen, e.g., also wrote Dialogues on Physic.

[4] *Dialogue of Wit and Folly.* This mediaeval *genre* lingered throughout the greater part of the century both in England and Germany, especially in the ballad form. Cf. Thynne's 'Disputation between Pride and Lowliness,' and a number of lost ballads recorded in the Stationers' Register: 'Dialogue between Age and Youth,' 'God and Man' (1568), 'Death and Youth' (1563). One of the favourite *Volkslieder* of the century in Germany was the Debate of the *Buchsbaum und Felbinger*. In Shakspere, *L. L. L.* v. 2, it will be remembered, the 'owl and cuckoo' still 'represent summer and winter.' Milton's *Allegro* and *Penseroso* may be regarded as the apotheosis of these *contrasti*.

and Nobility, where a Merchant, a Knight and a Plowman
dispute 'Who is a very gentleman?' And finally there is,
as in Germany, the *polemical* dialogue proper, ranging
from the tedious and undramatic discourses of Ochino's
'tragedy[1],' to the impassioned and eloquent debate of
Spenser's Eudoxus and Irenaeus, the stirring rhymes of
Roy and Barlow's *Rede me and be not wroth*, and of
John Bon, and the vigorous prose of William Turner's
Examination of the Mass[2]. It is a portion of this last
class that I propose to examine somewhat more closely.
The inquiry is practically confined to two comparatively
short periods: the first outbreak of English Protestant-
ism under Henry, and its brief triumph under Edward.

I.

The storm of Protestant dialogues which had swept Roy,
over Germany was perceptibly waning when the begin- Barlow,
nings of the English Reformation brought a new kingdom Tyndale.
within its range. Tyndale landed at Hamburg in 1524;
William Roy and Jerome Barlow, formerly Franciscans
at Greenwich, made their escape up the Rhine, the one

---

[1] 'A tragedye or dialoge of the unjust usurped primacie of the
bishop of Rome. Dedicated to Edw. VI.' More celebrated are the
'thirty dialogues' written after he left England, the 21st of which,
on polygamy, caused his expulsion from Zurich, 1563. He also
translated a German dialogue, 'Gesprech der flaischlichen Vernunft.'

[2] It is remarkable that Lucian, though his example was so fruitful
among a people whose possession of *esprit* was one day to be the
subject of a classical inquiry, should have been entirely neglected
among the English writers of original dialogue. Erasmus had long
ago translated the *Icaromenippus* (1512), and Bullock, in the year
of Hutten's final efforts (1521), the περὶ Διψάδων; while More, according to Bale, rendered three of the dialogues. The fragment
described by Collier (II. 280), and mistaken by him for a scene from
a modern Latin play, is a translation of the *Nekyomantia*.

probably in 1525, the other in 1527. These three men
led the first assault against Wolsey and English Catholicism, and a considerable portion of their polemic took
the form of Dialogues. The most important of these is
the *Rede me and be not wroth,* or 'The Burial of the
Mass,' the work of Roy and Barlow at Strassburg[1]. Roy
himself further translated a Latin dialogue on the Mass,
at Strassburg; and a third dialogue, that 'between a
Gentleman and a Husbandman,' issued from Tyndale's
circle at Marburg[2].

I.
*Rede me
and be not
wrothe,*
1527–28.
 The work of Roy and Barlow was certainly produced
between the spring of 1527 and that of 1528[3]. It was
apparently their joint work: Roy supplying probably
the original suggestion and the leading motive; Barlow
filling in the outline with details, and doing the whole of
the composition[4].

 The plot is simple and effective, though carried out
at immoderate length. The Mass is dead. His enemies

 [1] This has been well edited by Prof. Arber in his *English Reprints.* His concise but full introduction was the starting-point of
the following pages, and any further result they may render probable
is thus in a measure indirectly due to him.

 [2] MS. Cotton. Cleop. E IV. f. 121 contains a letter from Barlow
to the King asking pardon for his Lutheran works, among which he
further mentions a Dialogue 'inveying specially against St Thomas
of Canterbury, which as yet was never prynted nor published openly.'

 [3] See Tyndale's statement in the preface to his *Mammon* (quoted
by Arber, p. 11), according to which Barlow did not reach Strassburg before the former date; and More's statement in the *Supplication of Soulys,* 1529 (ib. p. 12), that the dialogue was published
before the *Mammon* itself appeared in May, 1528.

 [4] Tyndale says (*u. s.*) 'W. Roy, whose tong is able not only
to make foles sterke madde, but to disceyve the wisest that is......,
gat him to him and sett hym a werke to make rymes.' Mr Arber
interprets this as assigning 'to Barlow the expression and to Roy
the matter.'

at Strassburg have violently fallen upon him and slain
him.   The scene opens with a long lyrical lamentation
by a priest[1] for the decease of this all-powerful patron,
the source of luxury, 'the chief upholder of our liberty.'
He bitterly enumerates all the blessings which the Mass
has brought his order, and which end with its death.

> The masse made us lordis and kyngis over all,
>   Farre and nere every wheare havyng power.
> With honorable tytles they dyd us call,
>   Dredynge to offende us at eny houre.
> Then were we as fressh as the garden floure.
>   Under favoure of the masse,
>   Now deceased, alas alas.
>
> The masse made us so stronge and stordy,
>   That against hell gates we did prevayle.
> ....
> O faythfull masse, so constant and true,
>   In heven and erth continually.
> We now thy chyldren shall morne and rue
>   The chaunce of thy dekaye so sodenly.
> Constrayned we are all to wepe and crye.
>   Seynge that gone is the masse,
>   Now deceased, alas alas.

Hereupon the two servants of the priest, Jeffrey and
Watkyn, enter into discussion over the new tidings.
Watkyn, like Roy, is already at home in German affairs,
Jeffrey, like Barlow, is more familiar with recent events
in England.   Watkyn describes to his fellow-servant the

---

[1] Mr Arber says 'a *Strassburg* priest.'   There is nothing to
show this; and the words to which he appeals rather indicate that
the scene is *not* at Strassburg.   'I wolde heare mervelously fayne'
(observes Jeffrey) 'in what place the masse deceased.'   'In Stras-
brugh,' replies Watkyn, 'that noble towne, A cyte of most famous
renowne, wheare the gospell is frely preached:'—scarcely a natural
expression if the speakers were actually at Strassburg.   But it is
perhaps rash to press the language of so inartificial a production as
this.

last stages in the career of the fallen Mass, and the cause
of his death. He had not died of age, but his enemies,
Butzer, Hedio, Capito, Symphorian[1], had fallen on him
with 'a sharpe two-edged sword,'—the gospel,—and in
spite of Emser, Faber, Eck, Cochlaeus, and the Universities of Löwen and Köln, had slain him. Jeffrey
hears with amazement of this audacity, of which no one
in England had yet dreamed. The Mass being dead,
where, they next ask, should he be buried? In Rome,
the head see of Christendom, or in Paris, where he had
received so much favour, or finally in England? Jeffrey
suggests that he could not have a better burial place
than the gorgeous shrine of S. Thomas at Canterbury.
But the difficulties would be great, for in England the
strong are on the side of the Mass, nay they have just
caused his great rival, the gospel, to be publicly burned
in London city. This opens the way to a long, trenchant,
scathing satire upon the clerical party in England, and
above all the arch-champion Wolsey is assailed with all
the gross, ribaldry of the time. This satirical declama-
tion occupies the great bulk of the dialogue; indeed it is
so sustained that the principal speaker, who is now
Jeffrey, finding himself 'marvelously drye,' proposes
to adjourn for dinner; after which eminently English
interruption it is resumed with unabated zest.

   The whole dialogue is then substantially a vigorous
satire upon English affairs, in a framework,—the death
of the Mass,—suggested by recent events in Germany.
Only a man fresh from England could have supplied the
former element; only one familiar with Germany the

---

[1] Mr Arber in his preface (p. 4) goes out of his way to suggest
that by this 'Symphorian' the Lyonnais poet Symphorien Champier
is probably *not* intended. The allusion is of course to the Strassburg
Pfarrer, Meister Ziprian (Symphorianus Pollio).

latter. It appears just then to conclude that the former was the work of Barlow, who had just joined Roy at Strassburg, and that the framework or leading motive was supplied by Roy himself, who however, to judge from Tyndale's words, left to Barlow the whole execution.

For our present purpose the English element of the dialogue may be dismissed. The German element requires however to be more closely examined. Mr Arber points out an obvious difficulty in the interpretation of the 'death of the Mass'. 'In what place,' it is asked, 'did the Mass decease?' 'In Strasburgh,' is the reply; 'that noble towne...where the gospell is frely preached': and the chief agents in its fall are 'Hedius, Butzer and Capito, Celarius Symphorian,'—every one of them Strassburg men. Yet the Mass was not actually abolished in Strassburg until Jan. 1529[1], some months after the dialogue was printed.

Mr Arber has attempted to solve this *prima facie* difficulty in two ways. He points out that though the 'decease' is explicitly localised at Strassburg, yet various events are touched,—such as Erasmus' *de libero arbitrio* (p. 42), and the efforts of Löwen and Köln Universities (p. 43), which had no peculiar connexion with the Strassburg Reformation. 'So that this part of the Invective is but a dramatised representation of the Reformation struggle in Germany, and especially during the two years 1526-8 that Roy was in the country[2].'

He proceeds, secondly, to connect the dialogue immediately with the great and successful disputation at Bern in Jan. 1528, which was instantly followed by the

---

[1] Cf. Roehrich, *Gesch. d. Reformation in Elsass*, Pt. II. Chap. XI. and Lorenz u. Scherer, *Geschichte des Elsasses*. Baum, *Capito und Butzer*, has not been accessible to me.

[2] Arber, Introd. p. 6.

' decease' of the Mass in Bern, Constanz and Geneva,—
a disputation in which the Strassburg leaders Butzer and
Capito took part[1].

Without dissenting from this combination, it is still
not perfectly clear why Roy chose to localise the actual
decease of the Mass at Strassburg. The truth is that
though the Mass was not officially abolished there before
Jan. 1529, it had long before then ceased to be the Mass
known to the Roman church. The civic act of 8 Jan.
did not strike down a healthy and vigorous growth, but
merely ended an existence from which all character and
meaning had already vanished. It was the closing process of a gradual and prolonged dissolution. So early as
1524, a series of reforms or alterations had begun, which
sapped one by one the most vital characteristics of the
Mass. First the use of Latin was replaced by that of
German[2]; then the elevation of the host was discon-
tinued[2], and the dress of the officiating priest altered
from the imposing surplice to a simple black robe. The
peculiar gestures and attitudes customary at the celebration were next stopped[2]. And already in 1526 it was
possible for a Flugschrift writer to speak of the Mass as
' dying out[3].'

Finally, in the first days of 1528 came the conference
of Bern. The close alliance of Strassburg with the Swiss,
and their agreement, against nearly all the rest of Germany,
upon the question of the Eucharist, made this conference
as momentous for Strassburg as for the Bernese themselves. Butzer and Capito stood side by side with
Zwingli and Oecolampadius, bore the brunt of the battle

---

[1] Cf. Roehrich, *u. s.*

[2] Roehrich, *Geschichte der Reformations in Elsass.*

[3] *Neuwe Zeitungen von den absterbenden Messen,* quoted by
Roehrich.

and shared the victory. The Catholics were nonsuited
in default of appearance; the conclusive triumph was a
triumph not less for Strassburg than for Bern. As they
returned home to Alsace they may well have felt that
the struggle was over at Strassburg also; that the terrible
blow which the Catholic champions Eck, Faber and
Murner had inflicted on their own cause by not appearing
in its defence would tell far beyond the immediate
neighbourhood of Bern, and above all in Alsace, the
stronghold of the Swiss faith in Germany. To a Strassburg writer the collapse of the Mass in Switzerland under
the strokes of the Strassburg leaders, must have seemed
the final stage of the gradual disintegration all but accomplished in his own city; and but a small stretch of civic
patriotism was needed to localise that last stage also in
the city which had in any case taken an even share in
effecting it.

It was not then unnatural that Roy should make
his Mass 'decease' in Strassburg. But whence had he
this notion of a 'dying' Mass? or was he the first to
adopt this satirical personification of the essence of
Catholic ritual, and to describe its 'death'? There is
no doubt on the contrary that in this felicitous idea
Roy borrowed a genuine and characteristic piece of
German humour. Personification was the keenest
literary instinct of the day. Erasmus, and in a measure
Brandt also, personify folly; Eberlin von Günzberg per-
sonifies the fifteen arguments of Lutheranism; and
Thomas Murner in the *Grosse Lutherische Narr* achieved
a master stroke by personifying Lutheranism itself[1].
The title of the *Neuwe Zeitungen* quoted above shows

---

[1] He carefully explains in the preface that the 'great Lutheran
Fool' is not Luther but his party;—a Murnerian version of Porson's
satire on 'all Germans but Herman,—and Herman's a German.'

how near at hand lay the idea of personifying the
Mass, two years before Roy's dialogue. It is far more
important that just before he wrote there appeared
in Switzerland a prose dialogue in which the Mass
was not only personified with extreme vividness and
humour, but represented, in close analogy to Roy's
conception, as struck down with mortal illness, and
making her last will. Written by an eminent Bernese, and
produced a few days after the close of the disputation,
there is no doubt whatever of its meaning; it is the triumphant cry of Swiss Protestantism over the fall of the
Mass in Switzerland. From the 'deadly sickness' of
the Mass to her 'decease' is no very difficult transition;
but before I suggest the precise relation of this dialogue
to Roy it will be worth while to spend a few words
upon it.

Manuel: The dialogue on the 'Sickness of the Mass' was
Die krank- almost the last work of the notable Bernese poet, already
heit der
Messe.   mentioned, Niclaus Manuel[1]. It is incomparably superior as a piece of literature to the English dialogue of
several times its bulk; indeed its last editors hardly go
too far in placing it at the head of the whole literature
of the vernacular controversial dialogue of this period[2].
To most writers the dialogue form was merely a handle
for effective controversy, in the absence of a real disputation it was some satisfaction to create an imaginary one,
and maul or convert in effigy an opponent inaccessible

---

[1] Cf. the excellent reprint of his works, with memoir, in Baechtold and Vetter's *Bibliothek älterer Schriftwerke der deutschen
Schweiz*, Bd. II. The dialogue is printed at p. 216 ff. ('Ein klegliche Botschafft dem Papst zü komen,' &c).

[2] It would however have some severe competitors; e.g. the
Novella, attributed to Gengenbach, and the best of the dialogues
against Heinrich of Brunswick.

either to violence or to persuasion in his own person.
A few ironical compliments introduced the conversation:
once opened, however, all irony, all delicate literary
artifice was forgotten, and the writer plied his controversial hammer without a second thought. With Manuel
how different it is ! Painter as he was, the artist's sense
preserves him from sinking into mere polemics; from beginning to end the essential irony, the picturesque and
piquant phrase, never flag: the whole is a little drama
full of life and light, not a controversial tract.

The first speakers are the Pope and the Cardinal.
The latter enters in haste with bad news. 'Most holy
father, I have a letter from Germany, and nothing more
horrible and shocking ever came to my ears. Talk of
the destruction of Jerusalem!'

Pope. What is it? Concerneth it the whole world, or the
high? or the low?

Card. It concerneth the very best and mightiest, the rock
on which the whole priesthood is built.

Pope. Now in God's name ! it is the Mass. The bow has
long been strung; let it once be loosed and we are all shot.

They deliberate anxiously on means of relief. The
Cardinal is despondent, and points out the futility of all
the remedies successively suggested by the Pope. 'We
have a contrary wind, and all our oars are broken.' The
Pope proposes to call out all the strong and doughty
men to the rescue. 'In vain,' returns the Cardinal; 'we
have already hired at great cost Hans Strokehisbeard
and Claus Curseill, and others, but they might as well
have shot at the rainbow; and the poor Mass, seeing her
allies all falling off, fell deadly ill, and there is now little
hope of her life.' 'Could we not try the waters?' suggests
the well-meaning Pope. As a last resort the experiment
is made. The Mass is put into the bath, and the

famous doctors Rundegk (Eck) and Heicho (Faber)[1]
feel her pulse. 'Herr bis [sei, *imper.*] gelobt ! die
Mess facht an schwitzen, ich hoff es wöl besser umb sie
werden.' But alas, it is the 'death-sweat,' and the
'improvement' of the Mass is that of a twenty-year
horse, or of corn under hail. Eck then opportunely
reminds the company of the young lion which, born
dead, was brought to life by its father's roar ; and proposes to revive the Mass by a roar in concert. The
Catholic champions agree to this method of supporting
the cause and roar lustily. But the longer they cry the
weaker grows the Mass ; her eyes sink, her complexion
is as dough, her nose, like the dying Falstaff's, grows
'sharp and pointed.' Eck proposes to warm her chill
limbs by the fire of purgatory ; but alas, the peasants
have put it out with the holy water, and monks and
beggars are sitting there in the smoke with streaming
eyes. Faber calls for the holy oil to perform the last
unction ; but it appears that the sacristan has used it to
grease the boots of the *capellan.* At length all hope
vanishes. 'We might as well try to hang the sea on a
rainbow, like a sausage on a hook, as help this Mass.'
And he proposes that they shall all ride off home, keep a
cheerful countenance, and if any should ask, 'How is it
with Mass ?' answer, 'Wol, wol, marter liden wol! By the
torments of all the martyrs she is in the best of health,
and had a dance last night with the Pope's legate !'

The *Krankheit der Messe* is fitly followed by the
last Testament of the Mass, 'of her,' as it is affectingly
put, 'who has suckled, nourished and protected the entire
priesthood as a mother her child.' She arranges for the
disposal of her body and property, and for the order of
the funeral. One other touch of Manuel's pungent wit may

[1] Baechtold and Vetter ; *u. s. Introduction.*

be quoted, though it is too elaborate to be quite happy. ' My body,' writes the Mass, 'shall be buried under the eyes of the whole priesthood, and you shall drop holy water on the grave the whole time, for then their tears will be sincere.'

This effective satire became immediately popular, and was repeatedly reprinted and adapted[1]. At Strassburg, bound by so many links to Switzerland, where every movement of the Swiss Protestants found an instant echo, the report of it must have followed its production as rapidly as that had followed the collapse of the Bern disputation.   That Roy had yet seen the *Klegliche Botschafft* is scarcely credible in face of the inferiority of his own work; possibly he could not have read it if he had seen it.   But the idea of the personified Mass falling sick, abused by her foes, vainly succoured by her friends, and finally lying at the point of death, was one of those which in a country thrilling with excited hopes and fears at that very prospect, penetrates and is passed from mouth to mouth with incredible rapidity.   In Strassburg it must have been current talk at the moment when Roy conceived the thought of his dialogue.   As the most effective handle within reach for the elaborate assault upon the English clergy which he contemplated, he seized upon it—and then came the complaisant and industrious Barlow to give form to his conception[2].

---

[1] Cf. titles, including a Bearbeitung in Low German, in Goedeke, p. 301.

[2] I do not dwell on particular passages, which however here and there bear a curious resemblance. Of the bishop of Strassburg we are told:

> He spareth not to course and banne,
> Doynge all that ever he canne
> To revoke masse unto lyfe agayne.

2.

Dialogus inter patrem christia-num et filium contuma-cem. 1528.

Of the other two dialogues produced in Germany nearly at the same time little need be said. The 'dialogus christianus' between a 'pater christianus' and a 'filius contumax' remains neither in the original, of which no other notice appears to be extant, nor in the translation of it undertaken, according to Tyndale, by Roy. Considering the ideas with which Roy was pre-occupied at the time, we have no difficulty in believing More's assertion (*Supplicacyon of soulys*, quoted by Arber, *u. s.* p. 12) that it dealt with the sacraments. Much more remarkable and curious is the *personnel* of the dialogue. The speakers are father and son—so far there is nothing unfamiliar; what is I believe unexam-pled is their respective *rôles*. The genius of the Pro-testant dialogue tended to put the defence of the new teaching in the mouth of the younger, of the poorer man, while the elder, or the more powerful, or the superior in social ranks defended tradition[1]. Here how-ever, unless the title is delusive, the Christian, i.e. Re-formed, doctrines are urged by the father, and the obstinate opponent is the son. In the absence of the text it would be idle to dwell further on the anomaly.

And of Faber and Eck, Enser and Murner here as in Manuel, the chief protectors of the Mass,—it is asked:

'Did they unto masse no socoure?—
Yes truly, with wordes of greate boste,
They spared not to sende their oste,
Threatnynge with fearefull terroure,'

though, as the speaker proceeds to explain, they were not present, i.e. at the Bern disputation.

[1] As regards the father and son *motive* cf. e.g. the 'Bruderliche Warnung an M. Mathis Zell...' by Stephan Bullheym (extracts in Roehrich's *Mittheilungen* III. 94 ff.), where the cause of Zell and Reform is represented by Stephan against his father. Cf. the *Robin Conscience* in England.

An anomaly of a different kind would belong to the third dialogue in question, had it been written for a German audience or of a German society. The 'proper Dyaloge betwene a Gentillman and a Husbandman'[1] is a 'bitter cry' of two oppressed orders against the spirituality. There is little question here of religious beliefs, little allusion to the Mass or the sacraments, or purgatory. On the other hand the social root of the English Reformation is laid bare with great clearness and some force. In this respect the dialogue is a continuation of the epoch-making *Supplication of the Beggars*, 1527[2]. It has little of the intellectual equipment of that satire, of the statistics and dialectic which forced it home; it impresses solely by the simple pathos of personal suffering. Its heroes are not merely political spokesmen for oppressed classes, but foremost victims of oppression themselves. A certain emulation in misery finds place between the two as they tell their wrongs. Each will have it that his own condition is the worst. Both have suffered by the same exactions. The 'gentleman' sees the greater part of his old estates alienated to the clergy, under threats of purgatory if the owners did not yield. The husbandman finds himself rack-rented by his clerical landlords, while tithes and confessional charges, 'prestes dueties and clerkes wages, Byenge of perdones and freres quarterages, With chirches and aultares reparacion' consume much of what is left.

> 'We tourmoyle oure selfes nyght and daye
> And are fayne to dryncke whygge and whaye
> For to maynteyne the clargyes facciones[3].'

3. *Dialogue between a Gentleman and a Husbandman.* 1530.

---

[1] Printed at Marburg, by Hans Luft, 1530.

[2] This was translated into German by Sebastian Franck: *Klagbrieff der armen dürftigen...wider die reichen geystlichen bettler...* 1529 (B. M.).

[3] *Dialoge*, &c. ed. Arber, p. 139.

Such a dialogue was peculiarly English, in another
sense than that it dealt wholly with English affairs. The
fundamental situation would hardly have seemed plausible elsewhere. To represent peasant and knight
fraternising over their common misfortunes, would probably have occurred to no German pasquillist whatever.
Both classes might indeed be sufficiently hostile to the
old ecclesiastical order, but they fought in different
camps, they wanted different things, and their common
enmity permitted at most such a suspicious and half
involuntary alliance as that of Berlichingen. A strong
government, like that of Wolsey, might have forced
them to make common cause, like the 'Gentleman' and
the 'Husbandman' of the English dialogue; but in its
absence their class antipathy occupies as large a space in
the picture as the ecclesiastical conflict itself. If the
dialogue of the Gentleman and the Husbandman fairly
represents the state of English society of the time, the
truest picture of that of Germany, at least of South
Germany, is drawn in the Concilium, already mentioned,
of Utz Eckstein [1].

*Catholic
Dialogues.*   The characteristic qualities of the Protestant dialogues
are best thrown into relief by a glance at the work of
their rivals. It is comparatively scanty in amount and
mediocre as literature. The Catholic church in England
had no extraordinary satirist like Murner in its service.
John Heywood, whose satiric powers were perhaps not
less, devoted them mostly to exposing her abuses.

---

[1] A curious parallel to the English dialogue, with a characteristic difference, apparently occurs in a dialogue of which only the
title is accessible to me (Goedeke § 140, no. 40, b.): '*Ain schoner
Dialogus oder gespräch, zwischen ainem verprenten, vertribnen
Edelman und ainem Munch, welichen am unrechsten geschach*,'
belonging presumably to the time of the Peasants' War.

Skelton unfortunately died at the opening of the struggle[1]. And where the polemical dialogue was used distinctly against the Protestants, it is mostly constructed in a flat, unimaginative manner, without perspective, background, atmosphere, light and shade, and the *brio* which the defenders of an old cause commonly assume with more difficulty than its young assailants.   The best known of Catholic dialogues in the latter part of the century, those of Wingfield, published in his own name by Alan Cope, Wingfield, are as tame and lifeless as most of the dialogues pro- Cope. duced by either side at that date[2].   The dialogue of William Barlow upon the origin of the Protestant fac- Barlow. tions is of the expository kind, interesting chiefly for its autobiographical statements[3].   Nothing indeed in the controversial writings of the time approached two dialogues of Erasmus, translated into excellent English, Erasmus and issued about 1550 at a Canterbury press, without *(trans- lated)*. making much stir—the *Polyphemus* and the *De rebus et vocabilibus;* the former especially, with its admirable picture of the German *Reuter*, had comparatively little application to English conditions[4].

One among the Catholics was no doubt capable, if Sir T. he had chosen, of borrowing not perhaps the unsavoury More.

---

[1] It is difficult even to guess the nature of his *dialogi de imaginatione*, mentioned by Bale *sub nom.*

[2] Alanus Copus: *Dialogi sex contra expugnatores missae*, &c. Antverp, 1566.

[3] W. Barlow: *A dialogue describing the original ground of these Lutheran factions, and many of their abuses.*   London, 1553, 2nd edition.   Probably written about 1533, the date of his letter of recantation to the King (M. Cotton. Cleop. E. IV.) quoted p. 34 *note* 2.

[4] *Two dyaloges wrytten in laten by the famous clerke D. Erasmus of Roterodame*, &c.   Cantorbury, John Mychell *n. d.* (B. Mus.)—A *dyaloge between ii. beggars* licensed to Copland in 1567, was perhaps a version of the πτωχολογία.

though pungent pen of Murner, but the finer Attic weapon of Erasmus and Hutten.   But devoted as he was to the church, and prodigally as he spent his skill and learning in its cause, the huge volume that contains his best arguments for Catholicism could in no way rival one small but golden book in which he had embodied the more than half pagan inspiration of his early manhood. For the rest, this volume—a dialogue against Tyndale's book on the Mass—has pleasing qualities; but it belongs essentially to the less vivacious Ciceronian type.   Every circumstance which could provoke any scintillation of dramatic liveliness and seduce the attention from the flow of cogent reasons, is carefully refined away.   Cicero has familiarised us with urbane colloquies in Roman villas, where friends, united by common culture and the high breeding of the later Republic, carry on a leisurely exchange of views, and intellectual divergence is rarely accentuated by hot debate.   More has introduced something of this *urbanitas* into the uncongenial atmosphere of theological polemics.   The scene of the discussion is laid in the pleasant seclusion of the Chelsea library.   The opponent is not Tyndale, whose arguments are indeed mostly in view, nor any other ardent Reformer; but a personal friend of More's, who desires if possible to share his faith.   Shaken, in spite of himself, by Tyndale's arguments, he only seeks to have his doubts removed. And as if still further to relieve the tension of controversy, the friendly opponent does not himself appear, but is represented by a proxy, a 'Messenger,' who dispassionately reports his objections and receives More's replies. The whole of the prolonged argument, in four books, is conveyed in the form of an account of the conversation addressed by More to the friend who had occasioned it[1].

[1] *A dyaloge of Syr Th. More knyghte.   Newly oversene by the*

Little of the earliest heretic literature of England
survived the fitful persecutions of Henry's later years.
Roy's dialogue, all but exterminated by the successful
energy of Hermann Rinck, and proscribed in 1531[1],
was in 1542 too well forgotten to be worth proscribing[2].
The king's death was the signal for a flood of Protestant
literature, largely in the dialogue form, but scarcely at all
related to the earlier English efforts which we have discussed. Though Roy and Barlow however were forgotten
beyond recall, the German dialogues, which had in some
degree influenced the form of their polemic, remained in
immense abundance, making proscription out of the question. Even if no direct evidence were to be had, we might
infer that some of them fell into the hands of the fugitives from England whom neither spiritual song nor
religious drama wholly escaped. It will be seen, however,
that for at least one or two cases such direct evidence is
to be had. At the same time I have not hesitated, in
what follows, to allow the discussion to range considerably
beyond this nucleus of ascertained fact. It seems better,
in handling a subject from a somewhat unfamiliar point

said *Sir T. M.*, 1530. Some years later he wrote in the Tower another dialogue of essentially the same expository character: 'Comfort
against Tribulation,' in three books. Under the figure of the
miseries caused in Hungary by the Turks, he speaks of persecution
in general (translator's preface). His printer John Rastell put the
Turks to a very different use. Some originality belongs to his *A
newe boke of Purgatory...a dyaloge betwene one Comyngs an Almayne,
a christen man, and one Grangemyn, a turcke* (1530), from the fact
that the Turk is made to defend purgatory against the Christian
heretic.

[1] Cf. list of proscribed books at Lambeth, printed by Dr
Furnivall, *Political religious and love poems:* referred to by Arber,
u. s. p. 14.

[2] Arber, *u. s.* p. 8.

of view, to give a rather free rein to suggestion and conjecture, and, without insisting on them, at least to put
upon record even slight analogies which tend to support it.

II.

*Second
Period of
Dialogues.*
1547-
In the England of Edward the Mass was still the
centre about which theological controversy chiefly raged.
Henry's peremptory insistance on its observance long
after he had accepted other portions of the Reformed
'platform' gave it a somewhat factitious importance. In
regard to rejection of the Papal Supremacy Edward could
introduce no more thorough reformation than that
already accomplished by Henry : in regard to the Mass
he was, in Protestant eyes, a real Reformer. It was
natural therefore that satire should fasten upon this
single point ; and that the subject of the earliest English
dialogues, printed by fugitives at a foreign press, and
stifled at home, should be the absorbing topic of those
which now came out openly under Government favour.
The sacrament was dubbed with low nick-names—'Jack
in the box,' 'Jack of Lent,' 'Round Robin[1],' and the
old fancy of the 'death and burial of the Mass' was
revived just when it appeared to be an accomplished
fact[2]. Or the imaginary story is carried a stage further
back, and the Mass not undergoing 'death and burial,'
but being 'tried' with full legal ceremony, and 'condemned.' Or lastly we find the Mass exposed to the most
characteristic of all the methods of German dialogue,
that of opposing the 'Peasant to the Priest' and sapping

---

[1] Strype, *Cranmer*, p. 173.

[2] Ib. 207. 'A set of rhymes was now (1549) made about
the burial of Lent, and publicly sold in Winchester market.'

a solemn creed, like Langland long before, in the name
of the shrewd sense of Hodge.

Among the fugitives who returned on Edward's acces-   Scoloker.
sion was very probably one Anthony Scoloker, of whose
life absolutely nothing is known, but whose name appears,
as printer or as translator or both, upon a series of theological books of much rarity.   All of these were printed
either at Ipswich in 1547, or in London in 1548 [1].

By far the most interesting of all that is associated   1.
with his name, is the 'Goodly dysputacion between a   H. Sachs'
Christen shomaker and a Popysshe Person, with two   *Disputa-*
other persones more, done within the famous citie of   by A. Sco-
Norembourgh...translated out of the Germayne tongue   loker.
into Englysshe, by Anthony Scoloker.   Imprinted at
London by Anthony Scoloker.   1548.'   This was a
version, crude and faulty enough, it is true, of one of
those four dialogues which, with more than one spirited
hymn, were the fruits of the first Protestant fervour of
Hans Sachs [2].   All were produced in the same year,
1524, and dealt with various aspects of the great struggle.
In one, for example, he chastises the hypocrisy of the
Roman clergy [3]; in a second he plays the candid friend
towards some of the Hotspurs among his own party [4].

---

[1] They are enumerated in Ames and Hazlitt, and Dr Grosart
has thought it worth while to reprint the list as a contribution to
our knowledge of another Anthony Scoloker, the author of the
Daiphantus (1604).   Among them occur several translations from
German theology, partly anonymous, partly from Luther and
Zwingli.

[2] Cf. *Academy*, May 31, 1884, p. 386.

[3] *Eyn gesprech von den Scheinwercken der Gaystlichen und
ihren gelübdten, damit sy zu verlesterung des bluts Christi vermaynen
selig zu werden. Hans Sachs Schuster.*   (B. Mus.)—Discussion between Hans (Lutherisch), Peter (Evangelisch), and a Monk.

[4] *Ayn gesprech aines evangelischen Christen mit ainem Luthe-
rischen darinn der ergerlich wandel etlicher die sich Lutherisch*

The fourth, more directly dogmatic than these, describes a dispute upon the authority and testimony of the Bible, held at Nürnberg, between two informal champions of the rival opinions,—a Canon or *Chorherr*, and a shoe-maker,—the latter being naturally no other than Hans Sachs himself[1].

The shoemaker is discovered at the *Chorherr's* door, with a pair of shoes just finished,—a homely situation quite after the genius of these German dialogues. The shoemaker expresses his wonder that the *Chorherr* is not at church. He makes somewhat forced excuses,—among others that he has been feeding his pet nightingale, now drooping and silent with the approach of winter. 'But I know a shoemaker,' returns Hans with meaning, 'who hath a nightingale that beginneth now first to sing[2].' 'Yea, the devill of hell take that shoemaker and his nightingale, he hath railed on the holy Fathers and on us honourable gentlemen like a very pancake-boy[3].'

nennen angezaigt und bruderlich gestrafft wird. (B. Mus.)—Discussion between Hans (L.) and Peter (E.), turning in part on the zealous consumption of meat on Fridays by which many ardent Protestants testified to their sincerity. Cf. also *Die Unterweisung*, &c. (Goed. § 154, 14). The *Ein argument der römischen wider das christlich heuflein*, &c. (ib. No. 11), I have not seen.

[1] The full title is, *Disputacion zwischen ainem Chorherren und Schüchmacher, Darinn Das wort gotes und ain recht christlich weszen verfochten wirtt.* Hanns Sachs, MDXXIIIJ. (Br. Mus.)

[2] *Die Wittenbergisch Nachtigall, die man jetz höret uberall*—Sachs' song of triumph at the Reformation, and probably the most inspired lyric he ever wrote,—appeared in July, 1523. It is reprinted in the Stuttgart *Lit. Verein* edition of Sachs.

[3] *Ausgeholhipt wie ein holhipbub.* The point of the phrase is untranslateable, since *holhippe*, a sort of flat, sweet cake, had acquired the secondary sense of *schmähung*,—evidently from the habitual behaviour of those who sold them. Grimm, *WB.*, *s.v.* Scoloker blunders here.

This retort makes the way easy to the inevitable theological discussion. The fundamental question of authority
is soon reached. 'You regard not any council, then?'
asks the *Chorherr* of the champion of the Bible. 'Yea,
verily; that council which the Apostles held at Jerusalem.'

Chor. And did the Apostles then likewise hold a
council?

Sh. Yea,—have ye a Bible?

The *Chorherr* bids his *Köchin* bring forth the 'great
old book.' Unaccustomed to the order she brings the
more frequently desired 'Decretals,' a precious tome
anxiously guarded from spot or stain. She is despatched
a second time, and at length returns with a dusty and
cobwebbed volume, by the aid of which Hans gains an
easy victory.

The *Chorherr* appeals to his man-cook, who, however,
exults openly in the shoemaker's triumph, and closes
the *iam profligatum bellum* with a not inferior Biblical
artillery of his own. Furious at the betrayal, he dismisses the cook at a moment's notice. His maidservant
commiserates her master's misfortune, and hopes he
will not again incur the risk. 'Oh never fear,' he replies,
'I will take good precautions against him : "the burnt child
dreads the fire."' And he proceeds to forget his discomfiture in giving orders for a goodly feast with the
Caplan :—'Fetch me a capon or *twelve* from the market,
lay out the dice and the cards, and above all take away
the Bible[1]!'

---

[1] Scoloker has taken considerable liberties in his translation.
He has not merely given the *Köchin* a name, Katherine, and
altered that of the 'cook' 'Calefactor' from Heinrich to John,
but repeatedly slurred idiomatic and difficult phrases, missed the
finer *nuances* of wit and the finer turns of conversation, and

2.
*English
Dialogues
of the same
school.
John Bon
and Mast
Parson.*
Sachs' work evidently belongs, as already hinted, to the most characteristic type of Protestant dialogue,—that in which the humble layman, the peasant or artisan—expressed his sense of intellectual as well as moral superiority to the clerical representations of scholasticism. Sachs' shoemaker refutes the precentor, as Utz Rychsner's weaver refutes the parson, and both weaver and shoemaker are close portraits of the weaving or the shoemaking author.   Among the original English dialogues of this time is at least one which belongs essentially to the same type[1].   Of its origin nothing is known, except that it was printed, in 1548, by Copland.   A peasant, it will be remembered, ventures, under a mask of rustic εἰρωνεία, to question his priest upon the strange mystery of 'Corpsycursty.'   The priest has found John working betimes in his field[2], and opens the debate with a com-

committed at least two gross blunders.   The second of these is amusing, and suggests that Scoloker was ignorant of a very familiar proverb.   In the *Chorherr's* reply to his maid's warning immediately after the dismissal of the *Calefactor*—('Ich will mich nun wol vor im hyettenn, verprents künd fürcht fewer'), he ingeniously detects a reference to the fire just abandoned by the banished cook, and translates, 'I shall kepe me from him well enough, thou wicked and excommunicate knave, take heed of thy fire!'

[1] 'John Bon and Mast Parson;' ed. Hazlitt, *Remains of Early English Poetry.*

[2] Cf. a similar situation in the dialogue of Veltin Sendler: *Ein schön Frag von einem Bawren, wie er einen Pfaffen gefragt hab, ettlicher Artickel halben* (B. Mus.).—The *Bawr* is found working in his garden,—

> 'Es stünd ein Bawr in seinem garten
> In sawrem Schwayss thet er des abends warten.'

He is much less acute than John Bon, and puts his questions only at the instigation of a passing pilgrim.   His initiation into Reform is however as complete as it is rapid.   'Are ye the Anti-

pliment on his industry.   The talk is easily led to the
Corpus Christi procession, then the greatest English
festival, and John, professing bovine ignorance of the
nature of the sacrament ('Is Corpus cursty a man or a
woman?'), contrives to entangle his opponent in self-con-
tradiction and heresy[1].

If the 'John Bon' is constructed on the 'Peasant   3.
versus Parson' type of German dialogue, a second dia-   *Robin Conscience.*
logue displays that of the 'son *versus* the father.' This
is the so-called interlude of *Robin Conscience*[1]; where
the moral and Protestant son, Robin, refutes the worldly
aims of his father *Covetousness*, his mother *New-guise*,
and his sister *Proud-Beauty*.   It is true that the names
of the characters show that the piece is not to be entirely
separated from the Moralities among which Collier
includes it.   But the Moralities hardly ever arrange their
personnel so undisguisedly upon the type of the family as
is here done.   Virtues and vices confront one another,
the hero plays his part among them, and here and there
a casual hint of relationship is doubtless dropped; but
as a rule the relations of the persons are simply those of
the ideas they personify: they are allies or they are
opponents, but rarely fathers, mothers, sisters or brothers.
And the 'Robin Conscience' family, vividly drawn as it
is, belongs to the type which must be called normal in
the German polemical dialogues, so far as they deal
with family relations at all.   As in the *Bruderliche
Warnung an Mathis Zell* already mentioned, and in a

christ, or do we wait for another?' is his first greeting to his priest.
The priest on his part is drawn with a transparent hatred which
frustrates its own purpose and produces a gross caricature instead of
the lively portrait of 'Mast Parson.' 'Knowst thou not,' he asks
for example, 'that in all things we live and teach contrary to Christ?'

[1] Extracts in Collier, *Annals of the Stage*, Vol. II.

rather later dialogue (Goedeke, § 140, No. 51) *von der Beycht*[1], the militant energy, the quick conscience of the Reformation are here embodied in the son, while the father, as in those cases, represents with more or less energy the older faith. In the *Barbali* we have already seen an instance in which mother and daughter are similarly related.

The 'drama of debate' in England. The dialogues so far described all belong to the simplest type—the discussion between two persons which Wiclif apparently understood by the terms when he strangely called his own discussion between *three* the *Trialogue.* In Germany as we have seen the Dialogue had long ago attained far greater elaboration of structure. It had become, as in the *Rychstag* and the *Barbali*, a little drama of debate, with changes of scene and time, and a liberal diversity of speakers. In England this developed type of the polemical dialogue was hitherto unknown. Soon after the accession of Edward, however, appeared two remarkable examples of it; and it is significant that the earlier of the two is attached to the name

---

[1] *Ein hübscher Dialogus oder gesprech vierer personen, als unter Vater, Sün, Tochter und eynem Pfaffen, von der Beycht, wie unnd wem man beychten sol...*Jacob V. (Vielfeld), 1526. A brief account of this dialogue, of which a probably unique copy exists at Berlin, I owe to the great kindness of the librarian of the Königliche Bibliothek, Dr von Gebhardt, whose courtesies in this kind I am far from being the first to enjoy. The interesting analogy suggested by the title to the *Robin Conscience* scarcely goes beyond the relation of father and son which I have indicated. Instead of being opposed to the son, the daughter shares his disinclination to confess,—though from a different motive, viz. 'weil sie letzthin dabei eine schlimme Erfahrung gemacht.' She then disappears from the scene. The son finally goes at his father's request; but 'confesses' in such sort that the priest at first rejects him as 'Martinisch,' but is at length convinced of the justice of his view, 'und zuletzt sind sie éin Herz und éine Seele.'

of an eminent physician, long an exile in Germany, familiar with its language, and of all the English refugees perhaps the best acquainted with its highways and by-ways,—Dr William Turner. The particular form which the dialogue took in his hands, that of a Trial at bar, or ' Examination,' was itself quite familiar there.

The ' trial-motive ' lent itself to two distinct contro-versial purposes, neither of which was quite satisfied by the simple dialogue. One who desired to mediate between extreme views, or to discriminate between better and worse arguments, or in general to represent any unpopular *tertium quid*, could scarcely put his case adequately in a colloquy of two persons. He demanded a more compli-cated type of discussion, with more speakers, finer grada-tions of opinion, clearlier marked phases of development; —with room for a Glaucôn and an Adeimantus as well as for a Thrasymachus. Between the violent partisans on either side appeared the moderates, reasoning with them alternately, choosing and distinguishing, confirming and rejecting; and it was a natural and effective de-velopment to represent the advocate of moderation as at the same time the mediating judge, to whom the rival parties appealed or before whom they were summoned.

Uses of the Trial-motive in Dialogue.

On the other hand, the same motive was evidently equally available for a more ordinary kind of contro-versialist. If it lent itself readily to the purposes of the mediator, it also provided a telling framework for the most unmeasured castigation. Instead of being merely refuted in a private argument, and slinking away with no witness of his humiliation but the reader, the enemy was a prisoner at the bar, forced to listen to his own igno-minious condemnation and sentence, and finally dragged off to tortures in which theological vindictiveness could revel without check. The mere introduction of a *judge*,

listening with an air of impartiality to both sides of the
case before he pronounced upon them, was an appreciable element in the general rhetorical effect; to the
sympathetic reader his most unqualified verdict insensibly appealed with a certain authority; like a Greek
chorus, he seemed the impersonation of judicial reason
confirming the assertions of the advocate, a Philip of
evident sobriety setting his seal to the judgments of a
Philip obviously ardent and possibly biassed.

Trial-motive in Germany.   Both causes tended to keep the 'trial-motive' in the
repertory of the German writers of polemical dialogue.
Suggestions of it lay doubtless near at hand. The purely
literary *disputation* had continually exhibited it in the
germ : the Owl and Nightingale choose an arbitrator,
Pierre de la Broche and Fortune debate before Reason,
in the *Ackermann aus Boehmen* God is called in to decide between the Widower and Death[1]. On the mediaeval
stage too it was so familiar, that the procedure of the
law-court ranks with the Easter liturgy of the Church
among the *idées mères* of the modern drama. Among
contemporary German dramatists also the taste for
rhetorical disputation had already found vent in numerous
'trial' scenes; the *Fastnachtspiele* were particularly fond
of this solution for domestic difficulties, and numerous
versions of the *Susanna* story were making one of the
most striking trial scenes in literature familiar in every
great city of the land. It had thus been no striking
innovation when Utz Eckstein applied this method to
the purely polemical dialogue and gave his notable
attempt already briefly mentioned, to pacify the exas-
perated peasants, the form of a debate before a judge.
The delegate of the peasants 'Hans Eigennutz' pleads
their cause before the *Stadtgericht* of Fridberg ; the nobles

[1] Scherer, *Gesch. d. deutsch. Litt.* 268.

reply; when both parties have been heard, the burgermeister Herr Salomon, and the other *Herren des Gerichts*
take counsel together, and their sentence, to the effect
that 'man soll nicht schmehen obrigkeit,' is read by
Johann Scheidmann, the Town Clerk[1].   A mediator Witzel:
who found his task even more thankless than Eckstein's, *Dialogi.*
resorted to the same method a dozen years later.   The
three books of dialogues[2] of Georg Witzel are an
elaborate effort to restore the shattered unity of the
church on the basis of mutual concession[3].   There is
no attempt as in the *Rychstag* to simulate an actual
trial; the debate is a true colloquy held in the garden
of one of the disputants, whose wife is visible in the
background; the essential feature is that the honours
of the discussion do not belong to the advocates of
either side,—to the learned Catholic Ausonius, to the
ignorant but self-assured Lutheran citizen Teuto, the
host, or to the learned but equally self-assured Lutheran preacher, Core,—but to 'the judge' Palemon,
and his confederate Orthodox,—the latter the principal
advocate of the *media via*, the former the mouthpiece of

---

[1] *Rychsztag der Edlen und Pauren bricht und Klag zFriedberg
gehandelt auff dem Rychsztag.* Utz Eckstein. 1526. (B. Mus.)

[2] *Dialogorum libri tres.   Drey Gesprächbüchlein von der Religion Sachen in itzigem fahrlichen Zwiespalt auffs kürtzest gefertiget.*
Leipzig, 1539. (B. Mus.)

[3] Witzel (1501—1573) deserves to be remembered as one of those
who undertook to lead the forlorn hope of conciliation in a day
of unexampled sectarian fury.   Such an attitude was not easy to
preserve.   Already in this dialogue he leans perceptibly to the
Catholic side,—his satire upon Teuto, 'ein parteischer grossomodo'
who 'redet visirlich ding wie solche pflegen die sich's am wenigsten
verstehen,' and even on Core, is bitter in the extreme.   He ultimately became a Catholic and the compiler of a well-known Catholic
song-book.

Lycaon-gespreche. the author's authoritative verdict in its favour. It was reserved however for the unmeasured partisan to use the trial-motive with a picturesque elaboration to which neither Eckstein nor Witzel made any pretence. I have already briefly noticed the Lycaon-gespreche, in which the ruin of Henry of Brunswick is celebrated, somewhat prematurely, by his trial in the infernal court of Pluto. The only aim is here the humiliation of the prisoner, and every detail is made to enhance it. Of serious debate there is naturally none; and the whole weight is thrown upon the final catastrophe, the desperate intrigues of his infernal allies to save him, the indignant charge of the divinely sent judge to the doubtfully affected jury, the condemnation, and the portentous sentence in which Rhadamanthus exhausts the combined resources of the

Das Spiel von der Fasnacht. Greek and the Christian Inferno. Or, finally,—and here we are brought very close to the work of Turner,—instead of a real culprit, and an imaginary and poetic court, we have an allegorical figure, a popular personification, hustled by the serjeants and advocates of every day. A remarkable Fastnachtspiel[1], for instance, represents the trial of *die Fasnacht*, the genius of Carneval. The *precursor* appears with a warrant to arrest her, and promises the bystanders, in spite of her defiant resistance, that she shall be tried if any will accuse her,— 'that she may answer for her yearly plundering of all Christian folk.' The trial comes on; the advocates of the nobles, the citizens, the craftsmen, the peasants, the women, successively assail her, but she defends herself boldly, claims the merit of the Lenten fasting which her

---

[1] Keller, *Fastnachtspiele* No. 51. Though strictly speaking a drama, the 'Spiel von der Fasnacht' approaches so closely the method of the polemical drama of debate that I mention it here. The two classes merge in one another.

revels usher in, and is triumphantly acquitted by the sympathetic judge.

In the years when Witzel's dialogues were still fresh, W.Turner. and when the struggle with Lycaon was still agitating the whole North from Hesse to Saxony, Dr William Turner was probably beginning his long but laborious and fruitful German exile. A Northumberland man[1], he had gone to Cambridge, perhaps before 1530, and there became an ardent disciple of Latimer[2]. He appears to have lived there till towards 1540, when the new policy of the King made his position impossible. After a period of preaching in the English provinces he crossed the sea, took his degree at Padua, and then passed into Germany[3]. Here his versatile activity was divided between science and theological polemics. He travelled far and wide in search of rare herbs, and though for the most part living at various points in the Rhine valley,— Köln, Bonn, Strassburg, Basel,—few parts of either Upper or Lower Germany can have been unfamiliar to him. At the same time however he entered with great gusto into the theological war. He made it his work to

---

[1] Cf. Hodgson, *History of Northumberland.* Neither he nor Cooper (*Ath. Cantab.*) give a perfectly intelligible account of Turner's life. I have attempted at one or two points to clear it up.

[2] Cf. his *The Preservative or Triacle against the Poyson of Pelagius* &c. London 1551; dedicated to Latimer with these, among other words: 'About twenty years ago ye toke great paynes to put men from their evyl works,' and 'we that were your disciples had to do in Cambridge, after your departing from us, with them that defended praying unto Saintes;' &c. (quoted from the Bodleian copy, by Hodgson, *u. s.*).

[3] The chief ground for supposing that his flight took place in or soon after 1540 is the statement of his friend Gessner, 1555, that Turner visited him fifteen years previously. He was in any case at Basel in 1543.

expose the Catholic tendencies of the English bishops, representing them with more prudence than accuracy as acts of rebellion against the royal reformer who had lately enacted the Six Articles. The *Hunting of the Fox*[1] (*i.e.* the discovery of the hidden Romanist in the church) appeared at Basel in 1543, and so far impressed Gardiner that he wrote a reply[2], of which we can judge to some extent by Turner's rejoinder[3], where the 'Rescuer' (Gardiner) who had intervened in the Fox's favour, is in his turn confronted by 'the Hunter.' Their alternate objection and reply constitute this in a certain sense a dialogue, but it is of the stiffest mediaeval pattern; the whole suggests that he was using the dialogue form for the first time, with little consciousness of its capacities. A year or two later he returned to the charge in the *Hunting of the Wolf*[4], a work of greatly increased skill. The 'Hunter' is now joined by a 'Foster'; and both, unlike the somewhat abstract figures of the *Rescuing*, are

---

[1] *The Hunting of the Roman Fox*, &c. By W. Wraghton, Basil, 1543. (B. Mus.) This is not a dialogue.

[2] *Contra Turneri vulpem.* Bale, *Catalogus* &c. 1557, *sub nom.* 'Gardiner.'

[3] 'The Rescuing of the Roman Fox: otherwise called the Examination of the Hunter devised by Stephen Gardiner &c. Imprinted here at Winchester A.D. 1545. By me Hanse hit prik.' It was actually, of course, printed abroad; the 'by' before the printer's name perhaps represents the German rather than the English preposition. The substance of Gardiner's defence is pithily conveyed in Turner's dedication to the King: 'as soon as my houndes had found out [the fox]..., a certain sworne advocate of thys beste, drove my houndes from the beste, and saved his life bearing me in hande that the beaste *was no fox but on of your rede dear.*

[4] '*The Hunting of the Roman Wolf*, made by William Turner.' This title evidently belongs to the so-called '*Dialogue between a Hunter, Foster and Dean*,' of which a unique copy, without title-

palpable English burgesses, who have sat in parliament and are riding up to town in company with an acquaintance—a Dean, the partisan, in the discussion which follows, of the older faith.

These three pieces form a single group, carrying on the same image of a fox or wolf hunt, and differing mainly in the literary vivacity of the execution. The fourth, with which we are mainly concerned, is an entirely new departure. Almost every trace of the mediaeval disputation is now obliterated, a troop of well-distinguished characters replaces the routine two or three, and instead of a simple discussion, we have a *trial* with all the ceremony of a court. The Mass 'Mastres Missa' is discovered at the outset still at large, but betraying a large measure of the ὕβρις that forbodes misfortune. She loudly exults in her powers; she can break open purgatory, *Examination of the Mass*[1].

page, is at Lambeth. Since observing this, I find that Mr Hazlitt has seen their identity in Collections, 1st series. In the Handbook he had not seen it.—The date is fixed approximately to 1547 by a passage near the close: 'The wolf of Winchester about eight or nine years ago bit with his poison'd teeth doctor Crome and doctor Shraxton, whereof Dr Crome seeking remedye betime was helpt from the wolvish poison and madnes. But Shaxton deferring to long hath now the same poison that Gardiner had, and speaketh as like the wolf of Winchester as any wolf in England.' Shaxton's definite conversion took place in 1546; he had been deprived of his bishopric, by Gardiner's influence, in 1539.

[1] *The Examination of the Mass.* By Wm. Turner (Br. Mus.). Probably 1547. The plot almost implies that Edward's accession had already taken place; and on the other hand the terms of the notice in the *Preservative or triacle against the poyson of Pelagius*, &c. 1551,—'though this strife...were common to me with many, yet had I specially to do with...a Fox,...*and with a certain Wytche called Mastres Missa*' (quoted from Bodl. copy by Hodgson, *Hist. North. s. nom.* Turner), show that in that year (1551) it was no longer recent.

and release the damned; she is supreme in heaven and earth, for she can 'make God[1]'. An honest but ignorant listener, Master Freemouth, accuses her of profane blasphemy, first, to little purpose, before an old-fashioned Justice of the Peace, then before a wise and enlightened Judge, called, as in Witzel's Dialogue, 'Palemon.' Her cause is pleaded by two advocates Porphyry[2] and Philargyrus, who defend her with much ability but naturally without success, against the indictment of the prosecutor 'Knowledge[3].' Their attempt at once to defend the Mass by identifying it with the Last Supper, and to confine the right of administering it to a select priesthood, is crushed by unanswerable Biblical arguments. Finally judgment is given, and the unfortunate Mass is condemned to banishment within eight days from England, with a threat of severe punishment should she reappear. With a brief lyric lament at her fate she leaves the scene.

Turner's 'Trial' is undisguisedly English in colouring. The court is a London sessions' house; the officers, so far as they have any complexion, are English court-officers; the prisoner is an English 'wytch.' None the less does the whole scheme of the satire belong to a type of which the home was Germany, not England. The *Examination of the Mass* is the first native specimen of what I have called the 'drama of debate,' long before familiar across the sea. The particular form which it

---

[1] Such enumerations were already a commonplace of Anti-missal literature, cf. e.g. Manuel's *Testament of the Mass*, already mentioned.

[2] Cf. the use of 'Porphyrius' by Kirchmayer in the *Pammachius* as the counsellor of Antichrist.

[3] Cf. the title of Scoloker's lost dialogue, 'Simplicitie and knowledge,' where the latter also presumably represents the Protestant side.

takes,—a trial, had also, as we have seen, abundant analogies there; and finally the author was perhaps the best acquainted of his countrymen with the German speech and German land. Without pressing analogies of detail, such as the choice of the name *Palemon* (as in Witzel) for the judge, or the resemblance of Turner's ignorant Lutheran *Freemouth* to Witzel's 'grosso-modo' *Teuto*, there is ground I think for maintaining that some light is thrown by Turner's German exile on the work which appeared on his return.

Turner's effective satire did not remain unimitated. *'The En-* In the last days of 1548 appeared another 'Trial,' still *dightment* more elaborate and detailed than his, but unmistakeably *Mother* parallel in conception.   Two Protestants, *Veryte* and *Messe[1].'* *Knowledge*, meet and exchange news.   Knowledge mentions a certain sorceress, Mother Messe, whose unheard-of pretensions 'have brought the people into develyshe trade'; for she claims (like Turner's 'witch') to change the weather, release from Purgatory, and 'make God.' At *Veryte's* desire, *Knowledge* gives information to the serjeant, *Wisdom*, who at once sets out to arrest her. She is speedily found.   She greets the officers with insolent defiance, but is reminded that 'the world is not now as it hath been,' and finally submits,—not without an attempt to bribe her jailor, Antipas,—to go to 'suppe her porege in Newgate.'   What it is difficult to avoid calling the next 'scene' brings us to the session's house, at 8 o'clock on the following morning.   The judge, *God's word*, bids *Daniel*, the crier, inquire who has a suit. Mother Messe is put at the bar, and the twelve Apostles are impanelled as jury.   Then *Knowledge* as prosecutor brings forward the long and formal 'endightment' for

[1] *A new Dialoge called the endightment agaynste Mother Messe'*... 17 Dec. 1548 (Lambeth).

'treason, theft and murder.' She is defended, partly by herself, partly by her 'surtise' Master Stifneck and Master Covetous, who after her final condemnation to death, plead for a milder sentence, and succeed in getting it commuted to exile.

The 'Endightment,' upon which I shall not dwell, is evidently only a more elaborate treatment of the idea of the Examination. The preliminary scenes are proportionally longer and more detailed, the persons more numerous; their names are also more consistently allegorical, and more exclusively English. But the conception of the trial is identical; the Mass is, as before, a sorceress; as before she is accused by the advocate Knowledge; and if the judge's name suggests that the author's Lutheranism was warmer than his appreciation of Vergil, he at any rate pronounces the same verdict as the Turnerian Palemon. I regard the Endightment as a somewhat felicitous adaptation of Turner's plan, produced not many months after it.

Dialogus duarum sororum. The last of the dialogues of Edward's reign which calls for notice here, may be briefly dismissed. One of those accidents which even in our days count for much in international literature, brought into the hands of an English translator, a Dialogue which, like Sachs', was a production of Nürnberg. Wolfgang Resch the author, 'Formschneider' or engraver of that city, appears to have belonged to the large class of German satirists who devoted themselves to correcting the faults of the other sex. He calls his dialogue a 'Zuchtschul der bösen weiber,'—'a reformatory for shrews,'—or, in more detail, 'a proper dialogue *of two sisters;* the first a godly and virtuous widow of Meissen, the other a shrewish, obstinate and evil-tempered woman of the *Gebirge*[1].'

[1] '*Ein schöner dialogus oder gesprech, von zweien Schwestern,* &c. (B. Mus.). (Goedeke, § 140, No. 57.)

This I assume to be that 'dialogus duarum sororum' which is stated by Bale to have been translated, among other works, by Walter Lynne, 'e Germanico sermone in Anglicam linguam[1].' It is best described as a practical application of the Pauline doctrine of married life. Justina, the godly widow, exhorts her froward sister to live peaceably with her husband, and finally departs, leaving behind her 'as a New-Year's gift,' 'the Gospel and saving Christian doctrine of Paul.' The whole has scarcely more literary significance than that of an edifying treatise in a slightly picturesque form.

For our present purpose the period which followed *Dialogue under Mary.* the death of Edward may be briefly dismissed. Mary's reign was not favourable to an abundant harvest of so peculiarly Protestant a growth, and the few examples which remain, printed for the most part abroad, belong to an ordinary type. They are interesting however as contemporary pictures of England. Michael Wodde's Dialogue, written at Rouen in Feb. 1554, contains a lively portrait of one who had been in the opposition under Edward, returning with alacrity to the older faith in which he was bred, or as the Protestant author puts it, to the 'blind superstitions' in which he was 'noseled[2];

[1] *Illustr. Vir. Catalogus*, ed. 1548 (Additio).

[2] *A dialogue or Familiar talke betweene two neighbours, concerninge the chyefest ceremonyes that were, by the mighti power of God's most holie pure worde, suppressed in Englande, and nowe for our unworthines, set up agayne by the bishoppes, the impes of Antichrist...* From Roane by Mich. Wodde, 20 Feb. A.D. 1554. (Lambeth.)— The speakers are Olyver 'a professour of Gospell,' and Nicholas, a Catholic. Olyver meets Nicholas on his way to early mass. They exchange greetings. Olyver hints that his neighbour was not formerly found turning out so early to church. 'No, when there was nothing to do but to hear a priest babble. But I thank God I may see my maker again,' &c.—At the close, unnoticed in Mait-

and an anonymous work of some two years later, gives a
detailed account of the trial of Ridley at Oxford some
months before[1].

Elizabeth.   With the fervours and perils of its early days, the
Protestant cause lost much of its power of literary inspiration.   The peace of Augsburg in Germany and the
accession of Elizabeth in England opened an epoch of
comparative security and, in the region of what may be
called theological *belles-lettres,* almost complete insignifi-
cance.   Literary power steadily detached itself from the
world of Hebraic imagery within which it had so long
willingly moved.   In Germany the dialogue form sank
gradually into disuse as a method of theological controversy, and where it lingered tended to be little more than
a traditional trick of style, a literary fashion out of which
the zest and flavour had departed.   In England, where
its vogue had from the first scarcely amounted to a
fashion, its later course shows both less evident traces of
decay, and more complete independence.   It was freely
applied to a variety of secular discussions, the vexations
of the law, the Spanish invasion, the troubles in Ireland[2].

land's Catalogue, but apparently also by Wodde, is a short *Dialogue
or communication for two children, or unlettred folkes, profitable,* &c.
It is a catechism, similar to the *confabulationes puerorum* of Bale:
cf. A. Schröer, *Anglia* v. 146.

[1] *A trew Mirrour or glase, wherein we may behold the wofull
state of things in our Realm of England, set forth in a dialogue...
betweene Eusebius and Theophilus,* 1556.   (Lambeth.)

[2] Cf. under the first head, the *Newes from the North, otherwise
called the conference betweene Simon Certain and Pierce Plowman,*
1585 (B. Mus.),—one of the liveliest English dialogues of the
century, and not unlike that of W. Bullen.   Simon, mine host
of the Greek Omega, defends the character and public usefulness of
the profession against the charges of his friend Pierce.   A more
theoretic treatment of legal matters had been given long before
in the well-known Dialogue between a Student of the laws and

Towards the close of the reign the Puritans within the Church began to apply to the Church itself the method formerly used against the Catholics, but without any apparent resort to the older models[1]. Some measure of the degree to which the main literary current in England had diverged towards the close of the century from that still vigorous in Germany about the middle of its course, may be had by comparing Thynne's Disputation between *Pride and Lowliness* with Hans Sachs' treatment of a precisely similar subject,—*Gesprech zwischen der Hoffahrt und der Demuth*[2]. The long-drawn, sonorous quatrains of the former, with their pomp and luxuriance of phrase, show how far English verse had passed from any possible dealings with the cheerful hobble of Hans Sachs. German influence had passed, as will presently be shown, to a wholly different field. It remains, before turning thither, to review a great neighbouring literary *genre* from which the dialogue at its most ambitious moments was scarcely distinguishable, and in which the genius of Protestantism has deposited its most laborious monument.

a doctor in theology, by the eminent lawyer of the Inner Temple, St Germain (by 1531). Among the anti-catholic dialogues of the reign several of which exist at Lambeth, the most noted is the *dialogus contra tyrannidem Papistarum*, 1562, translated into English the same year (both at Lambeth),—a general survey of the European struggle with Catholicism, country by country as it then stood, at the moment when France and the Netherlands were about to enter on the conflict from which England and Germany had just emerged.

[1] Cf. Udall's *Diotrephes, the state of the Church of England laid open in a conference between Diotrephes a bishop*, &c. (ed. by Prof. Arber, English Scholar's Library).

[2] H. Sachs, Werke, *Stuttg. Lit. Verein*, Bd. 104.

CHAPTER III.

The Latin Drama.

THE very limited number of persons who have seriously examined the remains of our modern Latin drama, have hardly perhaps thought the oblivion which has overtaken it too hard a sentence. It has played the part of undistinguished sister to a woman of genius; overlooked in the more brilliant presence, and perhaps, with the knowledge that rivalry is hopeless, hardly doing justice to her own powers. While the native English drama advanced steadily throughout the century to the incomparable splendour of its close, the history of the Latin plays is a record of desultory production, without growth or advance[1], without vogue, without continuity. The thrice-refined dilettantism of the later Renaissance, the absorbed pursuit of classical elegance and classical phrase, which often, as in the miserable productions of Gager, involved a sacrifice of higher qualities without gaining its own object, has set its mark on nearly the whole of this hapless branch of art. It scarcely attempted to fertilise itself by any concession to the evidently more vital method of the sister drama, which, on its part, had rapidly appropriated as much of classical method as it could yet assimilate.

---

[1] Indeed one of the earliest, Grimald's *Archipropheta* is distinctly among the best.

The gulf between them remained fixed; the more se-
cluded drew little advantage from the popularity of its
rival; and while the latter remains in scores of contemporary prints, the former now lingers for the most part
in MS. at Oxford, Cambridge and London, where it is
seldom disturbed.

In Germany however the Latin drama had altogether *In
better fortune. Almost from the first it showed a robust Germany.*
individuality, a genial power of adapting itself to the
needs of the soil and climate without giving in to them,
which saved it from being either a feeble imitation of the
native growths, or a sickly exotic. It fell into the hands of
men for whom Humanism did not mean a doctrinaire reproduction of classical models, but a free use of whatever in
them was serviceable to the training of Christian citizens:
schoolmasters indeed for the most part themselves, and
writing in the first instance for those school performances
on which sixteenth century paedagogy looked with so
much favour. Under these conditions many refinements
of style and art were perhaps necessarily forgone; but on
the other hand the continual reference to an actual stage
and to the needs of actors all young and comparatively
unaccomplished in Latin, brought with it just that simplicity and boldness of handling, that rapidity of movement, that homely force of style, in which the modern
Latin drama of mere literature habitually fails[1]. And this
healthy condition was distinctly fostered by a kindred
development of vernacular drama, also in origin a school
institution, which in a manner mediated between the

---

[1] From the same motive, the strict and rhythmic iambic was
occasionally preferred to the looser and less easily remembered verse
of Terence and Plautus (so Macropedius, cf. his interesting preface
to the *Rebelles*); but less skilful writers found cogent reasons for
a different choice.

Latin drama and the still vigorous mediaeval Mysteries; borrowing its technique in part from both. Hence
the familiar intercourse which set in between all branches
of the drama in Germany and which is so hard to parallel
elsewhere. Their stock of subjects was in the main the
same, the same men frequently wrote in both tongues,
their plays were translated backwards and forwards.
Burgher and scholar sat as it were at the same banquet,
and were served as far as might be with the same dishes.
The Rathhaus, the school-hall, the Münsterplatz, or the
market-place was the scene of both; the Latin *Susanna*
of Sixt Birck was acted in a public garden of Augsburg,
the public *Brunnen* serving for the bath[1]; while the
whole populace of Strassburg flocked into the school-
court to witness the Latin *Saul*. Sometimes a Latin
performance before the school authorities, was immediately followed by one in German before the assembled
Rath in the Rathhaus, or in the open air in order that,
as was said, *beid gelert und ungelert Burger, Bawr, und
alle man den profectum wachs und zunemmen der Schulen
sehen und erfaren*[2]. At Magdeburg such a double performance was prescribed in the school-statutes, and took
place every year[3]; at Solothurn we hear of the *Acolastus*
being twice acted in an open place, first in Latin then in
German[4]. Frequently the comic scenes intended for the
groundlings were given in their idiom[5]; there are even
records of a performance of Frischlin's *Phasma* where

[1] Cf. the Epistle prefixed to the first edition.
[2] Baumgarten, *Juditium Solomonis*, 1561, quoted by Goedeke,
Grundr. p. 306.
[3] Cf. Goedeke, p. 306.
[4] Holstein, *Die Dramen vom verlorenen Sohn*, p. 43.
[5] A. Jundt, *Die dramatischen Aufführungen im Gymnasium zu
Strassburg* (*Einleitung*).

each speaker after delivering his Latin speech proceeded to render it in German[1]. And where the performances were wholly separate, and the German play, as was often the case, was acted by an 'honourable company of citizens,' often with the Burgermeister at their head, we hear of amicable loans of stage apparatus from the school properties[2]; while, on the other hand, the Rath not unfrequently contributed to the often considerable cost of the school-plays[3], and at Strassburg finally gave them an appointed income from the municipal budget. The school-drama had after all been warmly and emphatically prescribed by the founders of Protestantism; it played a recognised part in forming good citizens, and if the good citizen who was already formed found its language no longer easy, he still patronised it as a bulwark of morals and manners[4].

Under such conditions, the Latin drama could hardly aspire to the insipid perfections of academic art. It was barbarous,—as, in Ciceronian eyes, Erasmus' Latin was barbarous,—because it boldly laid hold of modern life, and wrote for modern, if not altogether for unlearned eyes and ears. It was not for nothing that it grew up in the atmosphere of great and almost republican cities, and that Augsburg, Strassburg, Basel, Magdeburg, were the theatre of a production to which Bristol and Norwich were wholly, and even London almost wholly, strange. But

[1] Hase, *D. geistl. Schauspiel,* 114, cit. Jundt, *u. s.*

[2] The Jesuits *e.g.* are said to have lent their *burning hell* to the Burgerschaft of Speyr.   Goedeke, § 149.

[3] At Rheinfelden, in 1602, at a performance of the Prodigal Son, the Rath presented the school with 12 gulden *and the calf.* Holstein, *u. s.*

[4] Sixt Birck's dedication of his Latin *Susanna* to the senate of Augsburg breathes a peculiarly lively sense of the bond between the city and the school-drama.

it had great and positive merits too, for which no 'product
of the circumstances' theory can altogether account.   In
England it enlisted barely one or two secondary names in
its service[1],—a Grimald, a Radcliff, an Udall; in Germany
the best dramatists of the century wrote wholly in Latin.
The best dramatic work done in Germany before Lessing
was done in Latin, says the most competent of living men
to pronounce[2]. The vigour and versatility of Macropedius,
the Aristophanic satire of Frischlin, the severity and
reserve of Reuchlin, the real pathos and passion which
glow through the too ornate periods of Brülow, entitle
them to a place in the most superficial view of modern
European drama.

A short history of this in England somewhat neglected branch of letters will best introduce what I shall afterwards have to say in more detail about its various points
of contact with our own literature.

I.

SHORT
HISTORY
OF THE
LATIN
DRAMA
IN GER-
MANY.

1.
The Hu-
manists.

Nothing perhaps so well illustrates the relative
slowness with which the technique of ancient literature,
in comparison with its style and phraseology won appreciation north of the Alps, as the heterogeneous and
even bizarre collection of dramas produced by the early
German Humanists. Several of the most conspicuous
masterpieces of German Humanists certainly approach
antiquity much more nearly by their style than by
conception or structure; the *Encomium Moriae*, the

---

[1] I do not reckon Cowley, whose *Naufragium Joculare* is
certainly one of the most brilliant of English Latin comedies but
falls, like the *Ignoramus*, outside our period.

[2] W. Scherer, *Gesch. des Elsasses*, 300.

Laus Veneris, for instance, are evidently built upon purely mediaeval motives. But the majority of their dramas betray a relation to the classical theatre at most by their respectable Latin. In 1470 was performed at Heidelberg the first drama produced by Humanism out of Italy,—the *Stylpho* of Wimpheling; some sixty years later, the publication of Gnaphaeus' *Acolastus* at length struck a fruitful vein and virtually originated the characteristic German school of Latin drama. These sixty years—three-quarters of which were the very heyday of German Humanism—were scarcely more than a period of desultory experiment in the history of this essentially Humanist form of art. At least four types of drama were put forth,—not, it is true, always with the same intention or with the same seriousness. The *Ludus Dianae* exhibited by Conrad Celtes before Maximilian at Linz in 1501, and the *Spectaculum* of Jacob Locher acted at Ingolstadt the following February, were scarcely more than pageants, allied on the one hand to the mediaeval *ludi,* on the other to the Court Masques,—pageants to the last in their loose structure and their indispensable splendour. In Celtes there is almost no pretence of action. Diana and her nymphs, Sylvanus and his Fauns, Bacchus, and his Bacchides come forward successively in three so-called acts; but their sole business is to express in flowing hexameters the favour naturally felt by the deities of hunting, love and wine for the young heir of the Roman empire.

Locher's *Spectaculum*[1] is dramatic in much the same sense as Scott's ' gathering of the Clans.' The first 'act' is as purely epic as a Euripidean prologue, a long narra-

1.
Pageants :
Celtes :
*Ludus
Dianæ,*
1501.
Locher :
Spectaculum, 1502.

---

[1] *Spectaculum in quo reges adversum Thurcum consilium ineunt,* s. l. 1502.

tive, in hexameters, of Turkish cruelties, followed by a
prayer from the chorus, to which the rest of the play
is a prolonged response.   In the second act the Pope's
legate is seen appealing, still in hexameters, to Maximilian as so many others had appealed, to march against
the enemy of Christendom; and the 'player-king' gives
the proposal that ready assent which the real one
found no opportunity of executing.   The third act is a
Council on a grander scale ; the kings of France, Spain,
England and Hungary deliver orations, and declare
their readiness for war.   Lastly, a lyric dialogue between
a 'Capitaneus' and the chief of Rhodes shows that the
eastern stronghold of Christendom is as combative as
the west, and the fourth act closes with a spirited call
to arms—

> en age rumpe moras liticen, dent classica vastos
> armorum strepitus, buccina saeva crepat.

The fifth act of actual war to which this should have
been the prelude Locher withheld, and history reproduced his aposiopesis.   Even where he deals with a
genuine dramatic action, as in the *De Judicio Paridis*[1],
he can scarcely be said to rise above that elementary
type of drama which consists in a series of set speeches,
and which was perhaps to be expected in a dramatist
who evidently knew his Ovid better than his Terence[2].

[1] Acted before the '*Achademia*' of Ingolstadt, July 1, 1502, and
printed s. l. the same year.

[2] Another piece of Locher's however, *de sene amatore*, is described as 'angeblich in plautinischer manier' (Goedeke, p. 133): of
this, as well as of his earlier *ludus de Thurcis* I unfortunately cannot speak.—As Locher is chiefly remembered as the translator of
the *Narrenschiff*, it may be worth while recalling the impressive
chapter in which, with the same reference to Maximilian, Brandt
gives full vent to the Turcophobia of the time, to which many
minds far less constitutionally despondent than his own were a prey.

A somewhat higher dramatic level is reached by a se-   2.
cond group of Humanist dramas to which Terence contri-   *Satiric*
buted scarcely more than he did to the shows and pageants   *dramas.*
of Humanism.   The social antipathies of Humanism   Wimphe-
were as little to be paralleled in the narrow domestic   *Stylpho,*
world of ancient comedy as its political aspirations.   1470.
Conventional satire against the ignorance and vices   *Codrus.*
of the Roman clergy, was scarcely more congenial than   Reuchlin :
pictures of crusading Christendom or mythological eulogies   *Sergius,*
of the last of the knights, to a school of drama which   1507).
reflected far more faithfully the political decay of Greece
than the still vigorous public life of Rome.   The satiric
dramas of the German Humanists show in plot and
structure very little trace of this influence.   Jacob Wimpheling's *Stylpho*[1] was produced in **1470** at Heidelberg,
where the future coryphaeus of Strassburg Humanism
and advocate of the aboriginal *Teutschheit* of Alsace,
was still a student.   It is little more than a student's
jeu d'esprit, though somewhat akin to the more elaborate
and brilliant *Return from Parnassus* of an unknown
Cambridge hand ; but it deals a blow with considerable
effect at the degenerate race of 'Roman Germans' who
crept into spiritual dignity by menial service at the
Roman court, one of whom presents himself to the
University chancellor armed with the papal recommen-
dation to a curacy, is put through an examination, like
the knight's son in the *Return*, and, like him, is dismissed ingloriously at the close, with the sentence that
he is *aptior ut porcos quam ut homines pascat*.   Equally
original from the point of view of ancient comedy is

---

[1] *Stylpho*, s. l. 1494.—By a strange oversight, repeated even in
the 'neu durchgesehene' edition of his and Lorenz's *Geschichte des
Elsasses*, Scherer refers to it as *unfortunately lost.*

the *Codrus*[1] of some anonymous Humanist, where a
pedagogue whose Latin was of the school of Villa Dei,
finding himself deserted by his pupils for more fashionable teachers, goes to Köln to learn for himself the new
way, but falls into the hands of Humanist students,
who make game of him as mercilessly as the 'pestiferi
poetae' who, a generation later, were the terror of the
correspondents of Ortuinus Gratius. Finally, the earliest
dramatic effort of Reuchlin, who will demand a fuller
notice presently, the *Sergius*[2], was a hit at the relic-
mongers. Reuchlin's language, style, and verse,—he
writes in a vigorous and flowing senarius,—certainly placed
him above both his predecessors ; but his plot,—the discovery of a skull, which after being washed and dressed
is worshipped as a Christian relic, and finally proves to
have belonged to a Mohammedan renegade,—is undramatic as well as unsavoury.

Later Pageants: H. Schotten. Neither of these two classes or types of drama can
be said to have made its fortune. Isolated cases cer-
tainly occur of *ludi* which do more naïve violence to
the primary law of drama than even those of Locher
and Celtes; particularly the so-called 'Imperial Play'
and 'Martial Play' of Hermann Schotten[3], 'Chronicle
Histories' of the rudest kind, where the 'divine victories'

---

[1] *Codrus* (MS.). Cf. Schulze, *Archiv f. Litteraturgesch.* 11,
328 ff., at present the only accessible account of this drama at first
hand.

[2] *Sergius.* First printed in 1507, and frequently afterwards.

[3] *Ludus Imperatorius seu Cæsareus, continens umbraticam
imaginem horum temporum regni Caroli V., illiusque divinas
victorias, imperii felicem exitum et laudem.—Ludus Martius, de
discordia principum et rusticorum Germaniae,* A. 1525, Colon.
1527. Hermann Schottenius Hessus was also the author of a well-
known set of *Confabulationes* for schools, translated later in the
century into English, like those of his fellow-dramatist Hegendorf.

of Charles, and those, less 'divine' certainly, of his nobles
over their peasantry, are fought once more, the com-
batants in broad undistinguished masses charging and
taking counsel, treating with heralds, &c., all with military
energy enough, but with no attempt at the psychological
colour without which war is a matter for the circus.
The purely satirical drama too had its isolated examples,—above all the savage and obscene attack of *and
'satiric'
dramas:*
Simon Lemnius upon Luther and his wife, powerfully
written in elegiacs, like Locher's *Ludus,*—elegiacs in S. Lemnius.
which every couplet becomes an epigram[1];—and the N. Frischlin.
three strange, barbaric but fresh and sparkling *Tendenz-*
stücke of Nicodemus Frischlin, to which the whole history
of the drama offers no precise parallel,—the *Priscianus*
Vapulans[2], the *Julius Redivivus* and the *Phasma.*

Setting aside then such anomalous or eccentric phases   3.
of drama as these, there remain, still within the circle of *'The*
christian
purely Humanist activity, two well-marked dramatic *Terence.'*
methods, each of which has its representative poet, and Chilianus:
Dorothea,
which far from occupying, like the former, merely a 1507.
curious page in the history of German drama, were
nothing less than the cardinal points towards which
nearly all its most characteristic work more or less explicitly tended.   On the one hand the pious effort of
the Nun of Gandersheim to create an immaculate Terence
out of biblical and legendary history, was far too congenial to the religious Humanism of Germany to be
wholly neglected; and her newly discovered writings,

---

[1] The *Monachopornomachia* is reprinted in Murr, *Neues Journal*
II. 85 (1791).   Cf. G. E. Lessing, *Schriften*, Th. II. Brief 7.

[2] A slight resemblance to this play may possibly be found, it is
true, in the Oxford *Bellum grammaticale*, where Priscianus likewise
figures, but where he 'beats' instead of 'being beaten.'   On
Frischlin, see below p. 100.

edited in 1501 by the discoverer Conrad Celtes, soon
found a disciple at one of the centres of religious Humanism, the young university of Wittenberg. The
Dorothea of Chilianus[1] 'eques Hillerstatinus,' produced
there in 1507, would have been the chosen companion
of the heroic maidens of Hroswitha[2]; and, though martyr-
doms are scarcely congenial to the modern stage, it can
scarcely be said that a subject was altogether ill chosen
which inspired Handel, and one of the most celebrated
sacre rapresentationi[3] of Florence, as well as the solitary
'religious drama' proper to which any great Elizabethan
put his hand. It is written in simple but not unskilful
prose, and follows the story with comparative fidelity, and
considerable effect. Naturally the daring imagination
with which Massinger at once enriched and degraded his
subject, is wholly out of the question.

4.
*'Modern
Terence.'*
Reuchlin:
Henno,
1498.

It was a stronger hand than Chilianus' however which
gave the decisive stimulus to the Latin drama. The
Sergius of Reuchlin, withdrawn on grounds of prudence
soon after its appearance, was followed a few months
later by his epoch-making *Henno*[4]. Its importance lay
in two things. It showed how a modern comedy-subject,
fresh and dramatic and at the same time perfectly

---

[1] *Comœdia Dorothee passionem depingens.* Liptzk. 1507.

[2] The resemblance is especially close to the *Dulcicius*, where
three virgins Agape, Chionia and Hyrena, after an attempt of the
præses to seduce them, suffer martyrdom. Cf. also the *Fides Spes et
Charitas.* The *Gallicanus* also deals with persecution.

[3] *La rapresentatione di S^a Dorothea* was reprinted very frequently
in the 16th century.· The authors of *The Virgin Martyr* may
possibly have known it, but it was certainly not their main source.
The singular error of 'Sabritius' for Fabricius, for example, (the
name of the prefect), has no place there.

[4] *Scenica Progymnasmata.* Argent. 1498. Cf. L. Geiger, *Reuchlin*, S. 89.

healthy[1], might be effectively made the base of a Latin
play; and its well-turned verses made clear that the true
medium was neither the epic hexameter of Celtes nor the
elegiac of Locher, still less the prose of Wimpheling,
Hroswitha and Chilianus, but the dramatic senarius of
Terence. The most effective part of the plot is drawn from
the famous farce of *Pathelin*, then some twenty years old.
The *drappier*, the astute advocate, and astuter *bergier* reappear in their familiar parts; a domestic Dromo borrows
the shepherd's weapon, and foils both draper and advocate with his impenetrable '*Ble.*' But this central
incident is placed in a different setting, which has a good
deal of merit of its own. It is one of the weak points of
Pathelin that it has two heroes, and that the second, the
bergier, is introduced, like a subordinate, without preparation, in the middle of the play. Dromo is, on the
other hand, from the first the mainspring of the whole
action. Sent by his master Henno to purchase cloth
of one Danista, with certain *gulden* (aurei) abstracted
from the private hoard of Henno's wife, Elsa, he contrives to secure both cloth and money, and to cheat
at one stroke the draper, his master, and his master's
wife. The draper accuses him; he seeks help from the
advocate, and the trial follows with the familiar result.
Pathelin and the *bergier*, the two heroes of the French

---

[1] In the prologue to the *Sergius* Reuchlin had specially insisted
on this:
> 'Non hic erit lasciviae aut libidini
> Meretriciae aut tristi senum curae locus
> Sed histrionum exercitus et scommata.'

It need hardly be said that the follower of Hroswitha had made the
same pretensions in the prologue to the *Dorothea*:
> 'Phyllidis hinc absint et Demophoontis amores,
> Pollutusque Davus, Pamphilus atque Cremes,
> Penelope......Hyppolitus.'

farce, are thus combined in Dromo, while the *drappier's*
double *rôle* of creditor and master is distributed between
Henno and Danista.   The new figures of Henno and
his wife serve too to repeat the principal motive of a
comedy, for which the *Cheater Cheated* would be a fairly
apt title ; Elsa cheats her husband by hoarding her gold;
he cheats her by abstracting it ; and both are cheated by
the cheater of the cheating advocate, the arch-cheat
Dromo, whose offences are finally condoned in a marriage
with his master's daughter, the stolen *gulden* serving as
his wife's dowry.   It is obvious that these changes, im-
provements perhaps, in structure, involved one loss for
which no technical perfection can console the lover of
high comedy.   As Dromo is responsible for the sins of
Pathelin as well as of the *bergier*, the advocate's *rôle*
loses nine-tenths of its humour; the exquisite double-
game between the *drap* and the *moutons*, the feigned
tooth-ache, the keen sense of fun with which he works
out the situation, necessarily disappear, and a comic
creation which may be mentioned without irreverence
beside Falstaff after Gadshill, becomes merely the unscrupulous pleader of every day.   The result, then, of
Reuchlin's remarkable attempt to turn a modern *farce*
subject into an ancient comedy may be summed up
somewhat thus.   Certain characters and incidents have
a Terentian or Plautine colouring : the wily Dromo, the
purloining of a buried hoard, the final solution of all
difficulties by marriage.   Finally, the admirably clear and
compact structure,—obtained, it is true, at the sacrifice
of a situation which lay wholly beyond the horizon of
ancient comedy.   The *Henno* is in so far typical of the
whole modern Latin drama of which it occupies one of the
most remarkable pages ; it told by high excellences of a
low kind, by success in satisfying the more mechanical

canons of art, by skill of structure, unity, singleness of plot; but it frequently missed in the search for them the more impalpable perfections which perhaps only a Molière entirely succeeded in combining with them[1].

It is possible that the popular drama of Italy may have contributed something to the *Henno*; and shortly after its appearance another Italian influence asserted itself in Germany which demands a moment's notice. It told entirely in one direction,—the comedy of vulgar love-intrigue. Three Latin plays by Italians were reprinted or translated in Germany between 1500 and 1520,—the *Poliscena* of Leonardo Aretino (Cracow 1509), the *Dolotechne* of Zambertus (Strassb. 1511), and

Italian Humanist Comedy in Germany. Aretino, Zambertus, Ugolino.

---

[1] I have intentionally taken no notice in the text of the interesting discussion raised by Hermann Grimm (*Essays,* N. F.), and ably continued by Geiger (*Reuchlin,* s. 80 ff.) upon the relation of the *Henno* to a German Fastnachtspiel, *Der kluge Knecht* (Keller, No. 107), which coincides with the drama in substance and in numerous details. Grimm, who first pointed out the resemblance, regards the Fastnachtspiel as the source of the drama, but neither Goedeke, Keller nor Geiger, nor, so far as I know, any one else, has accepted his view, though, through the uncertainty of the date of the former, it cannot be disproved. I have only two remarks to offer. 1. Whether Reuchlin or the author of the Fastnachtspiel was the first to use the *Pathelin;* both probably knew it independently. Dromo's magic monosyllable *Ble* is not likely to have been reached from the *bergier's Bée* through the medium of the *knecht's* quite different *weiw;* and on the other hand, the Fastnachtspiel name for the deluded tradesman, *Der Duochman,* is obviously a translation of *drappier,* not of Reuchlin's *Danista.* 2. Both Reuchlin and the *FNSp.* agree in giving *eight aurei* (*gulden*) as the price of the cloth, for the *nine francs* or *six écus* of *Pathelin.* A more exact comparison of the values of these coins in the 15th century than I can undertake would show whether the Roman *aureus* or the *gulden* better corresponded in intrinsic value to $\frac{3}{4}$ écu ($\frac{6}{8}$ franc); and produce an argument of some weight for the priority of the *Henno* or of the *FNSp.* respectively.

the *Philogenia* of Ugolino da Parma (a prose translation, Augsburg 1518). The common theme of Italian novels, —an *amour* carried to its issue by the aid of old women, slaves, *lenones* &c.,—reappears in a fairly attractive garment of Latin prose. The best appears to me to be the last, where a peasant girl's love for her seducer is pathetically drawn. It was probably from such works as these that a future schoolmaster of note, Hegendorff, produced his *nova comoedia*,—a slight sketch from a similar phase of life, which Goedeke has rather unreasonably praised[1]. 'New' as the author chose to call it, it merely gave a dramatic form to a subject already run threadbare by the novelists, a not yet hackneyed embroidery to a base and worn-out stuff. Hegendorff wrote in the prime of early manhood, but his work is the sapless leaving of an old literature, not the budding promise of a new.

II.
The Christian Terence.
The Dutch School.
Macropedius, Gnapheus, Crocus.

It was in the north, in Holland, still as ever to the forefront of Teutonic civilisation, that the work of Reuchlin was first worthily taken up and directed into a fruitful channel. His mantle fell directly upon a man of great eminence, probably of all modern Latin dramatists the one whose talent had the largest measure of genius,— George Macropedius, master of Utrecht school. By his side stand two contemporaries, whose first dramas, though written long after his, appeared before them,—William Gnapheus (Fullonius) of the Hague, and Cornelius Crocus of Amsterdam. All three appear to have arrived independently at the same solution for a practical problem which as schoolmasters they all had to meet: how, namely, to steep a boy's mind in the admirable colloquial Latin of Terence and Plautus without introducing him prematurely to a world of *lenones* and *meretrices*. All three found the solution in what may be generally called

---

[1] *Comoedia nova*, Lips. 1520, cf. Goedeke, § 113, 10.

the Biblical drama, or, as the strange phrase went, the
comedia sacra; but with differences in motive and *technique* which, as I have already hinted, cover almost the
whole region between the Christian mysticism of the
Dorothea and the worldly but perfectly fresh and pure
satire of the *Henno*, or at least tend to converge upon
one or other of the two venerable dramatic schemes of
which the *Dorothea* and the *Henno* were slight examples,—
the tragic struggle of a moral hero with 'the world,' his
unjust sufferings, persecution, ruin, or his triumph and
glory ;—and a career of *picaresque* or prodigal adventure,
issuing in a final restoration to grace and decency.   For
the former the Old Testament naturally offered abundant
examples ; as the *Judiths, Susannas, Esthers, Josephs,*
which presently inundated Germany, sufficiently showed ;
ancient comedy, on the other hand, none whatever.   For
the latter, Plautus and Terence were a mine of illustration ; while the Hebraic genius, to which such stories
were as foreign as they were congenial to the Greek, produced perhaps in the whole Bible but one instance,
though one of incomparable beauty,—the parable of the
Prodigal Son.   The latter commended itself to what
we may call the Left group, the champions of 'sacred
comedy,' the ardent Humanists, who vied with the old
comic poets, aspired to be the Terences or Plautuses
of the age, and to reproduce as far as was consistent with
a Biblical subject and a pious intention the art, the
colouring, the society, the atmosphere of Plautus and
Terence. Such, on the whole, was Gulielmus Gnapheus, the G. Gna-
author of the *Acolastus*[1], the most famous and the finest, pheus:
though not the first, Latin drama upon the Prodigal Son. *Acolastus,*
'Our age,' he writes suggestively in the prologue, 'has its 1529.

---

[1] *Acolastus*, Basil, 1534.   Performed at the Hague in 1529.

Tullies and Livies, its Virgils and Demosthenes, but of Menanders and of Terences none'; and it is the influence of Terence and not of the parable which dictates the choice of incidents, the complexion of the characters, and nearly every detail of the execution. The division of the inheritance, the return, the forgiveness, on which the whole emphasis of the Biblical narrative is thrown, are touched with extreme lightness; the elder brother, though casually mentioned, nowhere appears. On the other hand, what the parable passed lightly by becomes the main subject of the drama, and the reticent brevity of the *dissipavit substantiam suam vivendo luxuriose* is expanded into a series of striking scenes, painted with the genial vigour of Plautus, and a fearless use of his abundant material.

C. Crocus: *Joseph*, 1535.
A more austere school was represented in Cornelius Crocus. Gnapheus, originally Catholic, suffered prison and exile for Protestant leanings which finally led him into the camp of Zwingli, Crocus was an inflexible member of the old faith, and ended his days as a Jesuit in Rome. The Prologue to the *Joseph* reads like a counterblast to that of the *Acolastus*. Gnapheus' undisguised admiration for Terence and Plautus is replaced by unsparing criticism of their *fabulas vanas prophanas ludicras et lubricas*, which he elsewhere classes with the *crassissime facetae Facetiae* of Poggio. This does not however prevent his appealing to their authority on points of *technique*; from justifying the 'happy ending' of Joseph's trials by the *Captivi*, or the length of time which the action covers by the *Heautontimorumenos*. For the rest, the play belongs wholly to another school. The austere and dignified figure of Joseph (in whom, as in Isaac, the current theology saw a type of Christ), the stern but kindly Potiphar, the shameless wife, recall a similar group in one of the noblest tragedies of Euripides, the 'happier ending' notwithstand-

ing, more nearly than anything in the comic drama; and though the *Hippolytus* does not seem to have been in Crocus' mind, he writes throughout with a stately gravity of style which contrasts rather oddly with his predominantly comic metres. The 'comedia sacra' is already far on the way to become 'sacred tragedy.'

Between Gnapheus and Crocus stands the genial and brilliant figure of George Macropedius. Inspired by Reuchlin[1], but in no way his servile follower, with equal talent for comedy and tragedy, inexhaustible, if not very subtle humour, a genuine power of pathos, now throwing off Teniers-like scenes of boisterous jesting and domestic turmoil, now surrounding the last hours of a rich man divinely summoned to die with a mysterious horror, in its kind hardly to be paralleled in the drama elsewhere, Macropedius was in his chosen field the first of his contemporaries. Like Crocus, like Reuchlin himself[2], he refers disparagingly to the slippery scenes of the comic poets[3],—a sort of reference which was soon to be a hackneyed common-place of every prologue, but the very

G. Macropedius: *Asotus, pr.* 1537, *etc.*

---

[1] As he frankly confesses in the important preface to the *Rebelles* and the *Aluta*, 1540: 'Jo. Capnion...collapsum prorsus artificium comicum primus instauravit. Is mihi primus (ut verum fatear) ansam scribendi dedit, is me primus excitavit. Si praeter eum alii ante me scripserint, nescio: hoc scio, quod alios non viderim.'

[2] Preface to the *Sergius.*

[3] 'Non stupra virginum, aut dolos lenonios,
    quibus poetarum scatent comoediae,
    ......sed......probam
    e veritatis ore lapsam fabulam.
    quid fabulam? non fabulam sed mysticam
    e fonte puritatis haustam parabolam,' &c.
                                        Prologue to the *Asotus.*

The terms of this prologue evidently suggested the similar profession in that of Diether's *Joseph*, n. d. Augsburg.

play which is thus introduced, the *Asotus*, scarcely jus-
tified the disparagement, for it belongs quite to the
type of the still unwritten *Acolastus*, from a memory
stored with Terentian portraits and scenery, and not
anxiously scrupulous in their use.   But he was too versatile to commit himself to a formula.   With his great
countryman Erasmus and the mass of northern Humanists, he held to the faith that the ancient art-world was a
storehouse of admirable tools rather than of unimpeach-
able models.   If the *Asotus* belonged decidedly to the
Left wing of the Comœdia sacra, he was equally ready to
take up Biblical narratives into which the slightest trait of
Terentian character could not have been introduced
without dissonance :—' Lazarus the beggar,' ' Jesus in the
Temple,' 'Christ's Passion.'   But he was as far from
being fettered by Biblical subjects as by classical traditions
of treatment, and, after Reuchlin, no one so well deserves the praise of having naturalised the spirit of
modern comedy in the Latin drama.   The *Bassarus*,
Andrisca and *Aluta* are subjects almost as unconventional
as the *Sergius* itself : practical jests in low life, chastisement of miserly officials or unruly women, thefts of food
and wine, such as abound in the *Schwänke* of Ulenspiegel,
from which indeed the *Aluta* is directly borrowed ; and
in the *Rebelles*, a graphic picture of school-boy adventure,
we have the connecting link between this purely modern
comedy of Teutonic *espiéglerie* and the *bizarre* blending
of Plautus' genial worldliness and Hebraic solemnity
which created the *Asotus* and *Acolastus*.

The South-
west.
Sixt Birck,
T. Kirch-
mayer.

The new move made in Holland was instantly
followed up in Switzerland and Germany.   This was
the more natural because a vernacular drama of entirely
parallel tendency was then just starting into vigorous
existence.   The characteristic mediaeval conceptions of

the drama, sapped by the combined influences of Humanism and religious reform, were slowly giving way in every direction. The vast and often formless Mysteries, with their bold representations of the mysteries of faith, and the still more formless *Fastnachts-spiele* with their mostly gross and trifling plots, were irrevocably doomed. They satisfied the higher artistic sense of the new generation, its keener eye for structure and *technique,* as little as its quicker instinct of reverence. In the most remote regions of the land, from the Baltic to the Alps, the same solution almost instantaneously presented itself, and men turned as by a common impulse to the open treasury of dramatic subjects contained in the historical books of the Old Testament and Apocrypha, and the parables of the New, —the Romancero of the Jewish people[1].—Even before Gnapheus had touched the parable of the Prodigal Son, Burkardt Waldis in remote Riga had produced a German *Verlorener Sohn*[2], much less brilliant in colouring but also freer from the limitations occasioned by a comic model; and at the other extremity of the German population, the poet-painter Niklaus Manuel of Bern produced his *Lazarus* (1529), and Sixt Birck of Basel his *Susanna* (1532).

With this vernacular drama the Latin drama entered at once into easy relations. The *Acolastus* was immediately translated and performed, and its influence was very great[3].

---

[1] This 'solution' was not of course precisely without precedent even in Germany; an isolated *Susanna* or *Lazarus* occurs here and there among the MS. mediaeval *Ludi*, but it was nevertheless essentially a new departure.

[2] *De parabell vam vorlorn Szohn...*, Riga, 1527: reprinted in Niemayer's *Neudrucke.*

[3] In the remarkable prologue to the Latin version of his *Susanna*

German plays were re-cast ; men who had previously written in German began to turn their German doggerel into
senarii, or to compose afresh in Latin; and the use
of the Roman style brought with it a more or less
extensive adoption of Roman *technique.* The loose
continuity of the popular drama began to be broken
up into acts and scenes. The modern stage, with its
exits and entrances, its messengers and reports, its fundamental distinction between action *on* and action *off* the
scene, began to replace the naïvely symbolic scenery of the
mediaeval *Ludi*, in which the whole cosmos was visibly
represented, and every person concerned had his appointed
place, like the *domus* of the astrologer's chart, where his
whole procedure was always in view. The acts were
mostly divided by choruses, in short strophic metres which
waver between those of the Roman Ode and of the mediaeval Hymn; even the vernacular writers occasionally
attempted the first, and wrote German verse with a
scrupulous care which had long been utterly strange
to it, and is like a foretaste of the days of Opitz.

At the same time, however, it was plain that the
Latin drama had fallen into a society in which humanism and even sound pedagogy were only simple
forces among others even more urgent and exacting.
The placid atmosphere of school and church, scarcely
troubled by the distant ring of religious strife, in which
Macropedius and Crocus wrote, is exchanged for the
air of a turbulent southern city, in the heart of the
conflict. The Turks too, a negligible quantity at the
Hague, touched the imagination at Basel. The political
neutrality of the academic Dutchmen gives place to pronounced republican fervour ; and at the same time their

(1535), Sixt Birck refers to it in a way which implies it to have
been perfectly familiar to his audience.

Catholicism is replaced by the for the moment undoubtedly more stimulating faith of Luther.

This singular interpenetration of Humanism with
political Protestantism was summed up in two men.
Sixt Birck,—Xystus Betuleius as he rendered himself
(with the pun which no German Humanist willingly
forwent if it came in his way)—evidently wrote under
inspiration of the great civic communities of south-west
Germany and Switzerland, then at the height of their
splendour and independence. Born at Augsburg (in
1500), passing many years at Basel, first as student, then
as schoolmaster, and finally returning to his native place,
he breathed his whole life long the keen air of mingled
political and Humanist enthusiasm, of which precisely
these two cities were the most illustrious seats. His
dramas vividly reflect this bias. They aim, as he confesses[1], to train good citizens, to teach the ideals of
citizenship, reverence for the parent and care for the
child[2]. His heroes are strenuous, enduring men and
women, like *Judith* and *Susanna.* He crowds his stage
with motley figures of every rank and class, counsellors,
soldiers, magistrates, servants, artizans, priests, women
and children, with the obvious intention of making it an
image of the city. He delights above all in pictures of
the public procedure of city life ;—debates in council,

Sixt Birck:
Susanna,
1537, *etc.*

---

[1] The title-page of the *Judith*, e.g. explicitly describes it as
exemplum Reipublicae recte institutae; cf. that of the *Zorobabel:* 'in
quo typus est regni feliciter constituti, *unde monarchae discant*' &c.

[2] Cf. the dedication of the *Eva* to his wife:

> 'Hunc ludum tibi rectius quadrare
> O conjux puto, cui Deus benigne
> Prolem multiplicem dedit...
> Tu cultrix cole sicut Eva recte...
> In hoc gloria sola detur ipsi
> Qui prolem dedit elegantiorem.'

banquets in the hall, trials in court,—always with a
marked preference for formal speeches over dialogue.
The *Judith*, for instance, is, as Scherer remarks[1], almost
a continuous series of such scenes. The opening act is
wholly occupied with a solemn council, the capture of
Achior naturally involves a second; the consideration of
Holofernes' ultimatum demands a third; Holofernes
himself cannot dispense with a council of war, and the
triumphant return of Judith would have been incomplete without one more imposing gathering in which
'Bethulia' and Jerusalem rejoice together. The elaborate trial in the *Susanna*[2], the examination of the three
servants in the *Zorobabel*,—nay the very catechism to
which Eve's 'unlike children' are submitted on the occasion of an unexpected visit from 'Jova[3],' show a kindred
taste, which was indeed already fully developed in his
very first drama—*de vera et falsa Nobilitate*, where the
kernel of the action is an intellectual tournament between
two youths for the hand of one who has equivocally pronounced in favour of 'the nobler' of them[4]. And sometimes, as in the *Eva*, the earnestness of the strenuous
citizen is tempered by a genial and fatherly *bonhomie*,—
'Catonibus non ista, crede, scripta sunt!' he calls out to
the Zoïluses who lifted their hands at such a subject, and
he proceeds *sans gêne* to represent the venerable *Mütter-*

---

[1] *A. D. Biog.* art. *Birck.*

[2] In its various phases it occupies the greater part of Acts IV.
and V.

[3] It was based upon a prose fable of Melanchthon's, and suggested Hans Sachs' delightful version:—*Die ungleichen kinder Eva's,*
—in a language infinitely better suited than that of Terence to the
quaint household humour of the subject.

[4] The 'kernel' was itself derived from a 'debate' on the subject
by Bongarsus, which I have not seen.

chen ('matercula') marshalling her well-scrubbed children before the august Visitor.

From the author of the *Eva* to Thomas Kirchmayer is a transition analogous to that from Melanchthon to Münzer, or Ralph Radcliff to Bishop Bale. Totally strange to the imposing civic life amid which Birck grew up, he formed no enduring local attachments, and his career was a series of flights from positions which he successively made untenable. The family and the city have no place in his drama, as they had none in his turbulent Ishmaelite life. He condescends to no homely moralising, no practical counsel; he is an implacable idealist, who has invested his whole moral capital in hatred, and has none left for reconstruction. No gleam of human feeling relieves the iron rigour of his polemic against the 'diabolic rule' of Rome. The positive enthusiasm of Birck for his ideal republic turns into a fanaticism of antipathy which only permitted him to imagine vividly what he abhorred. If Birck resorts to the Bible for types of ideal citizenship,—Judiths, Susannas, Zorobabels,—Kirchmayer searches it for types of Antichrist like Judas and Haman, in whom the true Antichrist of Rome may be lashed in effigy; nay, in one lurid drama, of which I shall presently have to speak in detail, he attempts, with the aid of the Apocalypse, an unexampled historic picture of the papal rule.

T. Kirchmayer: Pammachius, 1538, etc.

To the end of its career the Latin drama of Germany showed traces of the school in which it had first taken definite shape. The *idée mère* to which it might be said to owe its very blood and nerve,—and which had borne fruit in natures so different as those of Reuchlin and Macropedius, Birck and Kirchmayer,—the union of Terentian style and *technique* to subjects at once 'true,' 'sacred,' and 'virtuous,'—was certainly no

Later dramas of the Terentius Christianus school.

I. C. Schonaeus.

passing inspiration which a new fashion could at once
put aside ; and so long as Latin plays were written, the
cast of mind to which it appealed continued to emerge.
Nay, the whole movement might even be said to culmi-
nate in this later time in which its authority was on the
whole less exclusive; no one, at any rate, laboured with
so single an eye to achieve a 'Christian Terence' neither
too pagan for piety, nor too Biblical for classicism, as
Cornelius Schonaeus, the rector of Haarlem ; though the
supreme honours for consistency of method ought perhaps to be awarded to another Low-German schoolmaster, Burmeister of Luneburg, who in 1623 corrected
the impieties of Plautus by a 'sacred' *Amphitryo*, in
which the beguiled Alcmene is replaced by the mother of
Christ. Schonaeus was well-known in England,—three at
least of his seventeen plays having been reprinted in
London almost as soon as they appeared [1], although our
Latin as well as vernacular drama had now emerged from
the phase to which they belonged. He is a cool, sober,
but not unskilful writer, handling the well-worn stories of
Joseph , Susanna, Judith, with scarcely a touch of the
enthusiasm which had once transfigured them in the
glow of Reformation politics, but with a shrewd calcula-
tion of effect which often gives him the advantage over
the men of dithyramb. His Judith is no personification
of Christian heroism, triumphing over the hated Turks,
like Birck's ; the crowded scenes, the incessant and mul-
titudinous movement, by which Birck expressed his
political meaning, are quite absent. Yet he at times
makes a more dramatic use of his scantier material. The
return of Judith, for instance, from the camp, is, in

[1] *Terentius Christianus, sive comoediae duae* (the *Toboeus* and the
Juditha), *Terentiano stylo conscriptae...quibus accessit* Pseudostra-
tiotes. London, 1595.

Birck, a fine picture of exultant triumph; but its whole force is in the given situation,—the unlooked for success, the humiliation of a great captain by a woman. She calls out to the guard at once:

> Ehem vigil, Oziae mox renuncies
> ut recipiat me victricem intra moenia,
> ...Moras abrumpe actutum, ille mox nuncia
> totam domum Israel per me esse liberam.
> *Tychophylax.* Io triumphus, ecquid hoc festivius aut laetius
> die illuxit? etc.[1]

The Judith of Schonaeus, on the other hand, remains the self-contained and crafty heroine of Holofernes' banquet. No eager outburst of the good news in the first friendly ear, but a dignified 'economy of truth,' taking nice account of place and person. It is not for the guard to have the first tidings:

> *Mel.* Cujus ego vocem hic audio? *Jud.* Cujus arbitrare?
> *Mel.* Nescio.
> *Jud.* Hem nescis? Judithae. *Mel.* Tune huc rever-
> teris
> Juditha, quam jamdudum interiisse putaveramus?[2]
> *Jud.* ...sed portam aperi, jam vos beavero. *Mel.* Nihil
> detrecto, ingredere. Age, nunc dic sodes Juditha,
> quidnam adferas bonae rei. *Jud.* Dicam, sed non nisi
> convocatis civitatibus optimatibus, etc.[3]

But while this original bent always had its representa-   III.
tives, the Latin drama showed in the latter half of the *Gradual*
century an unmistakeable alteration of front. The theory *preponderance of*
of the Christian Terence involved three assumptions, two *secular*
of which were distinctly fatuous, while the third was at *subjects and tragic*
treatment.

[1] Sixt Birck, *Juditha* v. 3.
[2] Schonaeus is fond of relieving the monotony of his senarii with catalectic, trochaic and scazontic verses at very frequent intervals.
[3] Schonaeus, *Juditha* v. 5.

least *borné*. It held that the drama ought to be *true*[1],
and that it must not *represent evil;* and it drew its ideas
of dramatic *technique* solely from ancient *comedy*, and
that of a single school. The work of writing drama inevitably weakened the two former prejudices, which had
indeed from the first been very fairly resisted. Without
conflict dramatic action could not be, and the very piety
which led the Christian Terences to array their hero in
stainless moral beauty, drove them to emphasise, nay to
exaggerate, the vices of his enemies or tempters, and
before they knew it, that pagan pen which had drawn
sin with so little reserve, and which they had begun by
indignantly throwing to the ground, was working vigorously in their own pious hands. The pretension of 'truth'
again, though it stood its ground longer, was certain to
have to give way in the end. It carried its dissolvent with
it in the other pretension, with which it was habitually
coupled, of 'sacredness.' The latter gave a sort of sanction
to any story drawn from the Bible; yet it was evident
that many such stories made no pretension to literal
truth. Criticism had yet breathed no suspicion against
the Pentateuch or the Book of Daniel; but the Parables
were in any case 'feigned'[2]. The Biblical recognition of
fiction told; secular stories, even pagan myths, gradually
established their claims; and *a fortiori*, secular history
could not be rejected. The subtly playful creations of
Teutonic fancy working on the austere hints of Jewish

---

[1] I cannot forbear reminding the reader of the admirable discussion
scene in Björnson's *Fiskejenten*, where a party of Norwegian
peasant-folk do battle with a travelled man of culture for this
apparently still stout and thriving prejudice.

[2] Cf. Macropedius' preface to the *Asotus* and Sixt Birck's
to his *Eva*, both of whom try to save their case by a distinction
between spiritual and literal 'veritas.'

thought, were freely admitted; the delightful *myth* of
'Eva' which Birch had introduced with a half defiant
apology, was followed, without one, by the equally delightful *Hansoframea* of Hayneccius[1],—the story of the
incorrigible fault-finder who has been forbidden heaven
on account of his unruly tongue, but contrives to enter
it by an oversight of Peter's wife, silences the stoutest
saints by the vigour with which he reminds them of their
earthly failings, and when the blameless Innocents, as a
last resource, are sent to drive him out, successfully cor-
rupts them with sweetmeats.   The parable of Dives
again was developed—not it is true wholly on German soil—into the striking *Hecastus*, almost the latest
play of Macropedius, and the yet more dramatic parable of the Prodigal Son became the germ of an unequivocally modern drama of boyish adventure and
license[2].

And subjects wholly without footing in the Bible were
not wanting.   Vergil, Livy and Ovid, competed with the
old chroniclers and contemporary *Flugschrift*.   Dido,
most international of dramatic heroines, wept the absence
of Aeneas in at least three German, as in several Italian,
French and English dramas; the stories of Palinurus,
Marcus Curtius, Andromeda, Lucretia, were treated at
least once.   And in modern history George Caleminus
anticipated Grillparzer in celebrating Rudolph's triumph
over Ottocar; while Rhodius of Strassburg unconsciously

---

[1] Martin Hayneccius, *Hansoframea*. Lips. 1581. A German
version 'Hans Pfriem,' immediately followed, and is reprinted in
Niemayer's *Neudrucke*.   The story is an old Märchen, noticed
by Grimm; it resembles the Fabliau of *Le vilain qui conquit paradis
par plaid* (cf. Lenient, *Sat. du Moyen Age*, 96) except that the
vilain does not display the peculiar *Naseweisheit* of Pfriem.

[2] Cf. section v. of the present chapter.

followed Marlowe in dramatising the S. Bartholomew
Massacre[1].

*The
Senecean
Renais-
sance.*   But the change went far deeper than the transgression
of a false orthodoxy in the matter of subjects; it affected
the very conception of the scope and capacities of the
drama. It may be said that the idea of drama as a *fine
art*, as something quite other than either a festive amusement or a method of paedagogy, for the first time took
deep root. And the process was much aided by the
new influence which the middle of the century brought
into vogue in Germany, as in England and France—that
of Seneca, with Sophocles and Euripides. The austere
temper of tragedy has often tended to bring with it a
similar austerity of method, a stern deference to canons of
art which the comic poet genially puts aside. Certainly
the tragedies of Seneca were likely to be unduly impressive in their ostentatious 'regularity' to men just
escaping from a pedestrian license of form, just divining
that the drama had a title to enter the world of poetry.
No one contributed more to effect this revolution than

*G. Bucha-
nan.*   George Buchanan, whose *Jephthes* (written at Bordeaux
1540–3, though first printed in 1554) is the earliest
tragedy composed north of the Alps in decidedly Senecean
form. Like the *Baptistes* which followed after a long
interval, it became very popular, partly through its extreme, though somewhat verbose elegance, partly by its
felicitous choice of one of the few Hellenic episodes in
Jewish history. It inaugurated a sort of parallel movement to the Christian Terence,—a 'Christian Seneca';
and the later alliance was both closer and more legiti-
mate than the earlier. With the doubtful exception of a
single parable, the Jewish records offered scarcely any

---

[1] *Colignius*, 1615. Of the dramas mentioned in this paragraph
I have seen only Frischlin's *Dido* and Brülow's *Andromeda*.

opening for the scenery of ancient comedy, and the
classical element therefore became for the most part
purely external—the phrase and rhythm, the division
into acts, or perhaps some subordinate Syrus or Dromo.
But with ancient tragedy they had many more points of
analogy, and accordingly, while the sacred Terence met
a very well-deserved death in the century of its birth,
biblical tragedy has kept in some sort fresh until our
own, though owing much of its vogue to sheer pietism,
as in Klopstock, and much to what, as in Byron, had all
the effect of sensational profanity. The Hebrew prophet
easily put.on the air of the Greek seer; the Sophoclean
Tiresias was a type of Elijah, of John, of Nathan;
Agamemnon sacrificing Iphigenia, of Abraham, or of
Jephthah; even the story of Joseph found a parallel
in the Egyptian adventures of Heliodorus' Chariclea[1].
And with all this went a feeling, more or less pronounced,
for the familiar appurtenances of tragic style; the dreams
which forbode the destined παθήματα before they arrive,
the messengers who report them when they are past, the
gnomic commonplaces about brief good-fortune and ill-
omened arrogance, the choice elaboration of phrase, the
weighty and sonorous verse. Even the hapless 'unity
of time,' warmly advocated by Scaliger, found a sturdy
Teutonic devotee in Balthazar Crusius, whose rigorous
use of it is however his chief title to memory[2].

Two men stand out in the history of the later Frischlin
Latin drama, both of them in some sort sharing in Brülow.
these tendencies, yet with a buoyant originality and

---

[1] Brülow's *Chariclea*, based on the *Joseph* of Hunnius (Scherer
ADB. art 'Brülow').

[2] Cf. besides his three dramas, *Exodus*, *Tobias*, and *Paulus*, the
little treatise *De dramatibus* (Lips. 1609), where he defends his
thesis with some learning.

vivacity which sufficiently distinguish them not merely
from the rank and file of modern Senecas but from a
Jodelle or a Norton.

N. Frisch-   The fascinating and pathetic story of Nicodemus
lin (1547   Frischlin cannot be given here. The network of errors
—1589).
and misfortunes which transformed the gifted and courted
Latin professor of Tübingen into the captive who found
his release, twenty years later, on the precipice of Ho-
henurach, has been unravelled with consummate art by
one well acquainted with the trials of German university
life[1]. A thorough and brilliant scholar, a facile versi-
fier, a boon companion full of wit and high spirits, he
was the most eminent man in the little town. He was
everything to all men; he could keep a company of
unlettered knights in a roar, or entertain his colleagues
with the choicer pleasantries of the common-room.
He was a chosen comrade of the duke himself, and of
that young prince whom Shakespeare years after made
immortal with a bad jest as the ' Cousin Garmumbles'
of the *Merry Wives*. When a court festivity was on
hand, it was Frischlin who had to write the after-dinner
play, and when the pageant faded it was Frischlin again
who had to sing of it in Vergilian hexameters rugged
with guttural names of guests who would have revenged
their omission, and not disdaining even the details of the
menu,—the parables in sugar and nativities in plumcake
in which the sixteenth century delighted. Something
then of the fantastic audacities of the true Court drama,
of the Masque, seems at first sight reflected in Frischlin's
most original dramatic work[2]; but they are the au-

---

[1] D. F. Strauss, *Frischlins Leben und Schriften*, 1855.

[2] He was extremely versatile, and wrote 'sacred comedies' and
Senecean tragedies,—a *Susanna* and a *Dido*,—as well as the dramas
here in view.

dacities of Aristophanes (whom Frischlin translated into Latin) rather than of Jonson. In the *Julius Redivivus* Caesar and Cicero, the antique masters in war and letters, ascend from the under world to visit the German inheritors of their empire and renown. Eoban Hessus, the 'king of the poets,' and 'Hermann' do the honours, and while Caesar is lost in amazement at the wealth and strength of Germany, her vineclad hills, her splendid cities and their elaborate fortifications, Cicero is forced by his remorseless interrogator to exhaust his vocabulary in eulogy of her Latin poets. The felicitous motive is not very dramatically carried out, and one cannot help contrasting this patriotic drama in which Germany is magnified by an auctioneer-like enumeration of her excellences, with the very different method of Shakespeare's English Histories. The others show the same power of turning abstractions into concrete dramatic action. In the *Priscianus Vapulans* it is the old grammarian who after being flogged ('murdered' as we should say) by scholastics of every profession, finds refuge with Erasmus and Melanchthon. In the *Phasma*, the chiefs of the rival sects are skilfully made to exhibit their various tenets, and are finally disposed of by the apparition (the Phasma) of Pluto. A striking scene for instance illustrates Anabaptist communism by the altercation of a new convert with his goodwife, who loves her husband (and her property), and is nowise disposed to accept his free permission to choose another.

Frischlin's sparkling comedies were eagerly read *The Strassburg School.* throughout Germany. In some sense he became a national poet. In a more popular society he might have helped to found a national drama. To make any approach to this was reserved for the great neighbour

city of Strassburg, where at the close of the century the
periodical plays of the Academy, long before established
by Johann Sturm, had become a permanent institution,
supported in part by the town revenues, and attended by
country people from the whole district.   It was here that
the first Greek plays were acted;—among them the
Troades, Medea, Hecuba, Prometheus, Alcestis.   Even the
Old Comedy was attempted, and Aristophanes, scarcely
known to what Gervinus has called the Aristophanic age
of the early Reformation, amused the ἐπίγονοι.   Then
came original plays.   For the sake of the unlearned spectators a German *argument* was provided.   But even with
this aid, a Latin play of the ordinary type, with its speeches,
its horror of visible incident,—its tendency to throw all
action into words, could scarcely have excited an audience which understood the words only in so far as
they were translated into action.   This was thoroughly
understood, and fearlessly acted upon.   "Our public,"
said Brülow, "cannot away with narratives, it will have
everything go on before its eyes ; we have to satisfy this
want : how then can we follow the laws of ancient
drama[1] ? "   The result was on the whole (so far as I can
judge from the very few specimens accessible to me),
fortunate ; at any rate the frigid solemnity which has
overcome all modern imitators of Seneca in his own
tongue is effectually dispelled.   Who would dream for
instance of meeting in a Latin drama devoted to the
fall of Sodom[2], the Elamite sack brought visibly upon
the stage, the enemy storming in, the people in tumult,
desperate fathers slaying their children, while the children,

[1] Quoted by Scherer, *Gesch. des Elsasses*, p. 299.
[2] Act III. Sc. 5 ; A. Jundt, *Die dramatischen Aufführungen im
Gymnasium zu Strassburg*, 1881, S. 59. The original is inaccessible
to me in either the Latin or the German form.

—the little boys and girls of Sodom—cry piteously for
their lives in language brimful of the quaint household
tenderness which is always lurking in some corner of
a German poet's heart :

> O weh, hertzliebstes Mütterlein !—
> Ach du güldener Vater mein !
> —Ach, ich bitt, schenkt das Leben mir,
> Mein newen Gürtel schenk ich dir !
> —Nim mein Kunckel und Seckel gut,
> Mein Nadel und mein Fingerhut !   &c.

The centre of the Strassburg school in the first two
decades of the century was Caspar Brülow [1], professor of
Latin at the Academy from about 1607.   Perhaps the
continual reference to an audience with whom spectacle
counted for much, made him even needlessly careless of
other parts of dramatic art. He freely chooses epic
subjects which only the highest skill could make fit
subjects of drama, such as Moses or Andromeda; gives
them a setting full of various resource and invention,
while the really stubborn material,—the *onyx au travail
rebelle*—is left almost in the rough.   The sudden appearance of the unknown Perseus, for instance, before the
doomed Andromeda, was not easily welded into the
texture of the action; but Brülow spends three acts
exclusively over Andromeda without a word of Perseus,
until, at the very moment when the fate of Andromeda
and the progress of the action imperatively require the
intervention of Perseus (IV. 1), Perseus most opportunely
appears.   That doubtless betrays a very infantine notion
of dramatic structure.   Yet the drama is effective and
moving, and sparkles with graphic descriptions.   Cas-

C. Brülow
(1585—
1627).

---

[1] Brülow, like Frischlin's follower, Flayderus, is a 'discovery' of
Scherer's. Cf. his *Gesch. des Elsasses*, p. 296 ff., and *ADB*.
'Brülow.'

siope's exultant joy in her own charms,—the fatal ὕβρις
which brings down the divine anger upon her (II. 1),—

> O colla mollicella! frons loquacula!
> O turgidula labella! lacteolæ genæ! &c.;

the account of the desolation wrought in the land by the
monster, the terror of the peasants disturbed by it over
their cheese and wine (II. 3, 4); and the spiced meats
and grinning boars' heads at the banquet after Andromeda's recovery (v. 2), are touched with evident gusto [1].
But none of the higher opportunities of dramatic life are
neglected: Cepheus' application to the oracle [2], his
wife's eager questions on his return and her amazement
to learn that she is herself the offender; the other questions, still more eager, of the tender, fourteen year old
Andromeda; the father's slow and reluctant answer; her
terrified prayer for life, passing (somewhat abruptly it is
true) into heroic joy that she is to have the glory of saving
the state,—in all this there is real and moving power.
Less elegant than Buchanan, without the robust geniality

---

[1] As a contrast between the ornate expression of the modern
school and the pedestrian, businesslike manner of the old, take two
descriptions of sleep. Birck's Judith describes the fatal slumber of
Holofernes thus laconically:

> dum stertit ipse somno profundissimo
> acinacem stringens gravem, seco caput.

This is Andromeda's account of the sleep in which she dreamed of
the monster:

> Postquam sopore nocte grato proxima
> labore telae fessa preli lumina:
> et umbra noctis iam polo decesserat
> frigida, repente visus &c.'

[2] In this scene I detect no resemblance to the demeanour of
Tiresias. The priest of Ammon gives his information with no tragic
reluctance.

of Frischlin, Brülow had a command of pathos and passion to which Frischlin hardly made pretence, and which
tend somehow to evaporate among the choice phrases of
the Scotchman.   Scherer, the best entitled of living men
to pronounce, declares Brülow to be decidedly the first
German dramatist before Lessing,—nay the superior of
any English dramatist before Shakspere[1]; and, with a
reserve to the latter statement in favour of Marlowe, I
am inclined to assent.

With Brülow I close this sketch of the Latin drama *Conclu-*
in Germany.   Of the promising growths blighted by *sion.*
the Thirty Years' War, none was so remarkable as the
school of drama at Strassburg.   For some years after the
war broke out, production continued here, as elsewhere,
seemingly unimpaired ; but after 1630 the stream decisively ebbs.   At the end of four generations, the vernacular drama reappeared, but in a form totally unrelated
to its German past : the Latin drama, which had been
the receptacle of the most distinguished talent of the
sixteenth century, and which at its close was the single
form of it still cultivated with abundant promise, expired
finally and without revival.

II.

A mass of literature so imposing as that just reviewed, THE BE-
could scarcely, in any case, have remained unknown GINNINGS
OF LATIN
among a kindred and neighbour people familiar with its DRAMA IN
language.   But England was at the same time bound by the ENGLAND
(1520—
close tie of proselytism ; it was the most promising field 1550).
of the blended spiritual and literary Renaissance of which
Germany was the native soil, and the Christian Terence
in some sense the flower.   Moreover, the very moment

---

[1] *Gesch. d. Els.* p. 300.

when the Christian Terence entered decisively upon its characteristic career was that at which this tie of proselytism was, as it were, officially recognised by the Reforms of 1535—6. What wonder if those who gathered in the fruit did not wholly neglect the flower, particularly when the flower was commonly credited with the virtues of fruit?

It is certain, at any rate, that soon after the date of the decisive öpening of the German school of Latin drama, the English enters upon a corresponding phase for which, so far as we know, nothing in its previous career had prepared it. Reuchlin, and in a sense Chilianus, also, prepared for Macropedius and Gnapheus; but if Radcliff, Grimald and Christoferson had any English predecessor in writing dramas at once classical in form and 'sacred' in subject, he has left no palpable trace behind. Absolutely nothing (it is true) has survived from the earlier period except titles and brief descriptions. But a moment's glance at these will show I think that the burden of proof lies on those who take an opposite view.

The earliest certain instance of an original performance in Latin in England,—apart, of course, from those of early mysteries, is the pageant of Luther and his wife which graced the ratification of peace and alliance with France in 1527; 'the most goodliest disguising or interlude,' runs the contemporary report, made in Latin and French, 'whose apparel was of such exceeding riches that it passeth my capacity to expound.' [1] Perhaps the presence

---

[1] Cf. the description discovered by Collier (*A. of St.* ed. 1879, I. 106 f.). Cavendish's account (*Wolsey*, I. 136, ed. Singer) clearly refers to 1527, not to 1514 as Warton thought. Like most of Warton's errors which relate to foreign history, this may still be found in Mr Hazlitt's edition (IV. 5), and has misled several of his successors up to Mr Collier.

of French ambassadors was the chief motive for the use
of Latin; in any case, the performance of a play of
Plautus in 1520, when French guests were also present[1],
is, with one exception, the only other early instance of
its occurrence at court. Equally meagre and sporadic
was the production at the schools and universities. The
Master of St Paul's, John Ritwyse, wrote a *Dido*, per- Ritwyse:
formed by the 'children' of his school before Wolsey *Dido.*
between 1522 and 1532[2]; in thus introducing the 'school-
drama' Ritwyse doubtless followed a German precedent,
but his subject belongs to the 'romantic-classic' school
of Latin drama favoured in Italy[3], where the moralised
amores of German paedagogy were unknown,—a taste in
no way surprising in the pupil and son-in-law of Lily,
whose training was altogether Italian. And lastly, Cambridge and Oxford had produced between them, by 1535,
three original comedies,—to which we may add a translation of the *Andria* in 1530. Thomas Artour, elected T. Artour:
a Fellow of St John's, Cambridge, 1517–18, afterwards *Mundus*
charged with heresy and forced to recant, wrote between *plumbeus,*
1520 and 1532, the year of his death, a *Mundus plumbeus* *Microcos-*
and a *Microcosmus*[4], and John Hoker of Oxford, a *mus.*
'comedy' *Piscator, or the fisher caught*, 1535[5]. The two J. Hoker:
former were most probably of the symbolical or mytho- *Piscator,*
1535.

---

[1] Collier, *u. s.* II. 89.

[2] He was appointed master in the former year and died in the
latter. Cf. Cooper, *Ath. Cant.*

[3] Tragedies on *Dido* were subsequently written by Giraldo
Cinthio and Ludovico Dolce (cf. Brunet *sub nom.*); Tiraboschi
mentions a MS *Didone* in the then unfamiliar *Sdruccioli* by Alessandro
Pazzo, nephew of Leo X. (t. VII. p. 1868); cf. Ward I. 199. The
first German drama on the subject is Knaustius', 1566.

[4] Bale, *Cent.* IX. 16.

[5] A. Wood, *Athen. Oxon.* I. 62. He graduated M.A. 1535, and
died after 1543.

logical type of the Mask ; the titles, at least, denote two kindred pieces of half scholarly, half popular, lore, which later became standing topics of the courtly mask-writers,— the parallelism of man and the world, [1] and the successive ages of the world. The most suggestive commentary is in the lines prefixed to Ford and Decker's *The Sun's Darling*, where the reader is assured that 'it is not here intended to present thee with the perfect analogy between the world and man, nor their coexistence,'... but [the succession of his four Ages, Spring, Summer, Autumn, Winter] [2].

Second Period (1535— 1550).

Palsgrave's translation of the Acolastus, 1540.

The first definite sign of the new influence was the translation published in 1540 by John Palsgrave of the epoch-making *Acolastus* of Gnapheus [3]. It is a purely paedagogic piece of work, intended to teach Latin phrase and style, but the translator had evidently conceived a high admiration of his author, and openly calls on his own countrymen to follow his example. ' I have chosen for my Latten authour to be Ecphrastes uppon, the

---

[1] On Nabbes' Mask: *Microcosmus* cf. Ward II. 374, and *note*, where the *Sun's Darling* is referred to. Gengenbach's *Die X Lebens alter* is a play of a very different school upon a kindred motive.

[2] The slender list of early Latin plays in England has been swelled through a not easily excusable blunder of Collier's. Describing a fragment in the Douce collection, printed by Rastell, (*H. of D. P.* II. 280), he says 'it appears to have formed part of a Latin play, possibly by Rightwise master of St Paul's and acted at court by the children under his care. The only part that is left is a scene between two characters Menippus and Philonides, in which M. is giving an amusing account of a journey he had made to hell.' The mere occurrence of such a name as *Menippus* ought to have sent Collier to Lucian, of whose *Nekyomantia* the fragment is, as may be supposed, a translation.

[3] *I. Palsgravi Ecphrasis Anglica in comoediam Acolasti*...Lond. 1540.

comedie entiteled *Acolastus,* not onely for bycause that I esteme that lyttel volume to be a very curiouse and artificiall compacted nosegay, gathered out of the moche excellent and odoriferouse swete smellynge gardeynes of the moste pure Latyne auctours, but also bycause that the maker thereof (as farre as I can lerne) is yet lyving, wherby I wold be glad to move into the hartes of your graces clerkes, of whiche your noble realme was never better stored, some lyttel grayne of honeste and vertuous envye.'

Whatever effect we may attribute to the excellent grammarian's appeal, it is certain that, in comparison with those that had gone before, the ten years which followed Palsgrave's translation were decidedly productive[1]. John Christoferson's *Jephthes* (1546), the ten comedies and tragedies (1540–52) of Ralph Radcliff, the 'plures comoediae' of Nicolas Udall and the *Christus Redivivus* (1543), the *Comedy of Fame* and the *ArchiPropheta* (1548) of Nicholas Grimald, are a respectable contribution, and what is more to the purpose, one at least of these dramas is extant[2], and we know enough of its author, Grimald, as well as of Radcliff, whose work has wholly perished, to be able to form some estimate of their aims.

*J. Christoferson.
N. Udall.
R. Radcliff.*

Radcliff and Udall, like Gnapheus, were schoolmasters writing in the first instance for their scholars, at Hitchin and Eton, but also, as we are expressly told, for the 'people'[3]. At both schools a play was annually acted, usually in Latin, but at Eton at least, English ones

[1] For the later history of the *Acolastus* in England, see section v. of the present chapter.
[2] The doubt chiefly concerns the *Christus Redivivus*, which is mentioned by Goedeke (§ 113, No. 30) as a Cologne print.
[3] Bale, *Cent.* VIII. 98: *Rad. Radcliff.*—Eton *Consuetudinary,* quoted by Warton and Collier.

were occasionally admitted, if sufficiently amusing, a concession to which we owe the *Ralph Roister Doister*. The
comedies to which Bale testifies, but which he does not
name, were doubtless written for these occasions[1]. Ralph
Radcliff is known almost exclusively[2] from the attractive
account which Bale has left of his visit to the Hitchin
school. A Lancashire man of good family, he had
adopted at the university the new faith to which the
greater part of young Cambridge, in the decade 1530–40,
was enthusiastically given. In 1538, the year in which his
friend Bale entered on his career as the dramatist of
English Protestantism, Radcliff opened a school in the
dismantled Carmelite monastery at Hitchin. The lower
part he transformed into an elegant and spacious theatre ;
and here every year he caused his pupils to perform plays
for the delectation of the country people, and their own

---

[1] Warton (III. 213) places the '*tragoedia de papatu*' also mentioned by Bale, among them. But in Bale this occurs among the
writings which Udall *translated for Queen Catherine*,—the others
being Erasmus' paraphrase to Luke, and to the Acts of the Apostles,
and Peter Martyr's treatise on the Eucharist. Can this 'tragedia
de papatu' have been Bernardin Ochino's *Tragedie or dialoge of the
unjust...primacie of the Bishop of Rome*, translated in 1549 by Ponet,
and given to Udall by an error of Bale's? It was a tragedy
emphatically of the kind *not* adapted for dramatic representation.

[2] I am assured by Mr Frederick Seebohm, who very kindly
made inquiries for me, that no old MSS. in any way connected
with Radcliff now remain at Hitchin, where his family still occupies
the site of his school. The family monuments in some respects
supplement, in others contradict Bale. It is usually easy to decide
between them. Thus, Bale is wrong in assigning the family to
Cheshire, instead of Lancashire; but his express assertion (*Cent.*
VIII. 98) that he visited Radcliff in 1552, undoubtedly disposes
of the vague statement of his epitaph that he ' died in the reign of
Henry VIII' (Salmon, *Hist. of Hertfordshire*, p. 165), even if we do
not press Bale's further words : *et nescio an...adhuc* (i.e. 1556) *vivat.*'

education in ease of manner and distinctness of speech[1].
His library, or '*musaeum*', soon accumulated a great store
of these plays, preserved there in MS. together with
speeches, letters, common-place books, extracts from the
classics, and other literary apparatus for the use of the
school; many of which Bale read during his stay. Bale
urged him to print, but Latin plays were still, as he well
knew, an unheard of commodity with English publishers[2],
and he replied by appealing to the classical excuse which
Horace has provided for literary reserve. *Spectacula
simul iucunda et honesta*, says Bale of these lost dramas;
a phrase which at once recalls the aims habitually professed in the school drama of Germany; and the comparison does not lose point when we examine the subjects. 'Pictures of Christian heroism' would probably
have fairly described their scope. The iconoclasm of the
Reformation can hardly have found so downright a representative in Radcliff as in Bale or Kirchmayer; rather,
one would suspect, the tendencies which made his native
county one of the last strongholds of Catholicism, and in
later days of Royalism, held him in the Conservative wing
of Reform. His heroes are almost exclusively drawn from
the records of steadfast endurance, of patient suffering,
not of violence and aggression. Griselda[3], Job, Susanna,

---

[1] Macropedius wrote with the same motive. Cf. the prologue
to his *Andrisca:*—

    Nam si in ea agenda exercearis sedulo
    linguae auferas stribliginem ac rubiginem.

[2] Grimald's two plays were printed at Köln; Buchanan's
Jephthes at Paris, and the *Baptistes* only in 1576 when his reputation was already European, at Edinburgh. The so-called *comedia
de vita S. Nicolai de Tollentino* of Galfredus Petrus, printed by
the Augustinian Ed. Soppeth in London, about 1510, is an exception
which proves the rule.

[3] *de patientia Griselidis*: either from Boccaccio or Chaucer.

the beggar Lazarus, the Melibœus of the *Parson's Tale*, Titus and Gysippus, and the martyr Hus—nay, even Judith, whose memorable feat was only the desperate resort of a people in the last straits of suffering,—these form a group of evidently related figures; and the subjects of his other two dramas, the *defection of Jonah* and the *burning of Sodom* obviously admitted of being treated in the same way, though it would be rash to assert that they were. It is more important to observe that six of the ten subjects are biblical, and that at least two of these were already renowned in the setting of the Latin drama[1], while the cognate history of the martyrdom of Hus had been handled by one of the most conspicuous of the second rank of Protestants, Johann Agricola, in a German drama of, it is true, very indifferent merit,—published the year before that in which Radcliff opened his school[2]. More than this, in the absence of his plays themselves, it is impossible to say[3].

The subject was already known on the French stage. A drama on Job by the famous Zürich surgeon, Jacob Ruof, had been in 1535, 'played very seemly by the citizens of Zürich in the Minster courtyard' (Stumpff, *Chronicles of Zürich*, quoted Goedeke, p. 302). Another by Narhamer, 1546.

[1] Besides Sixt Birck's Latin *Susanna* and *Judith*, both easily accessible in Oporinus' collection (1547) of Old Testament dramas, the former also in Brylinger's collection (1541), both subjects were favourites with the German-writing dramatists of Saxony (*Susanna*, Magdeb. 1534 &c.; P. Rebhun, *Susanna*, Zwickau, 1536; Jo. Greff, *Judith*, Wittenb. 1536). There was an early Italian drama on the Susanna story : *La Susanna*, by Tiburzio Sacco da Busseto ; (Tiraboschi, VII).

[2] Radcliff, like Agricola, probably drew his knowledge in detail of Hus' trial from the Acts of the Council of Constance, published, at Locher's instigation, by the noted jurist Hieronymus de Croaria (Hagenau, 1500).

[3] That the plays were all in Latin ought not perhaps to be taken

The case is somewhat different with the third of the N. Gri-
trio. Nicholas Grimald is chiefly remembered as the ^{mald.}
author of a considerable quantity of verse, preserved in
Tottel's Miscellany with that of Wyatt and Surrey, and not
altogether unworthy of the companionship. He is entitled however to an equally distinguished position in the
history of the English drama, as the author of the first
extant tragedy. For such, beyond question, though it
has scarcely been recognised, is his *Archipropheta, sive
Johannes Baptista*, printed at Köln in 1548, probably
performed at Oxford in the previous year. A Cambridge
man, born like Bale in the Eastern counties, Grimald
had migrated on taking his degree in 1540 to the sister
university. Two years later he was chosen Fellow of
Merton. At that time he was already busy with a Latin
drama on a biblical subject, the *Christus redivivus*,
printed at Köln in 1543[1]. Of several other biblical
works, which may have been dramas,—on the birth of

for granted. The opening words, however, which Bale quotes from
each drama, leave no doubt of this in at least two cases,—the
Griselda and the *Lazarus*,—where the quotation is obviously part of
a verse: 'Exemplar ut sim muliebris pa[*tientiae*]'—are the opening
words of Griselis, who must have been prologue as well as heroine;
'Viris mulierum garritum obstre[*pitantibus*]' is the less intelligible
opening of the *Dives et Lazarus*. Several other of the openings
probably formed parts of verses: the rest belonged to prose dedi-
cations. It may be added that the first of Radcliff's works cited by
Bale, the *Nominis ac Verbi, potentissimorum regum in regno gram-
matico, calamitosa et exitialis pugna*, may have stood in some
relation which we cannot now define to the elaborate working out of
the same idea in the *Bellum grammaticale* mentioned by Harrington
in 1591, in terms which show it to have been well-known (cf.
Halliwell's *Dictionary*, s. v.).

[1] Goedeke, *Grundriss*, § 113, No. 30. His English biographers
(including Mr Hazlitt in the *Handbook*) appear not to be aware
of this. I have met with no other trace of this piece, and describe
it as a drama solely on Goedeke's authority; Bale's omission of the

Christ, on the Protomartyr, on Athanasius,—Bale's notice
is the only record.   Removing in 1547 to Christ Church,
he lectured there on Rhetoric, explained Terence, Cicero,
Horace, Xenophon, and threw off at intervals the lyrics
afterwards collected in the Miscellany.   The *Archipropheta* belongs to the first year of his work at Christ
Church.

Grimald's was by no means the first attempt to treat
the dramatic climax of the career of John the Baptist.   The
fourteen 'books' which Bale devoted to the saint, must
have done justice in his ferocious fashion to these closing
scenes.   And within the previous half-dozen years, Jacob
Schoepper, presbyter of Dortmund, and George Buchanan, had unconsciously illustrated the opposite poles
of current dramatic method in dealing with the same
story.   A moment's glance at these will make Grimald's
subsequent work more intelligible.

Buchanan: The *Baptistes*—Buchanan's first work[1]—is conceived
Baptistes, in the severest style of Senecean tragedy.   The story is
1543
(*pr.* 1576). reduced to a bare outline; the dialogue is of the kind in
which development of action tends to degenerate into
one of thought, and development of thought into one of
expression.   There is no crowd of figures, no luxuriant
display of scenery, no touch of plebeian humour, no
attempt to refine upon a few broad and simple contrasts
of character.   The entire mass of hostile Judaism is
summed up in the Pharisee Malchus; sympathetic or
tolerant Judaism in Gamaliel; Herod is the conventional
Tyrant[2], and John the conventional *justus et tenax*, the
Com. or *Trag.* which he usually prefixes to dramas, would point
to a different conclusion.

[1] *Meus, quamquam abortivus, tamen primus foetus* he says of it
in the dedication to James VI.

[2] Buchanan seems indeed to have intended the drama to be above
all 'a vivid picture of the torments of tyranny' (cf. the *Dedication*).

Prometheus, the stubborn heretic who dies for his opinions. Even John's protest against Herod's incestuous
marriage is—perhaps from paedagogic motives—kept
almost out of sight, and with it disappears the real main-
spring of the story—his personal offence to Herodias—
and the tragic distinction of his fate.

No such criticism can be passed upon the work of
the Dortmund presbyter, the very title of which recalls
the fearless realism of the popular stage, the crimson,
headless neck and spouting blood of the Church altar-
piece. We see the prophet in the wilderness, unmistakeably the man of locusts and camel's hair, with a
crowd of disciples about him, and a crowd of Jewish
magnates suspiciously looking on. Herod approaches,
and the king has to hear himself branded with incest to
his face before his meanest subjects. He goes home in
trouble. The queen succeeds after many efforts in reading
the charactery of his sad brows, and henceforward knows
only one desire, to which John's arrest is the first step.
The banquet and dance, disposed of by Buchanan in a
brief and colourless *stichomythia*, gives occasion to a very
graphic and wholly unclassical scene. We see the servants busy about the loaded tables before the guests
arrive, we see the bustle of eating and drinking, the
passing of dish and cup, the commonplace amenities of
the dinner-table, the dance, the light promise, and then
the blankness of Herod's face as he hears the dictated
demand. Incoherent explanations break from him: for a
moment he is tossed between the two alternatives, then
hastily gives the order, and sinks back, deadly pale, with

J. Schoep-
per:
*Johannes
Decollatus,
vel Ectra-
chelistes,*
1546.

In the next century this application was made the most of; a
translation appeared in 1642 with the title: *Tyrannical government
anatomised.*

a muttered ' Pro Jupiter.'   The banqueters look at one
another, and wonderingly ask what sudden illness has
stricken the king: he recovers himself, protests that he
is perfectly well, and that it is rather for him to marvel

> ' quid vobis acciderit, quod non genialiter
> vivitis, ut paulo ante, quod haud exporrigitis frontem poculaque
> evacuatis.'

With all this tragic apparatus, however, we never lose
sight of the traditional association of the sacred drama
with Terence and Plautus.   Not only is the verse
throughout written in loose comic measures, but a distinctly comic figure is introduced in Herod's Fool.   To
the rigid technique of Buchanan such an intrusion would
have been intolerable; but Schoepper shared with the
majority of Teutonic Humanists the genial opportunism
which accepts a good inspiration without nicely scruti-
nising its antiquity.

Grimald: *Archi-propheta,* 1547 (*pr.* 1548).   Far more striking however is the blending of totally
alien schools of drama, in the work which Grimald com-
pleted the year following the appearance of the *Johannes
Decollatus.*   Without ever descending to deliberate imitation it is stamped in every page with an extreme
sensitiveness to the various intellectual influences which
then agitated the Oxford air.   The regime of Seneca
at the English universities was just beginning, as that
of Terence was drawing to its close; and in the drama
as in the schools they struggle visibly for the mastery.
John himself is drawn upon wholly tragic lines.   The
savage desert preacher, who only waits for the casual
appearance of Herod in his auditory to publicly denounce him, becomes a Teiresias, considerably reserving
his terrible message for the king's private ear[1].   On the

---

[1] Act II. Sc. 8.

other hand, versification, and several of the characters place it even less equivocally than Schoepper's in the ranks of the Christian Terence. The Oxford, like the Dortmund, Herod has a Fool—Gelasinus, who girds at the plotting Pharisees, tells bitter home-truths to the queen, and exchanges thrusts of tolerable humour with his fellow-servants, Syrus and Syra,—the latter a charming combination of gaiety and kindliness. But the chief beauty of the drama lies in another feature, for which neither Seneca nor Terence can be held accountable,— the passionate love—wholly romantic and modern— which unites Herod and Herodias[1]. Her insatiable hatred of John is not prompted by her injured dignity, but by the threatened ruin of her life with Herod. With genuine tragic art the ominous message of the preacher is immediately preceded by a picture, very tenderly drawn, of their still unclouded happiness (II. 4). On learning the truth, she gathers all the forces of her woman's nature into a single effort to turn her husband's purpose. Herod is half an Oedipus, but it was not from the horrified silence of Jocasta that Grimald imagined the Herodias who, after exhausting all argument in vain, overcomes him by her cry of wounded love:

> ......tu
> Hisce manibus (qua' ego lubens exosculor)
> His manibus inquam me iam occidito! sic ego
> Animam patiar mihi auferri cum sanguine.
> O mi vir, mi vir optime,
> Profari plura nequeo
> Prae lachrymis fluentibus.
> O mi vir, mi vir optime! (Act III. Sc. 7.)

[1] It is impossible not to be reminded of Calderon's far nobler and more moving picture of the love of the elder Herod and Mariamne in the *El mayor monstruo los zelos*.

In such passages one feels the lyric Grimald of the
Miscellany; and the drama is full of similar evidence.
Every opportunity is seized of substituting lyric measures for the regular senaries: long choruses divide the
acts; the very prayers of the Baptist and his disciples
are lyrical in form; the banquet scene is so profusely
inlaid with songs and music that the essential action is
somewhat starved; and a description of Herodias becomes, even in the mouth of a serving-man, a glowing
sonetto d' amore[1].

In spite, however, of these vivid reflexions of a
purely English poetic culture, Grimald's work belongs
distinctly to the German school of Schoepper, — the
school of biblical drama moulded, in regard to form,
and the mixture of seriousness and humour, upon ancient comedy, but freely admitting tragic motives, and
borrowing the tragic machinery of a chorus between the
acts.   Whether he actually knew the *Johannes Decollatus*
I will not pronounce.   Several external circumstances
make it easily conceivable.   Martin Gymnicus of Köln,
the printer of the only edition of Schoepper, became,
two years afterwards, the printer of the only edition of
Grimald.   The same channel, whatever it was, which
brought him in possession of Grimald's MS., may con-
versely have brought Grimald in possession of the
printed Schoepper.   And if a conjecture be permis-
sible, I suggest that this channel may well have been

---

[1] II. 3.

> cui formae fulgor ac decu' est eiusmodi, ut
> videatur esse divinum naturae opus.
> in oculis ipse amor locum elegit sibi,
> petis, protervis, claris, ludibundulis;
> ebori' instar candidi dentes.   labellula
> suffusa nativo quodam velut minio, &c.

John Bale, a friend and old fellow-student of Grimald's[1],
himself certainly acquainted with the Latin drama of
Germany, peculiarly interested in the history of the
Baptist, and at this very time living in exile in the
Low-countries. No one is so likely to have conveyed
the single foreign Latin drama (except the *Acolastus*), of
which we have direct evidence in England at so early a
date, as its congenial translator[2]; and so insatiable a
collector of literature assuredly did not send the *Pammachius* alone.

To the *Pammachius* itself I now turn, and its literary
history is remarkable enough to demand a section to
itself.

III.

In 1536, the Convocation of Canterbury, under the
guidance of Cranmer, accepted those 'Articles of Religion' in which the English Reformation was initiated
with a characteristic mixture of boldness and reserve.
Though some cardinal doctrines of the Roman church,
such as transubstantiation and confession, were still
insisted on, the news of this step was received with triumph by German Protestants. One among them, the
most trenchant and vehement polemic of his time, seized
the occasion to dedicate to the archbishop a drama of
remarkable qualities, and with a remarkable history, to
neither of which entire justice has in England as yet been
done,—the famous *Pammachius* of Thomas Kirchmayer[3].

T. KIRCH-
MAYER'S
*Pamma-
chius* and
J. BALE.

---

[1] In the *Catalogus* he mentions among Grimald's works an *Ad
amicum Joannem Baleum.*

[2] He translated the *Pammachius* before 1548.

[3] Printed 1538, and repeatedly afterwards; also translated
several times into German, as well as into Bohemian, and into
English. Of this last version nothing is known.

Kirchmayer has been already briefly noticed as the coryphaeus of the purely Protestant wing of the Latin drama.
His stormy and unlovely life is the fitting introduction to
the sombre work which was its most remarkable outcome.
Born in 1511, at Straubingen in Würtemberg, he studied
at Tübingen, and passed thence in 1536 to take the
pastorate of Sulza in Thüringen.   Here he produced the
Pammachius; here, four years later, he joined in the
literary hue and cry against the Wolf of Brunswick with a
drama not less famous, the *Pyrgopolinices*, where the duke
Henry, a modern Miles Gloriosus, is brought in intriguing
with Pope and devil for the burning of his towns of
Eimbeck and Nordhausen[1].   These two powerful strokes
on Luther's side did not prevent him from conflict with
Luther.   In 1536 he had published a commentary on the
first Epistle of S. John, in which he maintained the doctrine of Election in its most violent form.   Luther sent
him a friendly admonition, with a request that he would
keep his heresy to himself.   Indignant at this, Kirchmayer
despatched a series of propositions to Wittenberg, peremptorily demanding their acceptance or rejection.   Melanchthon was disgusted with his vehemence, and refused
to reply,—'non enim libet cum homine furioso litigare.'
The elector however, Johann Friedrich, pleased at the
chastisement of his enemy of Brunswick, took notice of

[1] A third drama, which immediately preceded the *Pyrgopolinices*,
is interesting as a Protestant handling of the *Every-man* motive
already several times treated by Catholics.   Kirchmayer makes his
meaning perfectly clear.   In *Every Man*, the soul of the dying
Dives is saved by 'good dedes.'   In the *Mercator* he is happily converted in time to the doctrines of S. Paul, and is saved by 'Faith,'
while three Catholics, less fortunate than he, suffer the penalty of
their obstinate reliance on their 'good works.'   The *Mercator* is
reprinted in Goldast's *Polit. Imperialia.*

the author, and employed him about his person. His
bitter and scathing verse, imposing by its sheer vehemence, made the parson of Sulza a personage in
Protestant Saxony.   For a time he succeeded in putting
the Wittenbergers themselves in the shade.   His com-
plaints against Melanchthon had their effect, and when
the duke attended the Reichstag at Speier in 1544, it was
Kirchmayer, and not Melanchthon, who accompanied
him. 'Probably,' adds Melanchthon, telling the story
with some bitterness to a correspondent, 'he thinks a bold
fellow like this a better man to pit against the moderates.'
The same year an inquiry was at length opened into his
alleged heresies; he chose not to await the result, and
quietly left Sulza.   For the next four years he lived an
unsettled life at Kempten and other places in Würtemberg.   But the disastrous opening of the Smalcald war
forced him again to fly, this time beyond the bounds
of the empire.   In Switzerland he passed some months
of considerable privation and suffering, solacing himself
meantime[1] with a work afterwards famous in England
as the 'Boke of Spiritual Husbandry,'—a sort of
theological application, in the bizarre taste of the time,
of Vergil's Georgics,—the 'Naogeorgica' in fact, as one
suspects he intended, of the Christian Vergil Naogeorg.
It owes indeed to Vergil not only the general structure
and plan, but a variety of graphic details scattered
throughout, and certain touches of a leisurely ornateness
which sits somewhat oddly on the vehement pen of
Kirchmayer[2].

[1] Cf. the closing lines of the *Agricultura Sacra* (Basil, 1550):
    Haec sacris super agricolis, ac arte colendi,
    casibus afflictus multis durisque canebam.

[2] It is divided into five books. The central topic, the sowing
and culture of the good seed, by ritual and study of the Bible, is

But the *Spiritual Husbandry* was not his only occupation. Since the *Haman*, seven years before, he had
ceased to write drama ; he now returned to it to treat a
subject made congenial by his own position,—the career
of a prophet neglected and unsuccessful like himself—
Jeremiah[1]. Finally, in 1553, appeared the colossal work
on the *Papal Realm*, by which English historians chiefly
remember him, an inverted *Fasti*, as the *Agricultura
Sacra* is a spiritualised *Georgics*, laying bare with the
inexhaustible patience of hatred the whole ceremonial
and customary life of the Roman Babylon[2].

With a head already sprinkled with gray[3], Kirchmayer
returned to Germany after the peace. He obtained a
living at Stuttgart which he held till 1558, when a sharp
decree of the duke of Würtemberg against the Zwinglians
forced him again to withdraw. Once more he took refuge
in the Palatinate, obtained another living at Wisloch,
and died there in 1563.

As the most conspicuous and vehement free-lance of
his generation Kirchmayer has sometimes been compared

---

prepared for by a long description of the character and accomplishments of the ideal 'Husbandman,' and his 'tools' (Vergil's *arma*,
G. 1. 160). Among the latter is the House, every detail of which is
minutely prescribed. It must be ordered simply yet pleasantly;
and abound with flowers and sweet odours. The 'Musaeum' above
all, is to be cheerful, bright and sweet ; the books in order gleaming
on the shelves, with the Bible crowning all. The third book deals
with the actual work of the pulpit, and Naogeorg discusses with the
authority of experience the difficulties of the unacceptable preacher.

[1] *Hieremias*. Basil, 1551. He also produced a *Judas Isca-
riotes*, Basil, 1552.

[2] 'Nunc age (he begins), magnifici mihi membra fidemque Papatus
    Et varios ritus, annique ex ordine fastos
    Musa refer, &c.

[3] Cf. the concluding lines of the *Agricultura Sacra*.

to Hutten, Frischlin and Murner. The comparison is doubtless in each case a somewhat flattering one. Though a fair scholar and a fluent writer, he is altogether inferior to Frischlin in versatility of talent, to Hutten in penetrating and overpowering enthusiasm, to both in intellectual brilliance, and even in command of Latin style; and his sufferings for his faith, though considerable, are scarcely entitled to be put beside Frischlin's dungeon, or Hutten's death in exile among the Zürich marshes. Nor had he, again, any claim to the racy and pithy language of Murner, or to the humour which humanises his polemics, and which permits him, for instance, to pleasantly introduce himself into his most important satire in the feline form which his opponents, in those days of polemical *Goats* and *Bulls*, readily deduced from his name[1]. Yet he has, in a lower degree, the capital talent to which all three owed a good part of their literary fortune,—of fusing the abstract stuff of political controversies into a concrete dramatic form. In a lower degree,—for the fusion is certainly incomplete enough; the polar antagonism of principles is far too distinctly visible through the often shadowy substance of their human representatives; the finer play of motive, the half-lights of moral *chiaroscuro*, tend to be merged in a crude glare of black and white; Pyrgopolynices, Haman, the rebellious Jews, the renegade pope, are simply *antithetic heroes*, whose essential badness is not palliated by any suggestion of moral struggle. Yet with all this, his best scenes are undeniably impressive, in their broadly but powerfully-sketched masses, their vague tumultuousness, their angry and sunless sky. Literary quality in some men reaches its highest point under the stimulus of polemics, in others ('*diverria nobil cosa o si moria*') it

[1] Cf. the illustrations to *Der grosse Lutherische Narr.*

vanishes as soon as they abandon the point of view of
pure art. Kirchmayer belonged emphatically to the
former,—nay, it is when he approaches the point of view
of pure art that his quality, such as it is, becomes merely
insipid. He is not among those who can ennoble an
indifferent subject by delicacy of handiwork. He shared
with most of his countrymen the incapacity to carve a
literary cameo. The Titanism of conception which was
the admirable side of the grossness of the age, had its
part in him, and he struck his chisel with the hammer of
Thor, rough-hewing his massive blocks with as little heed
to proportion as to finish.

Pamma-chius[1].

All these qualities are concentrated in his earliest
play. The *Pammachius* is a remarkable attempt to
give dramatic form to the Protestant version of the
legend of Antichrist. It is in a sense the representative
drama of the Reformation era; for nowhere had so elaborate an attempt been made to give the Reformation its
'place in history,' or to exhibit the middle ages in the
lurid light shed over them by the laconic dictum of
Wiclif and Luther: *the Pope is Antichrist*[2]. Dramatised
theology is no longer quite congenial to us, but it is difficult
to deny a certain ghastly sublimity to this strange drama,
in which the gradual evolutions of history are replaced
by a succession of colossal 'divine events,' by which the
whole creation is affected.

[1] On the *Pammachius* cf. Scherer in *Ztscht. für deutsches
Alterthum* 23, 190 ff., to which I am indebted for some hints.

[2] Among the chief mediaeval plays on *Antichrist* are (1) the
Tegernsee play *Vom Ende des Kaiserthums und des Antichrists;*
(2) the English Mystery *Antichrist*, (3) the Fastnachtsspiel *Vom
Endkrist* (ed. Keller, *Bibl. d. Stuttg. lit. Ver.* Bd. 56, No. 68).

In none of these is Antichrist=the Pope. In one the Pope
appears to be the *pater apostolicus*, a distinct figure. On the Antichrist here cf. E. Wilken, *D. geistliche Schauspiel in Deutschland.*

The story of Antichrist is a kind of trilogy-subject, with three distinctly marked antithetic stages[1]. Antichrist is the dominant figure of the second stage only; his reign is prepared for, in the first, by the dissolution of the Empire, and opened with the last Kaiser's resignation of his crown; it closes, in the third, with the second coming of Christ. In the mediaeval dramas upon the subject, the reign of Antichrist is scarcely more than a brief prelude to the final *Juditium*. But the identification of Antichrist with the Pope modified this treatment in two ways. The 'second stage' was changed from a visionary anticipation to a concrete historical reality; and, further, its proximate termination, the beginning of the end, was understood to be brought about by the Reformation. In early Christian days, when the second coming appeared to be at hand, the features of Antichrist had been detected without difficulty in Nero; and twelve hundred years later, the evil rule is still made to open in the age of persecution, at the very close, it is true, of that age, under the most remarkable of persecuting emperors, Julian[2]. The honours of Antichrist are no longer, however, bestowed on the Caesar, but on an imaginary contemporary,—the Pope Pammachius, to whom Julian, the last representative of the declining empire, resigns his

[1] Cf. Zezschwitz, *Das Drama vom Ende des Kaiserthums* &c. The introduction contains an excellent account of the development of the Antichrist legend. The drama has also been translated into German by Zezschwitz.

[2] Julian had already figured in the *Gallicanus* of Hrosvitha, but simply as the persecuting emperor. She is, I believe, the earliest predecessor of Ibsen in this field. Celtes' edition of her might well be known to Kirchmayer and have suggested his somewhat singular choice of a typical emperor.

crown. The opening scenes prepare the way for this consummation. The persecuted Christian pope and the persecuting heathen emperor are both weary of the contest, but by a somewhat violent exercise of ingenuity the remedies they severally seek are made to embitter their enmity and at the same time to invert their parts. While Julian resolves to abandon persecution, Pammachius is deciding to give up a creed inconveniently exposed to it, and in exchange for his divine office, to seek the alliance of hell. So attractive are the terms there offered to him, that when Julian approaches to make his peace, the ex-pope is already inaccessible, and the good emperor retires indignant at his corruption.

In Act II. we are introduced to the infernal court of Satan. His deputies relate their achievements during his enforced absence in the pit. He hears with indignation of the secession of Julian. In the midst of the discussion Pammachius and his councillor Porphyrius are seen approaching. They are at first taken for enemies, and the Fiend expresses his amazement at their audacity; but their suppliant attitude, and their obvious terror, which is comically described, restore composure. Satan very affably invites them to tell their story, and having heard it, congratulates them on their fortunate escape, and promises preferment,

> 'Vos bene sperate,' he concludes, 'amicitia mea nemini
> Negata est, nec qui voluit regni particeps
> Fieri, frustra est. Sed cedite dexteras,
> Et nomina vestra, quae sint, dicite, ut sciam[1].'

[1] The Satan of vulgar belief is hardly perhaps recognisable in these lines, nor indeed in any other of his utterances throughout the play. We cannot however infer that Kirchmayer, like Milton, deliberately deviated from the traditional conception; for it is clear that in regard to outward form, at least, he entirely adhered to it;— 'saevum, cornutum, hispidum,' &c. says Pammachius of his ally;

Preparations are then made for a solemn installation of the new potentate. A year is occupied in the manufacture of the throne and triple crown. Messengers are sent into every province of the empire to summon the people to the ceremony. With an alacrity that amazes Pammachius himself they obey the summons,—'Parrhesia' slipping in among them with a modest excuse,—'solam ambulare mulierem haud decet.' Lastly come Julian and Nestor, prepared for the worst. They find Pammachius already enthroned on the seat of the Caesars, while Porphyrius prepares to deliver the *Apologia* of imperial papacy; a long and elaborate oration, followed after some unavailing debate by the abject submission of Julian, who recites a mock *Credo* at the dictation of his supplanter; while Parrhesia, unable to restrain her indignation, is abruptly expelled, her mouth filled with mud, and returns to tell Veritas the tale.

In the fourth act the victory of Satan and his allies is complete along the whole line; Christ is vanquished by Antichrist, and in a speech of voluptuous rhetoric, the infernal leader calls on his comrades to begin the life of unrestrained pleasure which nothing can any more interrupt :—

> Totos genialiter consumemus dies,
> Nullus laboret, sed feriae sint perpetuae,
> Ludamus, saltemus, bibamus ordine.
> Et nullus ante ponat oblatum poculum,
> Quam ter quaterve exhauserit.
> Et si dies ad haec celebranda gaudia
> Breviores fuerint, pars addatur noctium, &c.

the associations of the literary medium insensibly made for a certain dignity and humanity of expression, whoever the speaker might be. The Devil of the Miracle-plays could scarcely have retained his nature in Terentian iambics. Even Marlowe's Mephistophilis owes much to the dignified traditions of blank verse.

He summons the whole ecclesiastical host to enjoy this
spiritual Cocagne; and monks, bishops, priests pour in
open-mouthed with expectation. A fierce struggle for
places begins, to the great amusement of Satan, who (remembering his *Bruder Rausch*) calls out for oak staves
to be put in their hands:

> 'Caedite, bibite, turbis, rixis, clamoribus,
> Alatis poculis resonet convivium.'

From this scene of infernal revelry we pass into heaven,
which with Kirchmayer, as with Milton, is far less
vigorously imagined than his hell. The universal infidelity is sadly observed by Christ and Peter. There
are scarcely seven Churches which have not received the
mark of the beast. A poor fugitive interrupts their discourse,—Veritas, for whom there is now no place on the
earth, bringing her tearful appeal for deliverance to
Christ. She reports that the allies are not content with
their triumph, but are preparing to scale heaven itself,
and boast that they have the keys. Peter is confident
that in that case they must have forged them. Christ
calms him with the assurance that Satan and Pammachius
will be assigned to a region which no key is needed to
unlock, and then proceeds to give Veritas prophetic
guidance for her future course. Since she can no longer
endure her exile, a place shall be found for her on earth,
but it will involve her in much trouble and perplexity.
Veritas eagerly assents, and only desires to be shown the
place; she is immortal, and can defy all the rage of
Satan and Pammachius. Christ then bids her seek out
a certain Saxon town upon the Elbe; there she will find
one Theophilus, who will receive her and learn her ways,
and lay bare all the sores of the Papal realm, and stir up
the sleepy Germans to revolt. Sleep has indeed fallen
on the victors. Satan and his confederates snore after

their heavy revel. The infernal messenger Dromo rushes in with the news that the Reformation has broken out at Wittenberg. 'O Satan, hearest thou not? Hast *thou* also learned to snore? *Sat.* Ah, who calls? Thou rogue, why dost cry so? *Drom.* Why do I cry? Why do you sleep at such a crisis? *Sat.* What sayest thou? *Porph.* Oh, I can scarce open my eyes. *Pam.* Who is it startles me thus from my sweet sleep?' Dromo then expounds the new teaching of justification by faith.

The most original part of the drama is perhaps the close. At the end of the fourth act, and the beginning of what should be the fifth, the author breaks off. The final act of a drama upon the captivity of the world could only be the close of the captivity at the second coming of Christ. But that being still unaccomplished, the dramatist will not represent it. 'Expect no fifth Act,' he tells his audience.

Kirchmayer dedicated his play in language of warm eulogy, to the archbishop of Canterbury. A book bearing this commendation upon its front, could not fail to be read in England, and there is no doubt that it rapidly became familiar in the Lutheran circles of Oxford and Cambridge. In the following decade, this is, as regards Cambridge, beyond question. A little before Easter 1545, the Chancellor of the University, Gardiner, learned with indignation that the 'youth' of Christ's College, 'contrary to the mynde of the Master and President,' had lately 'playde a tragedie called Pammachius, a parte of which tragedie is soo pestiferous as were intollerable[1].' *The Pammachius in England.*

Performed at Christ's College, March, 1545.

---

[1] MS. Corp. C, No. CVI. p. 437 ff. The performance is already noticed in Warton, though with characteristic inaccuracy he in one place (IV. 74) describes it as 'a libel on the Reformation,' in another (III. 302) as 'a dangerous libel, containing many offensive reflections on the papistic ceremonies.' The quaintness of the former description is obvious; but appears to have escaped Mr Hazlitt, who reprints

A peremptory demand for explanation (coupled with a communication as to the provision to be made for deceased cooks), elicited from Vice-chancellor Parker a somewhat equivocal statement. So far from the tragedy having been played by the 'youth' of the college against the will of the Master, the performance had had the full connivance or even approval of the college authorities; nay, the Master himself assured Parker that it had cost the college 'well nigh xx nobles.' He hastens however to add that they had taken precautions against scandal by requiring the omission of all offensive passages, and that all such passages had been omitted[1].

Moreover, Parker had met no one of the company that had been offended, 'albeit it was thought the tyme and labour might have been spent in a better matter.' This was far from satisfying Gardiner, who called upon Parker[2] to summon the masters and doctors of the University to a joint inquiry into the circumstances of the performance, so that 'by due examination of such as were there it may be truly known what was uttered.' He

the passage without remark. An account of the performance has lately been given for the first time, if we except Cooper's perfunctory notice, by Mr Bass Mullinger, in a monumental work of which it would be poor praise to say that it does for our common University something more than was done for Köln by Bianco, for Vienna by Aschbach, or for Erfurt by Kampschulte. My own account was obtained independently, from the MS. in the Library of Corpus College, before I was acquainted with his. I abridge many details given by him, but the event is too important from my somewhat different point of view to be dismissed with a reference.

[1] Parker's MS. is much erased at this point; he was evidently at pains to characterise the omissions in terms sufficiently severe for his critical correspondent. 'Where there is inspersed through the tragedie both slanderous cavillations and suspitious sentence' is his final combination.

[2] MS. u. s. Letter of April 23rd (not 3rd as in Nasmith).

hinted at the same time his suspicion that though particular offensive expressions might have been omitted, the context was of a nature to imply and suggest them; a suspicion, as we know, amply warranted. The meeting was summoned, and a second letter from Parker reports the result. As we might anticipate, the chancellor's threatening attitude did not tend to encourage unwilling witnesses. The company, whose sympathies were doubtless preponderatingly towards Reform, unanimously declared with more sincerity probably than candour, that there was 'no offence in the play,' or if there was, at any rate they had forgotten it[1]. A copy of the play in which the omitted passages were remarked, was less ambiguous evidence; and it is not surprising that witnesses by no means agreed as to their number and extent. In any case the perusal of the book only deepened Gardiner's anger. He found fault with what they had spoken and with what they had omitted; much that they confessed to have uttered was 'very nought'; some things they had omitted had been better spoken.

One cogent reason for resenting the public performance of the *Pammachius* was apparently not within Gardiner's knowledge: viz. that the fugitive heretic John Bale had already made it accessible to the vulgar in their own tongue. His translation is indeed attested solely by his own statement in the *Centuriae*[2]. Neither the work

Bale's Translation.

---

[1] Parker to Gardiner: '... the answer of all was that none of all the companye declared to them that they were offended with any thinge that now they remember was then spoken.'

[2] 'Pammachii tragoediam transtuli.' Any doubt as to the identity of this tragedy with that of Kirchmayer, is settled by Bale's quotation of the opening words of his original, which correspond with the first line of Kirchmayer's *Argumentum*. It is possible that the *Pammachius* was not the only tragedy of Kirchmayer translated by Bale. The notice in his Catalogus (edition 9, 1548): *Pammachii tragoediam transtuli*, appears in the second and enlarged edition of 1557: *Pammachii tragoedias transtuli*. Had he in the interval

itself nor any other notice of it has come down.   It was
probably never printed, and, like the mass of Bale's productions, if it escaped the fate of heresy under Mary,
certainly suffered that of dulness under Elizabeth.

The Cambridge performance was not witnessed by
Bale, who was then in Holland, a fugitive from the
equivocal Protestantism of Henry[1].   Whether he first
made its acquaintance abroad, or had seen it before he
left England, whether he translated it during his exile or
before it, whether his version was suggested by the noto-
riety of the Cambridge performance or was strictly an
occasion of that performance, cannot be ascertained[2].
What is certain, and what gives its chief interest to Bale's
laconic notice, is that the most unique and curious of
his own extant dramas was apparently written with the
example of the *Pammachius* in view.

Bale :
*Kynge
Johan.*

When the converted Carmelite sat down in the course
of the year 1538, to write 'comedies' in the spirit of his
new faith, he was entering on a still untrodden path.
No one had attempted in England to create a charac-

rendered also the sister-drama upon Heinrich of Brunswick, in
which, though it does not bear his name, the Pope as Pammachius
again bears a leading part?   The question is the more in point
because in the *Pyrgopolinices* Henry VIII. is introduced, in a
manner which in spite of Bale's professions of loyalty, cannot have
been altogether uncongenial to the exile, coquetting with the infernal powers, and indirectly in alliance with the more terrible and
consistent foe of Protestantism, who is immediately assailed.

[1] Cf. *Catalogus Scriptorum*, &c., sub nomine *Henr. rex*.   Bale had
fled on the death of his protector Cromwell, who, as he confesses,
had repeatedly since his conversion delivered him from legal troubles,
on the ground of his literary services to Reform (*ob editas comoedias*).

[2] The notice of the translation is the last in the list of Bale's
'comedies.'   But it cannot be inferred that it was the last in
chronological order, as he may naturally have named the whole of
his original writings before a translation.

teristically Protestant drama. Kirchmayer's essay in this
kind, simultaneous as it was with his own, cannot yet
have been known to him. The entire dramatic produce of this year,—and of his extant dramas, not less
than four[1] bear the date 1538,—is the work of a vigorous
but inexperienced mind, sufficiently pronounced in doctrine, but indecisive and confused in literary method.
He seems to have tried in succession the current types
of drama. The *God's Promises* follows with little change
the method of the Mysteries; there is the same attempt
to abridge the religious history of the world into the
limits of a stage, the same multiplication of slightly connected scenes, the same colossal defiance of the unity of
time. The *Baptism* and the *Temptation*, on the other hand,
recal the simpler subject and method of the Miracle
Play. Nor did they admit of more than a surreptitious
gratification of Protestant antipathy. The Romanist was
no doubt made to peep out under the vesture of in-
credulous Pharisee and tempting Satan, but a direct and
telling assault upon him was scarcely practicable within
the limits of a purely biblical drama[2]. The same limitations attached, with little qualification, to the plan of the
last of the four, *The Three Laws*[3]. The 'three Laws,'—
of Nature, Moses and Christ,—are sent out in succession
by Deus Pater, to preach to the world. All receive ill
treatment, at the hands of 'Infidelitas' and his sub-
ordinates: the Law of Nature flies, struck with leprosy;
that of Moses is blinded and lamed; the Gospel is burnt

---

[1] The *God's Promises*, *The Baptism*, *The Temptation*, *The Three Laws*.

[2] Except, of course, in a Prologue, where, as in the *Baptystes*, the assault might be direct enough.

[3] Printed, with valuable introduction and notes, by A. Schröer, in *Anglia* v.

for heresy; and then the *Vindicta Dei* falls upon Infidelitas.   Here the method of attack is virtually the same
as before.   A plot almost entirely suggested by biblical
history is made to yield a weapon of Protestant controversy by the simple process of writing 'Romanist'
under the figures of the Hebrew enemies of God.   The
'Idolatry' and 'Sodomy' which corrupt the Law of
Nature, the 'Ambition' and 'Avarice' which maim the
Law of Moses, are thinly disguised monks and priests,
like the Pharisees of the *Baptism*, and the Satan of the
Temptation.   And in the same way the divine vengeance
which befalls Infidelity represents, under the forms of
the old 'Juditium,' the collapse which, to the sanguine eye
of the Reformer, imminently threatened the Church of
Rome.   Only in the description of the troubles of the
'Gospel,' its heresy, and its fate at the stake, does the
historical basis of the action fall into line, as it were,
with the object of the satire.

*Kynge
Johan.*
In the remarkable drama which was first discovered
and printed in the present century, the change just
hinted in the *Three Laws*, appears considerably advanced.
The biblical scheme of the Mystery is frankly abandoned;
the action begins where the interest centres, under the
'Babylonian captivity' of the Church, and it culminates
in a 'Reformation' in which no trace of the 'Juditium' of
the Mysteries survives.   The King is represented defying a group of enemies, 'Sedition,' with his auxiliaries
the Pope and the Papal Legate, and the whole spiritual
power.   Through their machinations, reluctantly supported by the Nobles and the People, he is first excom-
municated, then forced to submit, and finally poisoned.
After his death *Verity* pronounces an encomium over him,
and reproves the Nobility and the Commons for their part
in his death.   They are easily moved;   For God's love

no more.   Alas ye have said enough'; 'All the world doth
know that we have done sore amiss.'   Verity urges them
to leave their evil ways, and her exhortation is cut short
by the entrance of Imperial Majesty, easily recognised as
Henry VIII., who hears with appropriate satisfaction
that his subjects have resolved to abandon the Pope.
The drama concludes with the inevitable hanging of the
leading spirit among the conspirators, Sedition.

The *Kynge Johan* is the most original of Bale's
works[1].   It is easy however to trace this and that element
in it to foreign suggestion.   The famous *Satire of the
Three Estates*, for instance, which became known in
England soon after its performance in 1539[2], at the
earliest, and must have dazzled many others beside Bale
with its polish and wealth of language,—evidently supplied the hint of the corresponding three classes of
John's subjects.   The spiritual and temporal lords and
the burgesses, and the suffering John Common-weale
who pleads his wrongs before them, are the principal
objects in Lyndsay's satire; with Bale they are less
important, but their resemblance is unmistakeable.   Lyndsay wrote as a high-minded layman, Bale as before
all things an ardent churchman.   To Lyndsay the worst
of ecclesiastical abuses was the legalised oppression
of the poor; to Bale this was but an incident of the
appalling 'Babylonian captivity' from which the true
Church, as he thought, had just broken free.

Of more importance, in my view, was another in-

[1] An interlude concerning King John had however been acted
at the Archbishop of Canterbury's in Jan. 1539 (1540), Collier (ed.
1879, I. 124).   This was possibly, as Collier thinks, Bale's play;
but for our purpose the question is unimportant.

[2] Mr Laing (Lyndsay's Works I.) throws doubt on the supposed
production of it in 1535 at Cupar, for which there appears indeed
to be no evidence.

fluence. It appears to me clear that the *Kynge Johan* owes much of its peculiar construction to a deliberate imitation of the *Pammachius*, and that it was this imitation which finally emancipated Bale from his clumsy efforts to build a Protestant drama on the ruins of the Catholic mystery. Kirchmayer had taken up the transformed *Antichrist* legend; Bale, without anxious fidelity, followed his lead; Kirchmayer had typified the Empire, whose ruin accompanies the rise of Antichrist, by the emperor Julian; Bale, to whom England naturally took the place of the Empire, found a parallel in the English king whom he has in his rough fashion canonised. For his purpose the analogy may well have seemed sufficiently close, between the 'apostates' of the fourth and of the twelfth century. Both confronted the Papacy at a time when its power had made a momentous advance. If Pammachius was a plausible representation of the newly independent bishops of Rome, Bale's Pope was *à fortiori* a less exaggerated portrait of Innocent. Like Kirchmayer's Julian, Kynge Johan is assailed by a conspiracy in which the Pope takes a prominent part; like him he first resists and then succumbs, though Kirchmayer has not, like Bale, allowed his hero the crowning glory of martyrdom. Finally, each drama closes with an attempt to represent the Reformation. Kirchmayer's superiority is indeed here decided; nothing in Bale is so effective as the scene in which Dromo suddenly awakens the sleepy fiends with the news that Truth has found a champion at Wittenberg. But with Bale also Truth ('Veryte') appears announcing the Reformation, despatched characteristically enough, not by Christ, but by the 'Imperiall Majesty' of Henry VIII., who shortly follows to receive her report and execute vengeance [1].

---

[1] In Lyndsay's *Satire of the Three Estates*, 'Veritie' was already

The infernal machinery which is so striking in the
Pammachius is not adopted in the *Kynge Johan.* Bale
was more at home among the abstractions of the Morality
than among the concrete forms of the Christian Inferno;
and a little band of Vices replaces the Fiends. As
Pammachius obtains the supreme rule of the world by
his alliance with Satan, so in Bale the Papacy only
reaches its full height when the Vice 'Usurped Power'
appears *disguised* as the Pope. A new epoch begins for
the Church in each case. This Usurped Power (*Dis-
simulation* tells the audience),

> For the Holy Church will make such ordinance
> That all men shall be under his obedience,...
> As Gods own Vicar anon ye shall see him sit,...
> He shall make prelates, both bishops and cardinals,...
> He will also create the orders monastical...
> And build them places to corrupt cities and towns, &c.

And the first sign of the new epoch is the overthrow
of the great enemy. Pammachius, strong in his new
ally, extorts submission from Julian; and the transformed Pope succeeds in breaking the stubborn spirit
of John.

To sum up. It would be too much to describe
the *Kynge Johan* as a consistent Protestant version of
the story of Antichrist, in terms of English history.
But it appears to me to have been evidently written
with a vivid recollection of the most famous Protestant version then known, and to have been coloured
at several points by its associations. John's resignation
of his crown, the full development of the Papal tyranny

used to represent the new 'Lutherian' doctrines. She enters, 'in hir
hand beirand the New Testament' ('in English toung') to convert
King Humanitas. But there is no further attempt to represent the
Reformation, to which Lindsay, however he may have sympathised
with it, never openly professed adhesion.

of which it is the first mark, and the foreshadowing of
final doom in the Reformation of Henry VIII., correspond exactly to the three moments of the Antichrist
legend as used by Kirchmayer: the dethronement of
Julian, the triumph of Pammachius, the Reformation of
Luther.

Bale's attempt to create a Protestant drama,—if the
phrase does not wrong a writer so innocent of all strictly
literary ambition,—was apparently rapidly forgotten.
The Moral-writers under Edward who shared his views
went elsewhere for their inspirations[1]; and such vitality
as the religious drama still retained under Elizabeth was
largely displayed in a set of *genre* subjects infinitely
remote from the epic breadth of the *Pammachius* and
the *Kynge Johan.* When the latter was once more towards the end of the century brought upon the stage,
he still indeed receives honour for having 'set himself
up against the man of Rome.'

IV.

KIRCH-
MAYER
and
J. FOXE.

'For nearly ten years he had been my Achates; in
England we dwelt together in the house of the illustrious
Duchess of Richmond, and now once more we are
dwelling together in Germany.' So wrote Bale from
Basel, in 1556, of John Foxe. The two Boanerges of the
English Reformation were bosom friends and house-
mates, as well as political allies; they shared the same
social *milieu*, the same learning, the same bigotry, the
same hatreds, admirations, memories and hopes; and it
will hardly seem unnatural if a literary influence which,
as we have seen, left some traces in the rude art of the

[1] Edward himself is said to have written an 'elegant comedy
called *The Whore of Babylon.*

one, also coloured in some degree the work of the other,
—the strange and lurid drama in which under a veneer
of classical expression, Foxe rivalled the crudest of the
mysteries in naïve prolixity of form, and it must be
added, in essential barrenness of thought[1].

Settled at Basel, and domiciled with the eminent
bookseller, Oporinus, the publisher of one of the best-
known collections of sacred Latin drama, Foxe was in
contact with the very heart of Protestant Humanism.   It
was inevitable that in such a *milieu* he should turn over
the writings of the Neo-Latin dramatists,—the more so
as he had himself written Latin plays in his youth.   His
own words at any rate make it clear that he knew them
very well.   Ardent Protestant though he was, he had not
disdained to turn over the *Asotus* of the staunch Catholic
Macropedius, nor the *Christus Xylonicus* of Barptholomaeus Lochiensis[3].   The *Christus Triumphans* does not

The Christus Trium- phans, 1556.[2]

---

[1] Bale *Catalogus*, 1556, sub nom. *Foxus*.

[2] The *Christus Triumphans* was translated into French 1562
(Genève, Jean Bienvenu), and into English by John Day, 1579:
late in the seventeenth century (1672 and 1676) two editions of a
reprint of it followed edited by 'T. C.' M.A. of Sidney Sussex
College, and dedicated to use in schools 'ob insignem styli ele-
gantiam,' a distinction which did it rather more than justice.
Foxe's original MS. exists in the British Museum (Lansd. 1073);
the most interesting of the corrections which abound throughout
are those which show that Foxe had originally chosen different
names for several of his characters.   In the first draft Nomocrates
was called *Dicalogus*, Adopylus (servus) *Dromo*, and Dioctes at one
time *Machonomus*, at another *Abadon*.

[3] Cf. the Preface to his play, where he asserts that in the
'Asotus reliquisque doctissimae Germaniae comoediis,' the chief
purpose is satire of human faults and vices.   The singular term
Xylonicus, used of Christ by Foxe, was apparently invented by
Barptholomaeus.   He says in the preface (*ad pium lectorem*), that
he has devised the title 'quod Christus ἐν ξύλῳ, id est in ligno,
positus sit νίκῃ, id est victoria.'

however stand in direct line with anything that had preceded it. Foxe makes indeed a claim to entire originality,
and addresses his audience with a complacency worthy
of a better poet:

> Silentium rogat
> poeta novus (novi spectatores) novam
> rem dum spectandam profert.

He aimed at no mere flagellation of particular vices
such as, in his view, was the object of the *Asotus* or
the *Acolastus,* nor yet at mere illustration of particular incidents in Biblical history or legend[1]. Even the
saeva indignatio against the papacy did not now give
the original impulse to his verse. One consequence
of the Protestant identification of the Pope with
Antichrist, had been to bring the second coming of
Christ and the final judgment, of which Antichrist was
the immediate precursor, indefinitely near. The far-off
divine event became an hourly impending catastrophe.
The moral earnestness of the Reformers was powerfully
stimulated by this solemn foreboding. The world however, as usual, failed to realise its peril and went its
way unconcerned, daily adding to its load of sins. To
startle it from its indifference was the aim of the
Christus Triumphans. 'Whosoever, writes Foxe in the
preface, regards as in a mirror the affairs of men, will
judge that the grain is ripe, and that the time is come for
the sickle of the reaping angel. Wherefore it seemed
not unmeet that I should prepare some writing wherein
setting forth the perils of our time, I might inspire to the

---

[1] 'Non licuit in hoc Dramate singula vitiorum genera, atque
crassiora vulgi flagitia, more veteris comoediae flagellare. Id enim
in Asoto, reliquisque doctissimae Germaniae comoediis, tum potissi-
mum in concionibus quotidianis,...abunde est praestitum.'—Foxe,
ad pium lectorem.

greater contempt for this life, and regard for that to
come.' For this purpose, he took up the most authoritative document of modern history known to the
Reformers. 'It sufficed, he observes, simply to follow
the Apocalyptic story, transferring to the stage just
so much of it as bore upon the affairs of the Church.'
We shall see however that this was by no means an
adequate account of the scope of the *Christus Triumphans.*

Though divided into five acts, the drama falls more *Its Plot.*
easily into three divisions, corresponding to the three
times of trial through which the ideal Church had passed.
They are represented by three tyrants, Nomocrates, the
Jewish law, Dioctes the Roman persecutor, Pseudamnus
the papal Antichrist. In the first scene Eve appears
mourning for her children, Psyche and Soma, who at the
command of Nomocrates, are languishing in confinement,
the one in Orcus, the other guarded by the lictor
Thanatos. But her lamentations are interrupted by a
confused noise above and Satan is seen falling headlong;
while shortly afterwards 'Christus redivivus' appears
leading Psyche out of her captivity.

The second and third acts represent the age of persecution. Nomocrates and his allies, the priest and scribe,
are joined by Dioctes the deputy of captive Satan, who
calls out the ten Caesars to his work. Ecclesia appears,
like Eve before her, lamenting the loss of her three
children, Europe, Asia, Africa, whom Peter and Paul
finally release from the bondage of Nomocrates. The
fourth act carries us on with breathless speed. In the
first scene the accession of Constantine terminates the
tyranny of Dioctes; but the good news is scarcely an-
nounced when we meet with Ecclesia disturbed as she
meditates on the 'halcyon days' she has enjoyed since

Dioctes fell, by the noise which announces Satan's release
from the pit.   He unites himself with the Pope, 'Pseudamnus,' and instructs him how to subdue the world
with the 'Circaean cups' of luxury.   The sons of Ecclesia
are easily won over with honours and high-sounding titles,
'Fidei defensor, rex christianissimus' &c., while Pseudamnus himself intrigues with the courtesan Pornapolis,—
Foxe's symbol for the eternal City.   But their triumph is
soon disturbed by the gathering signs of the Reformation.
Ecclesia falls into their hands, and mortifies them by her
persistent denial of the claim of Pornapolis to be
Ecclesia.   She is rapidly despatched to Bedlam, but in
the next scene Satan himself with his lictors overhears
one Hierologus explaining to Europus that Pseudamnus
is Antichrist, and Pornapolis *meretrix Apocalyptica*.
They are convulsed with fury, and fall upon the bold
preacher, who takes to flight.   The lictor Psychephonus
pursues him, and presently returns with a startling narrative of moving accidents.   He tells how he had been
rapt, as he thought, into Purgatory, where he found Scotus
and Aquinas lashing themselves in rage at the universal
neglect of the Mass; how at the same moment a countless host of heretics were seen quenching the fire of
Purgatory with oceans of water, and how lastly he had
pursued the heretic *Hierologus*, the ally of Ecclesia,
through the streets of a town, easily recognised as Oxford,
till the fugitive took refuge in Bocardo.   There he is left
in fetters, with his fellow heretic, Theosebes[1].

Then Anabasius is found reporting to Pseudamnus
and Pornapolis the current rumours about them.
He candidly advises them to give up the game,—
'Mundus quia diu Jam oculis captus, videre cepit.'

---

[1] Cf. Theophilus in the *Pammachius*, the Reformer with whom
Veritas was to find refuge.

Pseudamnus attempts to put off the charge: "'tis quite certain, he urges, that the Turk is the Beast.' So I told them, replies Anabasius, but they are keen heads, and they made it clear that what is foretold of the Beast does not apply to the Turk. Pseudamnus accepts the conclusion with phlegmatic indifference, but Pornapolis sinks fainting to the ground, with the weight of a mill-stone at her heart, begs that doctors 'quantum potest' may be immediately summoned, and is borne off the scene, supported by Pseudamnus and Anabasius. After this scene of grim theological comedy, the end rapidly closes in. Africus and Europus,—England and France—are reunited (somewhat prematurely in the latter case) to their mother, and she herself arrayed in her bridal robes, and attended by the chorus of virgins, listens to an Epithalamian hymn which hints not obscurely that the divine bridal 'is not long.'

Crowded with unnecessary figures, confused in structure, unimaginative in conception, and alternately undignified and pedantic in style, Foxe's 'Apocalyptic drama' was far from being comparable with the best of those *doctissimae Germaniae comoediae* whose example he had somewhat ostentatiously set aside. The difficulty of converting the visionary and loosely connected imagery of the Apocalypse into a compact and ordered drama was of course immense, even with all the new suggestions supplied by the Protestant reading of it, and Foxe struggles visibly in the toils. But was his work so independent of previous dramatists as he professed? On the contrary, he owed if not the original suggestion, yet some hints in the execution, to the more remarkable writer who had handled the Apocalypse before him. The *Pammachius*, as we have seen, was in no sense, like the *Christus Triumphans*, an attempt

Comparison with the Pammachius.

to 'versify the Apocalypse'; but it derived from it, and particularly from the mediaeval development of the legend, much of the groundwork of its story, some telling situations, and several characters. Naogeorg had not, like Foxe, begun *ab ovo*. The first coming of Christ and the beginning of the thousand years, the allegory of Eve and her children, the Jewish scribes and priests, the conversion of Paul, and similar extraneous matter with which Foxe encumbered the course of his drama, lay equally outside his scope. On the other hand, he had introduced a novel and piquant element in the Reformation. The allegoric figure of Ecclesia, of whom Foxe vainly strove to make a tragic heroine, a Hecuba mourning for her children,—is reproduced with much more originality in the banished Veritas and her talkative handmaid Parrhesia; entirely original are the final despatch of Veritas from the refuge she has sought with Christ, to the Wittenberg teacher Theophilus, and the vigorous picture which follows of the infernal court startled from its easy slumbers by the news.

Although Foxe throughout kept far closer to the original, he shared too intensely the polemical bias of Naogeorg to escape the influence of his far superior dramatic skill[1].

The appearance of Satan, for instance, after being 'unloosed,' has several traits in common. In Naogeorg Veritas, in Foxe Ecclesia hastily take to flight from his presence. His allies are more slow to arrive, and he grows impatient at the neglect.

---

[1] It is worth noting that the notorious performance of the *Pammachius* at Christ's, and the subsequent inquisition, which can scarcely have been unknown at the sister University, occurred a few months before Foxe's expulsion from Magdalen,—when he was already in the throes of conversion.

> Sed ubi primum meos quaeram vicarios?
> Quid agant miror, quod non ut semper hactenus
> Quotidiana ad me regni gesta perferunt[1].

His scout Dromo emphasises this in lacquey fashion:

> Vicariis magna hercle sunt negotia
> Hodie, ut non possint convenire principem, &c.

Similarly, in Foxe, Satan breaks forth exultingly:

> Salutem atque benedictionem Acheronticam
> Quotquot sitis,—

but suddenly stops in amazement:—

> At quid hoc? proh portas inferi,
> Itan' nemo gratatum huc provolat? semel
> Nec ex vinclis salutat reducem? Populus hic
> Friget. Vide, absentia quid facit[2]!

Again, the effective, though nowise Apocalyptical, scene in which Parrhesia listens to the diabolical plans of Pammachius and his ally Porphyrius, and through native incapacity for sagacious silence, breaks into irrepressible indignation, is roughly handled and rudely dismissed,— forms the most natural starting-point for the equally effective scene in which Ecclesia is caught by Pseudamnus (the Foxian Pammachius), Pornapolis, and the lictor Psychephonus. Ecclesia is seen lurking behind. 'Take care she does not betray us.' They angrily question her:

> heus mulier sodes
> Quae sis? *EC.* Ecclesiae equidem nomen fero. *PS.* Proh
> anathema. *POR.* Audin' hanc?
> *PS.* Haeretica......Schismatica......Wyclevista.....Anabaptistica[3].

---

[1] *Pammach.* II. I.
[2] *Chr. Tri.* IV. 4.
[3] *Chr. Tri.* IV. 8. Cf. *Pam.* p. 420.

She stoutly maintains that she is the true church, and
finally, as has been said, is despatched by Pseudamnus
'ad Bethlemitas.'

Parrhesia it is true at first affects neutrality, and some
humour is shown in her spasmodic efforts to maintain
it[1]: but her spontaneous outbursts are as unequivocally
hostile as those of Ecclesia herself, and far more vivacious.

> Ha, ha, ha, perelegans illuminatio

she exclaims, at the suggestion that the pope is arrayed
in gold and purple

> ut quasi sol omnes illuminet ecclesias:

and when the arrogance of Pammachius culminates in a
comparison of himself with S. Peter, she loses all self-
control :

>   Vah homines impii, summum mundi caput
>   Pedibus conculcant: te deus piaculum
>   Exterminet, ut illudis hominibus et deo.
> *PAM.*   Ejice mox mulierem multatam pessime,
>   Os collinito stercore, vel si mavis luto.
> *PAR.*   Quin mittis me pessime, tuasque res agis?
>   Heu etiam verberat, et faciem pingit luto...
> *POR.*   Abi in malam rem haeretica Wiclevitica.

The two salient points in the story, which it was part
of the originality of the *Pammachius* to have combined,
viz. the release of Satan, with the resulting development

---

[1] *PAR.* (*aside*). Num hic est Satanae regnum? *POR.* Quid
    ais? *PAR.* Nil equidem,
  Sed tussiebam.
And after a more irritating explosion:
>   *PAM.* Quin
>   Extrahas hanc mulierem per capillos Porphyri,
>   Pugnis in os ingestis? *PAR.* Sanctissime pater,
>   Meae loquacitati des veniam obsecro.
>   Magis ero muta quam piscis, &c.

of papacy, and the first shock given to his power by the
Reformation, are certainly treated with much difference
in detail, but the common contour is unmistakable.
The infernal council of Satan and his vicars, the distribution of functions,—war, persecution, corrupt doctrine,
vice, luxury[1]; the stupefied amazement with which they
learn the news of the Reformation,

> SA. Audis haec Pammachi? PA. Oh totus ardeo
> Iracundia, et animi perplexitate—

the appearance of the reformed teachers[2]; the angry
interrogations about their doctrine; lastly the dramatic
aposiopesis by which the 'divine event,' the second
coming of Christ, towards which the whole drama
appears to 'move' as its inevitable catastrophe, is finally
withheld;—Naogeorg cutting short the action at the
fourth act, and warning his readers that 'Christ in his
own day would play the fifth,' Foxe hinting even more
emphatically by the bride already arrayed and the
marriage hymn already sung, at the imminent coming of
the heavenly bridegroom :—all these analogies in the two

---

[1] The council in the *Chr. Tr.* (IV. 4) corresponds more closely
with the final council of the *Pammachius* (IV. 5).

[2] In the *Pammachius* we hear of 'Theophilus,' the doctor of
Wittenberg, with whom Veritas finds refuge; in the *Chr. Tri.* of
'Hierologus' and 'Theosebes.' The former, like Luther himself,
suffers merely threats at the pope's hands,—

> Si
> Quis Veritatem mihi jam et Paulum traderet,
> Simul et *doctorem illum scelestum*, in temporis
> Puncto cum ipsis omnes vorarem vestibus, &c.

It was natural that an English exile in 1556 should insinuate
that this pious wish had not been wholly ungratified; and that
Hierologus and Theosebes should be consigned to languish in the
Oxford prison from which Ridley and Latimer had just been released by death.

dramas, yield a strong presumption that the younger
writer, in spite of his silence, owed much of the form of
his 'unprecedented drama' to the greater artist and
equally fervid theologian who had led the way.

The German exile ended, and with it ended also the
Exile-literature of which Foxe and Bale were the chief
luminaries, an unlovely passage of English letters which
is nevertheless not without a sort of ghastly fascination
of its own. The Return was the beginning of a period
in which England rapidly acquired strength and prosperity, while Protestantism more gradually assimilated
the worldly graces, the genial culture, the bold and
brilliant imagination of which it had been incapable in
the first fever of youth. The first two decades of
Elizabeth's reign were in this respect a time of transition.
Literature still dealt largely in theological *motifs* but
with a less dominantly polemical purpose. The religious
drama particularly entered upon a phase not precisely
paralleled before or after, and which served to mediate
between the Catholic Mysteries and the Protestant polemical plays on the one hand, and the artistic secular
drama of the next generation on the other. The opening
of the reign is marked by a little group of plays in which
the literary charm of the Parables of the New Testament,
and of the many exquisite episodes in the Old which lie
somewhat off the main highway of Jewish history, seems
suddenly to have borne fruit. The Mysteries had passed
at a bound from Moses to Christ, and the Parables lay
naturally quite outside their plan. Now for the first time
the rich dramatic material of the books of Daniel, Esdras
and Esther, is utilised in such pieces as the *Enterlude of
the story of Kyng Daryus* (1565), the *Enterlude of Godly*

Queene Hester[1] (1561) and the *playe of Susanna*[2] (1568); while the parable of the Prodigal[3] was the basis of a play of which distinct traces are only apparent at a much later time[4].

Distinctly less remote than the authors of these crude pieces from the creators of the mature secular drama, wavering indeed visibly between the beautiful profanities of Italy and the austere ideal of the Calvinist preacher, is a young poet of the middle of Elizabeth's reign, whose work, almost by an anachronism, forms a last link in the series of English religious dramas which drew some part of their inspiration from the great German treasury of 'holy plays.' A brief notice of it will therefore naturally conclude the present chapter.

V.

George Gascoigne is a familiar figure in the genera- GAS-
tion which preceded Shakspere's. His *Iocasta* was the COIGNE: *The Glasse of Govern-*

[1] This seems to stand in no relation to the *Comoedia von der ment,* *Königin Hester* of the English Comedians. 1575[5].

[2] Sta. Reg. 1568–9. Extant in the last century.

[3] Sta. Reg. 1565–6. Perhaps the play of which a few fragments survive in the *Histriomastix*. It is scarcely likely to have been the original of the English Comedians' *Comoedia von dem Verlorenen Sohn.*

[4] It is a natural suggestion that this group of biblical *genre* dramas owed something to an acquaintance with the numerous plays of the same class which a fugitive in Germany must inevitably have met with wherever he went. But comparison, in the few cases where it is possible, shows that this influence can at most have affected the choice of subject. The rude *Darius*, for instance, is almost as unlike the elaborate *Zorobabel* of Birck as is possible for two plays upon the same story to be.

[5] The substance of this section has already appeared in the *Englische Studien*, Jan. 1886.

first tolerable translation of a Greek play, and the first
attempt to follow up the classical path opened by
Gorboduc. His *Supposes*, the first successful adaptation
of an Italian comedy, is immortalised by a notable
plagiarism of Shakspere, who used a considerable part of
its daintily artificial scenery to relieve the robust natu-
ralism of his Shrew, a Frank Hals with a background by
Moeris. On the other hand, his single original comedy,
the first fruits of the 'regeneration' of the once worldly
poet, has enjoyed only a *succès d'estime* in comparison
with either the *Steele Glasse* which adorns a later and
less severe stage of his repentance, or his juvenile and
rather frivolous *Posie.* Yet, as Mr Hazlitt truly says
(Gascoigne's Works, Roxb. ed., *Introduction*), *The Glasse
of Government* stands absolutely alone in the English
dramatic literature of the century; and he professes
himself unable to throw any further light upon it than is
implied in a very general reference to ancient comedy.
Under such circumstances, the slight suggestions which
I have to offer appear to need no apology.

The *Glasse of Government* was first printed in 1575,
and (in spite of Mr Arber, who in his introduction to the
Steele Glasse antedates the Dedication by just ten years)
certainly written not long before. It is a 'tragical
comedy' in five acts, and in prose. Two Antwerp
burghers, Phylopaes and Phylocalus, have each two sons,
the elder in both cases of the kindred of the Prodigal
son, while the younger are exemplary youths of an unreal type. Anxious for their welfare, the two fathers
seek out a wise and godly teacher, one Gnomaticus,
whose discourses, very unequally composed of classics
and of the teaching which Aristotle thought unwholesome
for young men, occupy much of the first two acts. Unfortunately, Phylautus and Phylosarchus, the two elder

sons, who learn the lesson soonest, are the first to forget it. The temptations of the town are let loose upon them in the person of a fascinating parasite, Eccho, who, after obtaining a holiday for them on the pretext of an invitation from the 'Markgrave,' introduces Phylosarchus to a local Cressida called Lamia, and her 'aunt' Pandarina[1]. And so, while the younger brothers are laboriously pursuing rhymes for a verse composition on Duty, Phylosarchus is already in the toils of the *meretrix*. The adventure soon comes to the ears of the two fathers, who anxiously take counsel with Gnomaticus. He advises that they shall be sent at once without warning to the neighbouring university of Douay. A sumptuous meal prepared for them at Lamia's house accordingly awaits them in vain, and the parasite and his crew are arrested by order of the Markgrave. Presently arrives a report from Douay to the effect that the 'Prodigals' have only changed the scene of their amours. Crime is added to vice, the plot thickens with increasing rapidity, months of action are crowded into minutes of narrative. Finally, while Eccho is still awaiting sentence, news arrives that the two incorrigibles have met their reward. Both in fact have fallen into hands not accustomed to pardon or indulge: Phylosarchus having been flogged for fornication in the city of Calvin; and his brother executed for murder in Calvinist Heidelberg. The two younger sons meantime, by a coincidence not infrequent in stories of this type, have reached distinction and influence in the same quarters;—the one as a minister at Geneva, the other as secretary to the Palsgrave.

Where are we to look for the origin of this singular

---

[1] This name, as Professor Ward observes to me, shows that the proper name was already understood in its *common* sense.

plot, with its pronounced didactic vein, its acute ethical contrasts, its rapid alternation of school and tavern scenes, its bold development of character in opposite directions? Doubtless, as Mr Hazlitt says, a certain element of it, especially the whole machinery of the *parasite* and *meretrix*, might be paralleled from Latin comedy.

But there are two peculiarities in its use of these Roman situations. There is an obvious attempt (1) to combine with them a pronounced Christian moral; and (2) to associate them with the life of a modern university. For these much closer parallels can I think be found elsewhere. To make this clear it will be necessary to resume a thread already briefly handled in the first section,—the dramas of the 'Prodigal Son.'

The Prodi-gal Son.   Unknown to the dramatic repertory of the Middle Age, all but unknown to that of France and England throughout the sixteenth century[1], the most finished of the parables had in Germany a vogue to which no other subject in literature approached. The variety of treatment displayed in the score or more of recorded versions of it[2] shows on how many sides the subject was congenial to the national mind. No other so effectively combined qualities which appealed to the Humanist with those

---

[1] The only example earlier than the *Acolastus* is Ravisius Textor's so-called 'dialogue' *de filio prodigo* (Paris, c. 1510), which is quite differently treated. The Prodigal is the heir of a miserly father, whose death gives him the first opportunity to deserve his name. There is accordingly no question of a return and forgiveness. The first known edition of Textor is 1536.

[2] Cf. on the whole subject: Holstein: *Das Drama vom Verlorenen Sohn,* 1880. An exact number cannot be given, as this class shades off by indefinite degrees into others. Several moreover are only surmised from their titles. A drama of similar tendency by Busslebius (1568) is described by Holstein *Archiv f. Litt. Gesch.* 10, 168 ff.

which had an attraction for the Reformer. The problem
of providing a 'Christian Terence' was materially lightened
by the example of a plot in which a genuine Terentian
intrigue led up in the happiest way to a Christian repentance and reconciliation. And, on the other hand, the
nature of this reconciliation itself made the parable a
capital weapon in the hands of the Protestant advocate
of 'justification by faith.'

These qualities were quickly seen, and the story was
seized upon, independently and almost contemporaneous-
ly, by three remarkable dramatists. With Georg. Macro-   Macropedius, as a Catholic and a schoolmaster, the Humanist   pedius:
Asotus,
motive is naturally predominant; and his *Asotus,* the   c. 1510.
firstfruits of his imitation of Reuchlin, is an almost
purely Terentian drama of intrigue, in which a bevy of
slaves, mistresses and parasites play their familiar part
about the dissolute son, and the final forgiveness is
simply the conventional accompaniment of a fifth-act
repentance. Nearly half the play is devoted to an
attempt, in conception just, but clumsily carried out, to
supply a motive for the division of the inheritance,—the
absence of which is an undeniable flaw in the otherwise
admirable art of the original. Asotus leaves his home
only on the discovery of an intrigue carried on there with
the aid of a slave in his father's absence. Totally
different was the handling of a new convert to Luther,
Burkard Waldis, and the crypto-Protestant W. Gnapheus;   B. Waldis
whose '*Parable of the Lost Son*[1]' and the *Acolastus*[2] gave   *Parabell
vam vor-*
the most decisive proof of the sincerity of the one and   *lorn*
brought the most damaging suspicions upon the other.   *Szohn,*
In Waldis there is no trace of classical influence[3]; the   1527.

---

[1] *De Parabell vam vorlorn Szohn,* Ryga, 1527 (ed. Milchsack).

[2] Acted 1529; printed 1534.

[3] He deprecates the comparison with the air of patronising

intrigues of Italian slaves and parasites are replaced by
the ruder devices of the Low German boor; with little
attempt to make new combinations, or to add anything
to the pathetic simplicity of the original, the garrulous
verse leads us tranquilly towards the climax, in which the
author's entire interest is centred, and which he has
spent all his resources to throw into relief, for not only is
it accompanied by a long and impressive moral upon the
need of justification by faith, but the whole drama is
preceded by a Prologue in which the diabolical origin of
the opposite doctrine is emphatically urged.

Gna-
pheus:
Acolastus,
1529.

In a sense intermediate between the play of Macropedius and that of Waldis, the *Acolastus* of Gnapheus is
superior to both. Without the structural excrescences by
which Macropedius had attempted to make the plot
more intelligible and Waldis to make it more edifying, it
felicitously combined just as much of the classical and
the biblical model as was capable of harmoniously
blending. Full justice is done to the intrigue, without
detriment to the intensely un-Roman *dénoûment.*

Acolastus, the Prodigal, is sent by his father into the
world, with the approval of a wise friend and counsellor,
Eubulus. He and his like-minded companion Philantus,
speedily fall in with two parasites of the astute Plautine
breed, Pantolabus and Pamphagus, who with the aid of

humility habitually assumed by the journeymen of Protestant art
towards the pagan masters of the ancient world. The reader is
begged to excuse his simple style,

> —dat unnser stilus ys szo slicht
> mit Terentio gar wenich stymbt,
> noch mit Plauto over eyn kumbt,—

and for a reason which betrays the infancy of criticism :

> de wyl ydt ys keyn fabel gedicht
> sonder up de rechte warheit gericht.

a *meretrix* Lais, make short work of his purse, as of his principles. The third act paints with extraordinary vivacity a glowing love-scene with Lais. In the fourth the ruin of Acolastus is consummated: he leaves the *lupanar* houseless and penniless. The climax has already been foreshadowed, with much art, in the steady faith of the friend Eubulus, that the Prodigal will not finally be lost. 'Eum fatis totum relinquito curandum,' is his reply to the anxious forebodings of Pelargus; and the fifth act effectively though very briefly records Acolastus' return, and his forgiveness, which is seasoned with reflexions, perilously Lutheran for a professed Catholic, on the justifying virtue of faith.

From the 'Prodigal son' to the dissolute student or the truant schoolboy, is not a very difficult step, and out of dramas of the *Acolastus* type grew a series of offshoots in which the motive of the parable is applied to the society of a modern University town. The informal adviser easily became a professional pedagogue, the steady son a blameless 'reading-man'; the ordinary contrasts of bourgeois life reappeared touched with the acuter antagonisms of town and gown. I am here concerned with only two of these comedies of school life: the *Rebelles* of Macropedius, and the *Studentes* of Stymmelius,—the latter a direct imitation of the *Acolastus*. *School-dramas*[1].

The *Rebelles* is certainly far from reproducing the compassionate ethics of the parable; on the contrary, it preaches with great zest the classical Old Testament doctrine of 'spare the rod and spoil the child.' It is the satiric revenge of a genial pedagogue, accustomed to flog out of sheer goodness of heart, upon tender mothers who founded an argument against the school on the '*clunes* Macropedius: *Rebelles.*

---

[1] On the School-dramas cf. especially Erich Schmidt's brilliant sketch, *Die Komödien vom Studentenleben*, 1881.

liventes' of their offspring. In the opening scene a mother laments to her plain-spoken gossip Cacologia, the cruelty of her boy's master. After mutual consultation they resolve to send him to the school of one Aristippus, with the proviso that he shall be taught *sine verbere.* A rumour of the decision reaches the boys, to their huge delight:

> O deum immortalem, ut est stultissima
> materna meus, nobis tamen ut accommoda!

The result is easily foreseen. Relying on their immunity, the boys gamble behind their books, quarrel, are detected, and finally agree to escape. Then follows the characteristic intrigue of the Prodigal story. They enter an inn, procure mistresses, are cheated at play, and make their way off with empty pockets. Finding a peasant asleep with a treasure, they rob him and return to the inn, where the host receives them with open arms. But their satisfaction is brief, for two 'lictors' speedily arrive, arrest the youths, and carry them off for trial. In peril of their lives, they despatch an urgent message to the mother. In frantic haste she summons Aristippus and rushes to the court, only to find that the trial, a mere five-minutes police-case, is already over, and that the prisoners, as a warning to others, are sentenced to death. The arrival of the master, however, diverts the threatened tragedy. He begs that the punishment of his own pupils may be entrusted to him; the judge without difficulty assents, and the boys are carried off to receive what is thus ingeniously made to appear the rare favour of a sound flogging.

Stymmelius : *Studentes,* 1549.

The *Rebelles* was printed in 1535, the *Acolastus* in 1534. In 1549 appeared the *Studentes* of Stymmelius, a piece much inferior to either, but probably even more

widely read. It is, as I have said, a free adaptation of
the *Acolastus*. Gnapheus had, somewhat perversely, neglected the telling contrast of the elder son; Stymmelius
atones for this parsimony by a liberal provision of three
sons and three fathers, whose divergent dispositions are
paired off against one another in neat alternation like the
squares of a chess-board. Eubulus, the wise friend, is
now the father of the prodigal, the sordid Philargyrus of
the son whose only ambition is learning, and the indul-
gent Philostorgus of the son for whom indulgence is
poison. Deliberation of the three fathers, as usual,
opens the play; followed by the despatch of the three
sons to the University. They seek out a teacher, one
Paideutes, who discourses unctuously of the advantages
of learning. Philomathes embarks on his course; the
other two speedily follow the way of Gnapheus' Acolastus,
with the difference, no doubt a concession to a respectable audience, that he is made to wrong an honest
girl instead of a professed *meretrix*. Her parents demand reparation: Eubulus, after much doubtful stroking
of his beard, reluctantly consents, and lacerated morality
is patched up in the approved way by a conventional
marriage. The impressive repentance and forgiveness
scene of Gnapheus is thus abandoned for a commonplace
dénoûment; and the *Acolastus* must be pronounced as
superior to the *Studentes* in moral weight as it is in
dramatic force and vivacity.

It is needless for my present purpose to follow further *Other*
either the dramas of the Prodigal Son or that special *'School'-*
class of them devoted to the school and university pro- *dramas.*
digal. Jörg Wickram's *Junger Knaben Spiegel*, one of
the cardinal works of early German Romance, is also
interesting as a step in the process by which the biblical
motive, steeped for awhile in the atmosphere of Terence

and enriched, if somewhat vulgarized, by the contact, became completely assimilated to German bourgeois life. Hayneccius' *Almanzor* ('Schulteufel') is a lively picture of 'Rebels' even more incorrigible than those of Aristippus[1].

Vogue of German School-dramas in England.

Before discussing the relation of Gascoigne's play to these three dramas, it may be well to review such external evidence as exists for his acquaintance with them. It is rarely possible in cases of this sort to bring a writer face to face with his source; to trace his steps to the very library, his hand to the very shelf, where it lay. But one may fairly be called on to show that his acquaintance with it would be exceedingly natural, that it penetrated well within his literary *milieu*.

I have already dwelt on the considerable vogue which several Latin comedies of Germany obtained in England in the course of the century. Conspicuous among those which obtained the honours of translation or reprint, were the *Acolastus* and the *Studentes*. Palsgrave's school-version of the former, the French translation, the London reprint of 1585[2]; the MS. copy of the latter made in 1570, the performances at Wittenberg and Christiania in 1572—3, twenty-three years after its first production, and above all the immense number of editions it went through[3], leave no doubt of the European celebrity of the two plays[4]. Of the *Rebelles* I have met

---

[1] Wichgrevius' *Cornelius relegatus*, which I know only from Prof. Erich Schmidt's account (u. s.), is said by him to be a picture of student-life much superior to the *Studentes*.

[2] In the library of Trinity College, Cambridge.

[3] My friend Dr Joh. Bolte, of Berlin, has kindly sent me a complete list of the editions from his own collections. They number 28, from 1549 to 1662; of which 11 (Frankfurt a. d. O., Antwerp, Köln and Strassburg) appeared before 1575.

[4] A reminiscence of the former play is doubtless also to be

with no distinct trace in England[1], where however three others of his dramas the *Andrisca, Bassarus* and *Hecastus* were probably known from Brylinger's collection, while his name was in any case familiar as the author of a standard treatise on letter-writing (*de conscribendis epistolis*) early reproduced in England. All three dramatists must have been well known at least by name and reputation, in the literary university circles to which Gascoigne belonged. But in 1572—3, circumstances carried him into the actual scene of the work of two of the three,—still the headquarters of the Christian Terence. He joined the prince of Orange in Holland, and, by the evidence of his own *Dulce bellum inexpertis,* found leisure for the victories of peace in the intervals of doubtful successes in the field. The Hague, Gnapheus' city, was also the home of the 'vertuous lady' whose intimacy proved so perilous to her frequent visitors[2]. Antwerp, where the scene of the *Glasse* is laid, he may not then have known[3]; but some parts of the plot, for instance the

found in S. Nicholson's *Acolastus his After-wit,* where Eubulus 'the auncient friend' (v. 705) and good counsellor, corresponds to the Prodigal's father of the same name in Gnapheus; while Acolastus himself is distinctly assimilated to the Prodigal. His mistress has played him false, and he returns, in an access of cynicism and despair, to Eubulus, who with difficulty prevents him from suicide. Cf. vv. 439 ff. where the analogy of the Prodigal is explicitly applied to the case of deluded soldiers returning home penniless, sufferers, like Acolastus himself, from the greed of gold.

> Poor playning Prodigals, now must they wend
> Back to the country with remorse and shame;
> But wher's the feasting Father, or the friend? &c.

[1] Dr Bolte enumerates six editions before 1575, published at Hertogenbosch, Köln, Regensburg and Utrecht.

[2] Cf. *Dulce Bellum,* st. 156 ff.

[3] That he knew it in the year following is shown by his *The*

episode of the Markgrave, show familiarity with its institutions, and the figure of Eccho, a gay fellow 'known to all the town,' has something of the air of a portrait. Gascoigne's attested knowledge of Dutch itself involved a certain acquaintance with Dutch society and its current literature.

The external evidence then rather favours the view that Gascoigne was not a stranger to works connected by so close an affinity with his own. The degree and nature of that affinity will be obvious from the sketch already given. Distinct copy of any one of them of course it is not; it is written throughout with a different bias; it is the work of a Calvinist, not of a Catholic or of a Lutheran; it is in the vernacular, not in Latin; in prose, not in verse. For all that, however, it assuredly belongs to the same dramatic cycle; it is an attempt, that is, to connect *Terentian situations* with a *Christian moral* in a picture of *school-life*. A brief examination of the play shows that it was written, like the *Acolastus*, with a very vivid recollection of Roman comedy. It is true that, with the majority of its modern imitators, he begins by explicitly condemning it. The play opens with this significant *avis :*

> A comedie I mean for to present,
> No Terence phrase; his time and mine are twain;
> The verse that pleased a Romain's rash intent
> Might well offend the godly Preacher's vein;
> Deformed shows were then esteemed much,
> Reformed speech doth now become us best...

So too in the first lecture of Gnomaticus (1. 4), we are warned that 'though out of Terence may be gathered many moral instructions among the rest of his

Spoyle of Antwerpe ('faithfully reported by a true Englishman who was present at the same') 1576.

wanton discourses, yet the true Christian must direct his steps by the infallible rule of God's word.' Another criticism occurs in II. 2.

On the other hand, this depreciation had definite limits. He could not only quote approvingly the profane poet's 'moral instructions':—'let shame of sin thy children's bridle be, And spur them forth, with bounty wisely used. So Terence taught, whose lore is not refused,'—but he can adopt his slippery situations and characters with as little compunction as the author of the *Acolastus* himself. He does so, however, like Gnapheus, with a 'godly' purpose, though one sufficiently unlike his. The dissipations of Acolastus serve to emphasise the beauty of forgiveness; those of the 'Rebelles' to strengthen the cause of rigorous discipline; those of Gascoigne's Phylosarchus to illustrate the time-honoured texts (suggested by the piety of his publisher): Fear God, honour thy parents. Still more than in Macropedius, the merciful climax of the parable vanishes, and is replaced by the stringent severity of Geneva and Heidelberg, where the final scenes of the prodigals appropriately take place. It may be noted that in the only other English Version of the Prodigal Son story of which we know anything in detail,—Thomas Ingleland's *The Disobedient Child,*—the solution of the parable is still more pointedly put aside: the prodigal actually returns to his father, but instead of receiving a lavish welcome, is with difficulty allowed a temporary refuge in his old home[1].

Assuming then that the *Glasse* comes evidently under the general category of the Christian Terence, I proceed

---

[1] A more distant parallel to the Prodigal Story occurs in Woode's *Conflict of Conscience,* with an equally emphatic Calvinist moral.

to examine in detail its relation to the three plays which further agree with it in applying this motive to the domain of *Studentenleben*. This will most conveniently be done by a summary.

I.   *A pair of 'prodigals' is contrasted with one or more steady and industrious students :*—(thus, in *G. of G.*, Phylosarchus and Phylautus with Phylotimus and Phylomusus; in *Ac.* Acolastus and Philautus with the elder brother, a *persona muta ;* in *Stud.* Acolastus and Acrates with Philomathes.   In *Reb.* the two schoolboys have no foil).

II.   *Parents, or parent and counsellor, discuss the problem of their son's education :*—(in *G. of G.* the two fathers, in the *Ac.* the father and counsellor, in *Stud.* the three fathers, in *Reb.* the two mothers).

III.   *Choice of a teacher, interview and arrangement with him :*—(in *G. of G.* the two fathers agree with Gnomaticus; in *Reb.* the mothers with Aristippus; in *Stud.* Philomathes with Paideutes).

IV.   *'Prodigals' leave their studies and involve themselves in vice, gambling and crime :*—(in *G. of G.* Phylosarchus is beguiled by Eccho and Lamia, in *Ac.* Acolastus by Pamphagus and Lais; in *Stud.* Acolastus by Colax and Deleasthisa; in *Reb.* the two schoolboys, who also inquire for 'Veneres,' by their host).

V.   *Anxious consultation of parents :*—(in *Ac.* this occurs after Acolastus' prolonged absence; in *Reb.* on the news of the prodigals' disappearance from school; in *G. of G.* both after the detection of the Eccho and Lamia plot, and on the news of similar *faux pas* at Douay.

VI.   *Disgrace of the prodigals.*   The different moral and theological bias of the four dramatists led them to handle this point with great independence: but none wholly excluded it. In the *Ac.* it is finally resolved into repentance and pardon; in the *Stud.* into wedded respectability; in the *Reb.* it is qualified by the substitution of the scholastic birch for the judicial axe. In Gascoigne alone, the 'wages of sin' are exacted to the full in the stern spirit of Calvin.

If I am not deceived then, there are plausible grounds for supposing that one of the most respectable pioneers of the great age of the English drama stood for a moment in literary contact with the most original Latin dramatists of the previous generation; that he met with their writings either in England, where they were in any case known by repute, or during the Dutch journey which immediately preceded the writing of his own play; and that he learned from them what no Roman or English dramatist could then have taught him,—the idea of a 'Glass of Government' in which the unsavoury world of Roman comedy is boldly adopted with a Christian purpose, while the story of the biblical Prodigal is worked out, much enlarged and still more extensively 'amended' in the sphere of the modern school.

With Gascoigne properly closes the discussion not only of the Latin drama, but of the entire *genre* of *theological belles-lettres* of which it was the most conspicuous class, and which the Reformation, comparatively barren elsewhere, produced with prolific energy in the country of its birth. Still in the vigour of manhood when Marlowe and Decker were at school, Calvinist 'by grace,' but a true 'Elizabethan' by nature, Gascoigne is as it were the meeting-point of the literature represented by the *Acolastus* and the *Pammachius*, and that other, not less vast or original, which is represented by *Faustus* and *Fortunatus*, by tales of magicians and witches, of fools and rogues, of Grobians and Owlglasses; a literature not, like the former, essentially composed of Christian materials, and called to life under a Christian inspiration, but a genuine and characteristic creation of the Teutonic genius,—a heap of fantastic and uncouth shapes, permeated and tinged no doubt at every point by Christian emotion, but in fundamental structure disclosing, unalloyed, the very native stuff of genial, lawless, untameable human nature.

PART II.

CHAPTER IV.

The Faustus Cycle.

No national reputation probably has ever undergone Intro- a greater change than that of Germany between the duction. middle and the end of the sixteenth century among its English neighbours. To the average contemporary of bishop Bale, and to the average contemporary of Jonson or Fletcher, the name had quite different associations. To the one Germany was the mother-country of the Reformation, the refuge of the persecuted Protestants, the seat of literary accomplishments and civic splendour which England could at the most barely rival. To the other, probably enough, it was famous only as a land of magicians and conjurers, as the home of Albertus and Agrippa, Paracelsus, Tritheim, and Doctor Faust[1]. It

[1] All, especially Paracelsus, are very frequently alluded to in the dramatists, for whom Paracelsus shares with Faust the position of the typical conjurer. Cf. e.g. Jonson, *Volpone* II. 1 (Nano's song— 'Paracelsus with his long sword'), *Epicoene* IV. 2 (*Ep.* 'Servant, you have read Pliny and Paracelsus, ne'er a word now to comfort a poor gentlewoman?) Cf. *Alchemist* II. 1; Glapthorne, *Hollander* III. 1; Fletcher, *The Fair Maid of the Inn* IV. 2 ('Were Paracelsus the German now living, he [Forobosco] would take up his single rapier against his terrible long sword'). Of Agrippa's fame the most notable evidence is Nash's well-known invention in *Pierce*

added a new fascination to the 'most wicked sorcerer' to
be a German; nor was there any better advertisement
for a tale of wonder than to be 'translated from the hye
Almain.'   Among the Jacobean dramatists, Germany is
as inseparably associated with magic as Holland with
'butter,' and Spain with arrogant manners.   'Wert not
better [to follow the court fashion],' asks Thorowgood in
Glapthorne, of the bookworm Holdfast, 'then to walke
like Faustus or some high German conjurer, in a cap fit
for a costermonger[1].'   In the *Alchemist*, Heidelberg is a
typical seat of alchemy, and a learned astrologer is called
the 'high almanac of Germany.'   The 'juggler with a
long name' whose services are desiderated in the *Magnetic Lady* is appropriately called Travitante *Tudesco*
(Tedesco)[2], and the association is only slightly different
in the boast of the 'upstart gallant' Fulgoso in *The
Lady's Trial*, that his mother was a 'harlequin,'

> In right of whose blood I must ever honour
> The lower Germany[3].

Penniless, where Surrey sees the fair Geraldine in the magician's
glass. He is also one of the traditional masters of Faust (*D. Faustus*
Sc. 1); cf. Jonson's notes to the *Masque of Queens* and *Newes from
the New World*. Tritheim's magical fame in his own day did not
suffer from the comparative inaccessibility of his magical writings;
but their publication in the next century gave it a stimulus.   Cf.
Cartwright, *The Ordinary*, III. 5,

> It would lay a devil
> Sooner than all Trithemius' charms.

[1] Glapthorne, *Wit in a Constable* (1639), I. 1.
[2] *Magn. Lady*, I. 1. Boy (to Damplay, who has declared that
'there be of the people that will expect miracles, and more than
miracles, from this pen'), 'Do they think this pen can juggle? I
would we had Hokospokos for 'em, your people, or Travitante
Tudesco.'
[3] Ford, *The Lady's Trial*, IV. 2.

The very language is regarded as peculiarly suitable for magical observations. 'In what language shall 's conjure in ?' asks Forobosco in Fletcher's *Fair Maid.* 'High Dutch I think, that's full in the mouth[1].'

And while this half humorous association gained ground, the serious prestige of Germany, the half filial reverence for her as a mother of learning and true religion, had almost vanished. The mutual relation of the two countries was in fact essentially altered. In nearly all the essentials of civilisation, Germany had steadily lost ground, while England had made a gigantic stride. In political development, in foreign enterprise, in literary brilliance, even in the wealth and size of her cities, Germany hardly entered the lists with England. Protestantism itself was become not less an English than a German institution ; the former colony of the new faith was now its most independent stronghold[2].

---

[1] Sir Epicure Mammon's library contained a work by Adam 'on the philosopher's stone in High Dutch'; *Alch.* II. 1), but the allusion is here doubtless to Becarus' well known theory about the language of Paradise, which comes in for a good deal of dramatic satire elsewhere (e.g. in Glapthorne's *The Hollander* II. 1, where the hero is called 'yon bird of Paradise, yon parcell Dutch,' and Sconce's remark in the same play (I. 94), 'like a Turke he answered me that all Hollanders were *Jewes*'). Jonson's spelling of such a name as *Hohenhein*, seems to show, what is not to be taken for granted in a man of his vast and curious erudition, that he was not acquainted with German.

[2] Among the accessory causes of the literary alienation of the two countries was, as Prof. Ward observes to me, the almost total abstention of Germany from the religious wars of the latter part of the century, which so deeply interested Englishmen. The vast majority of the German residents in England, moreover, who might well have been the medium of literary intercourse, belonged, far more exclusively than even at present, to the commercial class.

Neglect of German History.   Hence the almost complete neglect, as a serious study, of German political history; a neglect exceptional even in an age, like that of Elizabeth, very little prone to foreign history in general. An enthusiastic traveller had produced an account of Italy, admirable for its time, though apparently standing alone[1]; the translated Froissart and, later, the translated and continued Commines[2], went some way towards a history of France; the history of the Turks—a perfectly 'safe' subject in every European book-market in the sixteenth century—was familiar, long before Knowles, from T. Newton's *Curio*[3], to say nothing of the vivid light which had been diffused about certain episodes in it, such as the fall of Bajazet, by Greek and Italian, Spanish and German pens, from Poggio and Chalcocondylas to Spiessheimer (Cuspinianus), Paolo Giovio and Mexia[4]. But the history of Germany, as such, had as yet occupied neither any English historian nor any English translator[5]. It was indeed necessarily included in general history, and so in such chronicles as that compiled by Lanquet and continued after his death by Cooper[6]; as well as, of course, in the Chronicles of Carion continued by Fulk, and translated by the industrious

----

[1] Thomas, *The Historie of Italie*, 1549.

[2] *The Historie of P. de Commines*, 1601.—A continuation of the Historie *from...where Comines endeth, till the death of Henry the Second*, 1600.

[3] *A notable Historie of the Saracens...drawen out of A Curio*, &c., 1575.

[4] On the sources of the English treatments of this episode, cf. *The Academy*, Vol. 24, 265 f.

[5] Controversial pamphlets like Barlow's dialogue on the *Origin of these Lutheran heresies*, and narratives immediately suggested by personal experience, like Ascham's account of the State of Germany, are exceptions which prove the rule.

[6] *An epitome of cronicles*, &c., 1549.

Walter Lynne[1]; but its history was nowhere isolated and set in focus. There are scattered signs, it is true, of acquaintance with the German historians. The wonderful woodcuts of the fifteenth century compendium of history known as the *Nurenberg Chronicle* probably procured some currency for a picture of mediaeval Germany then unequalled for fulness and vigour[2], and at a later date other, more genuinely local, chronicles were certainly not unknown[3]. But the group of scholars who, at the opening of the Humanist age, laid the foundation of German historical writing, the Bavarians Aventine and Tritheim, and somewhat later Carion, the Swiss Tschudi and Kessler, the Rhinelanders Beatus Rhenanus and Wimpheling, the North German Albertus Krantz, can have been known at most to a mere handful of Englishmen. No one, probably, had the opportunity of being arrested by the story of Tell in Tschudi, on which his own country already possessed a drama[4]; and it is likely

[1] Carion's *Chronicle*, 1532, with the additions of Fulk up to 1550, was translated by Lynne in that year.

[2] Nuremberg, 1493, fol. Warton-Hazlitt, III. 233 *note*, suggest that Lyndsay may have borrowed from the cosmogony in fol. iv. [i.e. iii.] his own account in the *Dream*. I see however nothing in Schedel's language, which Lyndsay might not have found elsewhere.

[3] For that of Lübeck, cf. E. Howes, *Stowe's Annals*, 1631 (Sh. Soc.'s ed. of Harrison, II. 130), 'You shall understand that the citie of Paris was not paved until the year 1186, nor the citie of Lübeck in Germanie, in many years after, as appeareth by their severall chronicles.' As the capital of the Hanse Lübeck was comparatively familiar. Chettle's *Hoffman*, 1600, shows some geographical knowledge of its site. A 'Marquis of Lübeck' occurs in *Fair Em*.

[4] *Eyn hüpsch und lustig Spyl...von dem frommen und ersten Eydgnossen Wilhelm Thellen*. By Jacob Ruof of Zurich. It was originally performed at Ury—'dem löblichen Ort der Eydgnoschaft' —and printed in 1545.—Goed. p. 302.

to have been without the knowledge of an alternative
that Shakspere immortalised the Hamlet legend of
the credulous Saxo instead of that of the later Danish
historian, who so severely chastises the old chronicler,
and who was used by Sachs for his *Historie* on the subject.   And in so far as the German historians were read,
it was mostly for other purposes than to illustrate the
history of Germany.   Holinshed explores Aventine and
Krantz for the sake of his English chronicle; Reginald
Scot for stories of sorcery; Thomas Heywood for anecdotes of eminent women; and Beatus Rhenanus' annals
of his native land served only to inspire John Leland's
history of his own[1].   The name of Tritheim was familiar
enough, but it was a writer on occult arts and occult
writing, not a historian, who was currently associated with
it[2].   In the latter part of the century, Münster's admirable
Cosmography, which contained one of the best histories
of Germany then extant, was extracted only for its 'strange
stories[3],' or its account of remote parts of the world;
while a German historian who in European fame ranked
still higher than Münster, Philippson of Schleida (Slei-

---

[1] Cf. his laudatory epigram :

> Quantum Rhenano debet Germania docto,
>   tantum debebit terra Brytanna mihi.
> Ille suae gentis ritus et nomina prisca,
>   aestivo fecit lucidiora die;
> ipse antiquarum rerum quoque magnus amator
>   ornabo patriae lumina clara meae....

Quoted by Bale Cent. sub nom. Leland.

[2] Notwithstanding that his occult writings were first published in
the following century.

[3] *A Briefe Collection and compendious extract of strange and
memorable thinges, gathered out of the Cosmographye of S. Munster*,
1572.   Other Englishmen extracted his descriptions of Muscovy,
India, and Scandinavia.

danus), is significantly celebrated by Sir J. Elyot in an often quoted line—equally remarkable in prosody and sense—for his services to that native tongue in which he did not write[1].

The same indifference to the political history of Germany is reflected still more completely, as might be expected, in the drama.   The score or so of early plays which profess to be founded on German history, treat it with an open contempt much beyond what is demanded by the most exclusive pursuit of scenic effect.   Historic truth is not subordinated to dramatic truth, but simply ignored.   It is not merely that, as in Shakspere's Histories, incidents are rearranged, times and places altered, characters differently conceived, but that the whole action, scenery and *personnel* are transformed beyond recognition.   There is not the faintest sign that any dramatist studied a German chronicle[2] as Barnes, for instance, studied Guicciardini for his *Divel's Charter*, or as Marlowe studied the contemporary reports for his *Massacre*, Fletcher for his *Barneveldt*[3], and Chapman for his great French tragedies of Biron and Bussy d' Amboise[4].   Nay Chapman himself, if it was he, abandoned his relatively refined and even minute manner of painting

Dramas on German History.

[1] 'Et le gentil Sleidan refait l'Allemand.   Sonnet prefixed to *Perimedes*, 1588.   Cf. on Schleidan's writings, H. Baumgarten, *Sleidans Leben und Briefwechsel.*

[2] Prof. Ward has remarked (II. 388) on this reticence in as far as regards the Thirty Years' War.

[3] I agree with Mr Bullen, who has printed this remarkable tragedy in his *Old Plays* (vol. 2), that Fletcher had a hand in it,—'or at least a main finger,' as Decker has it.

[4] No doubt Spanish history was not less completely neglected in the drama than German,—and for a more obvious reason.   For the reverse side of the picture it is interesting to compare Cervantes' generally true and far from unfavourable portrait of Elizabeth in the *Española Inglesa* (the fourth of the *Novelas ejemplares*), and also

in the single German drama which goes under his name. The *Alphonsus* is merely a crude and sanguinary travesty of an imperial election dispute, in which the chief interest attaches to a wholly mythical love affair[1]. The play is

Hector of Germany, 1615. nevertheless probably the least unhistorical of the whole group. The *Hector of Germany*, professedly dealing with a contemporary of the Black Prince, is an audacious

Romantic dramas. revision of the history of the fourteenth century in the spirit of the seventeenth[2]. *The Costlie Whore*, though it falls in a period when the war had already made Germany relatively familiar[3], is nevertheless merely a combination of the legend of Hatto with a scarcely less romantic story of a duke of Saxony; Chettle's *Hoffman* lays at Lübeck the scene of a tragic story in which dukes and emperors take part, but which is a palpable coinage of the Elizabethan brain[4]. *Evordanus*, 1605, and *A*

Calderon's fanciful rather than fanatical caricature of Henry VIII. in *La Cisma de Inglaterra*.

[1] Cf. Ward II. 17, and Elze's useful edition of the play. I confess to great doubts whether it was Chapman's work.

[2] It was obviously inspired by the marriage festivities of 1613, the year of its composition. The action is divided between the Black Prince's adventure in aid of Pedro the Cruel (who is called 'Peter the hermit'), and an intrigue for the empire, in the course of which the Palsgrave seeks the alliance of the English king, visits England, and is entertained at festivities not greatly unlike those which welcomed his descendant.

[3] This is of course also the case with Glapthorne's *Albertus Wallenstein*,—a play doubtless more historical than any of those in the text; he could hardly indeed have altogether distorted contemporary events. His eye for history of such magnitude, however, is at most, that of a rough soldier.—Collier's unfortunate but not uncharacteristic suggestion that a play mentioned in Henslowe: *Albertus Galles* (1602), was likewise upon the story of Wallenstein, *Henslowe Diary* (p. 239), needs no comment.

[4] I offer this opinion as the result of a considerable number of hours spent, some years ago, in the vain search for its source.

defiance to Fortune, 1590, are romances attached in the loosest manner to German localities. The very names of the characters are foreign ; the 'duke of Saxonie' is an 'Iago' in the one, an 'Andrugio' in the other. And *Measure for Measure* is an Italian story localised, but without a trace of local colouring, in the imperial residence. The emperor himself appears for a moment, but only as a shadowy presence, on the stage of *Faustus* and *Friar Bacon;* the *Wisdom of Doctor Dodypoll* (1600) and Gascoigne's *Glass of Government* (1575) treat in the same irresponsible way, the courts of Brunswick and Heidelberg[1]. It is clear that with these ostensible dramatisations of German themes, history had little to do, and that more than one of them owed even its semblance of German locale to the contemporary fame of one of the half dozen princes,—a duke of Brunswick, an Elector of Saxony, or a county Palatine,—whom circumstances had made familiar in England.

The German history which was really read, must be sought in a lower region of literature; in the 'strange' and 'wonderful' News which English booksellers found it to their account to translate and publish. 'Wonderful strange Newes from Germany,' was the catchpenny title of scores of leaflets, now surviving mainly in the brief references of the Stationers' Register, which traversed the whole gamut of the sensational, the marvellous, and the horrible. They are but slightly caricatured in the marvellous reports from 'Lybtzig' and elsewhere, which supply the material of Jonson's Newsoffice[2]. Political history is almost entirely confined to a few reports of battles[3] (which after the opening of

'News' sheets from Germany.

---

[1] The former, of course, in far greater detail than the latter.
[2] Jonson, *The Staple of News*, III. 1.
[3] Thus: the capture and recapture of Jula by the Turks in 1566

the great war no doubt predominate), varied, at rare intervals, by an imperial coronation[1], or a court reception[2]. In its place we read of massacres[3], and earthquakes[4], storms[5], executions[6] and apparitions[7], monstrous births and bodies raised from the dead[8], fasting girls[9] and 'damnable sorcerers[10],' strange signs in the air[11], prophecies in the mouth of rustics[12] and of sages[13], visions of angels[14], mysterious glimpses of the Wandering Jew[15]. Even in the historical dramas already discussed,

(*News from Vienna*, Aug. 5, 1566); the defeats of the Turks in Croatia in 1593, already mentioned as the subject of a ballad, in Chap. I.; the taking of Stuben-Weissenburg, (*A true relacion*, &c., Nov. 9, 1601), and the battles of the Cleves-Jülich war.

[1] That of Maximilian II., 1565.

[2] That e.g. of Clinton, at the Hessian court, 1596. (*The landgrave of Hessen his princely receiving*, &c.)

[3] *Newes out of Germanie*, 1564 (true discourse of a murderer who had kylled 960 and odd persons, &c.).

[4] *Newes*, &c., 1597 (at Vienna); 1612—13 (at Münster).

[5] e.g. at Erfurt and Weimar, 1613.

[6] e.g. 'A bloody tragedy acted by 5 Jesuits on 16 young German frows, 1607'; account of executions at Prague, 1621; of 250 witches at Assenberg, 1612.

[7] e.g. 'strange sight' of ye sun and in ye elements at Basel, *Sta. Reg.*, 1566—7.

[8] e.g. Miraculous Newes from the Citie of Holdt, Münster, 1616.

[9] e.g. History of a Fasting girl, London, 1589.

[10] e.g. true discourse...of one Stubbe Peter, a most wicked sorcerer who in likeness of a wolf committed many murders, &c., 1590.

[11] e.g. 'strange sightes,' &c. about ye citie of Rosenbergh, the 19 Jan. Cast...1594.

[12] e.g. A prophecie uttered by the daughter of an honest country man called Adam Krause. London, 1580.

[13] Such as the countless 'Almanacs,' and the productions of 'prophets' like Grebner, and Graphaeus, 1598.

[14] e.g. 'Newes,' &c., of such an appearance at Druppa, 1613.

[15] 1612, a 'ballad' (the Wandering Jew at Hamburg).

the fragments of German material embedded in the
mass of romance, are chosen from what may be called
the News-sheet point of view.   The iron crown which
seres the skull of Hoffman, the thrilling death of Hatto,
the grandiose insult put upon Barbarossa by Alexander[1],
even the 'Saxon' wedding-night which is put to so tragic
a use in the *Alphonsus,*—only differ in their more heroic
associations from the common stuff of the Elizabethan
newsvendor.

The habitual 'strangeness' of the News from Ger- *Portents*
many takes a deeper tone as we pass to a branch of *and*
Prodigies.
literature which is in fact merely a collection of Strange
News theologically interpreted—a text full of marvels
with solemn annotations at the foot.   'These are the
prodigies and strange sights (studious reader), which at
this time I thought good to relate,...to the end that thou
mightest more plainly perceive that they were the certain
prognostications of changes, revolutions and calamities,
and the veritable tokens of God's wrath.'   Such is the
solemn language in which Conrad Lycosthenes[2], the

---

[1] 'Trod on the neck of German Frederick.'   This, like Bajazet's
cage and chain, had evidently taken hold of the English imagination.
It is pointedly referred to both in *Fortunatus* (where Barbarossa's
sudden decline is one of the four instances of the power of Fortune),
and in *Faustus* (ed. 1616), where Adrian quotes the exploit of his
'progenitor' as a telling precedent.

[2] He was at home in vast compilations.   He produced a translation of the late classic Obsequens' history of Prodigies, which
rivalled in popularity his own work: he also digested Erasmus'
Apophthegms in a more convenient order.   As Thomas Kirchmayer
says, in a rare mood of eulogy:

> Dicta olim veterum mixtim collegit Erasmus,
>   unde ingens studiis prodiit utilitas :
> Olim ea Conradus nidis communibus apte
>   disposuit, curis auxit et illa suis.

king of prodigy-collectors, closes his great work, the *Prodigiorum ac ostentorum chronicon*[1]. A quarter of a century later the English professor of theology who translated and supplemented Lycosthenes, expressed the same thought with more pregnant brevity by calling his work *The Doom*[2]. The collection of portents was indeed a recognised branch of Protestant work. Though of course not introduced by Protestantism, it received an immense stimulus from the fervour of Protestant piety, which, here as in some other cases, opened the way to a new superstition in the process of banishing an old. It was indeed pursued with almost equal zeal by the most rational and the most visionary of the reformed sects; the writers included Hedio the friend of Butzer, Manlius the follower of Melanchthon, Camerarius his biographer, the Swiss Lycosthenes and Jacob Ruof, and the Calvinist Batman. Nothing however could be more uncritical than their method. All the learned and all the light literature of the day was ransacked for examples; the flying sheet, the local chronicle, grave poet and solemn historian, Tritheim and Aventine, Sleidan and Krantz, Gesner and Münster, Brandt and Gengenbach,—were all made to contribute their stores. And

---

[1] Basel, 1557.

[2] Batman, *The Doome*, London, 1581. It is instructive to note the circumstances in which it appeared. The previous year had been marked by an unusual number of marvels. The great earthquake, recalled eleven years afterwards by Juliet's nurse, occurred on April 6. Two days later begins a stream of ' Reports' and 'Tidings,' 'Prayers,' 'Reflections,' &c., which for the whole month seem to have driven all other literature out of the field, and are still unexhausted at the end of the year. There were, in addition, earthquakes in other parts of Europe (e.g. at Rome), while an unusual number of monstrosities are recorded during November and December, in Germany. See the titles in the *Stationers' Register* for this year.

the width of range was only equalled by the perfect indiscriminateness of choice. The slightest anomaly was qualified as a portent; an accidental flaw, or even a signal excellence, in even the commonest object, at once constituted it a sign of doom. Curiosities of every kind are heaped together; comets, crosses in the sky, rains of blood, reports of misshapen infants and unusually fine game[1]; pretty myths like that of the Frankfurt maiden who turned everything she touched to silver, 'whereof a piece was sent to the prince and to Melanchthon,' and old stories from the days of the Basel council, like that of the nightingale which sang most sweetly to some heretical councillors as they wandered in a wood,— '*O ewig ewig wie ist das eine lange Zeit*[2],—' I judge it was a devil abiding in that place,' adds Lycosthenes, who tells the story—'and all they that were present at the conjuration fell sore sick, and shortly after died.' Such a literature naturally stimulated the diffusion of marvellous stories of every kind, and the more so as it threw the whole weight of emphasis upon their marvellousness. It resuscitated a mass of old material from sources often obscure or forgotten; and steeped them in an air of mysticism which heightened and exaggerated whatever strange element they possessed. And nowhere was it more readily welcomed and reproduced than in Protestant England.

It would have been superfluous to discuss these *The Faustus Cycle.*

[1] Seb. Brandt's description of a '*Hind* of notable and unaccustomed greatness given to Maximilian' in German and Latin verse, is used.

[2] A more illustrious 'heretical councillor,' M. Renan, has lately told us that he is accustomed to receive an anonymous warning couched in not dissimilar terms: '*Si pourtant il y avait un Enfer!*'

essentially insignificant masses of writing for their own
sake. They are, however, only crude specimens of the
most fruitful of all the kinds of influence which Germany,
after the literary decay of Protestantism, exercised over
England. The literature of marvels was almost the only
direction in which the literary communication between
the two countries remained relatively flowing and vigorous; one of the two or three 'lines of cleavage,' as it
were, along which the international barrier of unlike
language and custom yielded an easy passage. The
great mass of the German stories traceable in England at
all had this character; and scarcely any, without it,
seriously impressed the English imagination, or in any
way modified the course of English letters. The Portent
and the Wonderful Strange News are the plebeian elements
in this literature of marvels; humble kin, but still kin, of
'Famous Histories' which all the world knows by name.
Few of them contain the stuff of a *Faustus*, but they
flattered the same taste, they contributed to create and
sustain the intellectual atmosphere in which stories like
Faustus throve and bore fruit; the fictitious and mythic
elements in them bore the stamp of the same imaginative
mint.

The present chapter is an attempt to give a connected view of the whole of this literary cycle, so far as
it has left extant remains in England. I shall deal first
with the few slighter legends which found their way into
ballad or play; sombre tragedies, all of them, of the
'damnable life and deserved death' type, recording with
grim unction the 'doom' which overtook Hatto, or the
Wandering Jew, or the burghers of Hamelin. From these
it is an easy step to Faustus, by far the most important of
all the German acquisitions of the century,—and to the
series of reflex-Faustuses which in my view it is not

difficult to discern in the drama for half a generation afterwards. In Fortunatus the analogy to Faustus is of a different kind; the original legend has hardly a trace of the sombre colouring of Faustus; but both turn upon a command of supernatural powers, and we shall presently see the naive romanticism of the *Volksbuch* assuming, no doubt under the influence of Faustus, an incongruous air of tragedy in the well known play of Decker. Finally, the scanty traces of German witch-stories present a sort of hideous travesty of the Faust motive;—the diabolic intercourse in a more repulsive form, the supernatural powers put to a baser use. All these in different ways reflect the two antagonistic standpoints between which the German imagination in the sixteenth century incessantly oscillated. The exultant Titanism of the Renaissance, the delight in every vehement and defiant putting-forth of power; and, on the other hand, the horror of presumption, the disposition to see diabolic inspiration in every extraordinary achievement, and divine judgment in every sudden humiliation, which like some other articles of mediaeval faith was reasserted with still more urgent and impassioned emphasis by Protestantism[1].

I.

Nowhere are the limitations which controlled the LEGENDS. literary intercourse of England with Germany more palpable than in the case of the Legends. Of the vast body of traditional lore which was still current, not merely

[1] On the whole subject dealt with in the foregoing pages, I am much indebted to Prof. Ward's very full and stimulating introduction to his edition of *Faustus* and *Friar Bacon*;—at present, unfortunately for many students of Elizabethan drama, out of print.

in the mouths of the country people, but in literature, an infinitesimal proportion reached this country; and these, with hardly an exception, bore the drastic stamp of Faustus. Along the great river which every travelled Englishman knew, the story of Siegfried, in whatever homely form, must still have been alive. But neither he nor any of his brother heroes of the *Heldensage* is ever heard of in England[1], and indeed, if it were not that the ballad of 'God's terrible judgment upon Bishop Hatto' early found eager readers, we might reasonably suspect that the cultivated Englishman conceived the legendary river almost exclusively as the source of the excellent 'Backrach' and 'Rhinecow' which he drank at his ordinary. Even the two poets who first gave German legend a definite place in the English drama, Marlowe and Decker, know of the legend-haunted river nothing but its vine-clad banks, and the wild-boars whose tusks spoil the vintage[2]; and the *Masque* with which Beaumont celebrated the nuptials of the Princess Elizabeth at Gray's Inn is even more bare of local sentiment than the rococo Epistle of Boileau. A mere trace of the famous Drach-enfels legends occurs, noticed as if quite unknown, in the narrative of the journey of the Princess Elizabeth up the Rhine to Heidelberg after her marriage[3]. A

---

[1] At several points these legends were brought into curious approximation to English literature, as e.g. in Brandt's allusion to 'Frau Kriemhild' (*NSch.* chap. 42), omitted however by Locher, and naturally by Barclay also. So the Eilsam of the Rosengarten (*ib.* chap. 72).

[2] Marlowe, *Doctor Faustus*; Decker, *London's Tempe*, 1629, (Works, IV. 120).

[3] After mentioning that the Princess lodged for the night at 'Overwinter,' the narrative proceeds: 'Not farre from this towne, are seven great mountains standing close together with the fair castles. In one of which the people of the country report, that the

few ecclésiastical legends too, of European renown, attached a certain mystic sanctity to the great city of the
Lower Rhine where the Three Kings and the Eleven
Thousand Virgins had found their final resting-place[1].
But, as has been implied, the single genuine Rhine
legend which won a firm footing in England was that
which had long before turned the old *Miethethurm* of
the bishops of Mainz by Oberwesel into the terrible
Mäusethurm where the arch-criminal among them, Hatto,
met his deserved death.

Both Tritheim[2] and Münster had told Hatto's story *Bishop*
in the traditional form; and it was certainly known in *Hatto.*
England before the end of the third quarter of the
century.   In 1572 the author of *A briefe collection of
strange and memorable thinges gathered out of the Cosmographye of S. Munster* included this among them[3].

Divell walkes and holds his infernall Revels.' Continuation of
Stowe's *Annals*, 1613, p. 921.

   [1] An English version of the *Three Kings of Collen* was printed
by Wynkyn de Worde, without date.   The title runs: ' Prologus.
Here begynneth the lyfe of the three Kynges of Coleyn... as it is
drawn out of dyvers bokes and put in one.   And how they were
translate fro place to place.'   It was a translation of the Latin
narrative printed in 1481 by ' Bartholomaeus de Unckel' (date and
name given at the beginning of the index), and dedicated to Flor-
encius de Werelkoven.   The legend of S. Ursula and the 11,000
was scarcely less English than German.   After Lydgate's hymn on
the subject, however (reprinted by Halliwell, *L.'s Minor poems*),
it seems to have been wholly neglected in English.   In Germany
this was by no means the case.   About the middle of the century
a certain order called 'S. Ursula's Schifflein' was founded at Strassburg.   It was a century of *Naves* and *Naviculae.*

   [2] *Mon. Hirsaug. Chronica,* sub anno 967.   He professes to with-
hold judgment upon the *fabula*, but points to the still existing *Mu-
rium turris* and to the local tradition as arguments in its favour.

   [3] 'A thinge done at a towne in Germany called Bingium,'
fol. 16.

On Aug. 15, 1586, a ballad called 'The wrathful judgment of God upon bishop Hatto' was entered, among others, in the Stationers' Register. The form of the title suggests that the story was already generally familiar; plain 'bishop Hatto' was not the style in which a rhetorical ballad-monger commended an unknown hero to his readers. In any case it was familiar some thirty years later. In 1613 the narrative of the princess Elizabeth's Rhine journey speaks of it in a manner which implies this. 'After leaving Coblentz,' he records, 'we came to Brobgech, being there received by the bishop of Trier, and stayed in that place that night. Here standeth that castle in which by report a Germaine Bishop was eaten up by Rats[1].' Somewhat later, at a time of famine, the moral significance of Hatto's end presented itself forcibly. A very humble poet, and one of the flattest set of verses in the Roxburgh Ballads, was the result. It is headed: 'Bloudy newes out of Germanie, or the people's miserie from famine. Being an example of God's just judgment on one *Harto*, a Nobleman, in Germanie, of the town of Mentz, who, when the people were decayed' &c. This is followed by a rude woodcut representing three figures praying, presumably for the cessation of the famine. The opening verse gives a clue to the writer's motive, which was evidently not purely literary:

> When as my mind was fully bent
>   Some story for to rhyme,
> Amongst all others none I found
>   So fitting for the time.
>   ...it may well compared be
> Unto a song of joyful news
>   In pain and misery.

evidently a reflexion on some grain-hoarding Hattos of his own time.

---

[1] Continuation of Stowe, 1613.

A somewhat more interesting use of the story occurs 'The
in drama. The 'Comical History' of the 'Costlie Whore,' *Costlie*
Whore.'
acted by the company of the Revels, was printed in
1633. · The principal subject is the infatuation of the
Duke of Saxony for a Venetian courtesan. He proposes
to marry her, whereupon his son Frederick, indignant at
the unworthy alliance, quarrels with him. This does not
however prevent Frederick himself from entering on a
scarcely less palpable mésalliance, nor his father from
punishing the too sincere flattery. A certain contrast
and conflict of classes was thus part of the motive of the
play, and it may be that this accounts for the introduction in it of the Hatto-story. The rich bishop has
burnt among the rest the starving peasants, and afterwards suffered the vengeance of a God, who, in popular
legend, is usually on the side of the poor. When the
play opens, Hatto's funeral has just taken place. His
brother, who oddly bears the same name, is finally appointed bishop of Mentz[1] in his stead; there is a third
brother Alfrid, who narrates the terrible death of Hatto
to a fourth, the duke of Saxony. The first act contains
the most remarkable use of the story. Hatto the second
has just turned away some unfortunate beggars with
severity. But the beggars are 'sturdy and valiant,' and,
encouraged by the late notable 'example,' they plainly
suggest that he will probably share his brother's fate if
he does not listen to them: 'he will be eaten by rats
too !' Hearing the threat, his brother Alfrid intervenes
with prudent counsels :

[1] In the play this is throughout written *Meath*. The *h* of 17th
century handwriting was little distinguished from *z*. *Th* was
therefore in an English book an easy misprint for the unfamiliar
combination *tz*. The familiar name *Meath* would then easily effect
the further change of *n* to *a*. Dr Elze in his otherwise valuable
introduction to Chapman's *Alphonsus*, perversely suggests *Metz*.

> Good brother, stay yourselfe from wrathe,
> Thinke on the bishop and his odious death.
>
> *Hatto.* What odious death, I pray?
>
> *Alfrid.*   Eaten with Rats,
> Whilst he was living for the wrong he did
> Unto the poore, the branches of our God.
>
> *Hatto.* Tis true, and therefore call the poore againe.
> Come hither friend, I did forget myselfe.
> Pray for me, ther's some silver for thy wants.
>
> *Beggars.* Now the Lord blesse you, and keepe your goode face[1]
> From being Mouse-eaten: wee came thinking
> We should have some dole at the Bishop's funerall,
> But now this shall serve our turne, wee will
> Pray for you night and day.
>
> *Hatto.* Goe to the backegate, and you shall have dole.
>
> *Omnes.* O the Lord save thee.
>   (*Exeunt* B.)

Feeble as this passage is, it is the most notable that the English drama has devoted to the legend of Hatto.

The Piper of Hamelin. It was reserved for the Mérimées and Brownings of a later age[2] to put to literary use another story in which the moral accent, though less theological, is equally pronounced,—the famous legend of Hameln. It had indeed already found a corner in the great compendium of Verstegan[3], and was repeated thence later by Heylin in his Microcosmus; but its literary fortune for the present went, and perhaps could go, no further. Its delicate air of the marvellous was sufficient, on the one hand, to repel a good deal of seventeenth-century enthusiasm; while, on the other, it altogether fell short of the lurid supernatural horror which had made the fortune of *Faustus*.

[1] Mr Bullen's correction (*Old Plays*, IV. 238) for the corrupt 'fate'. The whole passage is, as Mr Bullen says, undoubtedly prose.

[2] I refer to the charmingly told version in the *Chronique du règne de Charles IX*. Simrock has modernised it in German.

[3] *Restitution of Decayed Intelligence*, 1605.

This supernatural horror is easily recognised, how- *The Wandering Jew.* ever, in another story, of which there are earlier traces, but which only in the early years of the seventeenth century obtained decided currency,—that of the Wandering Jew. Though not peculiar to Germany, it was known in England at this time mainly from a German source,— the *Wunderbarlicher Bericht* of Chrisostom Dudulaeus[1], the origin of a ballad entered in the Stationers' Register of 1612, under the title: 'Wonderful strange newes out of Germanie of a Jewe that hath lived wandringe ever since the passion of our Saviour Christ.' Of this ballad nothing more can be said unless we may assume it to be identical with that published by Percy on the subject. In any case it is clear that even then a vivid interest was excited by the strange figure who, like Faustus, is so profoundly isolated from the world he moves in, and, like him, suffers under the weight of a *privilegium* which, apparently exempting him from human limitations, in reality involves him in a unique curse[2].

II.

It is hardly an accident that, in turning over these DOCTOR FAUSTUS[3].

[1] *Wunderbarlicher Bericht, von einem Juden, aus Jerusalem Bürtig, Ahasuerus genanndt, welcher fürgibt als sey er bey der creutzigung unseres Herren...persönlich gewesen*, &c. This account refers to the most famous 'appearance' of the sixteenth century, that at Hamburg, 1547, attested by Paul Eitner, and afterwards recorded by Dudulaeus.

[2] Long afterwards the idea of the Wandering Jew supplied the framework of some vigorous sketches of London character: '*The Wandering Jew telling fortunes to Englishmen*, 1649;' reprinted in Halliwell, *Books of Characters*, 1857.

[3] The details of Marlowe's play and its relation to its German source have been amply discussed in recent years; and the present section makes no attempt to restate these familiar facts.

waifs of German story, stranded by chance upon the domain of English letters, and, as we have seen, receiving there at the best a somewhat lenten entertainment, we should have been continually reminded of one which had altogether better fortune, and not merely received a royal welcome from the first, but gathered in its train a crowd of followers, and left a memory which after the changing fashions of more than a century still remained fresh and green[1]. Almost all the elements of attraction which belonged to the rest are resumed and concentrated in *Faustus*; which is accordingly not merely by far the most remarkable of the German contributions to English literature, but the most vivid embodiment of their generic qualities, the central type about which they all converge. The wild pranks of Ulenspiegel, the diabolic feats of Friar Rush and the Kalenberger, of witch and wizard, the appalling shadow of an irrevocable doom which encompasses Hatto and the Jew, nay even the mere monstrosities of the flying news-sheet, the marvellous transformations, the unheard-of cures, the phenomenal crimes and adventures which tempted the penny out of the pocket of the town apprentice and the rustic Mopsa,—were all represented in the story of the infamous, yet irresistible doctor of Wittenberg.

All this, however, did not prevent Marlowe's choice of the subject for a drama from being extremely original. He was indeed habitually original in this matter. Where Shakspere loved to glorify a twice-told tale at the risk of

---

[1] The popular play of *Dr Faustus* had almost as remarkable a history in England as in Germany. The furore created by it in 1726 (cf. *Dunciad*, III. 308 and Pope's note on this 'miserable Farce'), and Mountford's *Faust Harlequinade* of 1698 show its singular power of interesting a generation less in sympathy than any other in English history with the class of subject to which it belongs.

provoking the charge of plagiarism, Marlowe chose to be the daring singer of 'unattempted things.' Neither waiting timidly on the popular taste, nor cautiously educating it, he flung himself with characteristic audacity into new and untrodden regions, and created a *furore* for an unknown name. No English dramatist had yet searched the annals of Turkey, when Marlowe drew the story of Tamburlaine from the pages of Mexia and Perondinus. No one had yet sought dramatic effect in the anti-Jewish fanaticism of the time, when he took from some unknown source the story of Barrabas of Malta. No one had put the ferocities of contemporary history on the stage when he drew with somewhat too tolerant a pen the closing years of the house of Valois. In 1587, a German *Volksbuch* was at least as unfamiliar ground to the playwright as a Turkish chronicle ; and the name of Faustus, if not wholly unknown, was far more obscure than that of the Scythian shepherd[1].

Once launched, however, *Faustus* had like *Tamburlaine* an enormous success. The name itself became a byword in the popular mouth, a stock term for the typical German ; and Shakspere could allude, more than a dozen years afterwards, to an incident in it, with the certainty that the point would be appreciated[2]. And we know that younger writers at least once, in 1602, attempted to make capital out of its popularity by extensive 'addycions,' to its slender bulk[3]. The many-sided fascina-

---

[1] Curious writers, like Reginald Scot, were probably familiar with the story, which occurs substantially in Weier's section on *Zauberey* in the *De praestigiis dæmonum*.

[2] The Host's reference to the horse-stealing 'Dr Faustuses' in the *Merry Wives*.

[3] Those formerly supposed to have been made by 'Thomas Dickers' in 1597 rest on the authority of one of Collier's forged

tion of the story, apparently so simple in its elements, brought it, in fact, instantly home to the imagination of all classes.   For one he was the incomparable trickster, the more potent and intellectual Owlglass, who could jest with the emperor and pass practical jokes with impunity upon the accursed Antichrist of Rome.   For another he was the magician whose extraordinary art had procured him the potent service of the devil; for a third the un-happy scholar whose tampering with forbidden knowledge had involved him in a horribly tragic fate.   The supreme attraction, however, and also the supreme significance of the subject in the English drama, certainly lay in his peculiar relation with the devil.   The absolute authority which he exercises over Mephistophilis, and which never-theless, like the Saturnalian authority of the Roman slave, only marks his complete subjection, has fascinated generations to which the relation was intrinsically much less credible than it was to that of Elizabeth.   The bond was in itself a piece of tragic material of the first rank; capable, even without any supernatural colouring, of pro-ducing situations of unsurpassed pity and terror.   Jeph-thah's sacrifice, Macbeth's fall, Lear's ruin, not to speak of the milder fate of the Merchant of Venice, are the result of compacts of which the conditions were imperfectly understood,—of 'one-sided contracts'; and where this pathetic half-ignorance is absent, as in the deliberately chosen fate of Antigone or Alcestis, we have the not less tragic compact of heroism, the wilful barter of life for the privilege of duty.   In Faust's case, the choice, though voluntary, is not altogether heroic; but the effect lost here is partly compensated by the appalling penalty; and his shrinking horror in the moment when it is about

entries. Cf. Warner, *Dulwich MSS.* My attention was called to this by Mr A. H. Bullen.

to overwhelm him, serves, like the last speech of Antigone, to make more pathetic a doom the bitterness of
which was less keenly realised when it was chosen.

Now the vital quality of the Faustus story lay in connecting this admirable tragic subject of the bond with a
figure whom the nativity of the English drama was fast
depriving of his old vested rights in the English stage.
For serious drama, the devil of the Mysteries, whose sole
capacity lay in miscellaneous mischief making, was played
out; his occupation was gone. But the fascinating invention of Mephistophilis and his bond made the devil
again dramatically possible, and gave him a new lease of
existence on a more developed stage than he had ever
known.

The process of imitation which began when *Faustus* *Imitations*
was still in the heyday of its first success, was not entirely *of Faustus.*
due however to the wish to borrow its piquant motive.
Dramatic zeal was supplemented by a very palpable vein
of English patriotism. Just as the Borde collections of
Scogan's and Skelton's jests were probably due to
patriotic rivalry with the newly translated 'Owlglasse,' so
the success of the German Faustus produced a keen
inquiry for English Faustuses. They were not far to seek.
Wittenberg, the chief of German universities in English
eyes had produced the chief of German magicians; and
both Oxford and Cambridge could produce a tolerable
counterpart of their own.

The story of one of these had already been told in *Friar*
the spirit of the most jubilant English patriotism. The *Bacon.*
chief figure of the *Famous Historie of Friar Bacon and
Bungay* was not merely a great conjurer but a national
hero, a champion of England on the field and, if one
may so say, in the laboratory. His arts reduce a re-
fractory French town to the will of the English king; an

old tradition attributed to him the design, only acci-
dentally frustrated, of protecting England from invasion
by surrounding it with a brazen wall; another, doubtless
much later, described as his crowning achievement the
triumphant defeat of the foreign magician Vandermast.

The resemblance of Bacon to Faustus had evidently
struck Marlowe himself. More than one touch shows
him to have drawn his picture of the German magician
with the fame of the English Roger Bacon in his mind;
'wise Bacon's works' are among those which serve for
Faustus' instruction (Sc. 1), and one of Bacon's most
famous mythical designs,—the casting of brazen walls
about the coasts of England,—is boldly transferred to
his German disciple.[1] At the same time the analogy was
evidently far from complete. The tragic horror which
hung over the name of Faustus was totally wanting in
the national legend of Bacon. Both had lived on
familiar terms with the powers of hell, both had reduced
the fiends to their service; but Bacon's authority over
them is not only not the fruit of any guilty bargain, but
is evidently regarded as an illustrious distinction, in-
volving in the worst case merely a loss of time that might
be better spent; and as if still further to destroy the
analogy, he is made to regret even this misspent time,
and to lay aside in a mood of timely and reasonable
repentance the powers which a tragic Nemesis violently
wrenches from the dying Faust. The popular story of
Friar Bacon is that of Faustus denuded of its gloomy
intensity, rewritten throughout in a major key, and culminating, not in fierce theological anathemas against
intercourse with hell, but in the philosophic reflections

---

[1] Sc. 1. 86, 'I'll have them wall all Germany with brass.'
Ward, *Faustus*, &c. p. vi.

of a Cornelius Agrippa upon the vanity of human knowledge.[1]

Such a story necessarily lacked much of the peculiar
power of the Faustus legend, which, as we have seen,
lay precisely in the tragic use which is made of the bond.
It happened, however, that the dramatist who took it up,
and who handled it with obvious reference to Faustus,
was perhaps of all his contemporaries the least sensitive
to the seductions of purely tragic effect. Imitator of
Marlowe as Greene at times appeared to be, he consistently forbore to follow him in the gloomier workings
of his genius. The triumphs of Barrabas, of Tamburlaine,
of Faustus, of Edward, of Dido, of Chatillon, end uni-
formly in ruin or death; Greene, whose own end was to
be so unhappy, refused to lead his heroes to a tragic
catastrophe; his Alphonsus remains powerful to the last;
his history of James considerably stops short of Flodden;
and his friar Bacon turns in time from his evil ways.
The joyous and light-hearted spirit of the Bacon legend
was on the whole quite safe in his hands. Bacon is still
the 'frolic Friar'; his feats, however adventurous, are
still inspired by good-natured patriotism and disinterested
humanity, as those of Faustus are by egoism, buffoonery,
or at best by a *Wissensdrang* which it is difficult to take
quite seriously.

Nevertheless, by one of those artistic inconsistencies
to which his discordant and unbalanced character made
him peculiarly liable, Greene at a certain point abruptly
abandons the light tones of his model. The repentance-
scene in the play is of altogether a more solemn cast
than that of the story-book. There, as we have seen,
Bacon has nothing worse to reproach himself with than

[1] Cf. the farewell speech of Bacon to his students in the *Famous
Historie*, quoted in part below. Ward, *ib.* p. xlvi.

the expenditure of time in pursuit of knowledge that
'serveth not to better a man in goodness, but only to
make him proud and think too well of himself. What
hath all my knowledge of nature's secrets gained me?
Onely this, the loss of better knowledge, the loss of
divine studies, which make the immortal part of man,
his Soule, blessed.' Far more poignant are the regrets
of Greene's Bacon:

> The hours I have spent in pyromantic spells,
> The fearful tossing in the latest night
> Of papers full of necromantic charms,
> Conjuring and adjuring devils and friends,...
> The wresting of the holy name of God...
> Are instances that Bacon must be damned
> For using devils to countervail his God.

There is however a remedy for his deadly sin,—one
superfluous in the case of the prose Bacon's venial
error:

> Yet Bacon cheer thee, drown not in despair:
> Sins have their salves, repentance can do much:
> Think Mercy sits where Justice holds her seat,
> And for those wounds those bloody Jews did pierce,...
> From thence for thee the dew of many drops
> To wash the wrath of high Jehovah's ire
> And make thee as a new-born babe from sin.

In other words, the Agrippa who has merely wasted his
life in vain speculation, passes for a moment into the
Faustus who has lost his soul by holding intercourse
with hell, and who can only be saved by the mercy of
Christ. The philosophic Bacon is suddenly immersed
in the *criard* lights and shadows of Lutheran theology
which gave so definite a character to the figure of the
German magician. And if he ends, like the prose Bacon,
and unlike Faustus, in calm seclusion, it is by virtue
of a theological remedy—the appeal to Christ—which

Faustus would have used if he had dared, but of which the prose Bacon stood in no need. Greene saves his hero from Faustus' penalty, but involves him in his guilt ; and the Englishman escapes the 'deserved death' of the German only to be associated, at the eleventh hour, in his 'damnable life.'

This was not, however, the only point in which Greene was influenced by *Faustus*. In spite of the extraneous accretions which had gathered about it, the latter still retained the unmistakable flavour of university society. Its hero was a Wittenberg professor; his disciples, his servant, Wittenberg scholars ; his pursuit of magic is undertaken after an experience of the vanity of all other studies for which only a university could afford scope. All the critical scenes of the story take place at Wittenberg[1]. A somewhat similar relation connected Bacon with the university of Oxford. But in the *Famous History* this connexion is almost entirely obliterated. The first chapter indeed describes his early successes there, but throughout the sequel, so far as appears, Oxford is nothing to him, or he to Oxford. He is an eminent conjuror patronised by the court, and if we can infer that he lived and worked at Oxford, it is at most from the implication of one of his adventures, that 'Oxfordshire' is not far off. But Greene, the 'Master of Arts of both Universities,' was more sensitive on this point ; and in his drama Oxford becomes very palpably the Wittenberg of Bacon. The awestruck Wittenberg scholars who are grouped about Faustus, are replaced by a little knot of Oxford doctors whose awe is scarcely less, though, in harmony with the characteristic tone of the story, it is much

---

[1] As Prof. Ward observes to me, the latest adapter of the Faust-story for the stage has shown his insight by laying its scene at—Nürnberg !

less mingled with theological horror[1]. And the rough serving-man of the *Famous Historie*, Miles, is handled with an evident eye to the poor scholar who serves Faustus, the third figure in importance after Faustus and Mephistophilis, and so little less popular than his master that he presently became the hero of an independent *Volksbuch* of his own. Like Wagner, the Miles of the drama is a scholar in his way,—Bacon's 'subsizar,' ' Doctor Bacon's poor scholar,' he is called,—and addicted beyond all the other characters, though few are quite free from it, to the foible of Latin scraps. Bacon's cutting raillery of him as 'the greatest block-head' in the university, who cannot speak one word of true Latin,' would have been a compliment quite out of the question to pay to the rustic Miles of the *Historie*.

And, finally, Greene has not only treated the Oxford of Bacon as a sort of English Wittenberg, but he has given his championship of English magic a direct point against the rival magic of Germany. The Vandermast of the *Historie* belongs to the French ambassador, and his defeat is only a new disgrace inflicted on the national enemy; but in the drama he is the champion of the German emperor,—one of the same race, Greene evidently thought (for he calls him a Habsburg) as the Charles who had witnessed the greatest exploits of Faustus. Vandermast,—'the German' as he is repeatedly called,—thus becomes the representative of the country of Agrippa, Tritheim, and Paracelsus,—names with which that of Roger Bacon could alone compete;

---

[1] We come, they say to Bacon,
              not grieving at thy skill,
       But joying that our academy yields
       A man suppos'd the wonder of the world.

and now Faustus was added, the pupil of Agrippa[1], and yet more mighty than his master.   The episode with Vandermast thus became a sort of mock trial of strength between the two countries.   The unskilful Friar Bungay succumbs to the superior art of Vandermast, but his defeat only relieves the subsequent triumph of Bacon. Faustus on the demand of the Emperor Charles, had brought up Alexander the Great: Vandermast as the champion of Frederick, produces Hercules: Bacon who sends 'the German' with Hercules back to Habsburg whence he came, triumphs implicitly over Faustus too; and King Henry's complacent remark, 'Now, monarchs, hath the German found his match[2]' (II. 126), is a formal record, as it were, that judgment has gone in favour of the countryman of the poet and of the audience.

A different distinction belongs to the hero of a se- *P. Fabell.* cond English Faust drama, which followed *Faustus* at an indeterminable, but probably not very long interval.   Peter Fabell, of Peterhouse, stood even nearer than the Oxford friar, to the doctor of Wittenberg[3].   All three are scholars, and university men, who have won command of supernatural powers by hard study.   But while Bacon, even in the vulgarest conception of him, retains something of the scholar to the end, in Fabell, as in Faustus, the scholar is rapidly obscured by the boisterous practical joker. Moreover, the pact, with which Bacon contrives to dis-

---

[1] *Faustus,* Sc. I.
[2] Cf. the lines VII. 23—25,

> Bacon, if he will hold the German play,
> Will teach him what an English friar can do.

W. Wagner (*Faustus,* Introd. p. xxxvii.) has briefly touched this point.
[3] The legend was probably as old as the century.   Fabell is said to have lived under Henry VII., and to be buried at Edmonton.

pense, is the foundation of Fabell's power, as it is of
Faustus'. Bacon secures the obedience of his spirit,
like Prospero, by sheer knowledge and art; Faustus and
Fabell only by pledging themselves body and soul.
While Faustus however loses his pledge and is carried off
in a tragic catastrophe of extraordinary impressiveness,
Fabell ingeniously eludes the fiend and secures a new
lease of authority and life [1]. Both Englishmen thus in
different ways have the advantage over the German :
Faust buys his power, and has to pay for it; Bacon
extorts it without pretence of buying: Fabell gets it on
credit and tears up the bill. The English Faustuses
might be less famous than the German, but they had the
prestige of success, and one imagines the complacency
with which an Elizabethan audience would regard the
national champions who had enjoyed all the privileges of
Faustus without paying for them. But apart from such
extraneous aid, the situation had dramatic piquancy of its
own; it shared the endless popularity of the whole group
of tales in which a natural superior is adroitly overcome
by one entirely in his power,—where for instance a Tanner
of Tamworth or a Miller of Mansfield resists the king,
or where, as in Jonson's play, 'the Devil' is, with very
little difficulty, proved 'an Ass.' If the English Faustus
did not thrill the audience by a tragic end, he at least
amused them by his clever evasion of it. For the rest,

---

[1] The *Smith of Apolda*, whose legend springs doubtless from
the same source as that of Fabell, does this three times successively
by the aid of three magical gifts bestowed on him by St Peter,—a
chair, an apple tree and a wallet, each with the property of holding
fast whoever touches them, which the fiend is simply enough induced
to do. In the Fabell drama only the first, the chair, is used. Cf.
Thoms, *Lays and Legends of Germany*, p. 160. He refers to one told
by Grimm in the note to 'die Spielhansel' in the *Kinder u. Haus-
märchen*.

the feats of Fabell are as trivial as those of Faust himself,
though not quite similar.   It is needless to dwell upon
the repulsive story, how Fabell, by the aid of his spirit,
personates a friar, and releases his friend's mistress from
the convent where she was confined.

   In spite of the analogy of its story, however, the B. Barnes:
Merry Devil is obviously hardly more than a boyish *The Divil's Charter,*
travesty of *Faustus*.   The tragic terror has altogether 1607.
melted away, and left a mere skeleton of grotesque
and trivial adventure.   Fabell is purely and simply the
Owlglass-Faustus, a boisterous and successful jester,
whose dealings with the devil, far from any suggestion
of tragedy, turn out to be the best jest of all.   Completely different was the treatment of a Faust-subject in
a drama played at Court some twenty years after the
first performance of Marlowe's play.   The author of *The
Divil's Charter*[1] was probably not unconscious that the
royal exponent of orthodox demonology was to be among
the spectators; and though without a spark of Marlowe's
tragic power, he has borrowed his most lurid colouring.
The story of Alexander VI. offered a unique opportunity.
On the very morrow of his death popular rumour began
to whisper that the pope had been carried off, like
Faustus, by fiends; and the powerful imagination of
German Protestantism produced a finished legend which
represented all his successes, including his election to the
papacy, as the fruit of a formal contract with the devil[2].

   [1] The *Divil's Charter*, by Barnabe Barnes, London, 1607.
   [2] The story appears, substantially as in Barnes, in Hondorff's
Promptuarium Exemplorum, Frankfurt 1572, and again in Widman's
colossal commentary to the Faust-book.   I have not met with the
trait of a *contract* in any of the Italians, the Italian conception of the
pope's history, where it assumes devilry at all, rather approaching
the *Don Juan* than the *Faustus* type.   I am indebted for the

The latter appeared as a protonotary[1], the contract was signed and sealed, and Borgia then received the pecuniary means of securing his election[2].   At the same time he was told the period of his authority, which, by a verbal equivoque like those associated with the fortunes of Pyrrhus and Edward II., was made to appear longer by seven years than it was destined to prove : *Sedebis Romae Papa, summa felicitate tui* [sic] *et filiorum annos XI et VII dies VIII post moriere*.   Not eighteen, but eleven years afterwards[3], the fiend arrives to claim his victim, who, after a lengthy explanation, is carried off to his doom.

This legend was certainly poorer in genuine tragic motive than the analogous story of Faustus ; and it was not for Barnabe Barnes to become its glorifying Marlowe.   This did not prevent him however from writing under the obvious inspiration of the dead poet.   The sensational details of the bond-scene were, to begin with, a precious contribution to demonological aesthetics, and the spectators are accordingly shown how "the devil... strippeth up Alexander's sleeve and letteth his arme bloude in a saucer," upon which the pope subscribes and delivers.   "'The remainder of the bloud," it is

reference to Hondorff and Widman, and for the Don Juan parallel, to Prof. Ward.

[1] In Widman, the appearance as protonotary is preceded by two others in much more eccentric forms.

[2] This trait must have been a relatively late addition, his enormous wealth as cardinal being well known to his contemporaries.

[3] The pope construes: 'annos xi. et vii., et dies viii.; post moriere'; the devil audaciously explains: 'annos xi., et dies vii.; octavo (die) post moriere.'   Neither Hondorff nor Widman gives these lines, which I suspect that Barnes composed.   Widman makes the term 19 years, made up of 11 and 8.

added (with a housewifely eye for cleanliness uncom-
mon in tragic poets), "the other divill seemeth to suppe
up[1]."

But Barnabe's appreciation of *Faust* comprised more
than a keen relish for its thrilling crudities.   He was not
insensible to the tragic power of Marlowe's work, and
in at least one or two points, seems to have borrowed
from his wealth of resource.   The fine trait of Faustus'
wavering after the signing of the pact, partly symbolised
in the conflict of the Good and Evil Angels, partly
made explicit in his own words :—

> When I behold the heavens, then I repent
> And curse thee, wicked Mephistophilis,
> Because thou hast depriv'd me of those joys.
>
> ....
>
> My heart's so harden'd I cannot repent:
>
> ....
>
> Why should I die then, or basely despair?
> I am resolv'd: Faustus shall ne'er repent.

reappears in the more matter-of-fact reflexions of
Alexander :—

> But Astaroth, this covenant with thee
> Made for the soule more pretious than all treasure
> Afflicts my conscience.—O but Alexander
> Thy conscience is no conscience; if a conscience,
> It is a leprouse and polluted conscience.
>
> ....
>
> I...cauteriz'd this conscience now sear'd up...
>
> ....
>
> In spight of grace, conscience, and Acharon
> I will rejoyce, and triumph in my Charter. (I. 4.)

The last scenes, which somewhat diverge from the
original, are remodelled with some help from *Faustus*.

---

[1] The resemblance of this scene has already been pointed out by
W. Wagner, *Faustus*, p. xxxviii.   There is no suggestion of the
signature in blood in Hondorff or Widman.

The fatal banquet is just over[1], in which the poison prepared for another has been furtively put into the cups of Alexander and Caesar. The pope retires struck with sudden disease. The fiends, the real authors of the mischief[2], assemble in preparation for the climax:

> *Astar.* Let Orcus, Erebus and Acheron,
> And all those Ghosts which haunt the pitchy vaultes
> Of cole black darknesse in Cimerian shades,
> Muster themselves in numbers numberlesse
> To daunce about the Ghost of Alexander....
> The date of his damnation is at hand. (v. 5.)[3]

Then we see the pope sitting, in invalid undress, between two cardinals. Like the Scholars in their last interview with Faustus, and the Old Man, they exhort him to repentance. The analogy is the more striking because, unlike Faustus, he does not anticipate the imminence of his end[4]. Like Faustus he is overcome by a

---

[1] Barnes, as well as Hondorff and Widman, follow Guicciardini's statement that the illness was a consequence of poison taken by mistake. Some doubt is thrown on this by Gregorovius (VII. 497).

[2] Guicciardini, followed in less detail by Hondorff and Widman attributes the error to an inexperienced servant. Barnes heightens the effect by making it the work of one of the fiends. (v. 5.)

[3] Cf. *Faustus* (ed. 1616,—a version undoubtedly produced before Barnes' play):

> *Luc.* Thus from infernal Dis do we ascend
> To view the subjects of our monarchy,...
> Mong which as chief, Faustus, we come to thee
> Bringing with us lasting damnation
> To wait upon thy soul; the time is come
> Which makes it forfeit.

[4] In Widman he is made to suspect his illness to be a premonitory symptom of the devil's coming: *Der Bapst gedacht nun, es wirdt die Zeit seyn, in welcher ich dem Teuffel mus meine rechenschafft geben, dann ohne zweiffel ist dieses .. ein angriff des Teuffels, der abfordert mein zeit und ziel.* In Barnes there is no hint of this, nor in Hondorff.

pang of remorse,—not, it is true, in the presence of the
Cardinals, whom he dismisses with an ironical request
that they should 'pray for themselves,' but in the soli-
tude which immediately follows:

> O wretched Alexander, slave of sinne
> And of damnation; what is he that can
> Deliver thy poore soule? Oh none but he
> That when thou didst renounce him cast off thee;
> Repentance is in vaine, mercy too late[1].

But the fit soon passes, and with fresh curiosity he
prepares to use his exorcism once more, and invoke the
fiends to show him knowledge of 'the manner of death[2].'
He draws a curtain and discovers 'the divill sitting in
his pontificals[3],' who promptly cuts short his desire. The

[1] Cf. Faustus' cry on the exit of the Old Man:
> Accursed Faustus, wretch what hast thou done?
> I do repent, and yet I do despair:
> Hell strives with grace for conquest in my breast;
> What shall I do to shun the snares of death?

[2] So Faustus' remorse is cut short by the second sealing of the
bond with Mephistophiles which procures him the sight of Helen.
The trait of sending for his conjuring book is represented however
both in Hondorff and Widman, who make it the immediate consequence of his illness. In both he desires to discover 'whether his
illness will be fatal.' It is possible that Barnes wrote 'the manner of
my death.' As printed the line is defective : 'To shew me now the
manner of death.'

[3] In its original form this trait is very old. Sanuto's diary
(quoted by Gregorovius, VII. 496) describes how the devil appeared
in the pope's dying chamber as an *ape*. *Et uno cardinale corse
per piarlo e preso volendolo presentar al papa, il papa disse lasolo,
lasolo, chè il diavolo. Et poi la notte si amalò e morite.* The notion
of the ape seems at the root not merely of the trait of putting on the
pope's robes, but in that, dwelt on by both Hondorff and Widman,
which makes the devil declare to the Pope's affrighted servant, *Ego
Papa sum, Ich bin Bapst.* Prof. Ward points out the similar trait
in the *Wagnerbuch*, cap. 2, where Wagner asks that the spirit
should appear to him ' in eines Affen gestalt.'

rest of the scene, with the squabble over the terms of the
pact, and the logical argument, necessarily bears little relation to the great finale of *Faustus*. With reasoning which
sounds very chill beside Faustus' outburst, and which is
also far less characteristically Christian, Alexander urges
that the soul is divine and necessarily imperishable. But
these things, as his opponent reminds him, 'should have
been thought upon before.' Then, driven from all other
resource, he calls upon the divine mercy: and the agonised
ejaculations of Faustus are replaced by such stuff as
this :

> Mercy good Lord, oh mercy, mercy, mercy.
> O save my soule out of the Lyons pawes,
> My darling from the denne of blacke damnation
> My soule, my dove, cover with silver wings,
> Her downe and plumage make of fine tryed gould,
> Help, help, help, above, stirre, stirre, stupiditie.

'He charms in David's words with Judas' spirit,' observes the devil with some force.

After a tediously prolonged scene of arguments and
protests, strangely in contrast with the speechless swift-
ness of Faust's end, Alexander is finally 'thrust downe.'
Then, as in *Faustus* (ed. 1616), come his former companions, the Cardinalls and Bentivoli :

> *Bent.* What is he dead?
> *Car.* Dead, and in such a fashion,
>   As much affrights my spirits to remember,
>   Thunder and fearfull lightning at his death,
>   Outcries of horror and extremity[1].

---

[1] Cf. the Scholars in *Faustus* (ed. 1616, *ad fin.*) :

> 1 *Scho.* Come, gentlemen, let us go visit Faustus,
>   For such a dreadful night was never seen;
>   Since first the world's creation did begin,—
>   Such fearful shrieks and cries were never heard.

The tragedy of Barnes does not exhaust the list of plays which the strange magnetism of Faustus has palpably affected. On imaginations of the most various cast, that one, profoundly simple, but overpowering situation, left an impression not easily effaced. The genial buoyancy of Greene, in his comedies so rarely broken by his accesses of tragic gloom,—the rollicking fun of the author of the *Merry Devil*, and Barnabe Barnes' vigorous but somewhat phlegmatic appetite for infernal horrors, all received a congenial stimulus from a drama which reflected little of any of these temperaments. In the case of Greene and Barnes it told, though not exclusively, in a tragic pathos more highly strung or more subtly and naturally varied; in a sombre shadow added to the pleasant old English legend, in a few suggestions of terror and pity infused into the gross outlines of a Lutheran *Bapstgeschichte*. In the next section we shall find the same transformation carried out, by hands more skilful than those of either Greene or Barnes, in a German *Märchen;* and one of so much independent interest and importance that it demands a separate treatment.

III.

The story of Fortunatus, as we know it, is an aggregate of very heterogeneous elements. The principal incident has been enriched with a series of episodes, loosely appended and easily detached. Scarcely any class of mediaeval fiction has failed to contribute to the medley

FORTUN-ATUS[1].

[1] Cf. Valentin Schmidt, *Fortunatus;* J. Zacher, in Ersch u. Grüber; and Tittmann's excellent introduction to the English comedians' version of the play. (Goedeke and Tittmann: *Deutsche Dichter des 16ten Jahrhunderts*, Bd. 13.)

some characteristic incident or colouring. Chivalric romances, religious legends, tales of magic are all represented. There are incidents which belong to the Lear-cycle, and others which belong to that of the Prodigal Son. There are motives from Italian novels and from primitive Teutonic mythology. Almost every country of Europe contributes to its scenery. We hurry to and fro between Cyprus, England, France, Flanders, Venice, Constantinople; we explore the Purgatory of S. Patrick and taste the genial hospitality of Prester John.

All the known editions of the *Volksbuch* contain substantially the same story. From the first German edition, published at Augsburg in 1509, and its numerous German successors, to the Dutch, English and Danish versions of the seventeenth century, the story everywhere unfolds itself in the same elaborate disorder, varying only in quantity of descriptive detail, or at most, in the omission or inclusion of some trifling episode. In outline it falls into four divisions. The first (chapters I.—X.) comprises the early history of Fortunatus preceding the encounter with Fortune which first entitled him to his name. The second (c. XI.—XXIII.) is the history of *Fortunatus and the purse*. After receiving the purse from Fortune, he enters on a career of successful adventure in Venice and elsewhere, and finally marries with great splendour in his native Cyprus. The third (c. XXV.—XXX.) contains the story of *Fortunatus and the hat*. After twelve years of domestic happiness the instinct for enterprise stirs once more in the old adventurer; disguised as a merchant, he visits the Sultan, robs him by a simple stratagem of the wishing hat, returns home and dies, leaving the purse and hat to his two sons Andolosia and Ampedo. The fourth (c. XXXI. to the end) contains the *Adventures of Andolosia*, his intrigue

with the English princess Agrippina, the loss, recovery,
and final loss of purse and hat, and lastly, the violent
death of both sons.

The German *Volksbuch* of Fortunatus was undoubtedly *History of the Volks-*
the source of all the English and Dutch, and probably of *buch.*
the French, versions of it now extant.   No Romance
version, whether Spanish, Italian or French, so old by
many years as the earliest German edition, that of Augsburg 1509, is known to exist.   At the same time this
edition itself contains evidences of a Romance source,
not easy to ignore.   Görres, who roundly declared the
story to be Spanish, pointed out that the French version
of 1670 was described in the title-page as 'translated
from the Spanish original,' and that Quadrio (perhaps
merely on the ground of this dedication) had stated that
it was written by a Spaniard 'non so da chi.'   Of more
importance than these vague assertions are the Romance
words sprinkled, without apparent reason, pretty freely
through the text.   These however by no means tend to prove
the case for Spanish.   The 'Porta de Vacha, das ist dye
Küport' of the 1530 (Augsburg) version[1], may point to a
Romance original, but *vacha* is nearer to the French
vache than to Sp. *vaca* or It. *vacca*[2].   In the 1550 version
(Frankfurt), 'pforte de vacca' is substituted.   In the

---

[1] The German versions of the *Volksbuch* fall under two classes,
represented by those published at Augsburg in 1509 and 1530, and
at Frankfurt in 1550.   The Augsburg texts, written in a Bavarian
dialect, are in many places ampler in detail and circumstance: they
use Romance forms more readily; the woodcuts also are wholly
different, and on the whole superior, though less elaborate.

[2] Zacher (Ersch u. Grüber s. v. *Fortunatus*) rightly disputes the
Spanish theory but does not explain these names.   Why should a
South German writer first go out of his way to speak of a *Porta de
Vacha*, and then translate it for the benefit of his readers?

English we have simply the 'cow-gate[1].' 'Zoyelier' again, as Zacher observes, is nearer to the Italian *giojelliere* (especially pronounced in the Venetian way) than to the Spanish *joyero*. The 1550 edition, which shows a dis- position to Germanise these Romance forms, substitutes *Edelstein-krämer*, the clumsiness of which may have hindered its use before. If the mention of 'Alamanelia,' the home of the maker of the wishing-cap, which does not appear to be the name of a Spanish town, proves the origin of the romance in Spain, the allusion to London may be taken to prove its origin in England. And what- ever force may lie in the argument that the name of the sleeping-draught, *Mandolles*, looks, or has been supposed to look, like Spanish, is not only neutralised by the fact that it is not Spanish, but this spurious resemblance is itself the strongest argument for doubting the Spanish origin of the romance in which it occurs.

Whatever part, however, a Romance hand may have played in giving the story its present shape, it was cer- tainly not of Romance invention. Its essential in- gredients are in the main Teutonic, and perhaps the most forcible argument for the view that the last *ré- dacteur* came of a different stock is the indifference to their import which has embedded and overlaid them with a mass of irrelevant additions.

1.
*Story of
Andolosia.*   One of these ingredients occurs, in an obviously more primitive form, in the tale of the *Gesta Romanorum* (chap. 120 of the Latin, chap. 54 of the English version), first

---

[1] If this is a bit of genuine local knowledge it stands alone. Louvain is eccentric in its street nomenclature: the modern town con- tains a *rue des Moutons*, a *rue des Corbeaux*, a *rue des Chats*. But the old maps and views show no gate of this name in either the inner or the outer line of walls. The *Porta lupina* is the nearest approach. I should add that I have seen no map earlier than the beginning of the 17th century.

referred to by Douce and Görres[1]. There the dying Darius bequeaths three gifts to his three sons. To the eldest he leaves what he had himself inherited; to the second what he had conquered; to the third three *iocalia*,—a ring, a necklace, and a rich cloth, of which the first gave him the favour of all, the second fulfilled all his wishes, and the third transported him wherever he wished to go. These three gifts, which obviously did not all belong to the original story, he successively loses through the seductions of a mistress. Her triumph seems complete when after Jonathas has carried her off by the aid of the cloth into a desert place,—'in tantam distantiam, ubi nullus hominum venit,'—she contrives, like Agrippina, to get the cloth into her own possession, wishes herself at home and leaves him there. The remedy is as in Fortunatus. The frustrated lover discovers as he wanders, water which blisters the flesh, and fruit which produces leprosy. Shortly afterwards he finds other water and other fruit which cure the inflictions of the first. He takes samples of both sorts, and sets out homeward. On the way he finds occasion to heal a leprous king with his second sample, and the renown thus acquired gives him the opportunity of punishing his faithless mistress with the first, and recovering his stolen treasures.

The hero of this undoubtedly eastern tale was already a Fortunatus in the germ, and his history attached itself without effort to the fancy, familiar in the west, of 'a child of Fortune,'—*der Sælden kint*,—a 'standing recipient of Good Luck[2].' The necklace and the cloth

2. *Story of Fortunatus.*

---

[1] Douce: Dissertation on the *Gesta Romanorum*, appended to his *Illustrations of Shakespeare.*

[2] Cf. 'Fortune's privates' in Hamlet's first conversation with Guildenstern and Rosencrantz.

found a parallel in two similar magic gifts, one at least of which was familiar to the oldest Teutonic mythology. The wishing-hat is evidently a last survival of that of the German Wish-God, Wuotan. The derivation of the inexhaustible purse is more puzzling[1], and it is perhaps fair to ask whether, in an age unacquainted with cheques, the gift of boundless wealth could well have been made in any other way.

The substitution of the 'child of Fortune' for the father, Darius, of the purse and hat for the less familiar necklace and cloth, and the development of the story of their acquisition, as a sort of *Vorgeschichte* to the adventures of the son, produced the main outline of the present tale. Then ensued a complicated process of expansion and accretion, the details of which it is impossible to trace with certainty. It is not difficult however to distinguish two classes of addition, which probably indicate successive stages or strata in its growth. There are, firstly, traces, not very consistently carried out, of a wish to give the tale a religious and moral colouring which it originally lacked. Fortune's offer of wisdom as well as of wealth, her injunction to feed the poor, and the elaborate foundations which her *protégé* accordingly creates at Venice and at Cyprus,— '100 ducats income for each priest and tombs in the Minster for his parents,'—the character of Ampedo, the douce, law-abiding citizen unknown to the *Gesta* story, who serves as a foil to his flighty brother Andolosia, the

---

[1] Grimm refers it to the cornucopia of the Roman Fortuna: 'mundanam cornucopiam gestans' Amm. Marcell. 22. 9. Grimm, *Deutsche Myth.* II. 870, E. T. Zacher, on the other hand (u. s. p. 485), argues for a Celtic origin, on grounds scarcely more convincing than those urged by Görres for the Spanish source of the whole romance.

hermit who exhorts the latter in the crisis of his fate to fix his mind on heaven, and provides him with the healing fruit which his predecessor in the *Gesta* owed to accident, and lastly, his use of the fruit, not merely for the punishment of his mistress, which completes the ambition of the *Gesta* hero, but for her final cure :—all these things look like the attempt of a possibly clerical *rédacteur* to mitigate the frank worldliness of a tale, the hero of which not only openly wishes for wealth above everything else, but is led by it to a happiness which apparently leaves him nothing else to wish for.

And then the story seems to have fallen into the hands of some professed manufacturer of romance, who was only concerned to load it with exciting adventures. The early history of the 'child of Fortune,'—told in ten chapters, without any attempt to explain how he came by the privilege; the exploration of St Patrick's Purgatory (c. 15), the elaborate courtship of the Earl of Cyprus' daughter (c. 21), the endowment of the faithful servant Leopold (c. 23), Andelosia's adventure with the French lady (c. 32), the Nunnery Scene (c. 41), Agrippina's marriage to the Prince of Cyprus (c. 42), the intrigue of the two earls for the purse, the violent death of Andelosia and Ampedo, and the execution of the earls (c. 48),—are additions which simply serve to turn a fairy tale into a romance of adventure.

Such is the ultimate form of the *Volksbuch* of *Fortunatus,* the first in which we know it :—a romance of adventure, the two central figures of which, in spite of one or two undeveloped germs of moral criticism, are treated frankly as heroes, and followed through successive enterprises with triumph when they succeed and undisguised sympathy when they fail.   Fortunatus' preference of riches to wisdom remains absolutely without retribution; if Andelosia wastes his gifts he is allowed to recover them, and his violent death, far from being conceived as a retribution, is made the direct result of his own valour and the ill-conditioned envy of his rivals, and is avenged amid the sympathy of all concerned by the still more terrible death of his assassins. Wholly different was the treatment of the story in an English drama, to the consideration of which I now turn.

Olde For-
tunatus.
1596—
1600.

The Comedy of *Olde Fortunatus*, printed in 1600, is the first extant representative of the *Volksbuch* in English[1], as it is also the first extant work of its author, Decker. This text, however, the only one we know, is plainly far from representing its primitive form. It is the result of at least two transformations;—one thorough and laborious, though in the absence of the original difficult to exactly define,—the other hastily executed at a sudden and peremptory call, and with palpable unevenness of work-manship. The case was apparently thus. In Feb. 1596[2], a play called the *First part of Fortunatus* began to run with great success at Henslowe's theatre. It probably dealt with only the first half of the story,—the history of Fortunatus the father[3]. Its attraction however, like that of most marvellous stories, rapidly wore off[4]; and it ceased to appear. Three years later, an attempt was made to revive it by adding the second half,—the history

[1] Of the later English versions, evidently fresh translations, not new editions of the old, some account will be found in the Appendix.

[2] Henslowe's date 'Feb. 1595' is Old Style.

[3] Not only is the original play described in the first entry as the *first part*, but Decker's is emphatically called *the hole history of Fortunatus.*

[4] Henslowe's Diary, ed. Collier, sub Feb. 3, 10, &c., '1595.' The takings were at first unusually large (£3 and more); but by May 24, they had fallen to 14s. and the play was withdrawn.

of Andelosia; and the task was put into the hands of
a young playwright, Thomas Decker, who had been
known for some two years to the London stage. Instead
of merely writing a second part, however, he incor-
porated the whole contents in a single play, recasting
for this purpose the already existing first part[1]. By the
end of November, 1599, the work was finished, and
on the 30th Henslowe sent him 20s. 'in full payment.'
But the very next day occurred a critical event for the
Olde Fortunatus. The play was ordered for performance
at court.

Under these new conditions extensive alterations *The play*
and additions were thought necessary, which apparently *composite.*
occupied not less than a fortnight, and certainly cost
half as much as had just been paid for the entire play[2].
It is clear therefore that the new work cannot have
consisted merely, as has been thought, in adding the
prologue and epilogue, though these were obviously a
part of it; nor could such additions be naturally described as 'altrenge.' The key apparently lies in this
phrase, together with the entry of Dec. 12, where Decker
is said to have received the large sum of 40s. *for the
eande of Fortunatus, for the corte.* In other words the
alterations consisted in (1) a re-writing of a portion of
the play, and (2) a substantial addition at the close.
Now it happens that the last scene in the extant text
corresponds, not only to nothing in the *Volksbuch*, but
to nothing in the rest of the play, with the exception of

[1] That he did this is probable both from the resemblance in
style, and from the sums paid to him for the work,—£6 in all,—the
usual payment for an entire original play being £8.

[2] Henslowe, '31 Nov.'; Decker receives 20s. 'for the altrenge
of the boocke of the wholl history of Fortunatus.' On Dec. 12, 40s.
'for the eande of Fortunatus, for the corte.'

two other scenes of the same stamp. In these three scenes, which bear the evident character not only of an after-thought, but of an after-thought conceived in just such circumstances as have been described, the two figures of *Vertue* and *Vice* appear as the rivals of Fortune in her originally unaided work. They plant the two trees from which Andelosia is to gather the sweet and bitter fruit; they woo him, as the Good and Evil Angels woo Faustus; and finally engage in a formal dispute for the mastery, closed by an appeal from Fortune to the greater 'Queen of Chance' before whom they stood.

1.
The tragedy of Fortuna- tus.
Reserving for a moment the consideration of these scenes, let us briefly examine Decker's treatment of the original story. Two years' experience of writing for the stage had strengthened the instincts of the practical playwright, somewhat at the expense perhaps of the vein of genuine though somewhat crude poetry which he undoubtedly possessed. He accordingly revises the story without ceremony. The work of one of the most romantic of Elizabethans is in curious contrast in this respect with that of the coryphaeus of the later Romantics, Tieck, whose two colossal dramas on the Fortunatus story[1] are a monument of the devout industry with which the Romantic school was wont to torment the most insignificant details of an old legend into the semblance of poetry. The incoherent string of adventures which both poets found in the *Volksbuch* had to be turned into a rounded whole. Tieck does this by complementing, by piecing out. Phrases become speeches, paragraphs scenes. Decker seeks the same end, in the main, by cutting away. He chooses the three most piquant adventures of Fortunatus,—the presentation of the purse, the stealing of the hat, and his death. The whole of his early history

[1] *Phantasus,* Bd. III.

is omitted ; the play beginning when he is already 'olde,' and his two sons of an age to take up the tale at his death. Tieck, in the spirit of the straitest Romantic orthodoxy, begins like the *Volksbuch* with his early adventures in Cyprus. The adventures of Andelosia are less curtailed, and at certain points even amplified. The punishment of the faithless Agrippina by the horn-producing apples was a trait too congenial to Elizabethan taste to be neglected ; Decker has accordingly made the two courtiers Longaville and Montrosse share the fate of the princess ; obtaining at the same time a better ground for the vengeance which here as in the *Volksbuch* they wreak upon the sons of Fortunatus.

But there is another class of alterations in which a more special influence is perceptible than the general needs of the stage. It is that of the tragedy of Doctor Faustus[1]. *Influence of Faustus.*

It is easy to see that the parallelism of the two subjects was of a kind to suggest still closer approximation. Fortunatus, like Faustus, receives exceptional faculties from a supernatural power, and accomplishes similar feats by their help. If Faustus plays a trick on the pope, Fortunatus outwits the Sultan ; and Agrippina is won as purely by magical means as Helena. Both stories, again, display, like true legends, the completest indifference to distinctions of time and space, and therefore presented the same kind of difficulty to the practical playwright ; and since both plays meet the difficulty by the same means, only in a few cases to be exactly paralleled elsewhere, the example of the earlier can hardly have gone for nothing with the later. The 'chorus' in both is

---

[1] A slight trace of the same influence perhaps appears in Decker's *The Gentle Craft,* acted 1599, the year in which he revised the *Fortunatus,* where the travelling Shoemaker is made to practise his art in the city of Faustus.

used to tide over, as it were, the hiatuses occupied with
rapid or otherwise altogether undramatic movement:
Faustus' early life, then his journey to Olympus before the visit to Rome; Fortunatus' journey to the
Sultan, Andelosia's robbery of his brother and capture
of Agrippina[1].

But a much more important point of contact remains.
The elements of tragic motive inherent in the legend,
though almost thrust out of sight by the discursive romanticism of the author of the *Volksbuch*, are in the play
brought into a prominence unprecedented in the literary
history of the legend. Fortune is not the benevolent
fairy casting favours on her favourite child, but a stern
goddess who confers them with contempt and calls him
inexorably to account for their abuse. His very choice
of riches instead of wisdom is made to assume the fatality
of Faustus's pact with the devil, and to play the same
part in his destiny; the prosperity to which it leads is as
hollow as Faustus's, and is cut short by the same inevitable catastrophe. At the fixed hour Fortune appears, like
Mephistophilis, to claim her victim; and his death-scene
accordingly has, scarcely less than Faustus's, the tragic
fascination which belongs to every sudden collapse of apparently boundless power. Like Faustus too, Fortunatus
in the critical hour bitterly repents his choice; Faustus
calls on Christ whom he had forsworn; Fortunatus begs

[1] Most probably just before Decker revised the *Fortunatus*
Shakspere in *Henry V.* (1599) had used the same piece of dramatic
technique to tide over the rapid marches and wide extent of scenery
required in a historical drama of war. Certain phrases suggest that
this too was specially in Decker's mind: cf. especially 'this cockpit'
of the first *Chorus*, with Decker's:

> For this smal Circumference must stand,
> For the imagin'd Sur-face of much Land, &c.

to be allowed to take the wisdom which he had re-
jected[1]; Fortune inexorably replies, in language of which
the Faustus-like colouring is undeniable:

> 'Thou hadst thy fancy, I must have thy fate;'

and finally, with the aid of a company of Satyrs, drags
away the body of her victim, as Faustus is carried off by
Mephistophilis and his crew of devils.   It is plain that
a Fortunatus who ends in this way was imagined under
influences wholly different from those which determined
the romantic Fortunatus of the *Volksbuch*, whose death is
only the natural and not unwelcome close of a career
sated with success.

In the story of Andelosia, the tragic motive is also
wholly due to Decker.   To the author of the romance,
as we saw, he is a hero to the last; his death is told
with undisguised sympathy, and savagely avenged.   To
Decker, on the other hand, he is a prodigal who has spent
his gifts in riot, *luxuriose vivendo;* and his ruin becomes
a retribution, of which Fortune is again the instrument:

> 'Fortune forgive me, I deserve thy hate;
> Myself have made myself a reprobate.'

What now is the relation to this essentially (in spite
of a profusion of Decker's usual robust comedy) tragic
story, of the detached scenes which were, in part beyond
question, added 'for the court'?   In my view, as I
have said, these represent a quite distinct theme,—the
rivalry of Fortune, Virtue and Vice, or, to use a term
steeped in the very odour of the court-poetry of the six-

2. The Triumphs of Virtue, Vice and Fortune.

---

[1]   *Fort.*   Take this againe: give wisdome to my sonnes.
Fortune.   No, foole, 'tis now too late: as death strikes thee
            So shall their ends sudden and wretched bee.

teenth century,—their successive *Triumphs*[1].   Only, it is
to be noted that it is Virtue who now finally triumphs not
only over Vice, but over Fortune, and who in the culminating scene pays the supreme compliment to the 'dred
nymphe' looking on :—

> Vertue alone lives still, and lives in you,
> I am a counterfeit, you are the true[2].

In other words, Fortune, who in the drama as originally
planned, was herself the supreme arbiter of the world,
bringing the destinies in her train, and overthrowing
greatness at her good pleasure, suddenly falls into the
position of one of a Triumvirate.   As a supreme power
she necessarily represented the forces of permanence and
therefore stood in no hostile relation to moral good.
Her parting injunction to the English king, which in the
first version probably closed the play, expresses the wish
of a Fortune at least tolerant of virtue :

> England shall ne're be poore, if England strive,
> Rather by vertue, than by wealth to thrive.

But Virtue personified, and a rival of Fortune, could not
thus coalesce with her ; the two figures necessarily stood
apart in sharp distinction, and it is curious to find
Fortune, immediately after uttering this exhortation to
Virtue in the abstract, discharge a bitter greeting to
Virtue in the concrete, as she enters 'crowned, with
Nymphes and kings attending on her.'

> How dar'st thou come
> Thus trickt in gawdy Feathers, and thus garded,
> With crowned Kings and Muses, when thy foe

---

[1] Cf. the *Triumphs of Love and Fortune*, pr. 1589, where the
alternate triumphs of each rival are merged in the final triumph of
Love.

[2] Decker's Works, ed. Hazlitt, I. 173.

Hath trod thus on thee, and now triumphes so?
Where's vertuous Ampedo? See, hees her slave,
For following thee this recompense they have[1].

When it is remembered that the latter passage belongs
to the opening of the last 'triumph' scene, which both
by Henslowe's testimony and by its direct allusions to
the queen, undoubtedly formed part of the alterations for
the court, we can hardly expect a more salient evidence
than this of the nature of the alteration. In other ways
too the resort to the Triumph-motive has injured the
original simplicity and clearness of the story. If Vice
and Virtue were to be effective rivals of Fortune, it was
necessary to make room for them in the action, to provide achievements for them. This was done by making
them the planters of the two trees, and the dispensers of
the fruit to the doubting Andelosia. The fruits, which
originally differed only medicinally, thus become emblems
of a moral difference ; and Andelosia's choice between
them recals the choice of Hercules, or that of Faustus between the rival solicitations of the Good and Evil Angels.
The eating of the apples is accordingly taken to indicate
a moral as well as a physical process, with the somewhat
awkward result,—since those who taste the apple of Virtue
are also the malefactors who murder Andelosia for the
purse—that the triumph of Virtue lies in facilitating a
breach of her own laws. Such inconsistencies, which it
would be easy to multiply, show how distinct the process
of working out the story of Fortunatus and his sons was
from that of patching on to it this frigid and artificial
allegory. There, as we saw, Decker, with the example
of Faustus before him, showed himself keenly alive to
the tragic capacities of the story : Fortune is the in-
exorable exacter, Fortunatus tastes the full fruit of his

[1] Works, I. 171.

error, and transmits it like the curse of Atreus to his
sons. Here, on the other hand, the moral tension of
tragedy gives place abruptly to the decorous and polite
conventionalities of the Mask, to the genius of which
a tragic ending was as uncongenial as tragic seriousness ;
Fortune, the merciless leader of destinies, dispenses a
general pardon, Virtue forgets all natural resentment in
her anxiety to triumph over her rivals, and the two
murderers, condemned to the wheel by the mortal king[1],
are let off with the 'terrors of an evil conscience.'

The *Fortunatus*, in spite of its first success, cannot be
said to have had any literary following. The play of
the English Comedians (printed in 1620), though the
work of Englishmen, does not strictly belong to English
literature, and demands therefore merely a word of
notice here. Like the rest of these barbarous pieces,
long the sole representatives for the German reader
of the great age of English drama, it is a meagre
epitome of its original—which was undoubtedly Decker's
play,—eked out however, at various points by direct
quotation from the German *Volksbuch*.

Some twenty years after this effort of his early manhood, Decker took part with Ford and Rowley in the
Witch of Edmonton. His old taste for dabbling in the
supernatural (it is difficult to use any more serious term)
had not left him,—we shall see another striking instance

---

[1] The contrast with the treatment of the *Volksbuch* is here
instructive. The murderers are there actually executed. Decker
therefore deviates from his authority, in the interest of the Mask-
treatment, to soften their fate, as he had previously deviated from it,
in the interest of tragic treatment, to make that of *Fortunatus* more
rigorous.

of it in the next chapter; and it is probable that we owe to him the scenes in which it is perhaps not rash to detect one more gross reminiscence of the pact of Faustus. But the league by which Mother Sawyer swears away her body and soul to the fiend Dog in her own blood, belongs to an altogether more vulgar phase of popular faith. The fashion of superstition had in fact changed, the realm of the imaginary itself was affected by the growing realism of the time, and the magician of legend was yielding the stage to the Witch of real life. In turning, as we now must, to the literature of Witchcraft, we shall involuntarily make a similar transition. It has been possible to deal with stories of magic, like *Faustus* and *Fortunatus*, with scarcely a reference to other than literary forces, but the literature of Witchcraft cannot be even discussed without some notice of the most horrible canker to which modern society has ever been a prey.

IV.

As the fourteenth century is, preeminently, the age of French, and the seventeenth that of English, witchcraft, so the sixteenth may be said to be that of German witchcraft. The lucid rationalism of the French Parliament had effectively restrained the persecution while its authority remained; and even after its complete subordination to the monarchy, it was only under the puerile and superstitious rule of Henry III. that the witch-trials recovered something of their former virulence and frequency. And England never knew the witch-fever in its most deadly and rabid form till the accession of a sovereign who possessed the talent of setting forth the mysteries of demonology in excellent Latin, and who

was impelled by a mixture of scholarly pedantry, kingly
absoluteness and childish timidity, to send his hundreds
to the rack and the stake. In Germany, however, the
ferocity of the witch-trials in this century was equalled
nowhere else. It was Germany too which made the
most notable contributions to the literature of witchcraft.
No more epoch-making books exist on the subject than
the *Malleus Maleficarum* of Institor and Sprenger, and
the *De praestigiis daemonum* of Weier,—the one the most
authoritative and final assault upon the whole class of
'sorcerers', the other the first powerful, though qualified,
effort in their defence. Bodin in France and Delrio in
Holland produced more elaborate and skilful books; but
they were deeply indebted to the *Malleus*, and the first
English rationalist Reginald Scot was not less deeply indebted to Weier. The depths of infatuation and the
greatest enlightenment and courage possible at the time
were equally shown in Germany. The influence of the
Malleus endured longer, and recovering from the temporary shock of Weier's work, helped to promote the yet
more terrible ravages of the next century; Weier was a
brave but ineffectual precursor of the Tanners and Spees
who two generations later, from the head-quarters of the
Inquisition, attacked a plague which the Inquisition had
contributed not a little to initiate, and prepared the
beginning of the end[1].

The Malleus Malefi-carum.   The *Malleus Maleficarum*, the chief object of the
attacks both of Weier and Scot, was no merely theoretical
work upon witchcraft. It was compiled by two of the
most active and fanatical of Inquisitors, as at once a text-
book and a defence, of their procedure; and its force
lay less in its arguments or in its learning, which were
poor enough, than in the extraordinary array of detailed

[1] Soldan-Heppe: *Die Hexenprozesse*, c. 23.

cases with which they confirmed every position. It was
the manifesto of a war which they were themselves
waging; a laborious attempt to extort the acquiescence
if not the approval of Christendom for the new crusade.
They prefaced it with the Bull in which Innocent
VIII. three years before had given them extraordinary inquisitorial authority over the greater part of
Germany[1]. This Bull declared that Germany was in-
fested by a number of persons of both sexes, who,
rejecting the Catholic faith, had entered into relations
with demons, and by their aid were spreading mischief
far and wide; destroying corn and vine, sheep and oxen,
and making the productive powers of the earth, of
animals and of man, barren and unfruitful. Some
persons moreover had been found who resisted the just
punishment of these sorcerers at the hands of the inquisitors. Over both classes an absolute authority, from
which the highest princes of the Church were not to be
exempt, was given to Institor and Sprenger; and it was
declared heresy not merely to practise witchcraft, but
even to be opposed to its punishment. 'Haeresis est
maxima, opera maleficarum non credere.' Even the
Bull however did not make their work entirely smooth
and the *Malleus* was accordingly designed to bear dowr
what remained of opposition, as well as to supply a text
book for other inquisitors.

This double aim is reflected in its arrangement. It
is divided into three parts, of which the first deals with
the theological theory of witchcraft, the second with its
practical effects and remedies, the third with the legal
procedure proper in investigating and punishing it[2].

---

[1] Cf. the Bull, *Summis desiderantes*, in the *Malleus*, ed. 1487,
etc.; also in Soldan-Heppe, I. 269.

[2] On the title-page the book is declared to be 'praecipue:

Three agencies concur, it is said in the first division, to produce the effects of witchcraft: the demon, the *malefi-cus*, and finally, *divina permissio*. Then in successive *Quaestiones*, the cardinal points of the theory are one by one investigated. The doctrine of *succubi* and *incubi*, on which so much of the popular terror of the witch de-pended, is naturally affirmed unconditionally, and the doubt, 'whether it was catholic to assert that human beings could be produced in this way,' decisively re-jected[1]. Then, by a process of exhaustion, the writers refute the supposition that some other powers than demons may be concerned. For neither *humana malitia* (Qu. 3), nor the *motores orbium* (Qu. 4), nor magic words (Qu. 5), nor the powers of the stars are capable of the same effects. The second division unfolds in detail the mysterious practices of the Witches: their pact with the Devil and its loathsome accessories, the nightly flight to the meeting-place, and the countless ways of injuring which they practise by his means. The third division lays bare the extraordinary system of procuring evidence and the not less extraordinary rules for applying it. Both were used and abused, if they were capable of abuse, to the utmost extent, nor could the inquisition have been carried on without them. It was through this system and these rules that the material on which the court worked was always forthcoming, and that the supply of accused persons even exceeded the enormous demand. No more ingenious device for making something out of nothing could have been found than the system of anonymous denunciation and examination by torture; and the inquisitors, by resorting to the worst methods of

omnibus inquisitoribus et divini verbi concionatoribus utilis et necessarius.'

[1] *Quaestio* 3.

ancient criminal procedure, effectually secured themselves against any lack of employment.   Their whole work was a process of reaping what they themselves had sown, and sowing what they intended to reap.

It was inevitable too that an organised inquisition such as this, armed with powers so boundless and so arbitrary, could not leave either the theory of witchcraft or the social status of the witch, as they were.   On the one hand, there arose a sort of orthodox doctrine of witchcraft, based upon the inspired pages of the *Malleus Maleficarum;* a mass of floating popular superstitions became a coherent and systematic theory; ideas purely local, or out of keeping with the rest, were dropped, and those that were everywhere implicit in the popular conception were dogmatically formulated.   The witch became the most distinct of personalities, with attributes every one of which was affirmed by the authority of the Church and the affirmation supported by her most terrible sanctions.   And, on the other hand, while the belief in witchcraft was defined, it took hold of the popular mind with unprecedented force.   The unscrupulous use made by the inquisitors of their power, far from raising general suspicion, apparently only confirmed the insane credulity which made the flimsiest accusation outweigh in the popular mind the strongest evidence of innocence.   Every chapter in the *Malleus* became a text to which new victims owed their fate, and which supplied a sort of divine warrant for new accusations.

Thus the *Malleus* acquired a double distinction in the modern history of civilisation.   It laid down a conception of witchcraft which has become classical in literature, and, if it were not for one deviation of supreme significance—*Macbeth,*—might even be called universal; and it started the frenzy of witch persecution on the career in which for two hundred years it hardly relaxed.

The *Witch* thus systematically defined bore few evident traces of the mythology of which she was a degraded representative. Though abundance of genuine Teutonic mythology may be picked up from the examples which strew the pages of the *Malleus*, to such things it is itself entirely indifferent. It deals only in the grosser ideas which, though traceable in germ in some Norse myths, were first made prominent by the well-meant efforts of the Christian priesthood. The Norn, the Valkyre, the Waldweib, are lost in the familiar and hideous caricature; Wuotan becomes frankly the devil; the free service of the god by the warrior-maidens turns into midnight gatherings devoted to the grossest kind of intercourse. The notion of a pact made by the witch with the devil, and of her sexual relation to him,—both unfamiliar to their prototypes,—came to occupy the very centre of the doctrine of witchcraft; and the literature of the subject teems with repulsive tales of *succubi* and *incubi*,—a horrible chapter of superstition which the German imagination accepted but which it cannot be accused of originating[1].

The Opposition.   The fever which, under the powerful stimulus given by Institor and Sprenger, invaded Western Europe, was

---

[1] As Reginald Scot suggests (*Discovery of Witchcraft*) much was probably due to the text: 'Viderunt filii dei filias hominum, quod elegantes essent; acceperunt sibi in uxores ex omnibus quas elegerant.' On the relation of the Witch to Teutonic mythology, cf. Grimm, *Deutsche Mythologie* 992 ff; Simrock, *Handbuch d. deutschen Mythologie*, § 129. The caldron and the stick probably derive from the sacrificial caldron and staff of the priestesses of Freyja; to whom also the cat, so habitually associated with witchery, was sacred. On the other hand the Teutonic element in the witch superstition is almost wholly ignored by Soldan-Heppe, *Die Hexenprozesse.*

not soon to be allayed. From the first, however, a few voices were raised in vain protest; in the middle of the century Johann Weier (Wierus) created for a time an effective diversion, which was not confined to his native country; and though the ample learning of Bodin and the skill and tact of Delrio renewed the *prestige* of the doctrine of witchcraft, an unconvinced though by no means noisy minority continued to dissent.

The opposition had principally three grounds. In the first place, just suspicion was aroused by the gross and injudicious unfairness with which the trials were carried on; by the gross venality of the inquisitors, their obvious preference for wealthy victims, their open encouragement of those who denounced them, their savage eagerness to convict, tempered only by the prospect of some better way of gratifying their avarice, or by their craven fear in the face of popular indignation. This was obvious to every calm observer, even to those who entirely shared the *Malleus'* view of witchcraft in theory. Cornelius Agrippa succeeded in rescuing an unfortunate prisoner from the clutches of an inquisitor by the mere cogency with which he insisted on the want of evidence. Cardan argued the hollowness of the inquisitors' case from their shameless persecution of wealthy Protestants as long as it was safe, their prudent abstention where they saw no prospect of gain. Weier and Scot both quote this passage with approbation.

Further, came the progress of positive science. Hardly any one yet dreamed of wholly denying diabolic, still less divine, participation in nature; on the other hand, under the auspices of men like Telesio at Naples, an incipient natural science was beginning, however unconsciously, to narrow the limits of the marvellous. Between the region of diabolic agency and of comprehended law, a middle region was recognised, in which phenomena were brought about, by human means indeed but still by aid of mysterious processes and occult qualities revealed only to profound study. This was the region of magic, closely related on the one hand to sorcery, in which phenomena of the same sort were accomplished by supernatural aid, on the other to natural science, in which ordinary intelligence sufficed. Of this sort of natural science, a branch in which Italians of every class had great proficiency, was the action of *poisons;* and so comprehensive was the inquisitorial view of sorcerers that it was not superfluous to distinguish from them even these. Tritheim's classification is very instructive. He distinguishes virtually three classes[1]: (1) those who do injuries by natural means, poison, &c.; (2) those who use mysterious words, charms, &c.; (3) those who either use the co-operation of demons, without having given themselves into their power, or who enter into an actual *pact* with them[2]. This distinction is highly characteristic of the confused and compromising attitude of the Rationalist reaction, in which Tritheim himself,—a firm believer in witchcraft,—must be denied a place. Scarcely any one was bold enough to deny diabolic agency altogether; if it was excluded in one region, it was allowed only more unlimited scope in another. In no one is this more striking than Weier, who passes, fairly enough, for one of the pillars of the reaction. His distinction rests wholly on his treatment of witchcraft in the narrowest sense,— the imputation of diabolic practices to old women. That there are sorcerers who deal in such practices he is perfectly convinced, and towards them, as well as the

Weier.

---

[1] Actually four; but the two last are rather subdivisions of one.
[2] *Antipalus Maleficiorum ;* cf. Silbernagel, *Tritheim.*

poisoners, he is not a whit more merciful than the inquisitors themselves. In the demoniac world he is not only a fanatical believer; he boldly enters upon a detailed description of its contents, divisions, territories and population, which he enumerates with the utmost precision[1]. Quite in a different spirit is his treatment of *witches*. Two things he sees are necessary. The belief that 'witches' fly in the air and hold intercourse with the devil has to be refuted, and its existence has to be explained. For both sorts of explanation his own experience as a physician served him in good stead. Thus he not only applies a rough but effective criticism to the witch stories,—asking, for instance, with characteristic *Derbheit* (apropos of the 'witch-broth' composed of dead children boiled to jelly), 'How dead, stinking flesh could have such power?'—but tries hard to account for the story by a discussion of the nature of imagination, illustrating with some resource its liability to delusions. He quotes e.g. the *Natural Magic* of Baptista Porta[2], to show how certain drugs produce a sleep in which occur dreams 'of travelling over sea and mountains—und allerley ander lügen'; and tells a story of an old woman who had been treated with the drug, and whose persuasion, when she awoke, of the reality of her travels was so absolute that no arguments could shake it. At the same time, with characteristic inconsequence, Weier introduces the hypothesis that the devil is capable of producing these illusions, and that many of those which occur are so produced; thus supplying the more skilful of his opponents, such as Delrio, with a weapon of which they did not fail to make use; for

---

[1] 7,405,926 is the total number of demons; they are subject to 572 princes.

[2] Weier, *De pr. d.* II. 34.

diabolic agency, however remote, being once admitted, it was impossible to rebut the practical conclusion of the witch persecutors except by asserting that one might be in a certain degree implicated with the devil without deserving death, which few persons were then prepared to do.   Hence Delrio was able to make a show of magnanimous impartiality in admitting, like the rationalists, that much witchcraft was mere delusion, since the casuistry of the Inquisition was quite equal to maintaining the equal guilt of being the involuntary subject of demoniac powers, and of deliberately engaging them.

R. Scot.   Reginald Scot followed the same lines[1].   Though not a physician himself he held enlightened views about medicine, and was acquainted with the German medical works which were so freely imported during this century. He quotes from Fuchsius, for instance, an explanation of the *incubus* or mare.   He attempts to account for the belief in them by the text *viderunt filii dei filias hominum quod elegantes essent*, &c.   He brands the folly of the interpreters of dreams[2]; and though he allows certain kinds of 'divination' to be lawful, it turns out that he only means that innocent form of prophecy which foretells the weather[3].

Equitable law and scientific medicine both helped to, raise the protest against the abuse which was so flagrant an offence to both : something is also due to the rise of a more spiritual theology.   Protestantism has indeed, on the whole, not a whit less to answer for than Catholicism in respect of the witch-frenzy ; the horrors of the perse-

[1] Scot was perhaps not the first Englishman to protest against the witch superstition.   The Sta. Reg. Aug. 23, 1576, contains the entry of a book called 'A warning against the superstition of wytches and the madnes of madmen,' but the title is ambiguous.

[2] *Disc. of W.*, X. 1.   [3] *Disc. of W.*, IX. 1, 2.

cutions in England and Scotland under James and
Charles, in North Germany under such princes as the
otherwise enlightened Heinrich Julius of Brunswick[1],
and in Sweden, fully equal the utmost barbarities known
in Catholic countries.	The total effect of Protestantism
was assuredly not to diminish the dread of infernal
agency, or to check in the smallest degree the morbid
disposition to trace it in the most innocent human
actions.	On the contrary, it sensibly deepened the hold
of the diabolic scheme upon the imagination by its
abandonment of the religious safeguards devised by the
Church.	The *alt böse Feind* was at last in grim earnest,
and the Protestant world fell upon those accused of
dealings with him, with the kind of exasperation which
might be looked for in a city swarming with invisible
incendiaries and suddenly convinced that the ordinary
channels of justice are corrupt.	But while it only
plunged minds of a superstitious cast more deeply into
superstition, Protestantism nevertheless offered to calmer
reasoners a formidable weapon against it, the value of
which was already perceived, though it was reserved for
the eighteenth century to put it to full use.	The theory
of direct and universal divine government which it opposed to the Catholic conception of a hierarchy of
secondary powers, contained the germ of the view which
later dissolved away diabolic agency altogether, and
referred the supernatural exclusively to a single source.
But already it showed a tendency to assert the direct
agency of God where Catholicism had seen the activity
of demons carried on ' with divine permission.'	As the
priest ceased to mediate between the worshippers and
God, so, for minds of this class, the demon-world retired
into the background, and the Creator was restored to

[1] Soldan-Heppe, u. s. II. 88.

direct relations with his work. Weier devotes the greater
part of the first book of his *Præstigiæ* to a determination,
in his minute style, of the limits to the power of the
Devil. Chapter III. for instance, recounts 'what Satan
cannot do,'—such as passing in and out of men at the
desire of others, reading their thoughts, &c. Chapter IV.
declares explicitly that the Devil is only the executant
and servant of God; and that the magician can do
nothing supernatural without other aid. To the witch-
mongers he says in effect : your proceedings are futile,
for the Devil is incapable of doing what you accuse the
witches of accomplishing by his aid. So his follower
Brentius, quoted by Scot: 'The imperial law con-
demneth them to death that trouble and infect the aire;
but I affirme...that it is neither in the power of witch nor
divell so to doe, but in God onelie.' Nowhere however
is this view more forcibly stated than by Scot himself.
'Certainly it is neither a witch, nor divell, but a glorious
God, that made the thunder.' And again, 'If all be
true that is alledged of their doings, why should we
beleeve in Christ bicause of his miracles, when a witch
dooth as great wonders as ever he did ?' And 'what an
unapt instrument,' he adds elsewhere, 'is a toothles old
impotent and unweldie woman to flie in the aier.'

It is to be noted that Scot regards his attack upon
the witch trials as a distinctly Protestant work. In his
eyes the witch persecution is a Catholic movement,
defended by Catholic writers, promoted by Jesuits and
Dominicans, sanctioned and encouraged by the Pope.
This view was the more natural as the earlier Reformers
had had to suffer from the zeal of the Inquisitors, who
found it convenient to bring a charge of sorcery where it
was not safe to charge with heresy[1]. And even in Scot's

---

[1] 'Sithens (says. Cardanus) the springing up of Luther's sect,

day, though the persecutions of Protestants as such had
declined with their growing power, the witch persecutions
were substantially a Catholic instrument[1]. Within a very
few years after his book appeared it was to become a
thoroughly congenial weapon in the hands of Protestant
superstition. In 1590 the decidedly Protestant Heinrich
Julius kindled with new ferocity the flames which his
father had allowed to burn more intermittently: James
VI. of Scotland initiated the same work with his *Demon-
ologie:* and in 1589, Henry IV. of France—Catholic only
by policy,—was so far from remitting the persecution
that it apparently surpassed that of Henry II. and did
not fall short of that under Henry III., with which even
Bodin had been satisfied[2].

The rationalist opponents of witch persecutions had *Witchcraft
however another enemy to reckon with, less terrible in in litera-
appearance than the Inquisitors with their array of argu- ture.*
ments and their practical power of enforcing them, but
less easy to vanquish because employing a more spiritual
weapon. Both Weier[3] and Scot loudly denounce the
poets, whose vivid pictures of witchcraft had stamped the
belief in it deep in the cultivated mind, and strengthened
the instinctive superstitions of the more ignorant.
Horace's Canidia and Vergil's Sibyl had played quite as
momentous a part in the history of superstition as in that
of literature[4]; and the revival of letters, in making them

these priests have tended more diligentlie upon the execution of [the
sentences], because more wealth is to be caught from them.'

[1] On the single prince of the empire who was charged with witchcraft, see Röse, *Joh. Friedrich von Sachsen.* [A. W. W.]

[2] Soldan-Heppe, II. 161.

[3] Cf. Weier's remark: Wie grosser und kunstreicher Poet, wie
herrlicher lügner, &c.

[4] Cf. also Lucan's Erichtho in Marston's *Tragedie of Sophonisba,*
IV. I. [A. W. W.]

better known, did not diminish their authority. Among
a wider circle the mediaeval romances, transformed into
prose *Volksbücher*, kept alive some memory of the vast
apparatus of mediaeval magic. Men who freely exposed
the shams of alchemy and astrology had no word against
the more terrible sham of witchcraft. Brandt has a
chapter against the 'achtung des gestirns' 'by which
every fool guides his life,' but none against the fools
who pursued witches. Ariosto's scathing picture of a
conjurer in *Il Negromante* had no companion-piece, nor
did his greatest successor in this field, Ben Jonson,
follow up his Alchemist with any exposure of the more
deadly social scourge. Fischart, who imitated Rabelais
in making merry over the makers of sham almanacs[1],
also followed Bodin in his furious assault upon Johann
Weier, and assisted in a new and revised edition of the
Malleus[2]. Nor was there the slightest reluctance to
make poetic and dramatic capital out of the witch
superstition. The keen instinct of the English playwrights seized unhesitatingly upon a subject so rich in
those combinations of crude realism and supernatural
horror which were the 'dear delight' of an Elizabethan
audience. Middleton's *The Witch*, Heywood's *The
Lancashire Witches*, and the *Witch of Edmonton* are
three prominent examples in which the witch superstition was treated with entire realism and with entire faith.
Rationalism in this as in other subjects lay beyond the
province of the playwright. Scot's book was evidently
well known to Middleton and Heywood, but they calmly
disregarded its arguments and utilised its facts. As a
store-house of facts indeed it had no rival in England,

[1] Fischart, *Aller Praktik Grossmütter*, 1572.
[2] Bodin, *De Magorum Dæmonomania*, translated by Fischart,
1581; *Malleus Maleficarum*, Frankfort, 1582.

and became for at least a generation a classic manual
of Witch-literature for English readers. As Scot had
drawn freely from the German assailants and exponents
of the doctrine, it would not be surprising to find this or
that trait from the *Malleus* or Weier occurring in the
work of the English dramatists who used him ; and in
fact it is easy to show that more than one stone which
had been hewn out of the quarries of Germany and
hurled to-and-fro in her literary battles, finally took its
place, more or less newly wrought, in the fabric of the
English Witch-drama[1].

In Middleton's *The Witch*, we have not merely
isolated traits derived ultimately from the German inquisitors, but a group of witch figures substantially
copied from a similar group which actually existed in
Germany early in the fifteenth century. The Suabian
Dominican Nider was the first to tell the story, in his
book on the *Maleficæ* written about the time of the
Council of Constance. It is repeatedly referred to in
the *Malleus*. A certain sorcerer named Stafus, living in
the diocese of Lausanne, was captured, forced to confess,
and put to death. He left a disciple Hoppo, who after

---

[1] I may dismiss in a note an instance genuine so far as it goes,
but too slight to dwell upon. The author of the *First Part of Henry
VI.* knew his Scot well, and several touches in his portrait of the
Pucelle carry us back through him to the German assailants and the
German exponents of the doctrine of witchcraft. Douce has already
pointed out that the terms of the Pucelle's last desperate appeal
(1 *Henry VI.* v. 3), are derived from Weier through Scot (*Illustrations of Shakspere*, II. 5):

> You speedy helpers, that are substitutes
> Under the lordly monarch of the north,
> Appear, and aid me in this enterprise !

The 'monarch of the north' is Zimimar, one of the four principal
devils who each commanded one of the points of the compass.

Stafus' death raised a certain Stadlin or Stadio[1] to the dignity of witch-master. Together the two proficients[2] perform the marvels of their art,—produce hailstones and noxious winds, cause children to fall into the water before their parents' eyes, transfer a third of their neighbours' corn and dung to their own barns, &c. Stadlin as well as the master Stafus was captured, and confessed his misdeeds[3]. Hoppo's end is not recorded.

This story was substantially repeated by Scot, with the important difference, however, that he represents all three sorcerers as operating together at one time. 'It is constantly affirmed,' he tells us, 'in the *Malleus Malefi-carum*, that Stafus...had a disciple called Hoppo, who made Stadlin a maister witch, and could *all* when they list invisiblie transferre the third part of their neighbours doong . . . into their own ground, make haile tempests and floods with thunder and lightning,' &c.[4]

It was in this form that Middleton, in quest of material to add pungency to an Italian intrigue, read the story[5]. He took over the group of three from Scot, but with several changes. The male wizards become old women, conformably with the superstition which discovered witchery more readily in the sex which was most exposed to the seductions of a masculine devil. Thus he speaks of 'grannam Stadlin.' ˙The masculine name of the principal, Stafus, is accordingly altered to Hecate,

---

[1] *Mall. Malef.* 'Stadio' in I. 15, 'Stadlin' in III. 6. Dyce, in his edition of Middleton, already gave the reference.

[2] 'hi duo' says the *Malleus*.

[3] *Malleus*, pt. II. qu. I. 6.

[4] *Discovery of Witchcraft*, XII. 5.

[5] In the story of Belleforest (No. 73), Rosamonde simply poisons her second husband Helmige (=Almachildes) without recourse to witchcraft.

and she is at the same time provided, like Shakspere's
Sycorax, with a son, a Caliban without pathos and without poetry, the foul and brutish Firestone[1].

The group, Hecate, Stadlin and Hoppo, thus repre-
sent the original Stafus, Stadlin and Hoppo of the
Malleus ; Stadlin's powers combine those of the original
Stadlin and Hoppo:

> Stadlin 's within ;
> She raises all the sudden ruinous storms,
> That shipwreck barks and tear up growing oaks.

Hecate, finally, is a much more important figure than
her Shaksperean counterpart. She does not merely
intervene at rare intervals in the meetings of her inferiors,
but mingles familiarly with them at all times. Shakspere's
Hecate is a queen, hedged about with the sombre
divinity of the lower world, and gaining a certain majesty
from the comparative passiveness of her part. Middleton's is an active ruler of her domain, ordering all that
is done there, superintending the goings-out and the
comings-in, and receiving all visitors in person. Macbeth
is hailed only by the three weird sisters, and never sees
their more dreadful mistress; his counterparts in Middleton, the lover seeking to make his betrothed's marriage
unfruitful, and the Duchess plotting her enemy's death,
are honoured with familiar consultations by the prosaic
Stafus-Hecate of the younger poet. In a word, Middleton's Hecate is as essential to the plot as Shakspere's
is otiose.

It is well known that this otioseness, among other
things, has been made the ground for denying Hecate a
place in the original version of Macbeth[2]. I am inclined

Hecate in The Witch and in Macbeth.

---

[1] Like Caliban he is called 'moon-calf.'
[2] Clark and Wright: *Macbeth*, Introduction.

to accept that view.   Few passages in any mixed play of
Shakspere's make a stronger impression of interpolation
than the first appearance of Hecate (III. 5), so gratuitous,
so wholly unprepared for, and so entirely unexcused by
an adequate motive.   For the motive which she actually
alleges is, on any hypothesis, feebly invented.   She, 'the
mistress of your charms,' 'the close contriver of all
harms,' has been neglected at the very moment when a
golden opportunity occurred of showing 'the glory of our
art'   But the 'close contriver' might certainly be expected to be on the spot when any business so important
as the meeting with Macbeth was arranged, which we
know was not impromptu[1]; and if by any accident she
was not, what is this petty accident or this petty cabal
to the reader of *Macbeth?*   Hecate may have good
grounds for her injured vanity, but they can hardly have
seemed sufficiently relevant to account for her otherwise
unprovoked appearance, except to a dramatist who was
intent at all costs on making her appear.   And if it be
said that she enters also in order to prepare the apparitions which subsequently appear in the second scene
with Macbeth, it can scarcely be supposed that the apparitions could not have been otherwise accounted for.   The
weird sisters of the first scene know apparently of no
limit to their power, and no superior;—'The three weird
sisters hand in hand, Posters of the sea and land, Thus
do go about, about;' they are to all appearance genuine
representatives in a clouded and obscure form, of the
mystic Norns; and the intrusion, almost at the eleventh
hour, of a fourth is as incongruous as it is superfluous.

It must be added too that, unlike as the functions of
the two Hecates are, they have a trait in common,—one

[1] Sc. 1: 'Where the place?—Upon the heath.—There to meet
with Macbeth.'

wholly foreign to the Witches of Shakspere. The Hecate of *The Witch* indulges unequivocally in the gross passions which the witch superstition, with peculiar loathsomeness, regularly attributed to its victims. Firestone is her *incubus;* if she gives Almachildes her aid it is with a view to his love, while her profession of Sebastian,

> I know he loves me not, nor there's no hope on't.
> Tis for the love of mischief I do this,

equally implies that, in her view, such love was the natural payment for her services. The Hecate of *Macbeth* has no amours of this kind; but she nevertheless in a single phrase indicates precisely this view of the nature and reward of her calling: 'All you have done Hath been but for a wayward son, Spiteful and wrathful, who, as others do, Loves for his own ends, not for you[1].' Those words, slight as they are, stand alone in the play: they are the glimpse of the cloven foot, the isolated hint of the vulgar theory of witchcraft, intruded not merely without any support in the remainder of the play, but in grotesque contradiction to the evident relations of the witches with Macbeth. Hecate was doubtless only confusedly remembering the passions of her own Middletonian phase when she startled the weird sisters with this warning against illusions hardly natural to those who 'seem not like the inhabitants of earth.'

I regard the Hecate of *Macbeth*, then, as a link, probably the last, in a series which opened with the story told for a ferocious practical purpose by the authors of the *Malleus*, repeated thence in the interests of fair play by Weier and Scot, and made by Middleton the groundwork

---

[1] This passage has of course been repeatedly noticed before. Cf. esp. Messrs Clark and Wright, *Macbeth*, Introd. p. x.

of a drama. The links may be slight, but it is not to be forgotten that the drama which this German story supplied with one element of its plot, was probably the first attempt in English to put a witch-subject to dramatic use. Middleton, though he apparently kept back his play for some years after it was written, was in this respect a pioneer. Others rapidly came forward to work along the same track; with one exception, however, they drew their witch scenery as exclusively from contemporary English society as their dramatic art from the contemporary English stage. That exception requires a brief notice.

Heywood (assisted by Brome): *Lancashire Witches*.
In 1634 Thomas Heywood embodied in a drama one of the principal events in the history of English witchcraft, —the great Lancashire trials of the previous year. The play which resulted,—the *Lancashire Witches*,—is interesting partly because it combines the two kinds of dramatic incident in which Heywood was most at home,— the domestic and the mythological. It unites a motive akin to that of the *Woman killed with Kindness* and the *English Traveller* with others drawn from that world of superstition and occult art of which Heywood had all his life been a persevering student and in which he was probably more deeply versed than any of his fellow dramatists. The character of the erring and repentant wife he had made his own; and the peculiar tenderness with which he repeatedly touched it was evidently something more than the stock pathos of a clever playwright. Mrs Generous in the *Lancashire Witches* is the sister of the erring wives in the *Woman killed with Kindness* and the *English Traveller*. She is not seduced from her husband, as they are, by a human lover; but she yields to the fascination of the powers of darkness and becomes a witch. Generous, her husband, views her fault like his earlier counterparts, more in sorrow than in anger, and

when she meets him after the commission of her fault
and confesses her guilt he forgives her in a scene little
inferior to the corresponding scenes in which Mr Frank-
ford and Young Geraldine receive the last penitent con-
fessions of another sort of guilt.   Popular superstition
which forms the main subject of the play, was particularly
well-fitted to enter intimately into a domestic drama.   This
application of witchcraft was essentially new in the
drama.   Middleton's witch and Decker's (the Witch of
Edmonton) are outside the pale of society,—the one a
dangerous sorceress, the other a despised though still
dreaded outcast.   Heywood, the dramatist of intimate
family life, gives us the witch who is also wife and
mother,—a motive far more capable of pathos than
either, though it can hardly be called original at a time
when the despised and outcast Mother Sawyers were not
seldom followed to the stake by the active housewife and
the fresh village maiden.

But the effect of this felicitously chosen situation
was impaired by an incongruous episode drawn from
Heywood's multifarious reading in German magical lore,
one evidently a favourite with him, for it was already
embodied in his vast repertory of supernatural learning,
the *Hierarchy of Angels* [1].

Johann Teutonicus of Halberstadt [2] is said to recount
how he took vengeance on some arrogant comrades
who taunted him with bastardy, by showing them the
image of their own fathers,—not the lords or knights
whom they took to be such, but much humbler recipients

---

[1] Book VIII. 512.   Halliwell *Dict.* under this play.
[2] I am unable to give the reference for this story.   Johann
Semeca (Teutonicus) was a canonist and ecclesiastical dignitary of
Halberstadt.   His commentary on the *Decretum Gratiani* is the only
one of his works accessible to me.

of their mothers' favours[1]. Such a story was quite congenial to the tendencies of the English drama, in which the triumphs of bastards had often been dwelt on with a curious relish of which the secret is perhaps to be found in Edmund's soliloquy. Whetstone is however a feeble successor of the doughty canon of Halberstadt. He is no magician, and the whole burden of contrivance is thrown, as may be supposed, upon his witch-aunt. By her aid Whetstone invites the gallants who have insulted him to a feast, pleasantly deprecating their shamefast apologies: 'What is that among friends, for I would fain know which among you all knows his own father?'—and triumphs like Teutonicus[2].

---

[1] Such reproductions of dead heroes were of course among the commonest feats of the old magician, as of the new spiritualist. Not to speak of obvious instances, I may mention that Heywood himself had quoted in the *Gynaekaeon* (ed. 1601, p. 101), Weier's story of the magician who summoned up Achilles and Hector for the delectation of Maximilian I.

[2] *The Lanc. Witches*, Act IV. The further detail of this somewhat repulsive story may be given in a note:—

'But tell me, gentlemen,' asks Whetstone, at the close of the meal, is there any amongst you that hath a mind to see his father?' *Bantam.* 'Why who shall show him?' *Whetstone.* 'Thats all one, if any man here desire it, let him but speake the word, and 'tis sufficient.' *Bantam.* 'Why, I would see my father.' Thereupon enters the form of 'a pedant dancing to music;' the strains done he points at Bantam, and looks full in his face. *Whetstone.* 'Do you know him that looks so full in your face?' *B.* 'Yes, well, a pedant in my father's house, who being young taught me my ABC.'...Whetstone explains the circumstances to Bantam's confusion and his companions' merriment. 'Why laugh you, gentlemen? It may be more mens cases than his or mine.' The images of their fathers in fact follow, 'a nimble Taylor dauncing,' and a stableman with switch and curricomb. Lastly, Whetstone caps his triumph by displaying his own father, no menial like theirs, but a gallant. 'Now gentlemen make me your President,' he exclaims in triumph: 'learn your duties and do as I do.' His vanquished persecutors are

This isolated and insignificant story is only interesting as an indication of the complex threads of legend and learning which went to the making of the witch of drama even more than the witch of common superstition. The various departments of magic were not curiously distinguished. The sorcerer was plundered to enrich the witch, as the witch to enlarge the powers of the sorcerer.

In the chapter which I here close it has been continually necessary to trench upon an apparently remote branch of the subject, which the idiosyncracy of the sixteenth century, particularly in Germany, brought into the closest touch with it. The dread of magic did not prevent it from calling up ludicrous ideas; the terrible sorcerer to one man was the ridiculous mountebank to another; the very extravagance of his feats made them laughable the moment they ceased to be imposing. Nay, in the same hands, the subject could become alternately humorous and awful without the slightest sense of strain; Faustus and Fortunatus use their giant's power like buffoons; from Faustus sealing his bond in his blood to Faustus making game of the pope, from the Ulenspiegel-like jests with the horse-dealer and the knight to one of the most thrilling death-scenes in literature, was a transition which assuredly neither German reader nor English spectator dreamed of resenting or finding strange. In the following chapter I propose to make the same transition, and to pass from what I have ventured to call the Faustus-cycle, to that literature of Jest which may be equally called, from its most national and on the whole most typical representative, the *Cycle of Ulenspiegel.*

at first inclined to resent this inversion of their position, but finally agree in good Elizabethan fashion to forget their differences in a revel.

CHAPTER V.

THE ULENSPIEGEL CYCLE.

German Jest-books of the 16th century. IF the wit of a nation were measured by its industry in collecting good things, Germany might have met the famous question of the Père Bouhours with complete equanimity. No literature is richer than hers in those compilations of amusing anecdote of which the sixteenth century was everywhere so prolific, and which owed their extraordinary development if not their origin to the new *II. Bebel:* literary influence of the bourgeois class. The first *Faceti-arum libri* stimulus indeed came from elsewhere; it was not the *tres,* 1506 naïve grossness of a Nürnberg Fastnachtsspiel but the *(pr.* 1508). elegant and pointed grossness of Italian Humanism *J. Pauli: Schimpf* which served as model for the *Facetiae* of Bebel[1]; and *und Ernst,* the second great Jest-book, the *Schimpf und Ernst* of *1519.* the monk Johannes Pauli, though owing much to Bebel, is still more closely related to mediaeval collections, such as the *Gesta Romanorum,* of moral *examples* for use in the pulpit. Bebel was the direct follower of the ardent and purely pagan Poggio; Pauli drew no small part of his work from the anecdotes which had lately been heard in Strassburg cathedral from the lips of the most

[1] Bebel's materials were indeed in great part German enough, adapted, with much trouble as he confesses, from native originals ('has nostras facetias, quas summa cum difficultate ad latinum eloquium commutavi'), but as a *raconteur* he is altogether out of the range of his successors.

remarkable preacher of the age, Geiler von Kaisersberg, as he illustrated its most famous moral satire, the *Ship of Fools*[1].

But when some years later, this beginning was fol-lowed up, it was in a different quarter. Soon after the middle of the century the production of jest-books came suddenly into vogue; but their authors are now neither scholars, as such, nor monks, but genuine citizens, often of official standing, and their contents, though in great part founded on either Bebel or Pauli, retain scarcely a trace of the formal elegance of the one, and but few of the moral earnestness of the other. Jörg Wickram, town-clerk of Burgheim, one of the most attractive figures in the literary history of Alsace[2], led the way; and he was rapidly followed by his fellow-Alsatians Jacob Frey, town-clerk at Maursmünster, and Martin Montanus of Strassburg; while across the Rhine the congenial vein was continued by Velten Schumann, Wilhelm Kirchhof, and Michael Lindener, the last-named one of the most extraordinary of the genial Grobians, the '*frommen, auserlesenen, bundten und rundten Schnudel-*

Later Jest-books.

---

[1] Pauli's preface, like his title *Schimpf* (i.e. Scherz) *und Ernst*, well illustrates the middle position which he holds between the Facetist and the preacher: He has written with three objects, [1] *damit die geistlichen kinder in den beschloszznen klöstern etwa zu lesen haben, damit sie zu zeiten iren geist mögen erlustigen und ruwen,*...[2] *auch die uff den schlössern und bergen wonen und geil sein, erschrockenliche und ernstliche ding finden, davon sie gebessert werden; auch* [3] *das die predicanten exempel haben, die schleferlichen menschen zu erwecken, und lustig zu hören machen.* Pauli has been admirably edited by Oesterley in the Stuttgard Litt. Verein Bibl. Bd. 85.

[2] Cf. especially for his share in turning the romance into the modern novel, Scherer's *Die Anfänge des deutschen Prosa-romans* (Quellen und Forschungen, XXI.).

butzen,' who ever spent wit and learning in giving a literary flavour to filth. Rough and gross-minded as many of these men were, nearly all had a practical, and in its way a moral, purpose, commonly disclosed with more or less sounding epithets in their preface or title-page. Pauli had chiefly had in view his own clerical order, though not without a hope that his moral examples might benefit an unruly aristocracy. Wickram and his followers write explicitly in behalf of the merchant class of the towns. The rapid growth of luxury had produced not only ampler leisure, but a higher standard of social intercourse, a more deliberate cultivation of amusing talk. To the noble absorbed in war and hunting, to the peasant immersed in the wearing labours of the field, society meant little more than the unceremonious drinking-bout that closed the day in castle or in tavern. But civic life brought with it countless occasions of more or less formal and involuntary intercourse, for which a store of '*Schimpfreden,*' '*boszen,*' '*spudelingen,*' '*grillen,*' '*tauben,*' and '*schwänke,*' was the best of equipments. The tedious sea-voyage, the long diligence journey across country to Nürnberg or Köln, or to the great national fairs of Frankfurt or Leipzig, the evenings spent in rough country inns (where supper, as we know, was often deferred till the last chance of more guests was gone[1]), the critical intervals of convivial intercourse in garden or banquet hall, the tavern, where folk sat, says Lindener, like a 'hültzner latern[2],' nay, even the

[1] Cf. the chapter on 'Deversoria,' in Erasmus' *Colloquia,*—a chapter from which Scott drew nearly every detail of the tavern described in *Anne of Geierstein.*

[2] Erich Schmidt in *Allg. D. Biog.* art. 'Lindener,'—a little master-piece (it is not much over a page) of combined wealth of detail and force of style.

briefer emergencies of being shaved or taking a bath[1], were all relieved by the possession of one of these com- pendiums of good things,—*Rollwagenbüchlin*[2], *Nacht- büchlin, Rastbüchlin, Wegkürzer, Wendunmuth* ('turn away gloom'), *Gartengesellschaft,* as they were christened with pointed reference to their intended use[3].

    I have purposely begun with these miscellaneous *Character-* collections of Jests from all sources, late in date and *istics of the German* loose in form though they are, as more representative of *Jest.* the whole compass of German humour, than the more specialised groups of anecdotes which, like the Histories of Amis or Ulenspiegel, attached themselves to a single famous name. Even with this advantage however, it cannot be said that the national powers of humour appear either brilliant or versatile, and far less if we look only to that meagre fraction of the facetiae currently read in Germany which was actually produced there. It is a humour with no trace either of the caustic subtlety of Italy or the ease and gaiety of France, and wholly

---

    [1] Even Bebel had had the tedium of bathing particularly in view. Cf. the dedication of his *Facetiae* to an invalid friend, the Abbot of Zweifelden, then taking the waters:—' aggressus sum ea commentari et fingere...quae maxime in thermis agentibus idonea et grata esse existimo.'

    [2] Like our 'railway-reading,' ' Eisenbahnlektur.'

    [3] Cf. Wickram's *Rollwagenbüchlin,* 1555 : *Ein neüws, vor unerhörts Büchlein, darinn vil guter Schwenck und Historien begriffen werden, so man in schiffen und auff den rollwegen, dess- gleichen in scherhaüseren und badstuben, zu langweiligen zeiten erzellen mag,...Allen Kauffleuten so die Messen hin und wider brau- chen,* &c....Frey, on the other hand, chooses the more romantic hours of the merchant's day for his *Gartengesellschaft* (1556): *Ein new hüpsches und schimpflichs Büchlein...darin vil frölichs Gesprächs Schimpffreden, Speywerck....wie ye zu zeytten die selben inn den schönen Gerten, bei den küilen Brunnen, auff den grünen Wysen, bey der Edlen Music, auch andern ehrlichen Gesellschafften,* &c.

alien to the fancy and pathos with which, since
Shakspere, it has tended to ally itself in England; it is
the rough humour of practical jokes, or the simple
humour of ignorant misunderstandings, or the gross
humour of some unequalled feat of obscenity, some un-
matched prowess at the table. To a great extent it turns
upon mere class distinctions,—distinctions singularly in-
veterate in Germany, and no less palpable in her literature than in her history. A whole family of jests sprang
from the casual, involuntary collision of divergent
customs, unlike moral standards, unequal knowledge;
foolish scholars come to grief at the University[1], ignorant
priests before their bishop or at the hands of some
shrewd peasant of their own flock[2], and the peasant
himself in innumerable chance encounters with priest[3],

---

[1] E.g. the amusing story of the Erfurt student who attempted
to write verses like Hessus by *measuring* his lines (Lindener,
Katzipori; Hub, *Die kom. Litt. des 16ten Jahrh.*, p. 334). Cf. *Wegkürzer* sig. C iii. (Hub, p. 325), of the ignorant scholar who appealed
to Maximilian to be made doctor ; *Schimpf und Ernst*, No. 95, of the
Count whose ignorance of Latin put him to shame before the Pope ;
and countless others.

[2] One of the best of these is that (Wickram, *Rollwagenbüchlin*
sig. D vii.), of the Pfarrer who required his people to substitute a low
whistle for the candid but offensive *Du lügst.* In the course of
a sermon on the creation, he committed himself to the statement
that the Lord, after creating Adam, 'leaned him up against a rail.'
A whistle interrupted him. 'Wie, du meinst ich liege?'—'Nein
Herr, ich wolt aber gern wissen, wer den zun gemacht hat.' Cf.
Schimpf und Ernst No. 585 (priest and citizen).

[3] E.g. the story of the shepherd who, having learned the prayer
Agnus Dei, miserere mei, uses it a year later in the form 'O Hammel
Gottes, &c.,' on the ground that the lamb by that time must have
become a sheep (Kirchhoff, *Wendunmuth* I. 244, and long before,
in our *C Mery Tales* No. 65). This class is particularly abundant
in Bebel. Far more rarely do we get a glimpse of genuine peasant
humour, as in the mock 'crowner's quest' held over the dead wolf

scholar[1] and citizen[2];—a clear reflexion of the strong
bias of town against country which animated both the
writers and readers of their jests. Tales of this sort are
like falling water,—they depend merely on a difference
of level. The eccentricities of particular districts and
professions supply another group;—the greed and uncouth dialect of the Saxon[3], the eccentric theology of the
Swabian[4]; the slyness of tailors, the incredible lying

(Frey, *Gartengesellschaft*, p. 69; Hub, p. 310), and the Rollwagen
story of one who horrified the pious pilgrims to the shrine of Mary
of Einsiedeln by declaring that she was his sister, having been,
as he afterwards explained, the work of his father, a sculptor.

[1] E.g. the students' goose-stealing adventure, turning on rustic
ignorance of Latin. An alarm being raised, *Habes?* asks one, *Habeo*
cries the second, *Cito fuge* replies the first; and the peasant reports
Messrs Citofuge, Habeo and Habes for the theft of his goose
(Lindener, *Rastbüchlein*, p. 131, Hub, p. 346). Cf. Hub. p. 344,
also from the *Rastbüchlein*, where a peasant casually drinking with
scholars takes their festive *Prosit!* for an intimation that there is only
brosi on the table.

[2] E.g. the peasant and the Strassburg barber (Pauli, *Schimpf und
Ernst* No. 601); the price of shaving is a pfennig; the peasant
demands to be shaved for a heller ($=\frac{1}{2}$ pf.), the barber shaves one
side of his face. Cf. the story of the peasants who came to a
painter with a commission for a painted Christ. 'Would they have
him painted alive or dead?' After consulting a while they reply
'Alive; and then if we don't like it, *so können wir in selber wol
zu tod schlagen.*' *Schimpf und Ernst* No. 409.

[3] E.g. *Wendunmuth* I. 206, a Saxon in an inn takes fish for
beans, and has to pay in proportion; *Rastbüchlin* LII. (Hub, p. 347),
and many more.

[4] E.g. *Wendunmuth* I. 265,—a Swabian peasant dying, and
indignant at the 'unreasonableness' of his death, appeals from God
to the Apostles; and ib. 266, where another in the same circumstances, assured that *Gott einen allenthalben finden kann*, tests the
assurance by concealing himself when the priest comes with the last
sacrament. He cannot be found, the priest returns unsuccessful,
and 'God' with him.

powers of smiths[1], the solemn follies of village alder-
men[2]. From the comedy of mere natural contrasts of
usage, it is an easy step to the more brutal but more
pungent fun of the practical joke in which these are
deliberately taken advantage of. And it is this fun of
the practical joke ('*loser Streich*,' '*Schwank*') which
above all others forms the staple of German humour in
the sixteenth century; so far indeed did it predominate over the rest that *Schwänke*—'pranks'—became a
generic name for the whole tribe of jests[3]. It is here that
the full force of German class-distinctions is felt[4]; the
peasant and the priest, whose separation from the burgher
society was the deepest, are still the principal victims;
and after them, with a sprinkling devoted to scholars[5] and

---

[1] The somewhat cheap amusement of *Lügengeschichten* was
cultivated with extraordinary zest in Germany; but for the most
part the result was merely extravagant nonsense, without the genuine
humour of e.g. Heywood's *Four P's*. Cf. e.g. the tame conclusion
of the parallel story of Six Students, who similarly compete in telling
the greatest lie, *Nachtbüchlein* I. p. 39, Hub, p. 352. The *Lügengeschichten* culminated in the adventures of the *Finkenritter*—an early
Münchausen—at the end of the century, as the *Streich* pure and
simple in those of *Ulenspiegel* at its commencement. There is
a large infusion of the *Lügengeschichte* manner in the more directly
satirical *Schiltbürger* tales.

[2] The famous *Schiltbürger* tales, a more classical form of our
Gothamites, are the veritable epic of the rustic Dogberry.

[3] *Jest* (gestum), like *joke*, had itself originally, of course, a reference to practical *feats;* the 'gestes' of Robin Hood mark the
transition, and correspond nearly to *Schwänke*.

[4] It is characteristic that in some of these books the distinction
of classes is made the basis of the arrangement. Thus the first book
of *Wendunmuth* proceeds from kings, nobles, doctors, students
to merchants, innkeepers, boors, &c. : and Pauli's work is throughout arranged under headings which connect it with the *Narrenschiff*
and the mediaeval *genre* of ' Satire on all classes.'

[5] One of the most celebrated is the story of the Magister of

soldiers¹, come the various occupations within the ranks
of the citizens themselves,—the innkeeper², tailor³ and
miller⁴,—whose discomfiture has always tended to
assume a comic air; while, very rarely, we have a glimpse
of the sanguinary struggles of *Rath* and *Bürgerschaft*
which made so much of the local history of the century
too bitter for a jest-book⁵. It was such things which stirred

Wittenberg (afterwards dramatised by Ayrer) who ventured to put
on the Fool's Cap under the protection of what he supposed an
impenetrable disguise of paint; but the painter had used water
only. *Wendunmuth* I. 139. Of a different kind is that—one of the
host of 'Pennal possen'—*Schimpf und Ernst* (No. 679), where a
student suspected by the Magister of his *Burs* of stealing a Vergil, is
convicted by a kind of mock ordeal (a piece of cheese is given to all
the students; the culprit will be discovered by his being unable to chew
it; to ensure the result a stone is secreted in that of the man suspected).

¹ E.g. the story, also dramatised by Ayrer, and bearing an obvious
analogy to a scene in *Twelfth Night*, how *Ein Schreiber bezahlt
einen Trommelschläger*, viz. by making him the bearer of a letter
which enjoins that he shall be treated as a madman. *Wendunmuth*,
I. 142.

² E.g. the story of the guest with a box which at the table d'hote
he insists on keeping on the seat beside him. The landlord charges
him twice for the extra place, upon which he fills the box with fish
and fowl:—*ich muss imm auch zu fressen geben, denn er ist lähr
worden* (*Katzipori* IV., Hub p. 332), and the well-known story
von dem gesang so die wirt gern hören, Wendunmuth I. 192, from
Bebel.

³ E.g. '*Ein Schneider wil im selbst ein bar Hosen machen,*' and
involuntarily scamps the work as if it were for a customer (*Wendunmuth* I. 231); cf. *ib.* I. 230-3. The story of *The tailor in heaven*
(*Rollwagen*, Hub p. 300) is a particularly riotous piece of popular
fancy.

⁴ E.g. *Wendunmuth* I. 288. The rapacity and cunning of the
'molitores' is repeatedly touched by Bebel also.

⁵ E.g. the story, rather a satirical fable than an anecdote, of the
town where the younger citizens had expelled the older, with
the exception of one who is secretly maintained by his son, and who

the loudest and most genuine laughter of sixteenth
century Germany; successful tricks which paid off an old
score or simply gratified unprovoked malice, 'jests' in
which the element of mere horse-play almost always
overpowered the wit, and sheer feats of audacious frank-
ness in that region of mere nastiness and obscenity where,
it has been said, 'comic ideas are to be had for the pick-
ing up by those whom they do not offend at the cost of
those whom they do,'—a region which, it may be added,
neither Wickram nor Frey, both of whom professed to
write only what was fit for the ears of 'erbare Frawen
und Junckfrawen,' by any means avoided.

Schwank-heroes (Amis, Ulen-spiegel, &c.). But the *Schwank* was not only the staple of the
ordinary Jest-book; it had its own more exclusive and
select domain.   No kind of anecdote more readily attaches itself to a familiar name; and the floating memory
of some facetious friar or parson, some rustic Autolycus,
some court-jester,—nay, of some altogether legendary
hero of another age, became a depository for the un-
claimed 'humour' of a whole country-side.   A literary
process of extreme slightness sufficed to convert these
loose accretions into the popular books of adventure
which go under the notorious and somewhat unsavoury
names of Amis and the Kalenberger, Leu and Rausch,
Ulenspiegel and Markolf, names which rapidly became
current symbols for the genius of practical joking in all
its moods and phases.   Amis is the German counterpart
of the famous personator of the Abbot of Canterbury:
the Kalenberger is the facetious parish priest, who out-

recovers his authority by the thoroughly *Märchen*-like expedient
of a lucky answer. The king tests the wisdom of the new Rath by
inquiring the best means of preserving salt from worms: they are
wholly at fault until advised, by the sole survivor of the old one, to
reply with a prescription of mule's milk. *Schimpf und Ernst*, No.442.

wits his parishioners, makes game of his bishop and extracts unintended bounties from his patron; Rausch, the young novice in the convent, who lays traps for the prior and the cook; Markolf, the foul but witty boor who paralyses the wisdom of Solomon with keen rejoinders and his modesty with the tricks of an unclean animal; Ulenspiegel, the knavish peasant, who retaliates on the haughty citizens with strokes in which the literature of the Schwank probably reaches its acme of fatuous insolence. In these homely yet vivid figures, and particularly in Ulenspiegel, the best known and the most purely national of all, the low life of the later Middle Ages of Germany lives before us; we hurry to and fro between tavern and workshop, highway and market-place, stable and scullery. Every line of Ulenspiegel vividly records the essential qualities of the society which made a hero of him; its gross appetites, its intellectual insensibility, its phlegmatic good humour, its boisterous delight in all forms of physical energy and physical prowess, its inexhaustible interest in the daily events of the bodily life, and the stoutness of nerve which permitted it to find uproarious enjoyment in mere foulness of stench. The whole interest of Ulenspiegel for us is social, not literary; all his jests together would scarcely yield a grain of Attic salt; we could not read the book but for the light which it throws upon a society which could and did.

Nor was the enormous success which these histories *Influence* enjoyed at all confined to their native land. In no other *abroad.* chapter of her literary intercourse with Germany did England contrive to appropriate so large a proportion of the total produce as exactly in this, where the acquisition was perhaps of least value. If Markolf, by far the most interesting of all, has left but few and scanty

traces, Ulenspiegel, the most repulsive, met with a reception in the England of Edward and Elizabeth only
exceeded by that which he had already found in the
France of Francis I.; the Kalenberger was the subject
of an English prose romance; while Rausch, in addition,
became the hero of at least two celebrated dramas, and
even won secure footing in our native folk-lore. To
follow out the fortunes of these four figures in England
will be the work of the present chapter.

On the other hand, Amis, Englishman as he was
reputed to be, remained unknown in that *stat ze Tâmîs*
where he was said to have lived; and Leu, 'the second
Kalenberger,' did not share even the moderate popularity
of the first. And of the whole series of miscellaneous
jest-books which began with Bebel, it would seem that
not one has left the slightest mark upon our literature,
with the exception (to a very small extent) of Bebel
himself[1].

---

[1] Two stories in the *C Mery Tales* 1526 are drawn from Bebel:
cf. No. 11, '*Of the woman that sayd her wooer came to late,*' with
Bebel, II. 69, *de quadam muliere citissime nubente post obitum primi
viri;* and No. 83, '*Of the parson that sayd masse of requiem for
Crystys sowle,*' with ib. I. 7, *de inscitia cuiusdam sacerdotis fabula
perfaceta.* Both are expanded, however, and probably separated
by one or two removes of oral tradition from Bebel's text. Cf.
Oesterley's edition of the Göttingen *C Mery Tales*, where the
references are given.—In later days, a writer who loved the bye-
ways of literature, Thomas Heywood, laid Bebel under contribution
for several of the stories in his huge repertory of curious things, *The
Hierarchy of Angels;* the most pointed of which is that of one
Daiglinus at Constanz, who remarked to a simple fellow that he
would make an admirable *consul*, having hitherto so carefully
husbanded his wisdom that none had escaped. Bebel I. 84, '*Pro-
verbium in parum prudentes.*' Heywood seems not to have understood Bebel's farfetched version of '*Bürgermeister.*' Cf. also the
story of an ass, p. 448. In regard to the later Jest-books of Pauli,

I.

I have tacitly assumed Markolf to belong fairly to the MARKOLF. class of genuine Teutonic jesters, the Kalenbergers and the Ulenspiegels, with whom we are here solely concerned. The assumption however needs explanation, and the extreme complexity of the legend makes it impossible that this should be very brief[1]. In England, France, and Germany a very slender germ of common tradition underwent developments in part quite distinct, in part mutually reacting, and finally in the sixteenth century almost indistinguishably blended; and it is necessary to attempt their separation.

The perplexed problem of the influence of the Rabbinical traditions of Solomon is for the present purpose of little concern[2]; the questions of the Queen of Sheba,

Wickram, &c., the few stories which they have in common with such English collections as the *C Mery Tales*, the *Merry Tales and Quick Answers*, are explained by the fact that both used a common source, usually Bromyard. In other cases, where the source is unknown, the Englishman has priority, as in the story of *Agnus dei* (*C Mery Tales*, 67—1526, and *Wendunmuth*, I. 244—1563).

[1] In addition to Kemble's in some points inevitably antiquated but still classical introduction to the Old-English *Salomon and Saturnus* cf. esp. Schaumberg, *Salomo und Morolf* in Paul and Braune's *Beiträge*, Bd. II. 1 ff., and Vogt, *Die deutschen Dichtungen von Salomon und Markolf*, of which however only the first part, an exhaustive account of the minstrel's epic *Salman und Morolt*, is yet published.

[2] The question of source is solved by Brunet in the airy fashion characteristic of a good deal of French scholarship: '[le dialogue] est d'origine grecque ou plutôt orientale.' *La France Litt. au xvme siècle, s. v.* 'Salomon.'—The materials are hardly complete enough to admit of a final solution.

the riddles of Hiram, furnished at the most the general scheme of confronting the wise king with a rival or an interrogator[1], a scheme which resolves itself at once into that, everywhere familiar in the west, of the *disputatio*. One form of such a *disputatio*, distinguished by its occasional high poetry and the mythic dignity of its characters, but not by essential form from the crowd of mediaeval catechisms and *Elucidaria*, is the Old-English *Salomon and Saturnus*, where Saturnus, as a 'Chaldaean Earl' of many travels and vast experience, probes the still vaster knowledge of the Jewish king on a variety of theological problems[2]. It shared however the general oblivion which overtook Old-English literature, and stands in complete isolation from the later development of the legend whether on the continent or in England itself. The essential steps in this development undoubtedly belong to the former. There the name Marcolf for the first time occurs in connexion with that of Solomon in the psalms of Notker, as engaging with the king, no longer, like Saturnus, in a disputation of the master and scholar type, but in a true polemical, yet still quite serious and decorous, debate[3]. The evidence of the earliest allusions in France, north and south, though slight, points equally to a discussion in which Marcolf is not yet the low jester Marcolf who ranks with Ulenspiegel and the Kalenberger, but a worthy antagonist, his rival in learning, whose name was wont to be coupled with his

---

[1] Cf. the arguments of Schaumberg u. s., who wholly rejects the notion of an oriental origin for the legend.

[2] Cf. Kemble u. s., and ten Brink, *Gesch. d. engl. Litt.* I. 113.

[3] Kemble u. s. p. 13; Schaumberg u. s. p. 33; 'Waz ist ioh anderes daz man Marcholfum saget sih *éllenon* wider proverbiis Salomonis? An diên allen sint wort *scôniû* âne wârheit.'

in the proverbial praise of wisdom and fair speech[1].
And from the probable fact that a very early form of the
dialogue received a clerical commentary[2], it is probable
that it dealt with theology, and that Marcolf was the
ingenious champion of a disputed doctrine,—or, as the
cleric Notker put it more strongly,—the pleader, in fair
words, for an untruth.

With the twelfth century however, the conception of Dialogue
Marcolf begins to change. The rival of Solomon is *of Salomo*
et Mar-
degraded into his parodist; the decorous sage of fair *culphus.*
speech becomes a boor, full of the gross though pregnant
humour of the people. The poetical catechism, the
serious debate, give place to a formal rivalry in shrewd
sayings, a competition of homely mother wit with divine
wisdom. The Latin dialogue in which this conception
was first embodied, is no doubt substantially represented
in the well-known *Collationes, quas dicuntur fecisse mutuo*
rex Salomo...et Marculphus; in the oldest version this un-

---

[1]   Cil que m'a vout triste alegre
     Sab mais......
     que Salomos ni Marcols
    Rambaut d'Auvergne, quot. Kemble and Schaumberg.
     Mes de tant soit chescun certayn
     Keu le monde nad si bon ecriveyn
     ni fieust à tant comme Salomon sage
     et com Marcun de bon langage.
          MS. Arundel 507, 81, quot. Kemble.
The latter testimony exactly coincides with Notker's *scôniû wort.*
In the later dialogue he is still *eloquentissimus,* but in a manner less
likely to attract either the poet or the preacher.

[2] Schaumberg agrees with Kemble in giving this very plausible
interpretation to a confused description in the *Hist. litt. de la*
France, tom. III. 565, of a MS. in the Bibl. Nat. : 'La quatorzième
pièce est adressée à un nommé Robert, à qui l'auteur fait l'honneur
d'un travail sur (les formules de) Marculfe et de commentaires sur
(les livres de) Salomon, &c.   Schaumb., u. s. p. 35.

doubtedly consisted of the interchange of proverbs alone; the framework of narrative which encloses this in almost every known version, though it can be but little younger, is easily separable[1], and belongs in part to a different school of humour.

A few words will suffice to characterise the former. Markolf's replies are in great part, as I have said, parodies, not less in style and manner than in matter. He mimics the solemn air of Solomon, and the comic effect is enhanced by the rhythmical balance which causes the successive pairs of saying and parody to recall to the ear the familiar parallel phrasing of Hebrew poetry. He utters ridiculous precepts relating to the least dignified parts of the body in the same gravely balanced antithesis which had just before conveyed a solemn ejaculation about virtue or understanding. What Solomon says of the temple or the council chamber, Markolf applies to the kitchen; regulations for men and women are copied for dogs and cats; spiritual analogies are followed out in the world of eating and digestion, or further still. Among these strictly parodic proverbs, however, are scattered others in which the contrast of peasant and king takes a less purely literary form, which we shall find made the principal motive of a later Markolf dialogue. The peasant Markolf as a poor man becomes a strict representative of his order; he is the boor, the *vilain*, liable to disastrous collisions with the rich and strong, and whose ethical code is a set of practical

---

[1] In the former for instance, we find Solomon alluding at the very outset to his famous judgment: *bene iudicavi inter duas meretrices quae in una domo oppresserant infantem* ('ubi sunt aures ibi sunt cause' replies Markolf); but in what the narrative shows to be the sequel, the whole scene is worked out in full, as if it had not occurred before.

maxims for steering his way with as few of such collisions as possible.   He opposes the practical egoism of
struggling men to the liberality, the 'courtoisie', of the
noblesse.   'Many are they,' says Solomon, 'who return
evil for good to their benefactors.'   'But he,' responds
Markolf, 'who feeds another man's dog, gets no thanks.'
'He shall himself cry,' pursues Solomon, 'who turneth
away from the cry of the poor.'   'And he loses his tears,'
rejoins Markolf, 'who sheds them before a judge.'

The framework of narrative in which the wit-combat
is embedded, is a succession of *Schwänke*, carried on for
the most part in Solomon's court.   The opening paragraph tells of his first arrival, and draws his portrait with
a graphic minuteness of detail quite foreign to the ordinary narrative style of these books, in which the pause
for description is unknown.   He is 'short and thick-set,
with a great head, broad, red, wrinkled brow; hairy ears
that hang over his breast, big bleared eyes, horse lips,
a goat's beard and hair, a stumpy nose, short fat fingers,
and club feet; shod in country clogs of a piece with his
dirty patched cloak and his scanty tunic.'   The narrative falls into three sections or complexes of anecdote,
which perhaps in part represent successive additions.
The first (besides a coarse practical jest of the lowest
Ulenspiegel type[1]) gives Markolf's explanation[2] of his
own wisdom : on the day when Solomon as a boy had
tasted the vulture's heart, his mother had thrown Markolf, then a child in the kitchen, its *skin*[3].   The second
is chiefly occupied by the solution of Markolf's well-

[1] *Cap.* 'Marcolphus Salamoni regi ollam lactis plenam offert.'
[2] *Cap.* 'Rex Salomon...introspexit domum Marcolphi.'
[3] This is omitted in all the earlier German versions, and can
hardly therefore belong to the earliest state of the narrative.   Cf.
Schaumberg, p. 4.

known paradoxes, and its consequences. Solomon chal-
lenges Markolf to watch a night with him. Markolf
repeatedly sleeps, and on each occasion a dialogue of
this type takes place : *Sol.* Dormis Marcolphe. *M.* Non
dormio sed penso. *S.* Quid pensas? *M.* Penso nullam
rem sub sole esse candidiorem die. ....*S.* Probandum est
hoc[1]. A series of similar puzzles is thus accumulated,
which on the following day he is called to solve. Milk
he shows to be 'less white than daylight' by putting a
bowl of it in the *dark ;* 'nature stronger than education'
by letting loose a mouse before the eyes of a cat which
has been trained to hold a candle[2], and 'women to be
untrustworthy' by inducing his sister to give information
that he carries a concealed dagger, with aims against
the king's life; the search for it, naturally fruitless,
speedily establishes his innocence,—and his thesis[3]. Indignant at this refutation, Solomon banishes him, with a
threat that the dogs will be loosed upon him should he
return : he obtains a hare however, sets it free before
the dogs, who pursue it instead of falling on him, and
presents himself once more unharmed before the king,
who condones his audacity for the sake of his wit.
With one other, somewhat grosser, piece of humour[4]
this second section closes, and in at least one MS.[5] the
entire story also.

In the rest there follows a fresh episode at court,

[1] *Cap.* 'Rex Salomon et Marcolphus per noctem vigilare
volentes.'

[2] *Cap.* 'Marcolphus...ex manica mures decurrere permisit.'

[3] *Cap.* 'Ad regem Marcolphi soror vocatur.'

[4] *Cap.* 'Marcolphus in faciem calvi salivam spuit.' The bald
man complains to the king, whereupon Markolph excuses himself:
'Non fedavi [frontem hujus] sed fimavi, *in sterili enim terra fimus
ponitur.*'

[5] Vienna cod. 3337. Schaumberg, p. 5.

ending like the former with a banishment, a threat, and
a successful evasion. The first story gives a new turn
to the familiar history of Solomon's judgment. Markolf
rails at the king's easy credulity: 'a woman has infinite
wiles,' and enforces his bad opinion of the other sex by
spreading a calumny about the king's prospective legal
reforms[1] which shortly brings the 7000 women of Jerusalem in fury to the palace to revile him. Impatient at
their taunts, Solomon exclaims that he would rather live
with dragons and lions than with evil women; Nathan
urges moderation;—'we must answer fools according to
their folly,' retorts the king. Markolf immediately starts
from his place: 'Thou hast spoken my mind, Solomon:
this morning you extolled women, now you revile them[2].'
In wrath at this treachery the king once more banishes
his antagonist, who as before finds means to reassert
himself by a coarse trick which nevertheless became
one of the most popular incidents in the story[3]. Ex-
asperated at the insult, Solomon orders him to be hanged.
Markolf begs only to be allowed to choose the tree, and
Solomon agrees. But to every tree which his guards
suggest, he discovers excellent objections; and after

---

[1] A law that every man should have seven wives. The women
are of an exactly opposite opinion: 'melius est ut una mulier habe-
ret septem viros.'

[2] *Cap.* 'Hic convenerunt mulieres ante regem Salomonem.'
This chapter is in subject a repetition of the episode with Markolf's
sister, and the mechanism by which the proof in each case is
obtained is also analogous. Markolf beguiles the women to be
unconscious witnesses against themselves.

[3] *Cap.* 'Hic Salomon venit ante furnum ubi Marcolphus jacuit.'
The king had ordered him 'not to let him see his face' again,—'ne
videam te in mediis oculis.' Markolf, in spite of his 'curta tunica,'
lies down in the oven in the position best adapted to conceal his
face.

leading him through Syria, Palestine and Arabia, they
are obliged to return to Solomon and report that they
had been unable to find any tree, though it were the
olive of Jerusalem, or the cedar of Lebanon, on which
Markolf *wished* to be hanged. Here in the longest
Latin versions the story ends, adding only that he 'returned home and abode in peace,'—the usual laconic
dismissal of a jester who has done jesting.

Markolf
and Aesop.

The Markolf thus vividly drawn was certainly indebted for certain hints to another legendary figure who
has been in recent times more than once associated with
him, the astute slave of the Greek philosopher Xanthus.
But I do not think these hints have amounted to much;
the imitation is in any case thoroughly independent and
original. Markolf is throughout the German boor and
is in no way assimilated to the Greek slave. The description of his person, though clearly influenced by that
of Aesop, is still quite distinct. Both are ugly, but
Aesop's ugliness is that of Thersites,—the 'pointed
head,' the 'squint eye,' the actual deformity of shape[1];—
while Markolf's is mainly borrowed from the mere grossness of brute life. Aesop is a distorted man, Markolf
an intellectual beast. Aesop's jests again are as strictly
those of his condition, as Markolf's are of his. They
are the tricks of the household slave as he waits at
table or goes to market, often merely perverse interpreta-
tions of orders, like those which Ulenspiegel inflicts
upon his masters the shoemaker and the tailor, and oc-

---

[1] Cf. the φοξὸς, φολκὸς, χωλὸς of *Il.* II. 212 ff., with the φοξὸς,
βλαισὸς, κωφὸς of the *Vita Aesopi*, which in fact adds explicitly:
τάχα καὶ τὸν ὁμηρικὸν Θερσίτην τῇ αἰσχρότητι τοῦ εἴδους ὑπερβαλό-
μενος. Thersites indeed was only 'the ugliest man in the Greek
camp;' this is improved upon in the case of Aesop, who δυσειδέσ-
τατα τῶν ἐπ' αὐτοῦ πάντων ἀνθρώπων εἶχε.

casionally accompanied by a touch of mere brutality like
his[1]. But this domestic, *kleinbürgerlich* trait is quite
wanting in the humour of Markolf. It can hardly be
doubted that the transformation thus effected was, if not
in origin, yet in all its later and more vivacious stages,
essentially the work of German, and probably of Low
German, humour. In France the narrative framework
remained unknown until the presses of Köln and the
Netherlands began to circulate the famous *Collationes*
through the length of Europe[2]; and the whole Markolf
literature that grew up before that date out of Germany
was founded upon the Proverb-contest alone. In
Germany, on the other hand, the entire story appears to
have been familiar almost as soon as it was composed.
The vernacular literature borrowed freely from it; the
minstrels turned it into romance, not disdaining even its
grosser incidents[3], some of which themselves betray the
influence of the native German art of the wandering
minstrels[4]. The whole was very early translated into
German[5], and again in the fifteenth century, as the
Frag und Antwort Salomonis und Marcolphi.

[1] Ulenspiegel's flaying of the dog may be paralleled by Aesop's
amputation of the pig's foot to make up the 'four pig's feet' which
Xanthus had ordered, Xanthus himself having privately abstracted
one from the dish with a view to obtaining a handle against his slave.

[2] They appeared in Italian as early as 1502 (at Venice), and
became the source of the Italian Markolf, Bertoldo.

[3] The adventure with Markolf in the oven occurs in the *Salman
und Morolt.*

[4] Cf. Schaumberg, p. 7, who finds traces of minstrel influence in
the typical numbers of the scene in which Markolf rouses the
women of Jerusalem: 'septem maritos,' 'septem uxores,' 'septem
milia mulierum.'

[5] The existing Latin *Collationes* do not however perfectly represent the source of the older translations, so far as regards the proverbs, which only to a small extent coincide.

Wholly different was the literary fortune of Markolf in France.   The narrative, as I have said, remained unknown there; neither its grossness nor its humour at all coloured the French tradition.   The dialogue however contained a sufficient measure of both, and it was moreover so rich in dramatic suggestion, the contrast of the two minds and characters was shown from so many points of view, that a fine literary taste might be expected to develope the subject rather by singling out particular aspects of it, than by mere accumulations, clumsily pieced together, as had been the case in Germany.   This was what actually happened in France.   The dialogue form remains to the end, with no attempt to complete or continue it.   But Markolf, the hero, has become a fraction of his former self; he speaks in one key, his ideas and illustrations all belong to one category, he is rather a personification than a person.   In the two poems in question, however, the key, the category, are at least widely different.   To the Count of Bretagne[1] Markolf is simply the ingenious *vilain*, Solomon simply the representative of *noblesse*.   The king praises valour, courtesy, generosity, compassion; the boor retorts by urging the pain of wounds, the dull stress of labour, the bitterness of poverty[2].   It is obvious however that the contrast of

---

[1] *Proverbes de Marcoul et de Salemon.*—'Ci commence de M. et de S. que li queus de Bretagne fist'—reprinted by Crapelet: *Proverbes et Dictons populaires*, Paris, 1831.   Cf. Kemble, u. s. p. 73, and Schaumberg, p. 31.

[2]
Seur tote l'autre hennor
est proesce la flor,
  ce dit Salemons;
Ge n'aim pas la valour
dont l'en muert à doulor
  Marcoul li respont.

noble and peasant by no means coincided over its whole
range with that from which it started; the type of French
chivalry in the thirteenth century was by no means
altogether in harmony with the wisdom of the Jewish
king.   And as the poem proceeds we find the wisdom of
'honour' and 'valour'—fair modern equivalents for
Solomon's 'virtue' and 'courage'—alloyed with the lower
wisdom of social refinement and personal ease, the
wisdom that eschews early rising and unpleasant noises.
Solomon in fact, the idealist of the old dialogue, ap-
proximates to the sheer egoism which is the standing
quality of Markolf; he is the refined, as the Markolf of
the Latin dialogue is the gross, egoist.   And even this
point of difference almost vanishes, for it is precisely the
absence of grossness which distinguishes the opponent
of the French Solomon from the older Markolf.   The
original antagonism of the two, accordingly, perceptibly
dwindles; until Markolf's replies cease to be retorts or
parodies at all, and become simply comments, or supple-
ments,—which carry on Salemon's thought in a new, but
not necessarily lower, region, or clinch his phrases with a
proverb. 'I love not poor pasture, nor toil beyond
measure,' quoth Solomon; 'snow in summer is against
nature' quoth Markolf[1].

[1] P. 195, stanza 1.   Cf. ib. 2, 3.

> Ge n'aim soulaz d'enfant
> ne doner à truant,
>   ce dit Salemons;
> ne ge feme plorant,
> ne de félon le chant,
>   Marcol li respont.
>
> Ge n'aim cri de mastin
> ne lever trop matin,
>   ce dit Salemons;

The author of the second poem[1], on the contrary, has
dwelt exclusively on Markolf the *railer at women.*   The
whole is merely an expansion of his abuse of the two
meretrices of Solomon's judgement[2].

Traces of   Ten Brink has more than once dwelt upon the strange
Markolf in failure of many literary growths which flourished luxu-
England. riantly on the continent to take root in England; and
no illustration can be more apt than that of Markolf.
One of the most vivid creations of the middle ages, with
a permanent freshness of literary motive which forced
it into celebrity at the very height of the Renaissance,
it has left in England no palpable trace beyond a few
allusions, a score of translated verses, a string of proverbs, and one or two characteristic jests.   Scanty as

ne ge mauvais cousin,
ne ève qui tolt vin,
Marcol li respont.

Cp. pp. 194, *stanzas* 2, 5 ; 199, *stanzas* 2—4.

[1] '*Veez cy une desputacoun entre Salamon ly saage, et Marcoulf le
foole.*'   MS. Trin. Coll., Camb., printed by Kemble, p. 77 ff.   I
quote the first stanza :—

Salamon dit.
Mortalité et guerre
Sonnt exil de terre,
Et destruizement.

Marcoulf responnt.
De putayne sonnd maux
Et guerres mortaulx,
Et perils des gens.

The British Museum *Dictz de Salomon avecques les responces de
Marcou fort joyeuses* is obviously a version of the same, but with
great variations.

[2] 'Ubi sunt aures, ibi sunt cause. ubi mulieres ibi parabole.'
Some of the old prints read *auce* (e.g. that of Landeshut, 1574),
which is plausible, as in the German version this saying is followed
by another about geese.

these are, however, their points of contact with the
Markolf legend cover almost the whole field of its
ramifications.

From the thirteenth to the sixteenth century, three
conceptions of Markolf appear to have succeeded one
another; and they are at once referable to the influence
of the only three versions of the legend which had any
chance of vogue in England. In the first phase he is
the cunning proverb-maker, a type, rather than a champion, of popular wisdom. It is as such that he appears
as the father of *Hendynge*, the impersonation of the
mixed wit and shrewdness which produces proverbs[1].
But Hendyng's collection was evidently, as Ten Brink
says[2], formed under French influence, and bears the
closest resemblance in form to that called *Les proverbes
au comte de Bretagne*, where each strophe is in the same
way clinched by a proverb, with the running burden,
ce dit li vilains, which the 'quoth Hendyng' of the
English proverbs is obviously meant to represent[3]. Neither Hendyng nor the *vilain* however at all represent,

(margin note: 1.
Markolf as
Proverb-
maker.
Hendyng.)

[1]
> Mon þat wol of wysdom heren
> At wyse Hendynge he may lernen,
>   þat wes Marcolues sone.

The opening stanza, in which these words occur, is only found in
one MS. (Ten Brink, u. s.); they are probably therefore not those of
the author, but they are evidently contemporary.

[2] *Gesch. d. engl. Litt.*, p. 392. Kemble, who as he himself admits
in a subsequent note, unaccountably omitted the allusion in Hendyng
when discussing the traces of the story in England, did not I think
see, what I hope will immediately appear, that it points to the
Bretagne Marcoul.

[3] To show the similarity of form I quote a stanza from each:

> Jà por estre cortois
> plus grevez nesserois
>   que por estre vilains;
> les tesches sont à chois

like Markolf, the *vilain's* characteristic point of view;
the precepts which Hendyng is made to sum up in his
epigrams is rather clerical in tone; with its zeal for
knowledge (2—5), charity (12), and temperance (36).
Nor is the *vilain* of the proverbs a typical man of his
class. At the very outset he is found regretting the
decay of the chivalrous virtue of honour, and applauding
the 'valour' that leads men to bear pain, the 'prowess'
that is the enemy of sluggishness[1]. And throughout,
his maxims, like Hendyng's, seem rather to give the
sanction of popular wisdom to universal morality than,
like Markolf's, to combat and trench upon it. Why then
is Hendyng called Markolf's son? From what I have
already said of the first French poem of Marcol or
Markolf, it will be plain that the transition from this
provided exactly the middle stage which we require from
the Markolf of the Latin dialogue, the foul-mouthed,

> mais qui prent du sordois
>   bien doit avoir du mains;
> qui d'onneur n'a cure,
> honte est sa droiture,
>   ce dit li vilains.
>
> Crapelet, p. 170.

> ȝef þou havest bred ant ale
> ne put þou nout al in þy male,
>   þou del hit sum aboute;
> be þou fre of þy meeles,
> wher so me eny mete deles
>   gest þou nout wiþoute.
> Betere is appel yȝeve þen y-ete,
>   quoþ Hendyng.
>
> Kemble, p. 273.

[1] Crapelet, p. 169, st. 2; this is the exact antithesis of
Marcoul's:

> Ge n'aim pas la valour
> dont l'en muert à doulor.

gross-minded parodist, to the excellent and honourable
'vilain' and his English brother Hendyng[1]. The Marcolf of the Count of Bretagne begins as an antagonist,
but his later utterances are often indistinguishable in
tendency from the king's, instead of parodying Solomon's sayings he *caps* them; and from the cap which
completes the step is small to the proverb which clinches.
With the disappearance of the antagonism, moreover, the
dialogue form at once became superfluous, and, when the
vilain replaced Markolf, was naturally dropped, or lingered only in suggestion conveyed by the 'ce dit' and
the 'quoth,' that the *vilain* or Hendyng spoke only the
final phrase.

Within 150 years from the Proverbs of Hendyng, a
totally different conception of Markolf had gained
ground. The kind of supremacy which he had won in
proverb literature, is exchanged for a similar supremacy
in the equally vast literature, to which I shall return in
the next chapter, of Fools. To Lydgate, whose somewhat gloomy morality and entire want of humour made
him a natural enemy of the whole tribe of Markolf's, the
'father' of the proverb-maker Hendyng becomes the
'founder, patron and president of the order of fools[2].'
The antagonist of Solomon becomes, what he had
never yet been, his direct moral antithesis; the rivalry,
which in the Bretagne dialogue was all but dissolved in
good fellowship, is now sharpened into diametric opposition; the satiric bias, the class feeling, the humour,
which had made the rough peasant appear rather more
than the equal of the divinely endowed king, are all

*2.
Markolf as
the Fool.*
Lydgate.

---

[1] This is of course not meant to imply that the figure Hendyng
was new, or a copy of the *vilain*; but only that it was through the
vilain that he came to be connected with Markolf.

[2] Lydgate: *The Order of Fools*, v. 5.

stripped away, and the supreme representative of wisdom is confronted—what could be more simple and natural? —by the chief of 'fools'[1].

It can hardly be doubted that this strong antipathy to Markolf was due, as Kemble has pointed out, to the second of the two French versions of the story; in which, as I have already said, the degradation of the German Markolf is carried still further than his refinement had been in the former. For Lydgate's 'fools,' like Brandt's, include not merely simpletons but actual wrongdoers of every kind; the 'order of fools' is a representative gathering of all the various forms of sin,—exactly sixty-three in number in Lydgate's view. The patronage and presidency of such a body could hardly be credited to a man who had not a well-assured reputation for positive wickedness. The pranks of the German Markolf could not possibly entitle him to that position; even his grossness is at the worst disgusting, not licentious; he hardly breaks the commandments and commits no deadly sin. Only the truly loathsome *Marcolf* of the French *dictz*

---

[1] Lydgate's moral contempt for Markolf is still better seen in his other allusion, in the *Moral of the Fable of the horse, the goose and the sheep:—Lydgate's Minor Poems*, p. 120 (Percy Soc.).

> A cherol of birthe hatithe gentil bloode;
> It were…A perilous clymbyng whan beggers up arise
> To hye estate…Clymbyng of foolis
> Unto chayers of worldly dignité,
> Looke of discrecioune sette jobbardis upon stoolis,
> Marchol to sitte in Salamons see,
> What follwithe after no reason no justice.

On the other hand, the allusions of Lydgate's contemporary, Audelay, to 'Marcol' (ed. Halliwell, Percy Soc. pp. 31, 50), show that, though called 'the more fole,' he could still be associated with homely popular wisdom; for he is made to 'warn' Solomon 'hou homle hosbondmen' are indignant at the sins of their rulers.

whose talk reeks in every line of the *lupanar*, can have been in Lydgate's mind when he made Markolf the 'founder of the order of fools.' The poem itself indeed directly gave the suggestion; for in at least one MS. it is entitled *Disputation de Salomon le saage et Marcolfe le foole*[1].

The moral poet of the dullest age of English literature was not however to pronounce the last word upon Markolf. The French version of the dialogue to which he owed his ill reputation, was still popular at the outset of the sixteenth century[2]; but it was now met by the formidable rivalry of a Latin dialogue, substantially equivalent to that on which both the old French poems had been founded, and enriched with the still more telling humour of the narrative which had gradually grown up about it in Germany. The *Collationes* are henceforth the standard edition of the Markolf story[3]; the humour which had vanished in serious morality on the one side, and in mere foulness on the other, reappears; the proverb-maker and the intimate of *putains* are equally replaced by the ingenious if gross jester of Solomon's court who, like Hans Pfriem, can neither be banished nor put to death.

3. *Markolf as jester.*

[1] Kemble, u. s. p. 77 ff. Lydgate's use of this poem is, perhaps, not the earliest trace of it in England. It was in any case in existence at least two centuries before him. But the *Certamen Salomonis et Marculphi*, attributed with little reason to Walter Map, and included by Kemble among the English traces of the story, cannot be claimed with any certainty as English, and I therefore make no further allusion to it.

[2] The French *Dictz* was translated into English early in the century, and twice printed, by Pynson in London and Leu in Antwerp. Both original and translation are reprinted in Kemble.

[3] The *Dictz de Salemon et Marcoul* (=the second French version) were printed only twice, about 1500; the *Collationes*, under various titles, went through at least a dozen editions.

The slight traces which remain of this third Markolf
are in fact concentrated about these two incidents, his
futile banishment and death-sentence. Transferred to
the English jester Scogin,—whose history is an agglomera-
tion of German and French, about a nucleus of native,
facetiae,—the story of Markolf's dismissal after the cat
and mouse trick, under a threat of loosing the dogs
at him should he return, and the device of the hare
by which he defies the dogs, became familiar English
jests[1]. The still more celebrated story of his second
banishment, the oven-trick by which he evades or re-
venges it, and the final piece of humour which saves him
from hanging, are also borrowed by the compiler of
Scogin[2], with some very unskilful attempts at improvement[3]. Both tricks became part of the standing stock
of court-jester legends. Not only James I's. fool, Archie
Douglas, but his tutor Buchanan, was credited with the
oven-jest[4]. In addition to the instances quoted by
Kemble, a trace of it occurs also in one of the most

---

[1] *Scoggin's Jests*, ed. Hazlitt (O. Eng. Jest Books), p. 124 f. Cf.
Kemble, u. s. p. 94. It must be observed that as the first extant
edition of Scogin is only of 1626, it cannot be certainly assumed
that this and the following story were originally contained in it.

[2] *Scoggin's Jests*, u. s. p. 152. This is quoted in full by Kemble,
p. 94.

[3] The servants commissioned to hang him are reduced to give up
their task from the irrelevant and absurdly invented circumstance
of having brought no food with them, while Markolf is abundantly
supplied with 'sucket' and 'marmalade.' At nightfall they leave
him, Markolf bidding them report to the king that he *would* not
choose a tree. This is obviously weak, for in declining to choose
he goes beyond his privilege, and the king might fairly have ordered
his execution *sine conditione;* whereas Markolf's position is unassail-
able : he is perfectly ready to choose, as soon as a tree 'on which he
would desire to be hanged' is found.

[4] Kemble, p. 96.

popular jest-books of the century, the *Merry Tales and Quick Answers* (No. 84), where 'a mery felowe in high Almayn,' who has displeased the great lord of the country by his scoffing, is taken by the earl's servants and condemned to be hanged. When at the scaffold he begs to be allowed one favour, which the earl agrees on condition that it does not concern his life. He specifies a certain degrading kind of homage to be paid him by the earl for three mornings after his death. The earl demurs, and lets him go. This story appears to be a confused recollection of Markolf and Ulenspiegel. The circumstances somewhat resemble those of Markolf's proposed hanging, but the 'condition' is eminently characteristic of Ulenspiegel, and is actually used by him in the 30th story of Copland's version[1]. There is here no 'lord' in question, but the town-council of Lübeck, and his fault is not 'scoffing,' like Markolf's, but cheating a wine-tapster, the degrading service being demanded of the tapster[2].

Such is, I believe, a complete account of the history of Markolf in England up to the end of the sixteenth century. If his name remained familiar in Germany, where Nigrinus (1571) and Bruno Seidelius (1589) could still mention the German *Collationes* among the most current of popular story-books[3], it was elsewhere remem-

---

[1] Lappenberg refers apropos of the Ulenspiegel story to that of Markolf, but not to this mixed version in the *Merry Tales.*

[2] For another allusion to the 'tree-choosing trick,' not quoted by Kemble, cf. Rabelais's Prologue to the posthumous fifth book of the *Gargantua:* 'Allez vous pendre,' he calls out to the *Zoïles emulateurs et envieux,*—'allez vous pendre, et vous mêsmes choisissez arbre pour pendage; la hart ne vous fauldra mie.'

[3] Cf. quotations in Goedeke, p. 117. A Fastnachtspiel *Marcolfus* was performed at Lucern in 1546, ib. p. 303.

bered only by curious scholars, like Burton, who uses the
old contrast of the wise king and the gross boor to point
a striking passage of the *Anatomy*[1].   Even in France,
where *calembour* and *espiègle* still attest the celebrity of
Markolf's brother jesters, pure Teutons though they
were, no permanent trace has remained of Markolf
himself, whose history owed to French pens so much of
its early diffusion and of its early form.   To these his
more fortunate rivals I now turn.

II.

DER
PFARRER
VON KA-
LENBERG.

No such venerable pedigree as that of Markolf belongs to the Pfarrer von Kalenberg.   Whatever amount
of legend may have gathered about him, the famous
parson is a historical figure, whom a credible tradition
localises as Weigand von Theben, at the court of Otto,
Duke of Austria[2], in the early half of the fourteenth century.   Kalenbergersdorf is still a village on the Danube,
below the wooded hill of the same name, well known to
Vienna excursionists.   The historical Kalenberger is
however hopelessly involved in the legendary reputation
which he in part inherited, and also in some degree
bequeathed.   A full century earlier we meet with a
similar though still more shadowy figure, Pfaff Amîs; and
at about the same interval after the traditional date of
his death, a continuation of his feats is ascribed to an
adventurer who assumed the cassock after a wild career
in the field, Peter Leu, 'der ander Kalenberger.'   All of

---

[1] Kemble, p. 93, points out this passage.

[2] The earliest authority for this appears to be Aventine (quoted
by Koch, *Compendium d. deutschen Lit.* 2, 354), who probably however took the statement from the book itself.

these have certain traits in common; and the most favourite jest was the least monopolised. The world-old topic of riddles, for instance, though steadily tending to give way before the more robust humour of the *Schwänke*, holds its ground in a few chosen forms inexhaustibly. Markolf, though overlaid with a later disguise of buffoonery, is still essentially a solver of riddles; Amis's most striking feat is that of the *soi-disant* Abbot in Bürger's ballad[1]; the Kalenberger not only solves the questions of his brother priest, but baffles him with others of his own. Even Ulenspiegel is, grotesquely enough, introduced (by an interpolator) into the university *aula* of Prague, and made to solve the still essentially similar problems of the doctors.

A hitherto unexplained tradition made Amis an Englishman[2]; the Kalenberger however, like Leu, is an

---

[1] This is one of the many points at which the medieval Rogue shews traces of a descent from, or a connexion with, Wuotan. Markolf is plausibly connected with Mercurius, his Roman equivalent; and the Abbot incident is paralled by Wuotan's personation of blind Gest and *asking* riddles of king Heidreck, a pardon to reward the production of any which he fails to solve. Cf. our Robin Hood, and the horse adventures of Friar Rush. Simrock, *D. Myth*, § 127.

[2] According to the Strichaêre, at the beginning of his *Amis*, (written between 1200 and 1250).

> Er het hûs in Engellant
> In einer stat ze Trânîs [Lappenberg conj. *Tâmîs.*]
> Und hiez der pfaffe Amîs.
>
> quoted Goed., § 43.

The mystical character of the land beyond the North Sea for the dwellers on the continent included at least two traits: it was an abode (1) of the *dead* (Simrock, *D. Myth.* p. 437), (2) of *elves* and *nightmares.* The relation between *elves* and the class of vagabond jesters like Amis is so intimate that the former association would be a sufficient mythologic ground for Amis' connexion with England. Cf. esp.

undoubted German, and a South German. Something
of the geniality of the South German temperament
belongs to his jests, and the appreciable interval in other
respects which separates him from the Saxon Ulenspiegel
is not without a hint of the relative refinement of manners
on the Danube and on the Elbe.

The future *Pfarrer* is described as coming up, a poor
student, to the court of duke Otto. His very first feat is one
familiar in legend. He arrives with an enormous fish for
the duke; the porter stipulates for 'half the reward,' and
the Kalenberger thereupon begs that this may consist in
a sound flogging[1]. Less equivocal gifts follow, and, the
cure of Kalenberg falling vacant, the needy student is
enstalled. He soon becomes notorious with bishop,
parishioners and duke. In his dealings with the last he
is hardly distinguishable from the pure court-jester. The
duke, for instance, has promised that 'nothing put upon his
plate shall be taken from him,'—whereupon he procures
a larger wooden trencher, several feet across, and leads
the duke's horse upon it. With the peasants, he is
naturally still less scrupulous. Encountering a party of
them, for instance, who desire an interview with the duke,
he persuades them that the duke is bathing and can give

Robin Goodfellow, and Friar Rush, the most mythic part of whose
history occurs in England. (O. Schade in the Weimar *Jahrbuch*, v.
382).—I am not aware whether another singular trait which possibly
contains a mythic element, has ever been explained; the association
of England with *madness*. Cf. the Gravedigger's allusion in *Hamlet*—
'[His going mad] will be no matter there, for there the men are as
mad as he,' [with Marston's *Malcontent* III. 1 cit. ad loc. in Clar.
Press Ed.—AWW.] and perhaps the following: 'Another did but
peep into England, and it cost him more in good morrows blown up
to him under his window by drums and trumpets, than his whole
voyage: *besides, he ran mad upon't.*' Ford, *The Sun's Darling*, II. 1.

[1] This is told of the Kalenberger in Bebel, *Facet.* II. 54.

them audience only in the bath; they accordingly strip, and are conducted, not to the bath but to the banquet-chamber, where the duke is feasting with all his court. The bishop too plays a somewhat ignominious part, too gross to be dwelt upon; and his moral censorship of the loose-living parson, has no other result than that the latter, being required to replace his youthful housekeeper with 'a woman of forty,' chooses, as her equivalent, *two* of *twenty*. The parson is finally transferred to another cure in Steiermark; and with the title of Kalenberger he seems to have put off the jester also, for we hear nothing more of him but his peaceful death.

The German book of the *Pfaff's* exploits is said to have been compiled early in the fifteenth century by one Philip Frankfurter, at Vienna; but the first distinct evidence of it occurs in the earlier years of the sixteenth[1]. It continued highly popular throughout the century, and till the beginning of the great war[2]. Probably about the end of Henry VIII.'s reign appeared an English version of it, under the title of '*The Parson of Kalenborow.*' It is now known in only a single, and that a slightly muti-lated copy[3]. The first sheet has disappeared, and with it the whole of the introductory chapter (the adventure with the porter) and a few sentences of the next; the last leaf seems to be also wanting, and perhaps contained the conclusion, which at present appears abrupt; but in

The English 'Parson of Kalenborow.'

---

[1] Bebel, *Facet.* II. 54: 'Sacerdos caeci montis de cujus facete urbaneque dictis integri libelli perscripti sunt.' The earlier mention by Brandt (*N. Sch.* LXXII. 24: Wer yetz kan tryben sollich werck Als treib der pfaff von Kalenbergk) does not imply, as Goedeke says (p. 117), that the book of his exploits already existed.

[2] It went through not less than four editions in the seventeenth century, the last in 1620. Goedeke, p. 117.

[3] In the Douce collection of the Bodleian.

any case not more than a few lines. The substance of
the history is therefore unimpaired. But, on the other
hand, the English version is by no means a mere translation; but a free and independent handling of the story.
Many incidents take a different complexion; obscure
hints are worked out, new motives supplied, entire narratives inserted, and that with a skill which gives them the
air of being rather portions of a fuller original restored [1].

Variations in treatment.   As a fair specimen of the handling in the two versions
I subjoin an extract from one of the earliest adventures
of the newly appointed Pfarrer with his parishioners.
Priest and people have been annoyed by the fall of rain
through the defective roof of the church, which the
community is too poor to repair. The former comes
to their relief by undertaking the repair of the nave if
they will repair the choir. They eagerly close with the
bargain :—

Without avysement takinge as gredy people [they] answered
their parson thus, saying Mr parson we thanke you of your gode
profer, yf ye be so content we wyll cover the quere because we
be nat able to cover the body of our churche, the parson hering this
was right glad and said he was content. Than the paysans began
the quere and ended it with all their diligence thinkynge that the
parson sholde cover the rest, and when they had done and
that theyr quere was covred they asked of their parson whan
he wolde cover the remenant, and he answered and said my frendes
yf ye have covred the quere ye have done that ye ought to do,
therefore be content for I am well content, I se wel that I shall
stande drye, and out of the rayne to do Goddes service, and
the best counsell that I can geve you is that ye cover up the reme-

---

[1] Douce's pencil-notes in the Bodleian copy show that he
speculated freely about its origin, but it does not appear that he
ever saw the German *Volksbuch*, nor has any one else, so far as I know,
compared them in detail. As the unique copy of the English
version is still difficult of access, I need hardly apologise for
devoting some space to the matter here.

nant, and than ye shall stande drye also. The paysans hering this were mervelously angry and curssed the preste, and began to crye out upon hym the one with a mischefe the other with a vengeauns, the third bid the deveyll bere hym away. Thus they were all abashed of their parsons subtyll wyles and yet they were fayn to cover their churche themselfe for any cost that the preste wolde do thereto or cause to be done, for he stode dry ynough to do goddes service, and thus he cared nat for them for they cared before as lytell for hym.

The corresponding passage of the original runs thus :—

> Es will doch recht sein, sie da sprachen,
> Und huben alle an zu lachen,
> Sandten des Richters Eidam ihm zu,
> Dass er den Pfarrherr bescheiden thu',
> Wie sie den Chor, nach seiner Wahl,
> Wollten schön decken überall
> Der Pfarrer sprach : Es gefällt mir woll;
> Darnach ich mich auch richten soll,
> Dass Gottes Haus werde geziert,
> Und das lang Haus gedecket wird.
> Die Bauern eilten mit dem Chor,
> Dass sie dem Pfarrherr kämen vor,
> Sie eilten mit dem neuen Dach
> Der Pfarrer verzog da sein Sach
> Wol mit dem Decken manche Wochen.
> 'Herr ihr habt nicht also gesprochen,'
> Dess sollet ihr euch immer schamen.
> So scharf sie da in ihn kamen
> Dass ihn da ganz erzürnt sein Muth,
> Er sprach : 'Es dünket Euch nicht gut
> Und dass ich hie im Chor steh' trucken,
> So deckt nun selber zu die Lucken,
> Dess ihr an mich da begehret.'
> Ein jeder sich da gesegnet'
> Und sprach zu derselbigen Frist :
> Ein seltsam Mann der Pfarrherr ist.
> Er sprach : Gesegnet ihr euch davor
> Ich steh' wohl sicher in dem Chor

Vor Regen und dazu vor Wind:
Versorgt euern Ort, ihr lieben Kind,
Wollt ihr nicht in dem Wetter stahn:
Nicht besser ich euch rathen kann.'
Er liesz sich die Bauern nicht erschrecken:
Die Kirche mussten sie wol decken,
Wollten sie da nicht werden nass
Wie unnütz mancher Bauer wass[1].

The divergence of these two narratives is evidently
not merely of the kind which results from the conversion
of verse into prose. The English writer has told the
story quite in his own way, adding and omitting, softening
and heightening, and perceptibly modifying the play of
character. His conception of the relation of priest and
people betrays the age of the Protestant Revolution.
The German villagers are still the abject inferiors of
their priest, and even at the moment of discovering his
gross treachery, go no further than to cross themselves
with a half awe-struck ejaculation: 'Our parson is a
strange man.' The Englishman clearly felt this mildness
intolerable, and his peasants are accordingly made to be
'marvelously angry,' to 'curse the priest,' and 'cry out
upon him'—'with a mischief,' and 'a vengeance,'—'and
the third bade the devil bear him away.' A similar touch
serves to adapt the parson to his new circumstances.
Towards the more childlike peasants of the German
tale he is blunt and overbearing; he meets their remon-
strances with open anger (*ganz erzürnt*): 'if they don't like
him to stand dry while they are wet, they can help themselves.' But to his less ceremonious English parishioners
he shews from the first an ironical respect, culminating in
the bland sarcasm, of which there is no hint in the *Volksbuch:* 'My friends, if ye have covered the quire ye have

[1] From the reprint in Hagen: *Narrenbuch*, p. 526 ff.

done that ye ought to do, therefore be content, for I am
well content.'

In other company it is the parson who is made to
display the vigour of abuse which the translator evidently
missed at certain points of his original.   The neighbouring priest 'der auch gar weise wass, und dauchte sich
auch also spitzig,' comes to test the Kalenberger with
hard riddles.   Foiled at every point he puts a good face
upon his defeat.   'Well, well,' he cries, 'I am beaten;'
but you must make amends for the injury by giving me
your lasting friendship,—and some of your best wine!'
And the Kalenberger vows he shall have it.   This genial
trait, together with, still more strangely, all the detail of
the wit-combat which it closes, wholly disappears from
the English version :—' In short conclusion, they argued
sore, but the parson held the overhand, whereof he had
grete honour.   Then said he to the old priest : Thou
gray-heded fole, thou hadest better not to have argued,'
&c.   'Now no more of this, said the parson,' and then
the Kalenberger consents as before, to make merry over
their good cheer.

But more substantial variations remain.   In the fifth *Additional stories.*
story of the *Volksbuch*, for instance, a repulsive trick is
told of the parson, which, as it stands, is a mere unprovoked piece of buffoonery. In the English version, however,
this tale is provided with a long *Vorgeschichte*, the effect
of which is to make the trick an act of vengeance upon
his clerk[1].   A more striking case occurs on the parson's
summons to his bishop.   The *Volksbuch* says simply:

> Er war gehorsam dem Bischop
> Er kam geritten und gegangen,

---

[1] The clerk has given him a quack prescription.   I cannot trace
any original for this story.

but in no way indicates the solution to the riddling
brevity of the second line.   In the English version, however, the whole story is given at length.   The parson

> sadeled a lowe lytell mare somewhat hyer than three horse
> loves, and so lept he into the sadell and set him on his journey
> with his one fote hanginge on the grounde and the other as yf
> it had been cast over the sadell, and so come to the bishop Courte
> where as the bishop lend before the gate; and the bishope thus
> seyinge laughd hartely and asked of the parson how he came so
> rydinge; the parson answered and sayde, my lorde I ryde nat, the
> bishop asked him, how then, goest thou on fote? he sayde nay my
> Lorde, I come hangyng on my Mare unto your grace, the which
> shall avantage me but lytell.   The bishop hearing this went away
> and thought he had ben folyisshe.

The quibble in this story was no doubt a very familiar
piece of *Volkswitz*; yet the English version has not the
air of a deliberate interpolation; and would an interpolator in the middle of the sixteenth century have
thought of the familiar description of the bishop 'leaning
before the gate' of his Court?

A third story, fragmentary in the current versions of
the *Volksbuch*, but completed in the English version is
that which narrates how the 'witziger und spitziger
Pfaff' of the riddle-contest is induced by his former
opponent to exchange his own more desirable benefice
for that of Kalenberg.   The Kalenberger privately distri-
butes *groschen* among the peasantry, with directions to
bring them as an offering to mass, and the strange priest
makes no difficulty in consenting to become the permanent recipient of so much generosity.   On discovering
the trick he gladly purchases the right to resume his own
benefice.   In all but a single known version there is here
an obvious lacuna, the parson's arrangement with his
peasants being abruptly cut short at the opening line:
Wist ir nit was im breu ist?   Hagen, in reprinting the

Pfarrer for his *Narrenbuch*, perceived the lacuna, but unfortunately read this line, *Wiszt ihr was in dem heu ist ?* and accordingly explains that the parson makes the peasants 'thrash hay, and bring the payment to mass[1].' It is obvious that this, as well as being nugatory, spoils the jest by making the peasants *earn* their contributions. The completion of the lacuna, with the true reading, was first given by Lappenberg from an old edition which he places about 1500[2]. But the English version had long before this discovery satisfactorily supplied the gap, in the chapter sufficiently described by its heading: ' Howe the parson gave shillynges to every one in hys parryshe to the entent that they should offer it the next daye at the olde prestis masse for to begyle hym to cause him chaunge benefices[3].' This is described in some detail, and the delusion of the ' old priest ' follows as before.

With the single, fragmentary old print which I have *Other traces of the Kalenberger in England.* described, at I fear tedious length, the career of the Kalenberger in England opens, and closes.   His failure is the more remarkable, as it occurred at the very time when the current tales of two heroes of native jest who strongly recall him, were formed into a collection which kept their memory green for a century,—the scholarly Scogin and the merry vicar, Skelton.   Several of his feats no doubt crept into English literature, but only through the accident of their having been borrowed to form a patch in the motley of the less worthy but far

---

[1] Narrenbuch, *Pfarrer v. Kalenberg*, note.

[2] *Wiener Jahrbücher*, Bd. 40, Anz. p. 19.   No hint is here given that this edition contains any of the other additions of the English Version.

[3] An unimportant trifle is that the amount for which the Kalenberger consents to resume his old benefice is forty instead of thirty pounds.

more famous figure to whom I shall immediately turn.
The German compiler of Ulenspiegel enriched his hero
with not less than five jests from Amis and two from the
Kalenberger[1], three of which were retained by the more
meagrely clad English Ulenspiegel. Of the five stories from
Amis—the mock painting, No. 27, the solution of the riddles proposed to him by the university of Prague, No. 28,
the teaching of the ass to read, No. 29, (both ludicrously
inappropriate to the character of the unlettered boor,
about whom universities felt little curiosity), the cure of
the patients in the Nürnberg hospital (by threatening
to burn the last to leave it), No. 17, and the adventure
as relic-monger, No. 31,—all but the third reappear in
the English version, (as Nos. 19, 20, 13 and 21). Of
the two taken from the Kalenberger, one reappears in
the English Ulenspiegel: the offer to fly from a tower-
top (No. 14, Copland No. 10); and from Ulenspiegel
this scion of the Kalenberger returned once more to his
own kin, for the story was embodied in the famous Jests
of Scogin[2].

[1] 'Mit zulegung etlicher fabuln des pfaff Amis und des pfaffen
von dem Kalenberg.' Ulensp. *Vorrede* (ed. Lappenberg). Lappenberg, (ib. p. 354), gives the references to these. They are given,
incompletely, by Kemble, *Sol. and Saturn*, p. 281.

[2] Hazlitt's edition (Old English Jest-books), p. 127. It is clear
that the compiler of Scogin drew from *Ulenspiegel* and not from the
Parson of Kalenborow. The promise to fly is in *Ulenspiegel* a
whimsical buffoonery without motive or pretext: in the *Pfarrherr*
it is a device to get rid of the parson's bad wine, which the thirsty
spectators readily drink while they await his appearance. The
story in Scogin shows no trace of this motive; and though its scene
is transferred to France, and its effect heightened by the introduction
of a Frenchman who, piqued by Scogin's failure, actually *does* fly,
in other respects it closely resembles *Ulenspiegel.*—It must be added
that as the first extant edition of Scogin is of 1626, it cannot be
assumed that this story, any more than those borrowed from Markolf,
belonged to the original collection.

III.

What the Kalenberger is to Lower Austria, and Leu ULEN-
to Swabia, Ulenspiegel is to Saxony, Hanover and Bruns- SPIEGEL.
wick. Magdeburg is the centre of his *terrain*, and thence
northwards to Luneburg and Rostock, westwards to Hildesheim and Hanover, southwards to Erfurt, he is everywhere at home. He has been well described as a wily
peasant who inverts the usual relation of town and country by making victims of the citizens. He does not
praʻtice exclusively upon townsmen; dukes, physicians,
priests and monks, are occasional though rarer victims;
but the chief sufferers are on the whole the typical men
of the burgher-class,—the tailor, the baker, the black-
smith, the shoemaker in their shops, the huckster in the
market-place, the *wirth* and *wirthin* in the tavern. He
takes service with a shoemaker, for instance, and obeys
his master's orders literally by cutting out his shoes very
large or very small (F. 27[1]); with a tailor, and being
required to make a 'wolf'—a current name for a kind
of peasant's cloak—cuts it to the shape of a wolf (F. 29).
He inveigles a priest into a virtual disclosure of what
had been told him in confession, and then extorts his
horse as the price of silence (F. 25). He cheats a farmer
of green cloth by laying a wager that it is blue, and
supporting his view by the aid of corrupted witnesses
(A. 68, F. 34[2]). At Magdeburg the flying adventure

---

[1] A=the number of the story in the Strassburg edition of 1519;
F = that in Copland's English version, containing about half the
tales.

[2] This is superficially like the Italian story in the *Merry Tales
and Quick Answers* (No. 58), 'Of the fole that thought himself
dead,'—where the 'fole' is successively met by a number of confederates who remark on his ill looks, until he is finally induced, on

already mentioned affords him a laugh at the whole town
(A. 14, F. 10). Another well-known legend with many
parallels tells of his mock alms to twelve blind men;
each imagines the money to be in the keeping of the
rest, and it is only at the close of a substantial feast in
the nearest tavern that they discover the true nature of
Ulenspiegel's δῶρον ἄδωρον (A. 71, F. 35)[1]. But his most
numerous victims are the innkeepers. He presents one
of his hostesses, at the close of dinner, with an account
'for the labour of eating it' (A. 33, F. 22), and punishes
another for her rash declaration that 'penniless guests
must pay with their coats,' by flaying her favourite dog
and presenting her with the skin (A. 82, F. 37). Here,
as often, Ulenspiegel's humour, such as it is, is lost in
his brutality. In another of his tavern-tales, one of the
best, it is over elaborate. Three guests who come in
late one evening after a delay caused by wolves, are mercilessly scoffed at by their host for their timidity. Ulenspiegel thereupon goes out, kills a wolf, brings its body
to the inn the same night, sets it up beside the fire, and
then loudly calls for drink. The host on going into the
Stube to fetch it, finds the wolf in possession of his
hearth, and rushes out in abject terror, only to be met

their authority, to believe himself dead. A much closer parallel
however is that of *Scogin's Jests*, p. 56, where the trick is transferred from cloth to sheep. In the latter form the story is very old.
It occurs in Bromyard and Pauli, and the former was the direct
source of Scogin. 'I know not,' says Mr Hazlitt in his note,
'whether this story occurs before.' I cannot help remarking on the
singular conception of editorship which allowed the editor of the
Old English Jest-books to neglect so obvious a source as Bromyard.

[1] This story, like those of the priest's horse and the blue cloth,
was turned into a *Fastnachtsspiel* by Hans Sachs. *Eulenspiegel mit
den blinden* is reprinted in Goedeke and Tittmann's selection of his
Fastnachtsspiele.

by the taunts of his despised guests of the evening
before (A. 78, F. 36).

No copy has ever been found of the Low-Saxon *History of*
original of Ulenspiegel, evident traces of which remain *the book*[1].
in the early High German versions. The first extant
versions take us to Strassburg, where in 1515 the earliest
known edition, and in 1519 that till recently regarded as
such and attributed to Murner, were published[1]. From
Strassburg it passed to Augsburg (ed. 1540) and Erfurt (ed.
1532—38) and northwards to Köln (Servais Kruffter's undated edition), thence to Antwerp (undated ed., 1520—
30), and from Antwerp to Paris and London. The Antwerp
edition,—a cento containing about one-half the stories of
the original,—was the basis of the French version of
1532 and its successors[2], and of the English version
printed, probably between 1548 and 1560, by William
Copland[3].

It was therefore only a mutilated Ulenspiegel which *Copland's*
Copland introduced to his countrymen. On the other hand *Howle-*
his Dutch original contained one new story, not in the *glass.*
Strassburg versions, but occurring as an evident interpolation in the undated Köln edition of Kruffter[4], that—

---

[1] For the bibliography I am dependent on Lappenberg (pp. 147 ff.),
as corrected and supplemented by Scherer (*Quellen u. Forschungen*
No. 21, pp. 27 ff. and 78 ff.),—the latter a most brilliant piece
of scholarship. The Strassburg edition of 1515, in London, was
unknown to Lappenberg. Scherer shows by a comparison of its
readings with those of 1519, that the basis of both was still a High
German edition. The original Low Saxon is thus separated from us
by at least two removes.

[2] *Ulenspiegel...Nouvellement translate et corrige de Flamant en
Francoys.* (Paris, 1532.)

[3] *Howleglass. Here beginneth a merye Jest of a man called
Howleglass, and of many marvelous thinges and jestes that he did
in his lyffe* &c.

[4] Scherer, u.s. p. 29. Lappenberg overlooked this.

perhaps taken ultimately from Markolf—of the young
Ulenspiegel's answers to a question about the way,
(Copland, No. 2)[1]; and Copland himself added a copy
of verses, which deserve a moment's notice as the first
indication of the impression made by Ulenspiegel upon
an English mind.   It is difficult to suppose that the particular English mind can have been that of the translator,
for they stand in complete antithesis to the history
which they close.   Instead of adding another to Ulenspiegel's feats, they introduce him holding a solemn
disputation,—in which for the first time in his life he is
distinctly worsted.   The undisguised fellow-feeling with
which his pranks had been told, passes abruptly into
stern reproof; the genial adventurer who compiled the
History, and in whom it was at least plausible to suspect
Thomas Murner, is suddenly replaced by a serious, staid,
and probably Protestant, London citizen, who doubtless
wrote with a purely moral aim, and a desire to put the
antidote within easy reach of the poison.   The verses
form a separate chapter, No. 44, immediately preceding
the final chapter which gives Ulenspiegel's death :—
' How Howleglass came to a scholar to make verses with
hym to the use of reason ' (No. 44).   In seven-line
stanzas, a form of literary art of which the boor of Kneit-
lingen is elsewhere quite innocent, he urges successively

---

[1] In the Dutch version headed: *Hoe Vlespieghel antwoorde eenen
man die nae den wech vraghede.*   Kemble, who notices the analogy
to Markolf, adds, by way of explaining why this story does not
occur in the High German : ' The German version knew well enough
that these questions and answers belonged of right to another tale,
and they are therefore not admitted into it ' (p. 322).   This reads
oddly in the face of the compiler's own frank admission that he had
added several stories from older books.   These nice scruples have
not counted for much in the history of Jest-books.

the irresistible might of Mars, Venus and Bacchus[1], and the scholar answers his grave objections like a moral poet. This is the strain of the English Ulenspiegel:—

> Venus a god of love most decorate,
> The flour of women and lady most pure,
> Lovers to concorde she doth aggregate,
> With parfyte love as marble to dure,
> The knotte of love she knittes on them sure,
> With friendly amite and never to discorde
> By dedes thought cogitation nor worde.

Scholar. Not to discorde? yet did I never see
> Know nor hear tell of lovers such twaine,
> But some fault ther was, learne this of me, &c.

But this rigorous view of Ulenspiegel gained little *Howlgla:* footing in England, or to put it more accurately, his *in Scotland.* name was never degraded as Markolf's had been, into a mere proverb for moral obliquity. In Scotland, singularly enough, the opposite was the case; the repulsive associations of the name appear to have there altogether extruded its humour; the word became a taunt if not an insult, and was introduced into the most acrid region of the polemical vocabulary. The very distortions it underwent show that it had become an everyday word in the lips of men for whom its original meaning was lost[2].

---

[1] So Lydgate, whose attitude towards Markolf is very similar, associates the 'order of fools' with the pagan gods:

> Bachus and Juno hath set abroche the toune.

[2] Its regular Scottish form was *Holliglass,* cf. Jamieson's article, where the information about Ulenspiegel, even in the English version, is still, in the 1880 edition, drawn wholly from Steevens, Reid, and—Ménage! The instance which he gives from Spotiswood ('He called them *holliglasses,* cormoraunts, and men of no religion') and those in Sempill's Satirical ballad on Patrick Adamson, archbishop of St Andrews (cf. the *Sempill ballads,* Edinb. 1882)

In England, on the contrary, Ulenspiegel gravitated
at once to the class of native jesters to whom he properly
belonged.   Under his English name he lost all foreign
associations, and became an inseparable member of the
brotherhood of Scogins and Skeltons, Robin Goodfel-
lows and Robin Hoods, from whom however he was
always clearly distinguished by the enigmatic symbolism
of the 'Owl on fist' and 'Glass at wrist' with which
he was invariably represented.   His History took its
place with theirs in the library of Captain Cox; and,
if a somewhat doubtful piece of evidence may be trusted,
all three, with the new accession of Lazarillo de Tormes,
were keenly relished by Edmund Spenser (which needs
good evidence) and roundly abused by Gabriel Harvey
(which is credible enough)[1].   It is therefore perfectly
natural to find them, a generation later, associated on
the stage, and Owlglass called in by Skelton, in his finest
'tinkling' verse, to play almost the only rôle still

both fall not before the last quarter of the century; Adamson was
appointed to the see only in 1575, (Spotiswood, *s. anno*).

[1] Cf. Collier, *Bibliographical Catalogue*, s. v. Howlglass, where
a MS. note in the Bodleian copy of the book is quoted, which
Collier, judged to be in the handwriting of Harvey, and to allude to
the poet.   In any case it is a contemporary testimony, of some
interest, assuming of course that it is genuine,—a proviso never
quite superfluous where Collier is concerned.—'This Howleglasse,
with Skoggin, Skelton and Lazarillo, given to me at London, of
Mr Spensar, xx. Dec. 1578, on condition that I would bestowe
the reading of them on or before the first of January imediately
ensuing; otherwise to forfeit unto him my Lucian in fower volumes,
whereupon I was the rather induced to trifle away so many
howers as were idely overpassed in running thorowgh the foresaid
foolish bookes; wherein me thought that not all fower togither
seemed comparable for false and crafty feates with Jon Miller,
whose witty shiftes and practices are reported among Skelton's
Tales.'

available in the mature Jacobean drama for a clown
of his rough breed,—that of leader in the Bacchanalian
fun of a Jonsonian Anti-masque. I give the often-
quoted passage below[1].

Even in the Anti-masque, however, Owlglass was
necessarily like every one else, little more than a show-
figure in a pageant; the wily peasant has no scope for
his jests, and is introduced less in his capacity of jester
than because his grotesque oddity of appearance contributed (like the monstrosities of a procession), to the
picturesqueness of the general effect. With his usual
minute care therefore, Jonson described every detail
of the Owlglass he had in view,—the crooked, apish
boy with fool's cap and feathers, glass and owl, astride
on his father's ass and probably, like the original Ulenspiegel, turning round to grimace at the groundlings[2].

This introduction into the *Fortunate Isles* is no doubt
Ulenspiegel's highest literary distinction. Once before,
however, Jonson had made more than one casual dra-

---

[1] *The Masque of the Fortunate Isles*, 1626:

> An Howleglass
> To come to pass
> On his father's ass;
> There never was
> By day nor night,
> A finer sight
> With feathers upright
> In his horned cap,
> And crooked shape,
> Much like an ape
> With owl on fist,
> And glass at his wrist.

[2] Thus the second story, which Jonson evidently had in view.
On this ground I describe him as a boy, though I am not confident
that Jonson meant this.

matic use of his name. When Sir Epicure Mammon, in the *Alchemist*, visits the laboratory where his base metal is being turned into gold, Subtle calls to his servant Face under the feigned name, 'Ulenspiegel'; and to Mammon he continues to be 'Ulen' to the end[1]. Jonson was the most finished adept of all his contemporaries in the irony of dramatic nomenclature; and he has given no better proof of it than in making one of the most cautious and crafty charlatans in literature conceal his identity from his most credulous victim under the name of a world-famous rogue[2].

Stories borrowed from Ulenspiegel. But the literary history of Ulenspiegel does not end here. His general likeness to the family of English jesters made it inevitable that their histories should here and there be enriched from his; and on the other hand, he had points of divergence from them all sufficiently attractive to palpably warp, in at least one case, the English tradition. Like Markolf, he was laid under contribution by the wholly unscrupulous compiler of Scogin; for a feat indeed which his own compiler had drawn from the Kalenberger; and which was as much in place among the freaks of an Oxford scholar, as of a German priest. But there was a different class of Ulenspiegel's jests, entirely his own, less easily assimilated to those of any English jester,—those of the mischievous apprentice, or servant. Skelton and Scogin are at bottom scholars,

[1] *The Alchemist* II. 1 etc.; *Poetaster* III. 1. These passages, like the last, have been referred to in almost all English accounts of Ulenspiegel.

[2] A still more remarkable piece of irony, over which he had no control, has associated Jonson himself with Ulenspiegel, whose upright burial (A. 95, F. 48) is probably at the root of the similar tradition once (if not still) current among the Westminster vergers, cf. *Quarterly Rev.*, No. 41, p. 108, and Lappenberg's note to the chapter in question.

with a strong dash of the court-fool; they cheat all classes from the king to the alewife; but they never take service. Nor, it need not be said, does Robin Hood. Robin Goodfellow is properly an elf, who rewards and torments men, but assumes no direct relation to them. Ulenspiegel, on the other hand, owes as much of his fame to his brief bondage with tailor and shoemaker, as to his roving adventures in taverns. And it was precisely the figure of Robin Goodfellow, uncertain and fluctuating in outline as it was, which took the impress of this new influence[1]. The early life of Robin (the first part of his 'Merry Pranks') is in great part modelled on Ulenspiegel; his mother's difficulties with him at six years old are those of Ulenspiegel's father[2], and they are followed by the adventure as tailor's man,—closely modelled on the 48th tale of Ulenspiegel,—the humour of which is of a kind as familiar to Ulenspiegel as it is alien to Goodfellow— that of taking a man precisely at his word[3]. But the child Robin was not the father of the man, and the 'second part' introduces us to a wholly different being Robin Goodfellow the 'sprite,' who is distinguished from Ulenspiegel hardly more by his fairy privilege of transformation, than by his fundamental good-nature. 'He alwayes did helpe those that suffered wrong, and never would hurt any but those that did wrong to others[4].' Ulenspiegel consistently follows the exactly opposite

[1] I follow here the suggestion of Lappenberg, u. s. p. 228.

[2] *Ulenspiegel*, chap. II.: whether put before or behind his father when he rides, the boy's behaviour is equally disreputable.

[3] The tailor in each case leaves his man with a hasty order: 'wirf die ermel an den rock,'—'Whip thou on the sleeves:' Ulenspiegel spends the night in throwing the sleeves at the coat, and Robin in lashing them to pieces. Cf. *Merry Pranks*, &c., ed. Collier, p. 8.

[4] *Merry Pranks*, u. s. p. 21.

principle, and the first Robin was only a second Ulen-spiegel.

In the much more remarkable story which will be discussed in the next section, we shall see the motive of the 'malicious servant' carried out far more consistently[1], and with supernatural associations wholly wanting to Ulenspiegel.   And so far as Ulenspiegel's literary in-fluence is at all traceable in after times, it would seem to have told in great part in the direction of this class of jest.   The solitary later translation in English[2] (1709) may well have stimulated the chap-book biographers who had their seat in the purlieus of St Aldermary's.   Several of their heroes show an unmistakeable family likeness to Ulenspiegel.   The scholarly or clerical jester of the sixteenth century is apparently extinct, and his place is taken by a bourgeois tribe of servants and tradesmen,— Tom Tram the apprentice, Tom Stitch the tailor, Tom Long the carrier, whose victims are for the most part their employers[3].   But they owe to Ulenspiegel at most a general hint; not one of their adventures, so far as my observation goes, is borrowed from, or modelled upon his; and though hardly at all superior in refinement or in point, they belong for the most part to a more civilised and artificial state of society.   On the whole it must be

[1] Two stories of Ulenspiegel were, as we shall see, transferred to *Friar Rush*, those in which he appears in a parallel situation, as servant in a convent.

[2] *The German Rogue, or the Life and Merry Adventures...of Tiel Eulespiegel*...Made English from the high Dutch. London, 1709.— An article in the *Quarterly Review*, No. 41, p. 108 (1819), in a brief notice of Ulenspiegel, confounds this with Copland's. The notice abounds with other errors, not worth pointing out.

[3] Editions in the Brit. Museum. The Quarterly Reviewer above cited, seems to me to go too far in asserting that 'these penny histories are all imitated from [Ulenspiegel's] jests.'

said that the fortunes of Ulenspiegel among us since the
16th century, have been, like those of Markolf from the
first, one more instance of the insularity which explains
so much in the literary as in the political history of
England. In Germany, in the Netherlands, in France
even, its popularity has never died out, and in all three
countries the whole interval between the gothic prints of
three hundred years ago and the critical editions of to-
day, is bridged over by a series of chap-book versions
continuous enough to show that they never ceased to be
read. England, on the contrary, during the whole period
from Copland to Thoms and Ouvry (who reprinted it
twenty years ago) witnessed but one attempt to revive it,—
the translation made in the heyday of that Augustan age
which has left so many strange evidences of its appreciation for the robust crudities of the sixteenth
century[1], and none more strange than this.

IV.

Markolf, the Kalenberger and Ulenspiegel, had all some FRIAR
degree of novelty. None of them had a precise parallel in RUSH[2].

---

[1] I will merely recall the furore created by *Faustus* in 1727 and
the new translation of the *Grobianus* in 1739.

[2] The active discussion of the Rush story dates from Thoms,
who discovered the English version of 1620 among Douce's books,
and reprinted it in the *Early English Prose romances*, vol. 1 (1827 and
1857). Soon afterwards Wolf and Endlicher discovered two editions
of a H. Germ. version at Vienna, and reprinted them with a suggestive introduction (*Von Bruoder Rauschen*, Vienna, 1835). In
the Weimar *Jahrbuch* Bd. 5, Oskar Schade reprinted the Low
Saxon version, the only one known in German before Wolf and
Endlicher, with the best critical account of the legend yet given.
Finally the Danish version of 1555 was reprinted by C. Bruun,
Broder Russes Historie (Kjöbenh. 1868), with an introduction, not
comparable in any way to Schade's, but containing some new

English legend; each represented a variety or shade
of humour which if not unprecedented was unfamiliar.
But this novelty lay within narrow limits. The jester
Markolf was only a more genial variety of Markolf the
'fool,' who had been familiar for centuries; the Kalenberger is a Skelton with a faculty for riddles; Ulenspiegel
a plebeian and unlearned Scogin. In complete contrast with these was the story which remains to be discussed. Neither English history nor English folklore
contained anything at all resembling the legend of Friar
Rush in its original form[1]; if his jests were of an ordinary
type, they derived piquancy from his wholly novel
personality and situation. And when we add to this
that his History is not a mere loose string of anecdotes,
but a connected narrative with at least a glimmering of
dramatic climax and catastrophe, it is not surprising that
he should have altogether outdone his rivals in literary
importance. The story of the disguised devil sent to
corrupt a convent of monks with delicious fare, had an
element of the same fascination which made the Faustus
legend unforgetable; and, as will presently appear, it
played a part not very far inferior in the English drama.

The historical Rush.   The historical germ of the Rush story is extremely
obscure. Its scene was undoubtedly the most famous
of Danish monasteries, the Cistercian convent of Esrom,
planted by bishop Aeskil, in the early days of the Order,
beside the wood-girt and legend-haunted Esrom lake[2].

suggestions. Nyerup, Thiele, Grimm and others, who only commanded a part of the material, will be referred to in the notes.

[1] The relation of Rush to Robin Goodfellow will be discussed
below.

[2] Hans de Hofman, *Samlinger af...Fundationer*, T. VII. p. 155.
The fact that the lake had its legend is not irrelevant. I have not
met with the mention of it elsewhere. 'Gamle Folk beretter,' says
Hofman, 'at denne Söe har tilforn været, ligesom en anden Engbond,

The dissolution of the convent at the Reformation, led to the destruction of most of its antiquities; but in Pontoppidan's day there still remained a huge gridiron and cauldron, and the tradition of a portrait, with inscription, of Rus the friar and cook[1].

The inscription, which has often been quoted, throws very little light on the legend[2]. At most the luxurious tastes attributed to the old priest, and the 'gray horse' which he bequeathed to the convent offer a slight foothold. The latest editor of any of the extant versions, Chr. Bruun, has attempted to supplement this meagre information from the scanty records of Esrom in the royal archives. A document of 1371 preserved there (Royal Library, gl. kgl. Saml. 4, 3124) contains an account of one Johannes Kraffse, a monk of Esrom, who 'at the devil's suggestion' had abandoned his orders and returned to the world[3]; the abbot applied for his excommunication, finally proclaimed in full form by the archbishop of Lund. This does not appear to

höstet, og at en Röst den Tiid sagde til Höst-Folkene: 'Staaer op at læse, Esse begynder at blæse;' derefter forlod endeel Moesen, andre blev af Vandet druknede.' No doubt many other lakes of comparatively recent formation have similar myths. A good popular description of Esrom and its legends is in Holger Bruun's *Gamle Danske Minder*, I. 294 ff.

[1] Pontoppidan says himself (*Danske Atlas* VI. p. 35): 'der skal endnu findes Broder Rusis Jerngryde og Rist.' Hofmann *Samlinger* &c. u. s. adds, rather naïvely, apropos of the unusual size of the implements, that 'the human bones dug up there show that the men *of that day* were of larger stature than now.'

[2]   Hic requiescit Jon Præst
            Qui semper comedebat det bæst, &c.

[3] C. Bruun, *Broder Russes Historie*, Kjöbenh. 1868, p. 13 ff. The MS. is difficult to read, and particular words are doubtful, but the sense is clear: instiganti scilicet dyabolo relictis religione et habitu monachali ad secundam [leg. *saeculum*]...est reversus, &c.

me to give much help. That the name corresponds with
that of the epitaph counts for little; particularly as the
two lives, so far as appears, were wholly different. Johannes' abandonment of his vows is not recorded of
Rus; while the apparent reference of the act to diabolic
suggestion, need mean no more than that the writer
applied to Johannes' sin the current theological explanation of sin in general. Finally, Bruun's attempt
to derive the name Rausch and Rus from this Kraffse—
'bold' he himself calls it—is I think inadmissible.
Kraffse or *Krause* might become in a German mouth
Rausch, whence *Rus* by simple translation. But the
loss of a sound so congenial to 'German lips' as *k*,
in a favourite combination like *kr*, is not to be so easily
disposed of.

But while this, as it stands, is certainly not an adequate hypothesis it must be admitted to be the nearest
approach to one yet produced. There only remain the
trifling suggestions of the epitaph. We find here not the
slightest suggestion of 'diabolica instigatio'; on the
other hand the *semper comedebat det bæst* offers a slight
foot-hold for the essential trait, prominent in every form
of the legend, that it was by means of the sixth deadly
sin that the devil sought the corruption of the convent.
'Jon Præst' was clearly conspicuous for his good
living. We cannot however suppose him to have stood
alone, a solitary epicurean in an ascetic community; the
common life of a monastery excluded so complete a
contrast; one would rather imagine him to have taken
a leading part in the more luxurious furnishing of the
Esrom table which, there as elsewhere, replaced the
early rigour of the Cistercians, to have been the Luther
of a dietetic Reformation, in whom his opponents readily
discovered an emissary of the devil.

This would agree with what evidently represents the oldest form of the legend known to us, the Danish prose *Märchen* printed by Thiele[1]. It tells simply that the devil, seeing the virtuous life of the monks of Esrom, assumed human shape, knocked at the door, and was admitted as cook's boy[2]. A favourable opportunity enabling him to dispose of his chief in a boiling cauldron he is appointed to his place. The virtue of the convent is now at his mercy ; and it is not long before the monks forget prayer and fasting over Ruus' exquisite cookery. Strife and wantonness creep in, and the monks are all but lost when a peasant, who has involuntarily over-heard a conclave of devils discussing their agent Ruus, discloses his true nature[3]. The abbot, summoning all the monks into the church, seizes Ruus, transforms him into a red horse, and commits him to the power of hell.

Such was probably the whole of the legend in its strictly Danish form. In the course of the fifteenth century it passed into Lower Saxony, was reproduced in verse with large additions, and this ampler version of the legend was then again transferred, about the middle of the sixteenth century, to its original home. The history of the myth in Denmark is thenceforth blended with that of the developed and in part foreign

---

[1] *Danske Folkesagn* II. 68 ; Wolf and Endlicher p. XVIII. It is given, in translation, by Schade u. s. and Thoms.

[2] To appreciate the significance of this choice of good living as the method of corruption, one needs to remember that in the mediaeval view, gluttony was one of the deadliest of the Deadly Sins, and that Dante could give even the *lussuriosi* a higher rank in the Inferno,—the second circle (canto V), than the *gulosi*, who occupy the third (canto VI).

[3] I cannot agree with Bruun that this scene, whether in the Danish or the German version, was the basis of the great scene in Lessing's fragment of *Faust*.

form of it given in the Danish poem[1], to which, with the cognate versions in Low Saxon and High German, I now turn.

The Low-Saxon, H. German, and Danish versions of Friar Rush.   All three substantially agree, but differ considerably in style. The first, undoubtedly the oldest, is written in the most unpretending manner of the rhymed chronicle ; it tells its story briefly, in simple sentences strung together with scarcely any articulation, and not the slightest rhetorical colour. Of the High German version this is also in the main true ; it shows also the weakness of an unskilful verse translation, often expanding without necessity, and altering without improvement[2]. The Danish version, on the other hand, belongs to a different

---

[1] The first Danish allusion to his name, which does not occur before the 17th century in historical documents, is in Christen Hansen's *Dorothea* (see Appendix), 1531:—

> Giiffve gwd hwer viil icke wære saa fuuss
> lligher uiss ssom them dieffvel broder ruuss.

(Bruun p. 17). Schade quotes it in modern spelling. The well-known testimonies of Hamsfort, and of Helvaderus (quoted by Pontoppidan), take us back only to about 1600, and may have been influenced by the legend. It is hardly worth while noticing the story solemnly recorded by Peder Resen and solemnly repeated by Wadskjär, *Poetisk Skueplads*, (Kjöb. 1741) p. 108, of a Copenhagen nobleman who in the early half of the seventeenth century was accustomed to frighten his children with Broder Ruus.

[2] Merely as an instance I quote the opening lines of the adventure in the hollow tree :—where the abbot sends for the cook to be his procurer.

> Dâr nâ to einer tît broder Rûs
> hadde gewesen to lange van hûs.
> he hadde to der koken nicht gedacht
> unde quam gelopen in groter jacht.
>   Schade u. s. p. 391, vv. 183—6.

phase of literary art. It is a free paraphrase by a skilful writer, obviously emancipated from the conventional manner of the mediaeval romance,—a writer worthy to follow, in the work of translating into his mother tongue, the enlightened and patriotic Christiern Pedersen, with whose type, if Bruun's judgment may be trusted, the 1555 edition was printed[1]. In his hands the narrative gains vivacity, the verse rhythm and flow, the style colour and freshness[2]. Almost any page would serve for comparison; I choose one from the last,—the abbot's charge to Rus as he commits him to his final fate.

In the High German (Strassburg 1515) version this is expanded thus :

> Uff einer zeit dar nach nicht lang
> rauschen sein schalckheit aber zwang.
> Er was zuom kloster auss gegangen,
> ob er möcht etwas news erlangen.
> Do mit het er den speiss vergessen,
> die die münch do solten essen,
> und do er das het überdacht,
> nach dem kloster ward im gach.
>
> Wolf u. s. sig. A vi

[1] On Pedersen see C. J. Brandt's monograph *Om Lunde-Kanniken Christiern Pedersen og hans Skrifter* (Kjöbenh. 1882), and his edition of Pedersen's Danish writings in 5 vols, the last of which contains his versions of the Danish chronicles and additions, full of fervid national pride, to Saxo.

[2] Bruun hardly overstates the case when he remarks, (with an exultation pardonable to a Dane in 1867): 'In the Danish *Broder Rus* there is an exuberant gaiety...which the German poems lack, and it displays a dramatic action which in the German will be sought in vain.' *Broder Rus*, p. 3. Cf. his illustrations pp. 4—9. No previous writer, German or English, had I believe noticed the distinct character of the Danish version, evident even in the extracts given by Nyerup.

This is the H. Germ. version, which, and not the Low
Saxon[1], was the basis of the Danish.

> Der apt sprach: 'hie leyt nit ferne
> ein berck, do solt du wonen gerne,
> solang bis kumpt der jungste tag,
> vor dem sich niemant verbergen mag.
> du solt auch [nie] kummen von danne
> das du nit beschedigst weib und manne.'

This becomes in the Danish :

> Abbeden suarede met alffvers tale
> jeg vil dig ey lenger forhale.
> Icke langt her fra jeg siger dig dette
> ligger et greseligt öde sted
> Der skalt du bo til euig tid
> oc aldrig mere komme hid
> Eller nogen sted i andre land
> du skalt ey skade quinde eller mand
> Du skalt ey skade fisk eller fæ
> ey hus, ey marck, ey skou eller træ
> Eller nogen anden verdsens creature
> men ligge der til domme dag oc lure[2].

[1] I am not aware that this has been pointed out. It is clear
however from internal evidence. The passage quoted in the text,
for instance, is represented in the Low Saxon by:

> de abbe to eme sprak 'hir licht verne
> eine borch, dâr schalstu gerne
> in singen unde ôk dâr tô lesen
> unde êwich dâr uppe wesen.
> du schalst dâr nummer mêr ute kamen.'

The special prohibition to injure mankind, on which the Dane
rings the changes for four lines, is only contained in the High
German. The Danish notion of a 'grim waste spot' is also obviously
due to the H. Germ. mistranslation *ein berck* for the L. Saxon *eine
borch* which reappears in the English *a castle*.

[2] The Danish version can however be concise as well as
elaborate; its length therefore, (rather over 600 lines) is not much
in excess of the H. Germ. (572 in Schade's reprint of Gutknecht's
edition): while the excess of the latter over the Low Saxon (428) is
a fair measure of its variations, which are mostly expansions.

One other peculiarity of the Danish version has not I believe been pointed out.   It repeatedly deviates from the German account, where this differs from the native Danish legend, to follow the latter.   Thus the abbot in the former asks Rausch's name, not on his first interview, but on despatching him as procurer.   The Danish version corrects this.   In both Danish versions too,—trifling as the matter is,—Rus takes one quarter of the slain cow, whereas the more robust Rausch carries off a half.   In more important deviations, however, the Dane follows his German authority even for the worse. To give a crucial instance, he fully adopts and even amplifies the dark picture which the Saxon had drawn of the original moral state of Esrom, in the face of the completely contradictory Danish tradition.   According to the latter it is the exceptional virtue of the convent[1] which attracts the diabolic assault, according to the former its exceptional godlessness[2]; in the Danish view the blamelessness of Esrom, like Job's, makes its conquest an alluring problem, in the German, its corruption offers it a temptingly easy prey.   The former is undoubtedly the stronger, as well as the more original, motive ; there is an evident awkwardness in the despatch of a tempter to men already committed to at least one deadly sin.   If it were doubtful, there are two testimonies

---

[1] The devil saw *hvor fromt og dydigt munkene levede paa Esrom kloster.*   This contrast is noticed by Bruun.

[2] Thus the Low-Saxon :

> Dâr weren moniken in ein dêl
> se weren junk und dâr tô gêl
> svarte cappen drogen se dâr
> se en deneden gade nicht en hâr.
> ein islik hadde dâr ein wîf:
> des quam under se manigen kîf.
> ere levent de duvel wol vornam, &c.

which would go far to settle it: that of Goethe, who prefaced his *Faust* with the prologue of the book of Job; and that of the shrewd playwright Decker, who in handling this very story of Rush, as we shall presently see, was led back by sheer dramatic instinct to the original legend, in the face of every version of it which he can possibly have known[1].

Rush's after-history.

I have still to speak of the most remarkable new feature of the German versions: the after-history of Rush. Transformed into a horse, he crosses the sea to England, possesses the king's daughter, and yields only to the exorcism of his former abbot, summoned for the purpose from Esrom.   As penance he is made to carry a load of lead for the abbey roof, the king's gift, together with the abbot himself, back to Denmark; and is finally banished to a solitary castle, with the strict charge, already quoted, to refrain from further injury to man or woman.

Schade is I think undoubtedly right in regarding this as modelled, in Lower Saxony, on the legend of St Zeno, which a still extant Plattdeutsch poem shows to have been current in the same district.   Zeno, like the abbot, has entertained the devil unawares in the disguise of his own son.   When the fraud is at length discovered the devil goes 'into the east,' and possesses a king's daughter.   Like Rush, however, he discloses the name of the man who is able to exorcise him.   Zeno is summoned; a devil in horse's shape bears him to the eastern

---

[1] Another case in which the later Danish version has described an obviously better motive of the earlier, is in the scene where the farmer whose ox Rus had slaughtered, is an unwilling witness of the devils' conclave from a hollow tree.   In the former, as in the German versions, he is made to take refuge there from mere fatigue; in the latter in order to wait the return of the thief, who has hung the remainder of the ox on a tree opposite.

court, where he casts out the fiend, and then returns
home as he had come[1]. An ordinary saint's miracle
legend was then grafted, incongruously enough, upon
the original Rus story. Rus's sharply defined task of
corrupting Esrom with dainty cookery is exchanged for
vague feats of possession; and the abbot once conspicuous for his vices is suddenly invested with the saintly
privilege of exorcism.

Such was the form in which the legend of Rush, *The Eng-*
after traversing Germany and Denmark, finally reached *lish Friar Rush.*
England. The well-known prose History, entered in the
Stationers' Register 1567-8, was already in every one's
hands by 1584, when R. Scot, in an often-quoted passage
referred his readers to it. The first extant edition (1620)
is a paraphrase very much looser than even the Danish,
and made probably from one of the High German
(Nürnberg) editions, which appeared between 1550 and
1582[2]. It is a rather verbose narrative, with not only a
host of new details, but so much fresh incident that it
stands to the German versions almost in the same relation which these bear to the original Danish legend.
In all these, for instance, the origin of Rus' adventure is
dismissed with a single phrase,—'the devil seeing the
evil ways of Esrom, disguised himself as a cook, and
knocked at the door.' But the translator saw his opportunity, and the story of Rush's journey is introduced
by a sketch of the diabolic council which authorises
it. So again, the adventure in which Rush, belated
at a distance from home, provides dinner for the convent by the extempore slaughter of an ox, is worked
up into an elaborate narrative which accounts for Rush's

---

[1] This description is based upon Schade's abstract (u. s.) of the
S. Zeno legend, which I have not myself seen.

[2] Cf. Schade u. s., p. 360.

long absence by help of a tavern scene, where he 'found good fellowes playing at cardes, and drinking and making cheare, then Rush made obeysance to them and sate downe among them,...and afterward he fell to play, and was as merrie as any man in the company: and so long he played and passed the time, that cleane hee had forgotten what he had to doe at home,' &c.; and when Rush at length reaches the abbey laden with his two quarters of beef, the translator once more calls us in on his own authority to see them dressed and cooked.

All this however was merely the result of the familiar attempt to adapt the simplicity and abstract language of the verse romance to the genius of an English prose story, with its insatiable love of incident, for crude detail, its anxiety to bring everything before the eye. But there are differences which strike deeper than these. The English Rush has obviously been modified by two distinct influences, one of them purely English, the other, like Rush himself, a quite recent result of intercourse with Germany. Ulenspiegel, though essentially of a different mythic type, bore too striking a superficial likeness to Rush to be kept completely distinct; and the mutual attraction was the greater since one of Ulenspiegel's adventures occurred in a convent. It is as a verger in the abbey of Marienthal that being told to 'count the monks' as they came to 'evening mass, he cuts away the steps by which they descend, and 'counts' their prostrate forms on the floor (No. 89). This, and the other still duller jest with the Hildesheim merchant, whom he serves as kitchen-boy (No. 64: being told to grease the carriage he greases the seat) are introduced into the English History of Rush, obviously because he also served in a kitchen and in a convent. Obviously too they are quite out of place there. Pure types of the merely wanton quibbling humour of Ulenspiegel, they are quite foreign to the politic devil whose jesting is only a mode of strategy.

More interesting is the second case. Robin Goodfellow, like Ulenspiegel, bore a certain but also only superficial resemblance to Rush. His 'merry pranks' are neither diabolic strategy, nor wanton outrage, but freaks of good nature tempered now and then by just resentment. We have already seen how his legend was mutilated under the powerful influence of the German Ulenspiegel: in revenge, the German Rush was now attracted still more completely by his. There were obvious points in the myth of Rush to suggest the comparison. If Rush was not originally a water-elf, as Schade supposes, his story was at least full of elvish traits[1]. The evil spirit disguised as cook recalled the household service for which Puck was famed, the swimming horse into which he is transformed was paralleled by equally familiar feats of transformation. That England was the goal of his journey was itself a trait of elf mythology[2]. It was therefore in no way an abstruse process which led to his intimate connexion with the native English kobold. This had consequences far more disastrous to the congruity of the story than the addition of the Zeno myth, far more than even the surreptitious dash of Ulenspiegel. Not merely is a story introduced

[1] Cf. Schade u. s. p. 382 f., where this is well worked out. Wright's essay (*Essays on the Middle Ages*, II. 1 ff.) contains a quantity of material on this head, rather loosely and popularly treated.

[2] On England as the mythic home of elves and nightmares, see Schade u. s. p. 383. Schade is wrong however in saying that the horse is Rush's 'original' form; the passage of the English version from which he argues implies the exact opposite. Rush is there said to be changed [from a horse, which he already was] 'to his original form,' viz., I suppose, that of a devil.

which though hardly founded on any extant legend of Goodfellow, is completely in his manner, but the central incident of the second part of the History is radically transformed in the same sense[1].   The first is the tale of Rush's intervention between an unfortunate married man and his wife, to the complete discomfiture of the interloping priest.   Rush's mission of corruption is here obviously forgotten.   In the other case, he passes still more explicitly through the whole interval which separates the devil from the good-natured kobold.   Instead of 'possessing' the king's daughter, he becomes the means of restoring her sanity.   Having taken service, as 'a poore young man,' with a gentleman[2], he is asked by his master 'as they went talking together,' whether he knew of any man 'that can conjure a spirit out of a woman's body.'   Rush makes no doubt of his ability to find one, passes across the sea to Esrom, fetches the prior, who performs the cure, and is then brought back as he had come,—a still closer parallel to the Zeno story, it is clear, than the German versions.   After this, the banishment of Rush into the castle, and his sudden resumption of devil nature, becomes still more incongruous.

But the process of assimilation to Goodfellow was destined to be carried still further.   By a chance certainly rather unusual in England, but by no means unexampled or anomalous as has been thought[3], Friar Rush

---

[1] This is briefly noticed by Lappenberg, *Ulenspiegel*, p. 228.

[2] The substitution of a 'gentleman,' for the 'king' of the original Rush legend is characteristic of the legend of Robin Goodfellow, a household spirit who does not haunt palaces.

[3] Wright (*Essays* &c. u. s.) goes so far as to suggest that there was a native English Friar Rush.   But similar transplantations abound in comparative mythology.   Even in quite recent times

passed from the pages of the German story-book into
the living folk lore of England. Long before the appearance of the English translation, he was a familiar
figure, in company with such popular favourites as the
Nine Worthies and the Prodigal Son, on the painted
cloth hangings of taverns;—the cloth being probably
imported, as such arras mostly was, from the Netherlands, the medium of almost every German legend which
reached us. Here however he was still distinctly the
disguised devil; the graphic lines in *Gammer Gurton's
Needle* make this clear[1]. A generation later he has
undergone a remarkable transformation. Not only has
the alien completely established himself in the fearful
fancy of rural England, but in the process he has put on
the likeness of the rest of the rustic pantheon whose
dominion he shared. From Christian he has passed over
into Teutonic mythology. The English pucks and gob-
lins have admitted him into their merry company ; and
the devil forgets his mission, and condescends, like Goodfellow, to play the village censor, and to stickle for
propitiatory bowls of cream[2].

something very like it has occasionally occurred ; only the other day
M. Maspero had to warn the Egyptological world that some tales of
his own collection, casually related to some Arabs at Thebes, were
already circulating in the country as quasi-native legends. And
probably not a few English children are brought up, as the present
writer was, in the faith of the German Santa Claus.

[1]   Saw ye never Fryer Rushe
    Painted on a cloth with a sidelong cow's tayle,
    And crooked cloven feet,......
    Looke, even what face fryer Rushe had, the devil had
        such another.

[2] The passage in Harsenet's *Declaration* 1604, has been often
quoted: 'If that the bowle of creame were not duly set out for

Rush in after literature. To all appearance however, this complete assimilation to the English household sprites, was confined to
the region of folklore. In literature, the literary version
of the legend kept its hold; and of the two dramas
which were probably based upon it, the only one which
is extant drops altogether the kobold element, and is in
fact, as we shall presently see, nothing but a set of
ingenious and in parts effective variations on the original
theme of the Devil-cook. Before discussing this name
at length, it remains to speak very briefly of the second,
to the nature of which the sole clue is unfortunately its
title and its author's name.

Dramas. 1. 'Friar Rush and the Proud Woman of Antwerp,' 1601. In July, 1601, Henslowe referred in his Diary to a
drama called *Friar Rush and the Proud Woman of Ant-
werp*, then in course of composition by two of the staff-
dramatists of his company, Day and Haughton. The
title gives no direct clue to the plot; for the 'History'
knows nothing of Antwerp, nor of any woman specifically
'proud.' It is nevertheless plausible to suppose that
the story of Rush's intervention between a wife and her
clerical lover has here been simply transferred to new
scenery and circumstances. Without discussing further
an insoluble question, I will merely raise one alternative
hypothesis. I shall have to notice, in speaking of
Decker's Rush drama, the remarkable Novella of Mac-
chiavel on the 'marriage of Belphegor,' to which Decker
has been supposed to owe more than is I think the case.
Belphegor is an Italian counterpart of Rush, despatched
by Lucifer on a special mission to earth, not to tempt
and corrupt, but to test, by a ten years' experience, the
truth of men's universal abuse of marriage. And the
whole point of the story lies in his taking as his wife one

Robin Goodfellow, the *frier*, and Sisse the Dairy maid, why then
either the pottage was burnt the next day, or &c.'

who is not only a 'proud woman,' but characterised almost solely by her pride [1]. Finding his domestic life at
Florence unsupportable, Belphegor makes his escape;
and, like the German Rush, devotes himself to 'possession.' The part of the prior is played by a former
benefactor of his, to whose exorcism he on several
occasions willingly yields, in token of his gratitude.
Finally however, conceiving that the service has been
sufficiently repaid, he refuses obedience, and all the
devices of exorcism fail to extract him from the possessed
princess, until it is intimated that the 'proud woman'
of Florence is on his traces; when in dire terror he
precipitately breaks out and takes flight to his native
realm.   It is obvious that this plot, which can hardly
have been unknown to the scholarly and cultured Day,
would give a point to the title of this lost play which on
the other hypothesis it does not possess.   I hasten however to turn from this perhaps idle speculation, to more
solid ground,—the indubitable Rush-drama which Decker
a dozen years later concealed under the fantastic title:
If this be not a good play, the Divell is in it [2].

For boldly planned and all-embracing infernal machinery, the play has no rival in the Elizabethan drama.
Faustus, not Mephistophilis, is the real starting-point of
the action of Marlowe's play, Prospero, not Ariel or
Caliban, of that of the Tempest; if the witches initiate
the plot of *Macbeth*, or Fortune that of *Fortunatus*, they
take no active part of it.   Here, however, the realm of

2.
Decker:
*If this be
not a good
Play, the
Divell is
init.* 1612.

----

[1] 'Aveva Onesta...portato in casa Roderigo insieme con la
nobiltà seco, e con la bellezza, tanta superbia, che non n'ebbe mai
Lucifero.' So again: 'l' insolente natura di lei.'

[2] I am not aware that Decker's play has been noticed by any
writer on the Rush legend, in connexion with it. I have accordingly
treated it at some length.

Pluto supplies both the first spring of action, and the main actors, who, after setting the intrigue afoot, dexterously guide it from point to point up to the desired catastrophe. The opening scene is an altercation of Pluto and Charon which reads like a rude reminiscence of Lucian. It is hard times with both, for 'Ghosts come not now thronging to my boate, But drop by one and one in;' and the royal table needs replenishing. To meet the pressing emergency, three fiends are hastily despatched to earth. Ruffman takes a Courtier's disguise, and makes for the court of young Alphonso of Naples; Grumshall puts on the citizen's 'treble ruffles' and goes to take service with Barterville, a well-reputed Naples merchant, and Shackle-soule, assuming the 'grave habit' of a friar, seeks 'the Friery best fam'd in Naples for strict orders.'

This opening scene was supposed by Langbaine to have been suggested by Macchiavelli's well-known *Novella*, already mentioned, on the marriage of Belphegor. Mr Halliwell, following him, asserts less guardedly (*Dict. of Old Eng. Plays*), that 'the principal plot of the play is founded on' the *Novella*. The latter statement is quite inadmissible, as any reader of the two works will perceive. The former appears to me very doubtful. Macchiavelli's tale, which is scarcely more than a *jeu d'esprit*, certainly opens with the despatch of a fiend to the earth in human shape, but, this fancy, of which he was certainly not the inventor, or the chief representative, is used as we have seen, with a motive and in a manner quite different from Decker's. It is simply a satire on marriage. The whole management of the scene is moreover different; Macchiavelli's Hades is the council-chamber of an Italian Senate, Decker's might pass for some tavern haunt of Thames watermen. Decker's fiends are the drudges of Pluto, abused for their indolence, flogged at will, and peremptorily sent where he chooses. Macchiavelli's are fiends whose advice he requests with the gravest courtesy and deference, and who give it with dignity and independence [1].

But the whole comparison with the *Novella* is in fact superfluous, for a much closer suggestion of the scene is to be found in the book which supplied, as we shall see, the foundation of the main plot,—the *Pleasant Historie of Frier Rush*. The opening chapter tells in its simple way after recounting the corruption of the friars, how the great Prince of Devils, when he 'understood of the great misrule and vile living of these Religious men, consulted to keepe them still in that state, and worse if it might be...*Belphegor* who was Prince of Gluttony, *Asmodeus* Prince of Lechery, and *Belzebub* Prince of Envie, with many other Divels assembled together... And as they were all assembled together with one accord: they chose a Divell to goe and dwell among these Religious men, for to maintaine them the longer in their ungracious living, which Divell was put in rayment like an earthly creature, and went to a Religious house...'

From this hint Decker took the whole conception of his play. The adventures of Rush in the convent would have been in themselves, however, too meagre fare for the highly seasoned palate of the playgoer of 1612, for whom double and treble plots were rapidly becoming an indispensable dramatic luxury; the monastic scenery was moreover unfamiliar and somewhat unreal. He accordingly produced two other stories, closely modelled on that of Rush, but carrying us into the two worlds in

[1] Although, he says, *dilettissimi mei*, I am king by divine will, yet *perchè egli è maggior prudenza di quelli che possono più, sottomettersi alle leggi, e più stimare l'altrui giudizio, ho deliberato essere da voi consigliato*, &c.

which the imagination of a London audience was most
at home,—the City and the Court. The main action is
accordingly woven of three distinct threads which only at
the close become in some degree entangled. The three
fiends do their work of corruption independently in their
three spheres. In each case they begin on virgin soil[1].
The young king announces intentions of the most
exalted virtue; his time will be devoted to old soldiers
and poor scholars; he forgives his debtors and bids his
prostrate courtiers kneel only to God. The merchant,
though without any virtuous prepossessions, has hitherto
kept within the verge of honesty. And the friars are
accustomed to spend the sad day wholly in religious fasts
and 'meager contemplation.' But a very brief experience of the suggestions of our worser nature suffices
to overthrow these unstable pillars of morality. A few
elegant phrases from Ruffman, the distinguished 'Hel-
vetian,' convince Alphonso that pleasure is the appointed
end of kings; and he is suddenly transformed into a
miracle of lust and tyranny, contemptuously dismisses
not only the old soldier and the poor scholar but his
bride, and is finally brought to the verge of ruin by her
father's vengeance. Old Bartervile, the merchant, falls
an equally easy victim to the snares of his cunning clerk,
and is presently found vigorously practising what he
calls the *true Citie doctrine*, that *Nature sent man into the
world (alone), Without all company, but to care for one;*—

---

[1] A judicious divergence from the *Historie*, where they are 'full
of wantonnesse' from the first. Decker is thus brought back by
sheer dramatic feeling to the original conception of the story, embodied in the phrase of the Danish legend, that the diabolic assault
was excited by seeing *hvor fromt og dydigt Munkene levede.* We
may perhaps detect here the influence of the grand prelude to the
book of Job.

And that ile doe. And the friars at once succumb to the
fascinations of rich fare provided for them by Shackle-
soule under the notorious name of RUSH.

The details of this last transformation are in
the main cleverly adapted from the romance. In
the first friary scene (Decker, ed. Hazlitt, III. 280)
Rush appears as junior novice, preparing the conven-
tual table,—'So; the Lord prior's napkin here,...his
knife and case of pick-toothes thus,' and *nimble as a
drawer in a new Tavern.* It falls to his lot to say the
grace which sanctifies the dinner of herbs and cold water,
and he does it in a fashion on which nearly all the
boasted asceticism of the convent goes shipwreck:—

> Hum, hum,
> For our bread, wine, ale and beere
> For the piping-hot meates heere:
> For brothes of sundrie tasts and sort,
> For beefe, veale, mutton, lamb, and porke,
> Greene-sawce with calfes head and bacon,
> Pig and goose, and cramd-up capon,
> For past raiz'd stiffe with curious art,
> Pye, custard, florentine and tart,—

and so forth through a gamut of continually ascending
exquisiteness to the climax of 'oyster-pyes, butter'd crab,
prawnes, lobsters thighes.' The burst of indignation
which follows is evidently not quite genuine, and little
difficulty is felt in assenting to the acute logic with which
Rush argues that *Anima sequitur temperaturam Corporis*,
—'and hee that feedes well hath a good temperature of
body, *Ergo*, he that feedes well hath a good soule.' One
only, the Sub-prior,—breaks the unanimity with which it
is resolved that Rush, who declines to be cook himself,
shall give the cook lessons agair.st night, 'for fare
abundant and delicious.' 'Rush thart some Angel!'

exclaims the prior, enthusiastically. 'Rather, mutters the Sub-prior, some divell sent to bewitch our soules[1].'

The following scenes are occupied with working out two motives, Rush's quarrel with the Cook, and his attempt to corrupt the isolated virtue of the Sub-prior. The former alone had any basis in the Romance. In the first scene (u.s. p. 303 ff.) the friars are met by the Sub-prior hastening under the lead of Rush to their Vines. 'Your Vines?' cries the Sub-prior,

> —this Serpent here,
> Has with that liquorish poison, so set on fire,
> The braines of *Nicodeme* and *Silvester*,
> That they in drunken rage have stab'd each other.

Yes, retorts Rush,—

> They bleede a little, but have no harme,—
> They brawld and struck, but I kept off the blowes,
> Yet the Sub-prior saies from me their quarrell rose.

And he proceeds to vindicate his character as one who 'repines to see vice prosper,' by telling a slanderous story of the Cook[2].

[1] The romance contains merely a general hint for this scene. It is only after the death of the Master Cook that Rush replaces him, and that the improved fare begins: 'Thus Rush became Maister-Cooke in the Kitchin, and dressed their meate mervailous well: for in the Lent, and in the Advent, both Fridayes and also other dayes, he put Bacon into their pottage pot, &c....insomuch that the Priour and all the Friers...said he did much better than their other Maister-cooke, &c.' (chap, III.). The antipathy of the Prior and Sub-prior is touched in chapter IV. but the idea of making the latter represent the moral Opposition is Decker's own.

[2] This scene combines a hint from Chap. IV. of the romance,— 'How Frier Rush made Truncheons for the Friers to fight withall,' and then plays the indignant peace-maker,—with the bias against the Cook there indicated by the act of putting him into the kettle (chap. II.); as well as with the general motive of corruption by good fare.

After a passage in which Rush vainly attempts to corrupt the insensible Sub-prior with gold[1], we arrive (p. 325) at a scene obviously founded on the eighth chapter of the romance. Scumbroth, the cook, who has proved less incorruptible, is found, like 'the prodigall child in the painted cloth'—all his money spent and gone, taking refuge in a grove near Naples. There, like the farmer of the *Historie* whom Rush has robbed of his heifer, he unwillingly witnesses the meeting of the Devils which discloses the character of Rush. 'Lucifer and divels' enter with thunder and lightning; Rush and his fellows follow; they 'sit under the tree all about him,' and Lucifer demands an account of their work in Court, City and Friary[2]. Rush is the last to speak:

Luc. Hath *Rush* lyen ydle?
Sha. Ydle? no Lucifer.
Scu. (aside). All the world is turnd divell. *Rush* is one of them.
Sha. Ydle? I have your nimblest divell bin,
    In twentie shapes begetting sin......
    I am fishing for a whole schoole of Friers,
    Al are gluttoning or muttoning, stabbing or swelling,
    Ther's onely one lambe scapes my killing,
    But I will have him[3].

---

[1] A speech here is in Mr Hazlitt's edition (p. 310), wrongly attributed to Rush, instead of the Sub-prior. The speech opens with the word '*Rush!*' which Mr Hazlitt or his copyist has converted into the name of the speaker, and placed in the margin.

[2] The romance describes how the Farmer 'came to an hollow tree wherein he sate him downe,...and he had not sitten there but a while; but anon there assembled a company of Devils, and among them they had a great principall Maister whose name was *Lucifer*, and he was the first that spake: and the first that was called, was a Devill named *Belzabub*, and with a loud voyce, he said unto him: *Belzabub*, what hast thou done for us?'

[3] Cf. the romance chap. VIII.; 'Then foorth went Frier *Rush* freshly, and with a good courage, and said: Sir, I am in a Religious

The cook, like the farmer, reports the real character of Rush to the Friars (p. 342). In the conclusion the friary becomes the centre of the action; the King in friar's disguise seeks refuge there from his enemies, Bartervile, similarly, from his dupes and creditors, and the whole issues in an infernal catastrophe, far inferior to the prelude, in which Bartervile appears in torments in company with the heroes of the most sensational contemporary crimes, Ravaillac and Guy Fawkes.

The play was evidently written with haste, and Decker's taste for the preternatural has allowed him to daub more than one page with the cheapest kind of pantomime devilry. But it has this ground of interest, that it shews once more, and more completely than elsewhere, the kind of flower and fruit which a very crude German legend was capable of yielding under clever treatment in the stimulating air of the Elizabethan drama. The mere reproduction of the story of the Friar is of little consequence in comparison with its widened scope. The 'diabolic mission' which originally served as a jest against the monks in an age when they were the mark for the abuse of every satiric pen in Europe, was extended to the more complex society of the seventeeth century, in which monasticism might claim to have handed over the better part, not only of its old wealth and power, but of its old vices to the City and the Court. No doubt there was something grotesque in this transfer

place, and I governe the Priour and his Covent as I will myselfe, and they have me in great love and favour?...Then said the maister Devill to Rush; if thou have done as thou hast said, thou hast done well thy part, and I pray thee be diligent thyselfe about thy businesse, &c.' The more churlish Lucifer of Decker only imitates this courteous rejoinder so far as to bid him, 'goe, ply your workes, our Sessions are at hand,' (p. 329). It is a singular inconsequence that the *Pluto* of the first scene is here replaced by the *Lucifer* of the romance.

of a mediaeval diabolic motive to a wholly modern world, in the spectacle of a devil bound apprentice to a merchant, counting crowns and studying mortgages like any Ralph or Robin of Cheapside; but this is the fault of Decker's genius rather than of his conception. For it is impossible to ignore that, with no other help than his sound playwright's instincts, and without a suspicion of its immense potentialities, he had stumbled upon the very idea afterwards carried out in Goethe's *Faust,*—the recasting of an old devil-story in terms of modern society. The polished urbanity of King Alphonso's guest, the ironical serviceableness of the merchant's clerk, already at isolated points recall the Mephistophiles of Goethe rather than that of Marlowe, and assuredly there is no scene in Marlowe's *Faustus,*—the immortal opening and close always excepted—at all equal in conception to Decker's pictures of the sudden transformation under temptation of a court of frail idealists and a convent of only half voluntary ascetics. Unhappily, however, Decker was after all little more than a hack with ideas, and the pinch of want probably contributed to make his work still less really significant than his total want of in-tellectual seriousness, of the brooding faculty, the austere enthusiasm of a great artist for his art, would in any case have permitted it to be.

The production of such a piece as the *If this play be not good* in the second decade of the seventeenth century was in some sense an anachronism, and the supernatural machinery, imperfectly welded as it was in the texture of an otherwise thoroughly realistic drama, was probably more congenial to the mob of all ranks[1], to the public

---

[1] It is a mistake to ascribe this taste to the 'groundlings' alone; the prologue in which Jonson uses the phrase is directly addressed to the 'grandees' upon the stage.

whom Jonson twitted with its untiring devotion to another
famous devil-drama—'your dear delight, the *Devil of
Edmonton*'—than to the more fastidious critics of whom
Jonson himself was the most eminent.   Nevertheless,
with all Jonson's evident disposition to be sarcastic over
the crude supernaturalism of the popular devil-drama,
they offered something which was capable of being
assimilated by his own far greater and more thoughful
art; and it is not difficult to understand how, four years
after Decker's play, he came to produce a devil-drama of
his own, in the prologue of which he implicitly courts
comparison with his two predecessors[1].

B. Jonson: Jonson had in fact so far the Aristophanic quality of
The Devil   genius, that he was at once a most elaborate and minute
is an Ass.
1616.   student of the actual world, and a poet of the airiest and
boldest fancy, and that he loved to bring the two rôles
into the closest possible combination.   No one so capable
of holding up the mirror to contemporary society without
distorting the slenderest thread of its complex tissue of
usages; no one, on the other hand, who so keenly delighted in startling away the illusion or carefully under-
mining it by some palpably fantastic invention.   His
most elaborate reproductions of the everyday world are
hardly ever without an infusion of equally elaborate
caprice,—a leaven of recondite and fantastic legend and
grotesque myth, redolent of old libraries and antique
scholarship—furtively planted, as it were, in the heart of

[1] Shew this, he cries to the grandees who cumbered the stage,

Shew this but the same face you have done
Your dear delight, The devil of Edmonton.
Or, if for want of room it must miscarry,
'Twill be but justice that your censure tarry,
Till you give some: and when six times you have seen't
If this play do not like, the Devil is in't.

that everyday world of London life, and so subtly blending with it that the whole motley throng of merchants
and apprentices, gulls and gallants, discover nothing
unusual in it, and engage with the most perfectly matter
of fact air in the business of working it out. The purging
of Crispinus in the *Poetaster*, the Aristophanic motive of
the *Magnetic lady*, even the farcical horror of noise
which is the main-spring of the *Epicœne*, are only less
elaborate and sustained examples of this fantastic realism than the adventure of a Stupid Devil in the play
before us. Nothing more anomalous in the London of
Jonson's day could be conceived; yet it is so managed
that it loses all its strangeness. So perfectly is the supernatural element welded with the human, that it almost
ceases to appear supernatural. Pug, the hero of the
adventure, is a pretty, petulant boy, more human by
many degrees than the half fairy Puck of Shakspere,
which doubtless helped to suggest him[1], and the arch-
fiend Satan is a bluff old politician, anxious to ward
off the perils of London from his young simpleton of
a son, who is equally eager to plunge into them. The
old savage horror fades away before Jonson's humanising
touch, the infernal world loses all its privilege of peculiar

[1] The conception of a 'stupid devil' (*dummer Teufel*) though
not precisely unfamiliar, had not obtained much currency in English
literature. The devil of the Mysteries was regularly beaten by
the Vice, but no attempt was ever made to emphasize the inferiority
of intellect possibly implied in this form of receptivity. The Merry
Devil on the other hand is far more distinctly a *stupid* devil; and
even the quick intellect of Shakspere's Puck betrays a flaw when
he involuntarily roughens the path of true love for the wrong pair
of lovers. In name, and in a certain pretty boyishness, the last
reappears in Jonson's Pug; but on the other hand he is much more
essentially dull than any of his predecessors, and his story is of
a wholly different cast.

terror and strength, and sinks to the footing of a
mere rival state, whose merchandise can be kept out of
the market and its citizens put in the Counter or carted
to Tyburn.

The characteristic conception of Decker's prologue,
that the world is becoming a full match for hell, and needs
to be attacked with the utmost art and policy, meets us
here in a more developed form.   Decker makes the
souls evade Charon and his pence, and Pluto angrily
forbids him to raise his fare lest men should find him 'so
damned deere, [They] will not come to hell, crying out
th' are heere Worse racke (*sic*) then th'are in tavernes.'
Jonson's Satan is equally politic.   Pug is 'too dull a
devil to be trusted Forth in those parts;...the state of
hell must care Whom it employs, in point of reputation,
Here about London.'   The trusted agents of fifty years
ago, the venerable Iniquity, the once terrible Vice 'in
his long coat shaking his wooden dagger,' are wholly un-
serviceable against an astuter generation, which breeds its
own Vices, as it does its own horses :

> We still strive to breed,
> And rear up new ones; but they do not stand,
> When they come there, they turn them on our hands;
> And it is fear'd they have a stud o' their own
> Will put down ours.   Act. I. Sc. I.

And the action fully confirms these melancholy forebodings.   Pug finds himself in a world where he and
his fellows count for very little,—a world immersed in
practical schemes and matter of fact business, in draining
swamps and finding a market for toothpicks;—and he
feels himself an anachronism.   The whole business of the
play goes on with scarcely an exception exactly as if he
were not present; he is the fly upon the engine-wheel,

fortunate to escape with a bruising; instead of spoiling human plans, he hangs helplessly in the background, or awkwardly intervenes to no one's disadvantage but his own. The *denoûment* of the general intrigue has no influence upon the *denoûment* of Pug's fortunes; he comes to grief through none of his misdeeds in connexion with the main plot, but on account of the preliminary theft of clothes which enabled him to enter on it. Thus the Stupid Devil, instead of being essential to the action, like the Merry Devil and the fiends of Decker, has really nothing to do with it. Notwithstanding the complete difference of treatment however, it is evident I think that Jonson was here working out in his own fashion the idea on which Decker had fallen in the effort to turn the old *Rush* story into a play,—of a diabolic romance of adventure, in the modern world, of a humanised devil not making compacts with the magician or the witch, but taking service with the city merchant and the country gentleman[1].

The Devil is an Ass nevertheless symbolises aptly enough the obsolescence of supernaturalism of every kind in our older drama, and Jonson's sense of it. The devil of the theatre was for the time played out, or survived only in the artless pantomime puppet show, or the wilfully eccentric art of the Masque; and Jonson's helplessly outwitted Pug is a type of the senile stage,—'sans eyes, sans teeth, sans everything'—which preceded his complete extinction.

The course of the present chapter has thus brought us close to the subject of the last, as the last here and there unavoidably anticipated the present. The keen mutual attraction of the ideas of roguery and devilry

---

[1] Pug enters the service of Merewater, as Lurchall that of Bartervile.

continually tended to fasten them on the same object. Faustus and Fortunatus use their magic powers in the very spirit of Owlglass ; and Rush, the Owlglass of monasticism, is taken for a devil in disguise. And the fact that, of the four stories we have reviewed, that of Rush alone got a serious footing in our literature, is one more evidence of that singular quality of the second-rate Elizabethan mind, which made the meanest story with a flavour of devilry often more fascinating than any degree of brilliance or beauty without it.   Precisely these four stories serve to illustrate the law which seems to have controlled so largely our borrowings from Germany—that where there was abundance both of better and worse work, we chose a very little—of the worse.   An inverted evolution seemed to have specially sanctioned the survival of the weakest and most unfit, and heaped the honours of literature upon buffoons like Owlglass and Rush, while it left the good jests of Markolf and the Kalenberger to grow musty in forgotten prints.

From the Jester we pass naturally to the FOOL :— one, however, whose motley is no longer the badge of privileged wit but the brand imposed by an indignant satirist.

CHAPTER VI.

The Ship of Fools.

Stultorum infinitus est numerus. These famous words
sum up as well as any others the fundamental axiom
of all satire, to which every generation of satirists has
given expression in every variety of accent, and phrase.
That the world is a kingdom of Fools is a conviction
easily detected beneath the fine urbanities of Renan,
the glittering irony of Pope. Uttered with more downright and brutal emphasis it is the commonplace in
which the decaying Middle Age invested its whole
capital of intellectual and moral scorn. The commonplace was piquant however, and the extraordinary
variety of expression and metaphor with which it was
seasoned never permitted it to pall. The whole range of
mediaeval institutions, the church, the court, the civic
gild, the monastic fraternity, were imported into the
kingdom of Fools; the animal world swelled its numbers
with 'asses' and 'cuckoos,' 'apes' and 'hares'[1]; pagan
mythology provided Venus and Bacchus for its di-
vinities[2]; Seneca and Solomon, Horace and Juvenal

---

[1] Cf. Zarncke, *Narrenschiff*, p. xlvii. ; Wackernagel, *Kl.
Schriften*, iii. 211; and Murner's *Gauchmatt*.

[2] Cf. Lydgate, *The Order of Fools*, ad init. Venus also presides
over Murner's ' Geuche.'

furnished a store of instances, and the treasury of vernacular proverb-lore an inexhaustible supply of illustration. The most intrinsically original of all these meta-
phors and fancies was due to Germany, and it served as
framework to what was long considered the masterpiece
of German satire, the *Ship of Fools.*

Writing in the last years of the fifteenth century, and
himself a loyal though somewhat backward pupil of the
Humanists, Brandt may be said to have given mediaeval
Fool-literature its last and crowning work. But if he
closed an epoch, he also initiated one. The *Narrenschiff* enjoyed the rare good fortune of winning equal
popularity in the world of scholars and in that of men
who run as they read. Translated into Latin elegiacs by
his disciple Locher, it became one of the classics of Humanism; it supplied More with the point of an epigram[1],
and Erasmus with the conception of his own no doubt
infinitely superior *Praise of Folly.*

And it also gave a fresh stimulus and in some degree a fresh form to vernacular satire both at home
and abroad. In England especially a long series of
writings, from Barclay and Skelton at the beginning of
the century to Tarlton at its close, betrayed the direct
influence of a book which held its ground here even
more persistently than in Germany, and in spite of an
incomparably more formidable competition. With all its
shortcomings it did us great service. It helped to bridge

---

[1] One of those against Germanus Brixius. I do not know that
it has been noticed before in this connexion :

In chordigeram navem et Antimorum sylvam.

Brixius en Germanus habet sylvamque ratemque,
    Dives opum terra, dives opum pelago ;
Utraque vis illi quid praestat scire? *vehuntur*
    In rate stultitiae, sylvam habitant furiae.

over the difficult transition from the literature of personified abstractions to that which deals with social
types. It helped to substitute study of actual men and
women at first hand for the mere accumulation of conventional traits about an abstract substantive; to turn
allegory into narrative, moralities into dramas, and, in a
narrower field, to prepare the way for the Character-
sketches of the seventeenth century, for the revivers of
Chaucer and the imitators of Theophrastus, for Overbury and Hall and Earle[1].

In England however as elsewhere Brandt had pre- *Fool-*
decessors, whose influence only in part coincided with *literature
in Eng-*
his and has to be carefully distinguished from it. This *land before*
distinction falls chiefly upon two Englishmen, the *'The Ship
of Fools.'*
brilliant author of the *Speculum Stultorum*, and the
poet who embodied his morose ethics in the *Order of
Fools*. Both differ from Brandt in starting with the
notion of a religious fraternity. The foundation of the N. Wi-
'Ass's Order,' it will be remembered, is one of the most *reker:
Speculum*
telling episodes of the *Speculum*. After a chequered *Stultorum.*
career of adventure at the university of Paris and elsewhere, the Ass, Brunellus, thinks of retiring from the
world. He weighs the merits of the various religious
orders in succession. Finding none perfectly satis-
factory, he conceives the idea of founding a new Order
which should combine the good points of all the rest; in
which, for instance, he might enjoy horse exercise, like
the Templars, share the liberal diet of the Dominicans,

---

[1] Prof. Ward has already expressed this view in a very full
article on Barclay in the *Dictionary of National Biography* : ' The
English Ship of Fools exercised an important direct influence upon
our literature, pre-eminently helping to bury mediaeval allegory in
the grave which had long yawned before it, and to direct English
authorship into the drama, essay and novel of character.'

the 'one Mass a month' of the Franciscans, the conver-
sational freedom of the Grandimontenses, and, finally,
borrow the privilege of that divinely founded Order of
which Adam and Eve were the first members, and have
a wife[1].

Lydgate:
'*Order of
Fools*'.

Wireker was a precentor of Canterbury under King
John[2]. The Ass's Order dates therefore at latest from
the outset of the thirteenth century. Two and a half
centuries later the 'Order of Fools' is already a common-
place of satire. It was in a certain sense carried into
practice by the Gild of the 'Enfants sans souci,' whose
Soties frequently, as in the *Roy des Sotz*, represented
a Fool-society modelled upon the gild itself[3]. And
Lydgate, in the score of octave stanzas which go by
this name, has given us the best means of learning what
a devout Englishman of his day understood by Folly.
His treatment is wholly different from Wireker's. The
religious order which Brunellus founded with so much
ceremony, has become a faded phrase to Lydgate, and
he barely enlarges on the allusion conveyed by his title.
Wireker sets forth conditions and privileges: Lydgate
does little more than drily enumerate the members,
and the inherent irony of his plan is dispelled at
every moment by an unseasonable earnestness. The
description of the 'sixty-three' Fools is quite without
dramatic life. Though written within two generations
of Chaucer's great *Prologue*, it is a mere catalogue

[1] *Speculum Stultorum*, sig. e.v. ' Novus ordo brunelli.'
[2] Bale, *sub nom.* Cf. the valuable disputation held (in indifferent
Latin before the celebrated Thomasius by Immanuel Weber,—*De
N. Wirekero*, Lips. 1672; the only detailed discussion of Wireker
that I know.
[3] *Ancien Théâtre Français*, ii. Cf. Mr Saintsbury's *Short History*, p. 123.

of isolated traits nowhere elaborated into a portrait, a sort of index of dangerous persons, as it were, calculated for practical utility rather than for aesthetic delight.

The *Narrenschiff* bears the closest resemblance to Lydgate's poem in plan. In both, a long series of *The 'Narrenschiff.'* vicious characters are collected and described under the rubric Fool. But the *Ship of Fools* would assuredly never have become the enormously popular book it was, had it been a mere summary of different kinds of 'Folly,' or even an analysis of the characteristics of various 'Fools.' In conception at least it was more. It was a series of vivid portraits, nay it was even a rudimentary drama in which a succession of Fools, the crew of a Ship bound on a mysterious voyage, appeared in person, and delivered each one his characteristic and self-portraying speech. The idea is no doubt very imperfectly carried out[1], but it is emphasised at the outset, and the impression lasts. We are continually reminded, even by the slightest touches, of the dramatic suppositions of the work; the Fools are charged or exhorted, sorrowfully chidden, or sternly threatened, peremptorily summoned and rallied. And this somewhat hesitating and precarious dramatic life is powerfully enforced by the invariably vivid woodcuts. When the description is most formal and abstract, or loses itself in parallels and 'examples,' the auxiliary art silently secures that the poet shall not be talked out by the moralist.

The advantage which Brandt thus gained over

---

[1] Cf. for example the chapters where the Fools speak in their own persons: thus the idle accumulator of books (ch. i): 'Den vordantz hat man mir gelan' &c., and the 'old' Fool (ch. 5), 'Myn narrheyt loszt mich nit sin grys.' So ch. 78.

Lydgate was however in but a small degree due to
Brandt himself. The ideas which he combined,—the
woodcuts, the procession or series of Fools, and the
Ship,—had all been familiar in German satire, though
they had never been associated in exactly the same way.
Figures of Fools with mottoes were a current form of
Flying Sheet, and had already been used as illustrations
in Vindler's *Blume der Tugend*[1]. The young and
vigorous Carneval drama had turned to account the
comic capacities of the Fool, and nowhere, except at
Nürnberg, was it more actively cultivated than precisely
at Basel, where the *Narrenschiff* was written. And the
Ship of bad characters, for ages a popular jest in
Germany, had been recently worked out in a *milieu* with
which he also stood in close connexion, and with an
effective touch to which he hardly made pretence.

1.
Fastnacht-
spiele.
Nowhere, in fact, in the early drama of Europe, did
the mediaeval taste for groups of parallel figures, of
which the Order of Fools was only one example, play so
large a part as in the German Fastnachtspiele. There
are traces of it no doubt elsewhere, and it was certainly
a conception of dramatic form which all the instincts of
mediaeval art tended to suggest and to confirm. Elsewhere however it either ruled only as a passing phase,
the defects of which were rapidly perceived and overcome, or else it was from the first so skilfully handled
that they were not felt. The English Morality was too
inartificial to deal more than occasionally (as in the *Four
Elements*) with this somewhat elaborate kind of artifice;
and its favourite theme—a struggle between good and
evil powers for the human soul—tended to merge all
finer grouping in a single absolute antithesis. The
French Morality, on the other hand, and still more, the

[1] *Allg. D. B.:* 'Brandt,' p. 257; Zarncke, p. xlvii.

Farce and the *Sotie*, was too lively to offer very salient examples of a device which inevitably tends to sameness, and the few which it does offer betray more anxiety to overpower this tendency than to emphasise it.   The 'five senses of man,' for instance, are brought on the stage; three Fools court the *folle Bobance*[1]; or the *Roy des Sotz* gathers his five subjects about him[2], but the rapid movement and the inexhaustible variety of combination easily carry off the repetition.   In Germany, on the contrary, the device of parallelism found extraordinary favour; and among the Carneval-playwrights of Nürnberg it became almost a stock principle of construction, like the double plot of our Jacobeans, applicable to any kind of subject, and always to be relied on for dramatic effect.   It flattered the taste for mechanical symmetry of form which has repeatedly haunted German literature, and which has frequently been exorcised only by help of a blind revolt against all form whatever.   A number of characters deliver successive speeches, each more or less artlessly setting forth his own peculiarities.   Frequently this is combined with the legal form of a trial or a consultation.   A youth comes into a law-court requesting the court's opinion upon the proper age for marriage. The judge appeals to the doctors of law in attendance; and their judgments, delivered in succession, constitute the play[3].   Another youth, desiring information upon the seven liberal arts, applies in turn to the 'seven masters'— Aristotle, Euclid, Boethius, Ptolemy &c., who one and all promptly satisfy his curiosity, in spite of his frank avowal that his interest in learning is strictly measured by its

---

[1] *Ancien Théâtre Français*, II. 265 ff.

[2] *Ib.* 223, ff.

[3] Keller, *Fastnachtspiele des 15ten Jahrhunderts*, No. 41: *der Jüngling der ain Weip nemen wil.*

utility in courtship[1]. Still oftener the action is modelled
on a regular trial; and the parallelism is furnished by
a successive examination of witnesses, prisoners, or
claimants. A number of suitors urge their rival claims
to a reward, or strive to clear themselves from a disgrace[2].
In *Die sieben varb*, in the same way, the seven colours
plead for supremacy before 'Frau Sunnreich,' who gives
the palm to brown, as 'the bond of love[3].'

Unexciting discussions such as this however occupied
little space beside those which gave play to the pungent
satire which was the genius of the *Fastnachtspiel;* and to
such an object the competition or examination of a
group of similar characters lent itself with the utmost
ease; the competitors or claimants were made ridiculous
by the prize they sought or by the story they told; the
string of pleading suitors became, in short, a row of
'Fools.' Thus in several plays, ten or more *liebe
Närrlein* are made to compete in the manner of
Heywood's Four P's, for the honour of being the
'greatest fool,' and recount their several adventures
in love, in order to prove it[4]. Or again, thirteen 'Fools
of love' are 'examined' by Venus. They recount their
adventures in turn, but the sentence falls equally upon
all:

> Seit ir durch weiber sein toren worden,
> So bleibt auch in dem selben orden[5].

---

[1] No. 96: *die sieben meister.*

[2] No. 12.

[3] *Ib.* No. 103.

[4] No. 14.

[5] No. 32: *Ein Spil von Narren.* Cf. No. 38, 'Ein FNSp. von
denen die sich die weiber nerren lassen' (*nine* fools, called ' der erst
narr,' der ' ander *thor*,' ' der dritt *esel*,' &c.). Also, No. 13, where
twelve fools of love in the same way tell their experiences.

Such processions of Fools were no doubt essentially
different from Brandt's; the Fools are all of a single
type; there is no suggestion of the Brandtian thought
that all sins are reducible to forms of folly.   But there
was all the dramatic apparatus for carrying out that
thought, suitable by its very simplicity to a poet whose
aims in art were very humble, and who was much more
anxious to convert the world than to amuse it.

Even more than to the Fastnachtspiele however *The Ship.*
Brandt owed the form and the spirit of his satire to the
device of the *Ship*.   The old satirical fancy of a 'Ship of
boon companions' was of purely German invention, and
before Brandt, exclusively of German currency.   Teichner's *Schif der Flust*, Jacob van Oestvoren's *Blauwe
Schute* and Jodocus Gallus' *Monopolium des Lichtschiffes*
all had in common, with different shades of emphasis,
the representation of a crew of ruined revellers and
spendthrifts¹.   In the two latter the irony is heightened
by the introduction of an 'order' or gild to which only
ruined revellers are admissible, with a formal scheme of
privileges and conditions, and a list of members drawn
out of all ranks of society, from the alchemist who had
melted his fortune in the crucible, to the bishop who had
mortgaged his income to buy his title².   A satirical
device of this kind evidently came of the same stock as
the 'Land of Cockayne.'   It also reflected a somewhat
less genial, a somewhat more resentful and vindictive
criticism of the riotous living at which it was aimed.

¹ ' All die von grôzem gut Chœmen un vieln in armut' (*Sch. d.
F.*); 'allen ghesellen van wilde manieren' (*B. Sch.*), 'qui, cum prius
essent multarum divitiarum...onere gravati, dispensante cum eis
ebrietate...sunt de gratia Dei ab eisdem...hodie *levificati*' (*Monop.
d. L.*).   All three are printed at length in Zarncke, p. lxi. ff.

² *Monopol. des Lichtschiffes*, Zarncke, p. lxix.

Cockayne was a *bonâ fide* paradise of the improvident, in which the one condition of prosperity was to take no thought. But the Ship was a paradise only in the imagination of its crew. They crowd eagerly on board, and sail gaily away, but their destination is not what they anticipate. The worn-out spendthrifts of Teichner's *Ship of Ruin* are bound for the havens of 'Emptymouth' and 'Hollowcheek' in the land of spare living[1]. Those of Jodocus Gallus' *Lichtschiff* decree that the dullest on board shall stand at the helm, and that no one shall take any thought of danger. They show the easy temper of Cockayne exactly where this can be done with least impunity—in a ship at sea. And Brandt expressed this pointedly by calling his ship of 'good fellows' the Ship of Cockayne[2]. Their voyage is accordingly as full of perils as that of Odysseus, on which it is with some felicity modelled. They put out merrily from 'Narbonne' with 'Narragonia,' their final port, inscribed on their pennon. They wander helplessly along the seas, searching every port and every shore, but vainly, for none knows where to land; dreaming of an Eldorado but heedless of compass and chart; half crushed in the Symplegades, barely escaping Scylla and Charybdis; some lulled by the Sirens to fatal sleep, others swallowed by the Cyclops, and many more entertained by the cannibal Laestrygones who

> sunst anders essen nüt
> Dann narren fleisch zu aller zyt
> Und drincken blut für irn wyn.

At length, broken by the waves, borne astray by the wind, despoiled of its crew and bereft of all help and

---

[1] *Schif der Flust*, vv. 6, 25 etc.
[2] *Narrenschiff*, chap. 108.

counsel, the Ship of Misfortune is swallowed up in a whirlpool.

The 'Ship of Cockayne' is thus the direct equivalent of the 'Ships of Ruin,' which preceded it, and Brandt in so far merely added one more to the mediaeval satires upon prodigal riot. His plan however was far more comprehensive than this. Prodigal riot was but one among the hundred and odd types of human infirmity which he gathered under the head of Folly, and to which he extended in a strangely loose fashion the image of the Ship. It was to this, rather than to its confused and feebly executed imagery, that the *Ship of Fools* owed its lasting influence, if not exactly its immediate attraction, above all in England, where, as I have said, it was destined to become one of the main starting-points of modern satirical portraiture. It is necessary therefore to examine its contents somewhat more closely.

Without any pretence of philosophic nicety, we may distinguish six different notions which Brandt at various times attaches to his cardinal term Folly, and under one or other of which all his Fools may be grouped. Some of them have always been recognised as marks of Folly; others reflect the curious idiosyncracy of Brandt's age, and of Brandt himself. The inclusion of a large number of more or less criminal offences, for instance, is perhaps the most original feature in an ethical system which for the modern mind is full of originalities. We have offences against religion,—blasphemy[2], 'contempt for God[3],' or for another life[4], desecration of festivals[5]; *Classification of Brandt's Fools.*

I. *Vicious or criminal offences*[1].

---

[1] This term fairly expresses the judgment of Brandt's age upon the faults mentioned below, some of which we should regard more leniently.

[2] Cap. 28.   [3] Capp. 86, 87.

[4] Cap. 43.   [5] Cap. 95.

offences against the law and common morality,—oppression[1], crafty dealing of various kinds, forging[2] and appropriation[3], dishonest borrowing[4] and extortionate usury[5], slanderous falsehoods[6] and hollow flattery[7], with lust[8] and adultery[9]. All these are actions by which society suffers, while the offender may in a certain sense gain. They are consistent at any rate with a considerable share of the worldly happiness of which 'Folly' is commonly thought to involve the loss.

2.
Insolence.
The second class of Fools are also unpleasant to their neighbours rather than conspicuously or directly injurious to themselves; the insolent and quarrelsome people, who take offence at the slightest provocation[10] or correction[11], and carry every petty squabble into the law-courts[12]; or wantonly injure, and sneak away to avoid the consequences[13]; petty tyrants like the civic officials[14], rough oppressors like the knights[15], insolent upstarts like the peasants[16].

3.
Riot.
The third class are also far from innocuous to society, but they do themselves still worse harm. Among the forms of Riot the sober and peaceable lawyer of Basel sternly condemned every kind of dissipation and the slightest breach of orderly social observance;— dancing[17], and gambling[18], heavy eating and drinking[19], disturbances and bad language in the streets[20], or in church[21], or at table[22], and above all on the occasion

[1] Cap. 10.   [2] Cap. 102.   [3] Cap. 20.
[4] Cap. 25.   [5] Cap. 93.   [6] Cap. 105.
[7] Cap. 100.   [8] Cap. 50, cf. 49.
[9] Cap. 33.   [10] Cap. 25, cf. 42, 53, 64, 72.
[11] Cap. 54.   [12] Cap. 71.   [13] Cap. 69.
[14] Cap. 79.   [15] Cap. 79.   [16] Cap. 82.
[17] Cap. 61.   [18] Cap. 77.   [19] Cap. 16.
[20] Cap. 62.   [21] Capp. 44, 91.   [22] Cap. 110 a.

most notorious for both,—the Shrove-tide festivities[1];
wantonness of idle students[2] and workmen[3], butlers
and cooks[4]. And with these may be classed those
who indulge in even innocent forms of the superfluity
which to Brandt's ascetic temper seemed itself a sin;—
superfluity of wealth[5], of talk[6], of books[7], of benefices[8];
outlay of precious hours in the saddle[9], or with the gun[10].

The fourth class, like the third, is closely connected with the Folly of Cockayne; but their fault is
one of neglect rather than of commission. People who
neglect their children[11], or do not provide for old age[12],
or for death[13], or for the accidental mischances which
to men of Brandt's cautious temperament appear to
be always impending[14]; or again, the merely lazy and
indolent, the maid who slumbers at her wheel and the
man who loiters at the mill[15]. But neglect of duty was
a relatively small offence in Brandt's view if it merely
ended in inaction. It was at least consistent with being
quiet and sober and thinking of oneself no higher
than one ought to think, virtues on which he is never
weary of insisting. The Fools, on the contrary, who
incur his most vehement and persistent criticism, to
whom he returns again and again, and who, if any,
may be said to touch the very heart of his satire, are
those who neglect their own duty to meddle with
another's, the officious Atlases, represented in one of
his woodcuts, who try to put the world on their own
shoulders[16], the Fools of *presumption.*

4.
Sloth.

---

[1] Cap. 110 b.	[2] Cap. 27.	[3] Cap. 48.
[4] Cap. 81.	[5] Cap. 17.	[6] Cap. 19.
[7] Cap. 1.	[8] Cap. 30.	[9] Cap. 74.
[10] Cap. 75.	[11] Cap. 6.	[12] Cap. 12.
[13] Cap. 85.	[14] Cap. 70.	[15] Cap. 97.
[16] Cap. 24 (*von zuvil sorg*).		

Brandt's fertility of illustration on this head is infinite. His ethics are not drawn from the Gospel, for
they are without a suggestion of altruism; but the Gospel
itself did not urge a more unqualified abasement of pretensions, a more complete 'lowliness of spirit.' He has
nothing but scorn for heroic rashness. The 'unhappy
Faun' who strove with Apollo, and was flayed for it,
is his chosen type for those who attempt what is too
hard for them[1]. And commoner sorts of pretension are
denounced with what reads like the tirade of an egoist,
but is really only a severe application of the practical
maxim that, for society's sake, men must attend to
themselves first. To ignore the mass of men is the
beginning of wisdom. 'He is a wise man who knows
his own business, and no man else's.' 'Whoever would
satisfy all the wants of mankind must indeed rise early.'
'It takes a great store of meal to stop everybody's
mouth.' 'He is a fool who runs to put out another
man's house when his own is burning, or who pushes
another's boat on with a loss of speed to his own[2].'
'The father who gives his children bread when he is
starving should be flogged to death[3].' And an attack
upon the monks for seeking their own salvation at the
expense of the world from which they withdraw, is
answered by the plea that every one must think of his
own soul first. 'If I had *two* souls, I would gladly give
one for my fellows.' Another remarkable chapter is
devoted to the fashionable Fools who travel and return
no wiser than they went, according to the domestic-
minded proverb, approvingly quoted by Brandt, which
declares that 'a goose flies away and a gander flies

[1] Cap. 67.   [2] Cap. 58.
[3] Cap. 90. 1 ff. This was a current proverb; cf. Zarncke,
ad loc.

back,' and the students who thronged the universities
of Paris and Bologna; a cry heartily echoed by Barclay, as
afterwards in more classical prose by Ascham.   The possi-
bility of getting wisdom by travel Brandt did not indeed
wholly deny, but it was mainly confined to wise pagans
like Ulysses and Pythagoras; and a more sincere homage
is paid to the still wiser pagan who never left his native
Athens.   Brandt lays bare the kernel of his moral nature
in thé suspicion that 'he who wanders cannot perfectly
serve God.'   At other times he dwells rather on the
perils of travel than on its futility.   A wise man should
stay at home, or if he find himself by chance at sea,
make for the shore as swiftly as possible.   The Eldorado
is far off, and you are more likely to be drowned than to
reach it.   Such was the view of a Basel doctor just two
years after the discovery of America.   Less amiable
kinds of presumption are touched with hardly more
severity, such as frivolous ambitions[1], worldly marriages[2],
or meddlesome quarrel-making[3].   And then comes a
whole series of chapters devoted to assailing the common psychological ground of this class of Folly,—idle
confidence in one's own powers[4], or virtuousness[5], or
good fortune[6], or in God's mercy[7], or in the speedy
death of one's rich relatives[8].

Lastly, we have the class of mere simpletons whose
title to belong to the order of Fools has always been
recognised: the people who 'cut themselves with their
own knife'—are trampled on, as Brandt says, by the
ass[9], who disobey their doctor[10] or make foolish exchanges[11], or who are fatuously credulous[12] or fatuously

6.
Perversity.

[1] Cap. 92.	[2] Cap. 52.	[3] Cap. 7.
[4] Cap. 60.	[5] Cap. 36.	[6] Cap. 37.
[7] Cap. 14.	[8] Cap. 94.	[9] Cap. 78.
[10] Cap. 38.	[11] Cap. 89.	[12] Cap. 41.

communicative[1], or generally weak and unstable in character, incapable of breaking a bad habit[2] or keeping a good resolution[3].

Summary.   Such is a general view of what Brandt included in his gallery of Fools. Compared with other attempts of the same kind it is extraordinarily comprehensive, and also singularly German. It is a picture of the infirmities of German society in the year 1494. Eccentric as at certain points it may seem, it is in its main lines in perfect harmony with fifteenth century ethics and nomenclature. Lydgate, for instance, views folly from a scarcely less catholic standpoint, and his sixty-three Fools are recruited from every class of Brandt's five score. Thus the '*insolent*' Fools are represented by him 'that is cursed and hathe therof deynté' and him 'that bostith of his cursidness' (st. 13, 11); the '*riotous*' by the 'night motoner' (st. 15) and the 'night rowner' (st. 21)[4], the '*self-neglectful*' by 'him that castithe away his cloke in showris,' sleeps when the fox is in his fold (st. 19), drinks beer when he might drink wine (st. 16)[5]: the '*presumptuous*' by 'the lusti galaunt that weddithe an old wiche' (st. 15), or 'sekithe warre and hathe hjmself no myght' (st. 9). On the other hand, the proportionate emphasis laid upon these

---

[1] Cap. 39; 101.   [2] Cap. 5.   [3] Cap. 84; cf. 96.

[4] That this was a perfectly natural use of the term Fool (it is scarcely so to us) is also shown by the interesting *Sermon joyeux des Foulx* (Viollet-le-Duc II 207 ff.) where one of the four classes of fools is that which 'per plateas nocturno tempore currit.' (ib. p. 213).

[5] This very English conception of Folly is the main point of *Jyl of Brentford's Testament*, a century later; it also appears to survive in the old Highgate ceremony of 'swearing on the horns,' the oath consisting in a promise 'not to drink small beer when one could drink strong,' &c.

classes is very different. Brandt has his own country
in view, and he gives enormous space to the riotous
sensuality for which Germany was then and long afterwards a bye-word, while he has little to say of the subtle
duplicities of which, as the patriots of the next generation exultingly boasted, the guileless Teuton had
never been accused[1]. It is precisely this vice however,
upon which the main weight of Lydgate's indignation
falls. The deceitful fool, we are told, is the most heinous
of all, who

> may hoppe on the ryng,
> Foote al aforn and lede of right the daunce:
> He that al yevithe and kepythe himself nothyng[2],
>   A double hert with fayre feyned countenaunce,
>   And a pretence face trouble in his daliaunse,
> Tunge spreynt with sugre, the galle kept secret,
>   A perilous mowthe is worse than spere or launce,
> Thoughe they be cherisshed, God lete them never the[3].

The note thus struck almost at the outset is recurred
to throughout the series. We hear of fools 'with two
faces in one hood (st. 2)', simulating (st. 5), 'flattering
and faining' (st. 10), 'promise-breaking' (st. 11), and
faith-violating fools (st. 12). On the other hand, Lydgate
is in various ways less complete. The sexual offences
on which Brandt repeatedly dwells, have no place in
his list[4]. The horror of presumption, of superfluity,

[1] Hutten : *Inspicientes.*

[2] Lydgate and Brandt thus each describe the same trait under
their favourite rubrics.

[3] I quote from the Harleian text printed by Halliwell for the
Percy society. A slightly different one is in EETS, Extra Ser.
No. 8.

[4] Brandt's inclusion of them may probably be explained by the
associations of the term *Gauch*, which was both an equivalent for
Narr, and also, in a special sense, as we see from the *Gäuchmatt*,
referred to breaches of chastity.

of self-confidence, which colours so much of Brandt's satire, is scarcely perceptible.   But what was far more important for the literary influence of Brandt was, as I have already hinted, the profusion of concrete figures, types of classes, of professions, trades, spiritual and secular offices, with which he illustrated what no doubt was primarily a classification by moral qualities.   There is nothing in Lydgate like the sections of the *Narren-schiff* on the beggars and vagabonds, on the fraudulent tradesmen, on the apprentices, on the monks, on the peasants, on the idle serving-men, on the courtiers, several of which, like that on the *Grobians* which will be discussed in the next chapter, themselves became independent and fruitful literary starting-points.

And this feature of the book was relatively even more important for England than for Germany.   Its concrete and individual pictures of society were there hardly so much relished as the fantastic and humorous imagery of the Fool, in which they were disguised.   The *Narr* was the most popular of satiric types[1].   The Aristophanic imagination of the time made a plaything of him, and sportively maltreated him with huge and riotous enjoyment.   He was 'conjured' and 'cast,' crowned with the proverbial 'cap,' immersed in the

[1] The motive of the *Ship* on the other hand, remained after the first generation comparatively dormant.   Geiler's *Schiff der Busse* and *Schiff der Heil*, with the *Ursulenschifflein*, are purely devout works which recall it merely in their titles.   In the field of satire there remain only Gengenbach's *Narrenschiff vom Bundschuch* (on the insurgent peasantry) and perhaps Sachs' *Der vollen Säw gefehrliche Schiffart* (Zarncke, p. lxxii.).   In England also, as we shall see, and in France, the *Ship* had only a transient success. Badius Ascensius' characteristic adaptation to the other sex in the *Nef des Folles* rapidly followed the original.   Symphorien Champier's *Nef des Princes*, though wholly unlike in motive, perhaps owed its form to this source.

proverbial 'bath,' 'swallowed' by one enemy, extracted
from the labouring intestines of another[1]. The wild
humour of *Narrenschneiden* was, however, not wholly
congenial to the somewhat realistic genius of English
satire; and, in spite of Lydgate's precedent, the Fool
in Brandt's sense remained practically locked up in
the pages of his translator. No other catholic and universal satirist formed himself upon his model; and the
crew of Fools begot for the most part only crews of
knaves, beggars, courtiers, and court-jesters,—separate
detachments of the *innumerabilis numerus stultorum*,
which the private experience of each writer, rather than
his moral judgment, led him to single out for special
chastisement. What they lost in breadth however,
Brandt's English successors gained in distinctness, in
vigorous and vivid realism, in fulness of detail. If they
were worse moralists they were better artists, and if
they borrowed but fragments of his large and dignified
ethics, they can fairly claim to have brought his fragments of art, his broken and confused hints of imagination, into roundness and completion.

I

Nowhere is this contrast more striking than in the KNAVES.
first of these productions[2], the remarkable fragment Cock
Lorell's
Bote.

---

[1] Cf. the *Narrenbeschwörung, Narrengiessen, Narrenkappen,
Narrenbad, Narrenfresser*, and Murner's *Lutherischer Narr*, of all
of which, except the last, extracts are given by Zarncke.

[2] I do not propose here to speak of Barclay's translation, though
much might be said of its innumerable variations upon the original.
On Barclay see, besides Prof. Ward's article in the Dictionary, to
which I have already referred, a pamphlet by J. Seyffert: '*Alexan
der Barclay's Ship of Fools*,' which contains many suggestive re-

known as *Cock Lorell's Bote*[1]. Whoever the author may
have been, we owe him not merely a piece of writing of
high antiquarian and philological interest, but one of the
most vivid pictures we possess of vagrant life, comparable
with 'Robin Hood' and the 'Jolly Beggars,' and the delightful beggar-scenes in Frischlin's *Frau Wendelgard*, and
in contemporary literature paralleled only by a poem
which it doubtless contributed to produce, the *Hye Way
to the Spittel House*. It is certainly not without many
marks of a seriousness as genuine as Brandt's, though less
bitter; but this is broken by flashes of half suppressed

marks. Seyffert however makes us a present of some unsuspected
facts when he not only takes Barclay to Basel but actually introduces him, it is true with a *vermuthlich*, into 'the circle of scholars
there, of which Johannes a Lapide was the centre' (p. 1). This is
however only a natural enlargement upon Jamieson, who assumes
the continental journey, for which there is no evidence at all, as a
matter of fact, naïvely grounding it upon Barclay's account of the
continental towns which were the favourite resort of *Fools*.

[1] *Cock Lorell's Bote*. London, n. d., but about 1510. In col:
Wynkyn de Worde. The best edition is that of Rimbault for the
Percy Society. The editor's list of early allusions to the poem
omits, however, the earliest of all, that in the *Hye Way to the
Spittel House*, v. 1058 ff. He refers, but only in a general way, to
the influence of the *Narrenschiff*.—All the five woodcuts in the
Cock Lorell's Bote are free imitations of originals in the *Ship of Fools*.
None stand in very obvious relation to the text. That at B ii., (a
Fool, with outstretched tongue, standing before a tree up which a
magpie is ascending to her nest) is from the chapter *Of to much
speaking or babbling*. That at B iii., (the hunter whose dogs are
divided between the attractions of two hares running in opposite
directions) is taken from the illustration to the chapter *Of him that
together would serve two masters*. Those at B v. and C ii. are identical, and are freely adapted from the *Universall Ship* (*Schluraffenschiff*). That on C iii. (four Fools playing cards round a table)
is also freely adapted from the chapter on *Card players and
dysers*.

sympathy with the wild outlaw life. Something of the atmosphere of the greenwood is transferred to the scenery through which the 'Bote' makes its endless voyage; and Cock Lorell is hardly more the chief of a Ship of Fools than a naval Robin Hood among his merry men[1].

The fragment opens abruptly with what is evidently a description of the crew. Knavish tradesmen of every craft are crowding to the Bote at the summons of Cock Lorell, the 'corryer' whose ill-dressed hides 'wolde drynke water in fayr wether'; the shoemaker and cobbler struggling for a piece of leather, which they end in tearing to pieces; the butcher 'all begored in red blode, His hosen greasy upon his thyes,…He had as moche pyte as a dogge.' At this point appears, with an abruptness which the lost opening pages would probably have explained, a pardoner, bringing the muster-roll of what is now seen to be a 'religious fraternity' of knaves, and a list of the privileges which the pope is pleased to grant them, both of which he reads:

> The pope Darlaye hath graunted in his byll
> That every brother may do what he wyll......
> Also Pope Nycoll graunteth you all in this texte
> The coughe and the colicke the goute and the flyxe,
> With the holsome tooth-ache.

He adds the equally equivocal grant of land for a chapel, in the most notorious part of Southwark Bankside. This is followed by a long enumeration of the names of the crafts represented,—a store-house of the trade-nomenclature of the early sixteenth century;—'Cock Lorell cast asyde his hede, And sawe the stretes all over sprede,

---

[1] The Robin Hood cycle was still in vigorous growth, and had yet to receive some of its most notable elements, such as Friar Tuck. Cf. the excellent dissertation of H. Fricke: *Die Robin-Hood Balladen* (1883).

That to his bote wolde come, Of all craftes there were one or other.'   Each has his office in the ship, his particular rope to haul &c.

Then follows the spirited account of the voyage :— Cock Lorell blows his whistle, the crew set up the rowers' cry and smartly strike the water,—'men might here the ores classhe,'—and gaily spread the sail; away they go, singing merry ballads and blowing trumpets 'for joy'; pulling to shore now and again to dance 'with all their might,'...'sweryinge and starynge heven hye,' or drinking about St Julian's tonne[1],—'they would not have virtu ne yet devocyon, But ryot and revell with joly rebellyon,'— until the sun goes down, and 'pale Lucina' rises with 'her silver stremes' that make the world as light as if it 'had be paved with whyte.'   And then they set off again, up hill and down hill, to traverse England through and through, 'vyllage towne cyte and borowe,' 'from Garlic-head to knaves' in;' the poet watches the departing ship till he can see it no more, and then turns sadly homeward.   On his way he meets a rout of monks and nuns, all eager to join Cock Lorell; and anxiously inquiring where he is to be found,—δεόμενοι ἐς κόρακας ἐλθεῖν, καὶ παρεσκευασμένοι, but unfortunately, like Euelpides and Peisthetairos ἔπειτα μὴ 'ξευρεῖν δυνάμενοι τὴν ὁδόν,—bent on 'going to the dogs' but unable to discover where 'the dogs' are. And he reckons the whole following of the Bote at 'the thyrd persone of Englande,'—a modest figure which Brandt's more pessimist arithmetic would hardly have ratified.

It will be obvious from this sketch that the poem was the result of a not entirely successful attempt to fuse two conflicting though kindred motives; the travesty of a

---

[1] *Torne* in the original, a misprint, as the rhyme shows, but reproduced without comment by the editors.

religious order and the Ship of Fools. Most of the first
part is only a new variety of the Order of Knaves. The
pardoner's roll-call of the members of 'this fraternite,' his
announcement of special indulgences, and of the grant of
land for the chapel[1], place Cock Lorell in the company of
the Markolfs and Brunellus', the founders of new Orders.
Tradition too dwelt almost exclusively upon this aspect
of him. For a century afterwards he was, if not the
'founder,' the 'confirmer' of the 'Twenty five Orders' of
knaves[2]. But the constitution of the crew, their 'offices'
and above all the voyage, are obviously drawn from the
Ship of Fools, and from Barclay's version of it. The
members of the 'fraternity' are approximately what
Brandt called 'Craftsmen-fools,'—they are the rogues of
the whole commercial and artizan world, gathered out of
every craft and calling[3]. The opening lines of Brandt's
Gesellenschiff (cap. 48) contained the germ of this :

> Eyn gsellen schiff fert yetz do här,
> Das ist von hantwercks lüten schwär
> Von allen gwerben und hantyeren, &c.

[1] Cf. in Lydgate's *Order of Fools*, the similar allusion to a papal
grant: 'Nullatenses ensealed hathe his bulle To all suche, that none
of hem shall the.'

[2] So e.g. Awdeley, on his title-page, to which I shall return. It
is hardly worth while inquiring whether 'Order' in this phrase has
the same meaning as in the 'Order of Fools' (Lydgate), which, though
it has 63 members, is itself single. It seems likely that the word,
originally used with a distinct reference to the Monastic orders,
afterwards resumed its etymological sense of 'rank'; so that the '25
orders of knaves' would mean so many 'rows' or subdivisions of
them. Cf. the title of the *Tincker of Turvey* (1630)......'with the
Eight Several Orders of Cuckolds marching here likewise in their
horned Ranks.'

[3]   'Of every craft some there was,
          Shorte or longe, more or lasse.'   p. 11.

The vast majority are true crafts, and the names show the great

careless and hasty workmen, as he proceeds to tell us,
journeymen who fancy themselves masters, 'tailors who
take long stitches,' 'masons who leave large joints,' 'car-
penters who make much sawdust' and the like.   And
Barclay had given the satire a somewhat keener point by
turning the slipshod workers into downright scamps:—

> Some make theyr ware unjust and disceyvable...
> Such as coveyt the byers to begyle
> With flaterynge wordes fals and dysceyvable,...
> And all other...
> Whiche make theyr warke not true and profitable
> But counterfayte and pleasaunt to the iye
> And nought in profe, men to abuse therby.

The Voyage.   The crew of the 'Bote' are then essentially Brandt's
'Gesellen.'   But when we come to the voyage and its
adventures, the history of the Gesellen ceases to offer a
parallel, Brandt having, as usual, very speedily acquitted
himself of the imaginative part of his work.   Once however, and only once, he had ventured upon a genuine
and detailed account of a voyage,—the voyage of the
'good fellows' to Narragonia or Cockayne; and it is this
voyage of the *Schluraffenschiff*, not that of the *Gesellenschiff*, from which the idea of Cock Lorell's is immediately
derived.   The *Bote* is therefore a fusion of the two
chapters.   Such a fusion had been much facilitated by
the translators.   Locher had brought these originally
remote passages (capp. 48 and 108 in the original)
together at the end of the book[1], and had also given

specialisation which English trades had attained even at the beginning of the sixteenth century. A few however are only ironically
described as crafts, e.g.:

> Swerers, and outragyous laughers,
> Surmowsers, yll thynkers, and make brasers
> With lollers, lordaynes, and fagot berers, &c.

[1] In Locher they are separated only by his own *Excusatio.*

them somewhat analogous titles[1]; while Barclay besides
following him in this, as was natural, had placed at the
head of one chapter in his version a stanza which reads
like an introduction to the other, so vividly does it refer to
the vices of craftsmen rather than to those of Cockayne.

> Here shall Jacke charde, my brother Robyn hyll
> With Myllers and bakers that weyght and mesure hate
> All stelynge taylers: as Soper; and Manshyll
> Receyve theyr rowme.

Most of the dramatic incident is suggested by this
chapter as it appears in Barclay, with some hints however from the prologue. The spirited account of the
Fools rushing in from all sides to get a place in the ship,
(Brandt, Prol. v. 20 ff., Barclay, ed. Jamieson, I. 13), has
furnished the framework of the first part of *Cock Lorell*,
where Cock receives the applicants for admission as they
successively appear, and especially the vivid picture on
p. 8:

> Then Cocke caste a syde his hede,
> And saw the stretes all over sprede[2]
> That to his bote wolde come.

The numbers left behind, who struggle for precedence, or
wait vainly on the shore, (Brandt *u.s.*, '*Ein schiff möcht die
nit all getragen Die yetz sind in der narrenzal,*' Barclay:
They run to our shyp,...we are full lade and yet forsoth
I thynke A thousand are behynde whom we may not re-

---

[1] Locher calls the *Schluraffenschiff* 'Latina navis seu barca socialis,' adding that it is intended for all who have not secured a
place elsewhere; the *Gesellenschiff*, 'socialis navis mechanicorum.'
So Barclay: 'The universall Shypp and generall Barke or barge
wherin they row that yet hath had no charge,' and 'The unyversall
Shyp of crafty men or laborers.'

[2] Cf. Brandt's phrase (not in Barclay): 'all strassen, gassen
sindt voll narren,' *Prol.* v. 10.

receyve &c.) reappear in the troop of monks and nuns
whom the poet meets as he returns,

> To mete with Cocke they asked how to do,
> And I tolde them he was a go;
> Than were they sad everychone,
> And went agayne to theyr home[1].

The voyage itself is lineally derived from that of the
Ship of Cockayne, by a process however which wholly
changed its character. In Brandt the whole weight of
description is thrown upon the disasters and the im-
providence of the crew.   But his opening lines contained
a hint which in the hands of the translators became the
nucleus of a new and different narrative. 'We have
brethren in all lands,' he says; 'and through all lands we
travel, from Narbon to Schluraffen land.' This was a
tempting topic for a fluent Latinist, and Locher expands
it into some thirty lines, informing us, with a Vergilian
profusion of names, of the geographical distribution of
Fools among the countries of the world[2], England holding a conspicuous place.   Such an opportunity for edifying his countrymen was naturally not lost upon Barclay,
and the single couplet devoted to England is in its turn
expanded into four stanzas :—

> In Englande is no Cyte, nor shyre towne
> Boroughe ne vyllage howe pore so ever it be
> Nor noble Palays of such a grete renowne

---

[1] Cf. Brandt's chapter on the idle pursuivant (No. 80, *Narrehte
bottschafft*) who finds himself left behind on the strand.

[2]   Ex Asia veniunt rutilo sub sole creati
> Stulti: nobiscum qui cita vela trahunt;
> Finibus e Lybiae veniunt...
> Migrant Hesperii: migrat quoque Gallia tota...
> Ad navem veniunt gentes quas ultima Thyle
> Finibus extremis quasque Britannus habet, &c.
>   *Navis Stultifera*, fol. cxxxiv.

But some maryners sende must they unto me[1].

.   .   .   .

Now must we leve eache sympyll haven and porte
And sayle to that londe where folys abounde and flowe
For whether we aryve at London or Brystowe
Or any other Haven within this our londe
We folys ynowe shall fynde alway at hande.
                        The Ship of Fools, II. 308, 9.

And to increase the divergence, the Odyssean narrative
of peril which should follow is turned into a sermon,
in which the Cyclops and the Sirens, Scylla and Polyphemus, loom dimly through a mist of moral interpretation.   In a word, the Ship of improvident 'good fellows,'
destined to be borne through continual misfortunes to
final ruin, performs the less tragic rôle of a grand tour
through the world, to pick up the Fools who are everywhere eagerly awaiting it, and nowhere more than in the
harbours and cities of England.

Finally came the author of the *Bote*, and completed
the transformation; for in his hands the voyage is, on the
one hand, entirely without misfortune, and on the
other, entirely English.   He has localised it, and if he
has not altered its moral, he has at least successfully obliterated the imagery by which the moral was enforced.
A genuine realist, with a keen eye for detail, for local
colour, and an extraordinary intimacy with the London
life of his time, he had little in common with the clerical
poet who prided himself on the elevation of a Muse which
would not deign to sing of 'Philip the Sparowe.'   He
has given us then in a sense impossible to Barclay, a
genuinely English ship and a genuinely English voyage,
a crew of Londoners, painted with a variety and humour
which sufficiently contrasts them with the monstrous

[1] So 1570 edition.   The first edition, followed by Jamieson, mis-
prints *unto come.*

features of Brandt's Fools, commanded by a noted
English rogue, and traversing England from end to end.
—'They sailed Englande thorowe and thorowe, vyllage,
towne, cyte and borowe[1].' And the voyage appears to
have no other destination or end. Joyous and heedless
as they are, their heedlessness has no unfortunate consequences. They 'blowe their trumpets for joy,' 'sprede
their sail as voyd of sorowe,' sing merrily and loud,
dance when they will in the deepening twilight, 'with
swerying and starying heven-hye'; they even drinke the
tonne of the patron saint of thirsty travellers; but no
more bitter consequence follows than the unwelcome
interruption of their revel by the boatswain's whistle, and
then every man takes his oars and they sail gaily off, 'up
hill' and 'down-hill,' to gather in the knaves of England;
—while the poet wanders away, not in the grim triumph
of Brandt and Barclay, but sadly 'to mowe shames tere.'

II.

COURT-
IERS.
Skelton:
' The
Bowge of
Court.'
The author of the *Bote* was an innovator in English
poetry. Consciously, or unconsciously, he broke em-
phatically with the tradition which, since Chaucer and
Langland, had practically confined serious verse to the
regions of classical or sacred story and moral allegory.
His portraits of 'knaves' are certainly not at all com-
parable in literary refinement with those of Chaucer's
pilgrims, but they were equally an attempt to find the
material for literature in close observation of real life instead of in allegorical subtleties. This was the more striking

---

[1] Two of these bear a curious resemblance to Narbonne and
Narragonia,—the point of which was only intelligible to one who
knew German;—'they sailed from *garlick-head* to *knaves-in.*'

because the scheme of the *Ship of Fools*, which as we have
seen, was borrowed in the *Bote*, lent itself with peculiar
ease to allegory.   Even Brandt, to whom his 'Ship' was
hardly more than a telling framework for his collection
of apologues, an alluring embroidery, as it were, to catch
the popular eye, treats it, at least once, with unmistakeable symbolism.   And to a poet already formed in
the conventional manner it must have offered material
hardly surpassed for suggestiveness.

Such a poet was the great English satirist of the age
of the Reformation.   The remarkable poem which he
called *The Bowge of Court* (court-rations) was probably
produced within a dozen years of Barclay's translation
of the *Narrenschiff*, for its satire on court-life is pointed
by no allusion to the patron of whom he became from
about 1522 the bitterest assailant.   That he knew and
read this translation is certain, in spite of his unfriendly
relations with its author.

His *Boke of the Three Foles*, as Dyce long ago pointed *The Three*
out, is merely a paraphrase, with a commentary, of three *Foles.*
chapters of it.   [1]In manner this little work contains but
few touches of the Skeltonian 'pith'; its three prose
apologues are conceived in the serious tone of the
preacher; quoting examples and drawing morals, appealing and exhorting; and they probably indicate that
at least one English parson followed the example of
Geiler von Kaisersberg at Strassburg, in founding sermons
on the *Ship of Fools*[2].   While Geiler however held up
the entire gallery of Brandt's Fools for the warning of

---

[1] His lost 'Nacyown of Folys' (*Garl. of Laurell* v. 1470, Bale
Cent. sub nom.) was also presumably written under the influence of
the Ship.

[2] I know no other indication however that it was ever so
used.

his audience, Skelton fastened upon three only,—the
Envious, the Voluptuous, and those that wed for wealth.
It is not difficult to understand the motive for this
choice. Few chapters in the *Narrenschiff* could have
better expressed the characteristic bitterness with which
Skelton incessantly assails the follies of worldly station
and of those who struggle for it. Voluptuousness is for
him in a special sense the vice of high rank; it is by
taking *Liberte* and *Fansey* into his service that the grandee
Magnyficence, in the Morality of that name, prepares
his own ruin; and in the *Bowge of Court*, Ryot is one
of the seven vices that man the ship of good fortune.
In the same way Envy was the vice of those who sought
high station, and *wedding those old wyddred women, whych
have sackes full of nobles*, a means of attaining it hardly
preferable to the extortionate devices of the conjurer
which he was one day to lay bare in the lost tragedy of
the '*Negromansir.*' Thus the little treatise which Skelton
presented to the most illustrious contemporary example of
worldly greatness, was but a prose anticipation of or
comment on the vigorous teaching of his more famous
poems; on the pictures of deluded greatness and frustrated ambition, of courtly vice and courtly insecurity,
which were the *raison d'être* of the *Magnyficence* and the
Negromansir, which were traced with even keener zest in
the *Speke Parrot* and *Why come ye nat to court*, where the
folly of the Court is incarnated in the person of Wolsey
himself, and which, finally, were carried out with an
imaginative brilliance which Skelton nowhere surpassed,
and, as I believe, by aid of the same famous satire to
which he owed his 'Three Foles,' in the *Bowge of Court*.

*The
'Bowge of
Court.'*   The poet finds himself, it will be remembered, one
autumn evening at Harwich. He is agitated by the
mental conflict between his poetic ambition and the fear

of failure.   The recollection of the great poets of old
incites him to follow in their steps; but *Ignorance* (i.e.
the conviction of his own ignorance) advises him to throw
away his pen; and he reflects characteristically that

> of reproche surely he maye not mys
> That clymmeth hyer than he may fotynge have;
> What and he slyde downe, who shall hym save?
>
> (vv. 26—8.)

Harassed with these thoughts he goes to rest, and
presently dreams that he sees

> a shyppe, goodly of sayle,
> Come saylynge forth into that haven brood.

She casts anchor there, the merchants go aboard to
examine her cargo, and Skelton follows after them.
The owner is the lady 'Saunce-pere', and her merchandise
is *Favore*.   Skelton, who appears under the name of
Drede, would fain come to her throne, on which is
written in gold letters, 'Garder le fortune, que est ma-
velz et bone!''   *Daunger*, one of her ladies, sternly
repels him; another, *Desyre*, encourages him, and gives
him a jewel, *Bone Aventure*, which ensures the favour of
Fortune, under whose guidance the ship sails,

> Fortune gydeth and ruleth all oure shyppe;
> Whom she hateth shall over the sea boorde skyp.
>
> (vv. 111 f.)

After this introduction, the poem proper begins.   The
vessel is no sooner fairly started on its way, in happy
independence of wind and waves, than the poet per-
ceives among the crew seven 'full subtyll persons.'
These prove to be, Favell 'full of flatery,' Suspecte,
Harvy Hafter the cunning thief, Dysdayne, Ryotte, Dys-

---

¹ I prefer, with Dyce, to follow the MS. reading, as it is not certain that Skelton wrote modern languages correctly.

simuler, and Subtylte. *Drede* attempts to join them, but
they receive him with marked disfavour: 'They sayde
they hated for to dele with Drede.' In a succession of
highly dramatic speeches the 'Subtyll persons' express in
their several fashions, their hostile sentiments towards
the intruder *Drede.* Favell displays his insinuating smooth-
ness of speech, Ryotte comes 'russhynge all at ones,' 'a
rusty gallande, to-ragged and to-rente,' boasting loudly of
his revels and amours. Drede's position becomes in-
creasingly perilous; finally he sees 'lewde felowes here
and there' bent on slaying him:

> And, as they came, the shypborde faste I hente,
> And thought to lepe ; and even with that woke,
> Caughte penne and ynke, and wrote this lytyll boke.

> (vv. 530—2.)

The *Bowge of Court* is then an allegorical picture of
the follies and the perils of court life. Every feature
and incident has to be interpreted with reference to the
court. The ship stands for court-favour, the continuance
of which is at the mercy of fortune. The crew stand for
the vices which flourish under court-patronage. The
hero, *Drede*, represents the diffidence which shrinks from
the treacherous privilege of court-favour, and rarely obtains it. Skelton's satire had therefore obviously a far
narrower scope than Brandt's. He is strange to the
impartial pessimism with which Brandt had made as it
were the round of society, holding up his unflattering
mirror to every class in turn. He strikes at the class
which private antipathies and personal humiliations
rather than moral instinct had led him to detest, and at
it only.

Among the rest, however, Brandt had as we have
seen included this class. One of the few chapters in
which he dwells for a moment upon his own images of

the Ship is that in which he sarcastically provides for the ' Fools who seek court favour' a private, select vessel of their own :—

> They coveyt a shyp for them selfe to attayne
> Therfore for them this shyp I nowe ordayne.
> Great lordes servauntis wyll nedes sayle apart
> Alone by them self they coveyt for to be,
> For they ne can well use their craft and art
> Of gyle and flaterynge among the comontye.
> ...With the comon Folys for that they wyll nat mell
> I ordayne to them this Barge here present
> Lyst theyr fraude myght be theyr owne impedyment.

And then the reference to the court is made explicit :

> The kynges Court nowe adayes doth fede
> Such faynynge flaterers.......
> No man in Court shall nowe a lyvynge fynde
> Without that he can bowe to every wynde [1].

Here we have not only the figure of the Fools of court-favour borne along in a ship, but a suggestion of the hostility to outsiders which reappears in an allegorical form in the antipathy of Skelton's 'subtyl persons' to Drede.

Skelton has not, any more than the author of Cock Lorell, spoken of a crew of *Fools*, or, as his allegorical plan would rather have required, a crew of *Follies* [2]. 'Subtyl' however as they are, they show close affinity to the Brandtian Fool [3]. They are sanguine and improvident;

---

[1] *Ship of Fools*, II. 211, 'Of flaterers and glosers.'

[2] As More had already done in the epigram quoted above, p. 324, 'Vehuntur in rate Stultitiae.'

[3] Besides the flatterers themselves, several of Brandt's Fools are as 'subtyl' by their very calling as Skelton's,—e. g. the forger (cap. 102), the speculator in corn (cap. 93), or the usurer (ib.).

buoyed up with overweening confidence in their future,—
the confidence which is so strongly emphasised in the
Narrenschiff, and which Brandt, who had not read Hume,
regarded as an unqualified disaster for society.   They
will 'have no dealings with *Drede*,' the personification
of diffidence and caution.   They travel in a ship guided
by Fortune herself;—'they could not fail, they thought,
they were so sure;' Fortune is 'theyr frende, with whome
ofte she dyde daunce.'   Yet Fortune, as the golden inscription on the throne of Saunce-pere significantly
warns them, is 'evil and good,' and the ship that she
'guides and rul·s' is hardly in better condition than the
Ship of Cockayne, which drifts about at the mercy of
every accident; while it is significantly added that
'whom she hateth shall over the sea boorde skyp,'—
like the unfortunate Cockayne mariners who fall victims
to Scylla or the Laestrygones.   The blind chance to
which Brandt's light-hearted sailors abandon the guidance of their ship is in fact *personified* in the 'Fortune'
who guides the *Bowge of Court* and enjoys the absolute
confidence of its crew.

Skelton has thus, in my view, used the Ship of Fools
in a manner curiously analogous to that of the author of
Cock Lorell.   There it was the chapter on idle tradesmen,
as here it is that on flattering courtiers, which supplies or
suggests the *personnel* of the crew, while in both, on the
other hand, their bearing on the voyage, and the fortune
and destiny of the ship are modelled on the impressive
but quite unconnected episode of the *Schluraffenschiff*.
The ship which proves so unfaithful to the confidence of
the Fools of Cockayne, is for Brandt the type of insecurity: Skelton makes it the symbol of what in his
view was the most unstable of human things, court-
favour, crowds its deck with the only apparently 'subtyl'

persons who put their trust in it, and typifies its insta-
bility by setting Fortune at the helm,—the allegorical
equivalent, as I have already suggested, of the 'blind
chance' which controls the destinies of the Ship of
Cockayne.

III.

What was after all to be the fate of the Ship? This BEGGARS.
was a topic which as we have seen both Skelton and the
author of Cock Lorell had somewhat lightly touched and
which Brandt, except in a single case, had left to be inferred from the general bias of his satire. In other words,
the prospective ruin of the race of Fools, Knaves,
Courtiers, remained at the most a looming catastrophe in
the dim and distant future. It was reserved for a London
man of business to invert this course, by bringing what
may be called the economic aspect of Folly into the
immediate foreground, and introducing an analysis of
the forms of worldly foolishness by a vivid picture of
the ruin and beggary to which they led.

The plan of the *Hye Way to the Spyttel-House*[1] is ex- Copland:
tremely simple, but not ineffective. Copland takes refuge *The 'Hye Way to the*
from a passing shower in the porch of the Spyttel-house, *Spyttel-*
and falls into a conversation with the porter, suggested *House'.*
by the motley throng of 'people, as me thought, of
very poore estate...with bag and staff, both croked,
lame and blynde' who beg admission at the doors. Is it
open to all, Copland inquires, to come there for a night's
lodging,—'losels' for instance, 'myghty beggers and

[1] Hazlitt's *Remains*, vol. IV. p. 1 ff. Cf. also Dr Furnivall's
account of it in his valuable *Captain Cox* volume, p. cii f. It will
be seen that my analysis somewhat differs from his.

vacabonds,' and the whole race of vagrants and impos-
tors?   This leads to a number of very graphic sketches[1]
of vagrant life; the old soldiers, real or feigned[2], the
shabby scholars[3], the itinerant quacks[4].   And then, becoming impatient of the porter's loquacity, Copland begs
for a more summary account 'of all folk in generall That
come the hye way to the hospytall.'   The porter agrees,
and, with a warning that it will be tedious, launches out
into a detailed description of the classes that, as we
should say, are 'on the road to ruin,' which occupies the
remaining half of the poem, and constitutes its *raison
d'être*[5].

It is with this latter part that we are specially concerned.   A palpable difference separates it from all that
goes before.   There is nothing in the first five hundred
lines to suggest that Copland was doing other than versify
his reminiscences of an actual incident and an actual conversation.   The wholly inartificial incident itself and the
date, perfectly void of significance, which he assigns to it
are not characteristic of deliberate invention.   And the
porter's talk is genuine talk; with all his discursiveness,
he tells for the most part only what might be supposed
to engage his hearer's curiosity if not to enlarge his
knowledge.   He does not recite moral commonplaces,
he does not assume the accent of the professional moral
reformer whose business is merely to reiterate things
liable to be ignored rather than forgotten.   He does not,
in a word, pass from conversation to sermon or satire.
With the second part however this is hardly the case.

---

[1] I cannot agree with Mr Hazlitt that the literary merit of the
dialogue is 'of an infinitesimal kind.'   It is one of the most vivid
and vigorous productions of the time.

[2] v. 279 ff. [3] v. 391 ff.
[4] v. 430 ff. [5] vv. 565—1089.

Copland, no doubt, keeps up the illusion very well.   He
puts his questions and receives the replies with the same
ingenuous curiosity as before.   But that does not obscure
the fact that the talk which was before full of minute
detail and special knowledge, is now, for the most part,
such as any close observer of the world at large might
arrive at for himself.   The opening verses strike the note
of this changed manner at once; for they are almost
identical with the opening stanza of Lydgate's enumeration of Fools.

> The chief of foolis, as men in bokis redithe,
>   And able in his foly to hold residence,
> Is he that nowther lovithe God ne dredithe,
>   Nor to his chirche hathe none advertence,
> Ne to his seyntes dothe no reverence,
>   To fader and moder dothe no benevolence,
> And also hath disdayn to folke in poverte,
>   Enrolle up his patent, for he shall never the[1].

This is Copland's version :

>   There cometh in this vyage
>   They that toward God have no courage,
> And to his worde gyve none advertence;
>   Eke to father and mother do not reverence;
> They that despyse folk in adversyte[2].

The *Hye Way* catalogue of prospective paupers is
thus tacitly connected at the outset with the traditional
lists of Fools.   The remainder does not belie the analogy.
For it becomes obvious as we proceed that it is not, as
it professes, a catalogue of prospective paupers at all,
but of those only whom their own vice or fatuity leads
to pauperism ; not a summary of 'all folk in generall that
come the hye way to the hospytall,' but only of those

---

[1] Lydgate, *Order of Fools*, vv. 9—16.
[2] *Hye Waye*, vv. 573—7.

who incur this 'vyage' by their own folly. Yet a *bona
fide* discussion of the grounds of poverty in the fourth
decade of the sixteenth century could hardly have ignored the effects of enclosure, or of the economic tyranny
which had just before been exposed with trumpet-tongue
in the *Supplication of the Beggars* and the *Dialogue of a
Gentleman with a Husbandman.* The *Hye Way*, in spite
of the compassion for poverty displayed at the outset,
contains no allusion to such things. Barely two or three
of Copland's three score incur their ruin innocently. The
rest fall easily into a classification analogous to that
adopted for the *Ship of Fools.* Thus we have a class of
more or less criminal or riotous offenders: the irreligious[1],
the vicious priest[2], the glutton[3], the drunkard[4], the lecher[5],
the pander[6], the swearer[7], the slothful[8], the adulterator
of food[9]. The others fall generally in two groups,—
the 'fools' of apathy or of presumption. They give too
much liberty to their children[10], or their wives[11], or their
servants[12], or their debtors[13], they neglect their estates[14], or
their households[15], or they help others when they are in
more need of being helped themselves[16], go to law for
trifling causes, draining their purses in bribes before the
trial[17], or in costs after it[18]; they take barren farms at
extravagant rentals[19], or marry before they have the

---

[1] v. 574.   [2] v. 583 f.   [3] v. 818 f.
[4] v. 914 f.   [5] v. 830 f.   [6] v. 687 f.
[7] v. 850 f.   [8] v. 866 f.   [9] v. 693 f.
[10] v. 806 f., *Ship of Fools*, cap. 6.
[11] v. 736 f., and *Gyl of Brentford.*
[12] v. 768 f.   [13] v. 802 f.
[14] v. 613 f.   [15] v. 824 f.
[16] v. 727 f., *Gyl of Brentford*, passim ; *Ship of Fools*, cap. 58.
[17] v. 619 f., cf. *Ship of Fools*, cap. 71.
[18] v. 637 f.   [19] iv. 786 f.

means[1], or court a reputation for generosity by giving unnecessary sureties[2].

At the same time it is clear that the scope of Copland's satire is narrower than Brandt's[3]. His subject is beggary and he keeps within the limits of the forms of Folly which issue in it. He excludes therefore both the successful criminal and also his less fortunate brother whom the 'road to ruin' conducts not to the Spyttel-House but to Tyburn[4]; while Brandt's scheme, which took account of the punishments of another world—where, as he warns one of his Fools, 'thou shalt have gall a thousand-fold for thy little honey-drop here,'—could have included the entire range of crime[5].

[1] v. 700 f., and *Gyl of Brentford.*   [2] v. 706 f.

[3] As a direct proof of familiarity with the *Ship*, I may quote the illustration of mistaken self-neglect :

Brandt, cap. 58, *syn selbs vergessen :*

> Wer leschen will eyns andern husz
> So im die flamm schleht oben usz
> Und brennt das syn in alle macht
> Der hat uff syn nutz wenig acht.

Copland, v. 724 f.

> They that dooth to other folkes good dede
> And hath themselfe of other folke more nede,
> And quencheth the fyre of another place,
> And leveth his owne, that is in wors cace,
> When it is brent, and woteth not where to lye.

[4] Cf. vv. 882 f., where the extortioners and thieves are deliberately excluded. So the envious, for a different reason, v. 982. All three are included in the *Ship of Fools.* Cf. also, in the latter, as instances conspicuously outside Copland's scheme, the fools that marry for wealth (Barclay, I. 247), and those that take many benefices (ib. I. 156).

[5] Another source of divergence is that Copland's plan confined him strictly to those whose folly brings disaster on themselves primarily. Thus Brandt's idle servant (cap. 81) is blamed for impoverishing his master, Copland's (v. 778) for ruining himself.

In this deviation, however, Copland has merely, like the author of the *Cock Lorell* and Skelton before him, applied the idea of a series of Fools to a particular class. His are the fools who come to beggary, as theirs are the fools of commerce and of the court.

IV.

ORDERS OF KNAVES AND FOOLS.

About the time when Copland was thus attempting to classify the world of beggars, the beggars were developing an actual classification of their own, the full disclosure of which, a quarter of a century later, took respectable England by surprise and contributed a quite novel element to the methods, as well as to the materials of social satire. These vagrants and outcasts, the *débris* of organised society, had organised themselves. They had official chiefs and various grades of subordinate rank, each with nicely defined powers and privileges, and bearing enigmatic titles which enhanced the vague prestige which they inspired in the uninitiated public. No wonder that to the printer Awdeley, who first gave a detailed account of the system, it at once recalled the most celebrated English tradition of the kind, the 'Order of Knaves' founded by the rogue Cock Lorell; and that he called his exposition, with direct allusion to this, the ' Fraternity of Vagabonds[1].' It was another evidence of

---

[1] To leave no doubt about this, he introduced the beggar-chief or 'Upright man,' on his title page, holding fraternal colloquy with the king of thieves :—

> Our brotherhood of vacabondes
> If you would know where dwell
> In Gravesend Barge which seldome standes
> The talke wyll shew ryght well.

the same reminiscence that he appended to it a new, and in part I suspect original, version of the Order of Knaves itself.

The *Quartern of Knaves*, or *serving-men*, thus closely associated with the Fraternity, belongs nevertheless to a distinct literary genus. The latter is a matter-of-fact account of a real society, an abstract of titles and offices, the first sketch of an Alsatian *Debrett*. The other is a satirical classification of social types, like the 'Bote' or the '*Ship.*' Both take the form of a *catalogue raisonné* of cant-titles, but they differ as a glossary of names differs from a discursive explanation of *nick-names*. The Vagabonds' titles are of their own coinage, invented by rogues for rogues, with an eye, as a rule, either to disguise or to euphemism. Those of the 'knaves,' on the contrary, are in the main the objurgatory epithets of their masters,—brief and sarcastic catchwords out of the immemorial bill of charges against those that serve. Hence we have, instead of the mere descriptive sketches of the *Fraternity*, a series of satirical characters: Unthrift, for example, 'that will not put his wearing clothes to washing, nor black his own shoes' (No. 22); Ungracious, he 'that by his own will will bear no manner of service, without he be compelled thereunto by his rulers' (23); *Nunquam* (24)—'he that when his master sendeth him on his errand, he wil not come again for an hour or 2,'—a good comment on the familiar exclamation of an impatient master in the dramatists ('*When*, Lucius, *when?*' &c.); *Obloquium* (6) 'hee that will

Awdeley: 'Quartern of Knaves.'

To which 'Cock Lorrel answereth:'

> Some orders of my knaves also
>   In that Barge shall ye fynde:
> For nowhere shall ye walke I trowe
>   But ye shall see their kynde.

take a tale out of his master's mouth and tell it him-self [1].'

The Quartern of Serving-men thus added yet another to the English class-satires. Connected with the *Ship of Fools* only through the link of *Cock Lorell's Bote*, it approximated, in a certain matter-of-fact way, more nearly than either of these famous books, to the social satire of the next century. Neither of them dealt very largely in pure analysis of character. In the *Bote* it is willingly sacrificed to description, in the *Ship* to morals and parallels. Awdeley's efforts in this kind it will be seen are wholly unpretending as art, but they were quite clear and decided in method. They were a step, distinct, how-ever minute, in the long and slow advance of literary realism, in the better sense, upon the territory of me-diaeval allegory. This advance was stimulated by every influence which led to the study of society at first hand; and we owe not a little to the maligned vagabonds whose eccentric life drew them perforce into literature. The most malicious study of a real rogue differs from a mere effort to personify roguery; and though an allegori-cal meaning might still be conceivably attached, yet every fresh trait made it both harder to secure and easier to dispense with.

The Twenty-five Orders of Fools. While the order of 'Knaves' was thus preparing to ripen into a satire of manners, the older and more famous order of Fools was undergoing a revolution of

[1] Cf. also, especially, Jefrey Godsfo the swearer, *Ingratus* the unthankful, Nichol Hartles, who 'when he should do ought for his master his heart faileth him.' Is it credible that such names as these I have quoted, figured in the list of a professional rogue? Or did Awdeley, as I should rather conjecture, revise and supplement the original list? This is supported by the fact that the older tradition knew of only *twenty-four* orders of knaves (Copland's *Hye Way*, v. 1065).

form.   The fantastic literary fashion of 'quarterns,' which
had converted the 'twenty-four' knaves into twenty-five,
did not spare the 'one order, without number, of Fools[1].'
Gyl of Brentford's foolish legatees are already an exact
quartern ; the first count producing twenty-four,—'nay,
set in one mo, she interposes, to make a hole quarteron[2];'
and the twenty-five orders of Fools here tacitly an-
nounced, are at length assumed without question in the
well-known and important ballad of which I have now to
speak.

The ballad of the 'xxv orders of Fooles[3]' is attached even more closely to the *Ship* than the parallel
'quartern' of knaves is to the *Bote*.   If Cock Lorell
'confirmed' the latter, if his 'knaves' were to be met in
the same company, the new twenty-five orders of fools
were entirely recruited from Brandt's crew.   Not only
are their characters directly suggested by as many chapters in the *Ship of Fools*, but in nearly every case they
are described more or less in Barclay's words.   Thus the
sixth Fool, who preaches without practising, is described
by the author of the ballad :

> He is a foole which to others doth preach and tell,
> And yet this foole is ready himself to go unto hell.

obviously from Barclay's introductory stanza to the
chapter on Fools of this class :

> So he is mad which to other doth preche and tell
> The waye to hevyn, and hym selfe goth to hell—

So, e.g. Fool [VII] :

> He is a foole, and ever be shall,
> That others judgeth and himself worst of all—

[1] In the *Hye Way*, v. 1069.
[2] *Gyl of Brentford's Testament*, v. 214.
[3] Reprinted by the Philobiblon Society, *Old Ballads and Broadsides*, p. 128 f.

is from Barclay's corresponding chapter (I. 152):

> He is a fole, and onys shall have a fall
> Syns he wyll other juge, hym selfe yet worst of all.

Fool [XII.]:

> This fooles golde is his God, wrongfullye got,—

corresponds to Barclay [I. 29]:

> Gold is your god, ryches gotten wrongfully.

Nearly every stanza is constructed on the same principle[1]. The ballad is thus a mere epitome of the *Ship*

---

[1] The following list will give a fairly complete notion of the
composition of the piece. The references are to the chapters of
Brandt, and to the page and volume of Barclay (ed. Jamieson).

Fool I. Sins against right and law=Cap. 47 (B I. 230) *von dem weg der seligkeit.*

    II. cannot get wisdom with age=Cap. 5 (B I. 47) *von altten narren.*

    III. causes lying and slander=Cap. 7 (B I. 53) *von zwietracht-machen.*

    IV. always borrowing=Cap. 25 (B I. 133) *zu borg uff nemen.*

    V. disdains wisdom=Cap. 8 (B I. 57) *nit volgen gutem rat.*

    VI. preaches and does not practice=Cap. 21 (B I. 111) *ander stroffen und selb thun.*

    VII. judges others=Cap. 29 (B I. 152) *der ander lüt urteilt.*

    VIII. eschews wisdom=Cap. 107 (B II. 281) *von lon der wissheit.*

    IX. scorns neighbours=Cap. ?.

    X. cannot keep secrets=Cap. 51 (B I. 243), *heymlikeyt verschwigen.*

    XI. improvident for age=Cap. 70 (B II. 43) *nit fürsehen by zyt.*

    XII. avaricious=Cap. 3 (B I. 29) *von gyttikeyt.*

    XIII. delights in strife=Cap. 71 (B II. 48) *zancken und zu gericht gon.*

of Fools, and to all appearance an epitome made at hap-
hazard by some one quite free from the dominant antipathy to certain types of Folly which so powerfully
colours the choice of Brandt and Lydgate.   It is quite
without bias,—and 'without savour.   Both qualities become still more palpable when it is compared with the
rich and nervous humour of the earlier and native
quartern in *Gyl of Brentford*.   There the changes are
rung upon a genuine English conception of folly through
a host of pleasant proverbs,—the folly, half absent-
minded blundering half short-sighted imprudence, of the
man who lends his horse and walks himself, gives all
and keeps nothing, forgets his fork when he goes out to
dine, bids his friend drink first when he is thirsty, or in a
score of similar ways violates the sturdy, honest, un-
chivalrous self-regard of middle-class England[1].   But this

XIV.   foolish messenger=Cap. 80 (B II. 86) *von narrehter
          botschafft.*
XV.   neglects divine punishments=Cap. 88 (B II. 136) *von
          plag und stroff gottes.*
XVI.   disobeys parents = Cap. 90 (B II. 147) *ere vatter und mutter.*
XVII.   flatter=Cap. 100 (B II. 210) *von falbem hengst streichen.*
XVIII.   credulous=?.
XIX.   prevents neighbours doing good=Cap. 105 (B II. 235)
          von hyndernisz des gutten.
XX.   seeks no remedy in misfortune=Cap. 109 (B II. 249)
          verachtung ungefels.
XXI.   slanders=Cap. 53 (B I. 252) *von nid und hassz.*
XXII.   behaves ill at table=Cap. 110a (B II. 259) *von disches
          unzucht.*
XXIII.   seeming wise=?.
XXIV.   rashly risks death=Cap. 45 (B I. 225) *von mutwilligem
          ungefell.*
XXV.   walks about in church=Cap. 44 (B I. 220) *gebracht in der
          kirchen.*

[1] Cf. Dr Furnivall's short criticism in his *Captain Cox*, p. ciii.,
as well as his (privately printed) edition of it.

old English quartern of Fools was now ousted from its
place by the epitomised Brandt, as Lydgate, the father
of English Fool literature, had been ousted by Brandt
himself.   The English Fools were driven from their own
order, and the German Fools installed in their place.
We have no more vivid illustration of the popularity of
the *Ship of Fools*, which it remains to follow in its final
phase.

V.

THE SHIP
AMONG
THE LATER
ELIZA-
BETHANS.

The *Ship of Fools* shared with no second English book
of its day the privilege of being read for nearly a century
after it was written.   Skelton was perhaps better remembered than Barclay, but it was a half-mythical jest-
book rather than his own verse which kept his memory
green; and the question 'Who now reads Skelton?'
might probably have been asked without serious error
fifty years before Cowley asked it.   The *Ship of Fools* on
the other hand had a sufficient combination of attractive
qualities to resist, or rather to appeal successively to, the
changing fashions of several generations.   A preacher's
manual to the merry Vicar of Diss, a model of social
satire to the author of *Cock Lorell* and his successors, it
was to a much larger public a book of sheer amusement,—a book put on the same shelf with romances and
jest-books, with *Howlglass* and the *C. Mery Tales*.   Laneham, it is true, classes it among the 'philosophical' books
of Captain Cox's library, but 'philosophy' with Captain
Cox and Laneham meant *Gyl of Brentford* rather than
More or Elyot.   'We want not also,' wrote another
country-gentleman some years after Laneham's well-
known letters, 'pleasant mad-headed knaves that bee
properly learned and well-read in diverse pleasant bookes

and good authors; as Sir Guy of Warwick, the Four
Sons of Aman, the Ship of Fooles, the Budget of De-
maundes, &c....'¹.   This reputation it doubtless owed
entirely to the wood-cuts.   And it is probable that the
wood-cuts facilitated its popularity with that somewhat
different class of readers of Laneham's generation who
favoured the new literary fashion of Emblem-books.
Brandt wrote a quarter of a century before Alciatus, the *Emblem-*
accepted founder of emblem-literature; but the majority *books.*
of his wood-cuts are nevertheless genuine emblems,—
literal representations, that is, of symbolic sayings, which
differ from later specimens only in so far, that their
symbolism is drawn from German proverbs and not from
ancient fables.   And Brandt's peculiar pessimism, again,
is only distinguished by its absolute sincerity from the
official despondency of the Emblematists; the uncertainty of the future, the littleness of man, the imminence of death, is the first article in his creed as in
their profession; and one of Brandt's most forcible
illustrations of it—Death and the Fool—was adopted
not only into the most famous of all German Emblem-
books, the Dance of Death, but into the common stock
of European imagery².   It may thus have been no accident that the first English Emblem-book, Van der Noot's
Theatre for Voluptuous Worldlings, was succeeded in a
few months by a new edition of the *Ship of Fools;* and
that in this new edition Barclay's clumsy English rime-
royal is accompanied, as if to propitiate more elegant
tastes, by Locher's Latin version in elegiacs, the conven-

---

¹ *The English courtier and the country-gentleman*, 2nd edition,
1586.
² *Narrenschiff*, cap. 55, *nit vorsehen den tod* (a Fool overtaken
by the skeleton Death and trying to elude him), embodied in later
editions of the *Todtentanz*, as 'Der Narr.'

tional metre of Emblem-writing.   But the *Ship of Fools*
had less fragile and casual grounds of popularity than this.
The Brandtian 'Ship' was never again imitated on the
same scale as is the *Bote* or the *Bowge of Court*[1], but it
survived even in the palmy days of the drama as an inexhaustible source of allusion.   It would even seem to have
found its way into the comic legend-lore of London, to have
been localised in the Thames, and been seen regularly
plying for hire between Billingsgate and Gravesend in the
form of the well-known 'Gravesend barge.'   Awdeley, as
we saw, had already treated this barge as the equivalent
of Cock Lorell's Boat, itself merely a local Ship of Fools;
and among the dramatists the Thames is the almost in-
variable highway of the Ship.   Nash makes it call at the
Isle of Dogs[2]; Greene brings it down from Oxford to
Bankside[3]; and perhaps it is not too bold to detect a

[1] The 'ballett against the Ship of Fooles' (*Sta. Reg.* 1567–8)
was however presumably a satire upon a collection of 'Fools' in the
manner of the '*XXV Orders*,' but using the Ship as framework.   It
can hardly have been an attack upon the book.

[2] 'Here's a coil about Dogs without wit,' says Summers, in
Nash's *Summers' last Will and Testament*, provoked by Orion's
praise of dogs; 'if I had thought the Ship of Fools would stay to
take in fresh water at the isle of Dogs, I would have furnished it
with a whole kennel of collections to the purpose.'

[3] 'I will make a ship,' says Ralph to the Oxford doctors in
Friar Bacon, 'that shall hold all your colleges, and so carry away
the *nini*versity with a fair wind to the bank side in Southwark.'
'And I,' adds Miles,

> 'Will conjure and charm,
> To keep you from harm;
> That *utrum horum mavis*,
> Your very great navis,
> Like Barclay's ship,
> From Oxford do skip
> With colleges and schools,
> Full laden with fools.'

suggestion of this association in the voyage to Gravesend, which the Cobler of Canterbury and his friends
beguile with stories of Fools of a particular class,—the
'eight orders of Cuckolds'[1]. Another London institution seems to have also been constituted a local Ship
of Fools. From at least the middle of the sixteenth
century the 'voyage' of the cart of condemned criminals
from Newgate to Tyburn was a current jest, obvious to
any one familiar with the doomed ship bound for Narragonia[2]. Less specific allusions abound. Whether a

---

[1] At the same time the *Cobler of Canterbury* (1590) like its successor the *Tincker of Turvey*, is of course a direct imitation of the
method of the Canterbury Tales. And it is not to be forgotten that
a voyage, with its enforced leisure, is one of the most natural of
frames for a series of stories like this. Clough's *Mari Magno* will
occur to every one ; *Westward for Smelts* is a contemporary example more in point, where a set of fishwives tell tales to their
Thames waterman as he rows them home.

[2] Cf. e. g. the close of the *Ballad against Unthrifts*, Philobiblon
Soc.: Ballads and Broadsides, p. 226 f.

> ' Then some at Newgate do take ship
>   Sailing ful fast up Holborne Hil ;
> And at Tiborn their ankers picke,
>   Ful sore indeed against theyr wil.'

So S. Rowlands, *Knave of Clubs:* ' A politique Theefe,' ad
fin. ' for Newgate voyage bound.'

Can this transition have been assisted by a mere mistake?
Barclay's chapter on the ' way of felicitie' contains a description of
the *cart of sin*. This cart is in the woodcut drawn by the 'sinner,'
but Barclay's words are ambiguous, and the author of the *Twenty-five
Orders*, copying them, apparently understood that the offenders
were drawn *in* the cart:

> ' Many fooles the carte of sin doth drawe,
>   Nourishing their sinne against all right and law;'

and this stands at the very outset of his list. To a London citizen
did not this inevitably suggest the Tyburn cart? And the ' cart of
fools' would inevitably become a Ship of fools.

satire upon loose livers[1] or a grave exposure of delusion were on hand, the 'Ship waiting for its freight of Fools,' was an allusion that never lost its flavour[2].

The day had gone by however, when it could be anything more. Such importance as the book still retained as a constructive and moulding force in English literature, belonged to it not as a piece of humorous imagery, but as a collection of satiric types. It would even appear that the full scope of Brandt's satire was now for the first time appreciated. His imitators hitherto had applied the method of the ship only to particular classes —to knaves, courtiers, paupers, serving-men. All of them were strongly biassed by the instincts and prejudices of their own. They felt the well-to-do shop-keeper's hatred for knavery, the disappointed aspirant's antipathy to the court. Booksellers, printers, parsons, not one of

---

[1] The 'Ship of Fools' is however to be kept apart from the somewhat analogous notion of a Ship of Drunkards, which appears in T. Heywood and Cowley, but has in England at least a different history. The fancy of a number of topers persuaded that they are on a voyage, provisioning the ship, hauling ropes, &c., appears (1) in Athenaeus, II. 5; (2) in Jan Enenkel's *Wiener Meerfahrt* (1200—1250), where this is told of a group of Viennese (repr. by Hagen, Gesamtabent. LI. cf. also *Zt. f. d. Alt.* 17, 354); there can here naturally be no question of Athenaeus; (3) probably from Enenkel, in Aloysius Passerino's *Historia lepida de quibusdam ebriis mercatoribus*, Brixen, 1495 (Mussafia in *Germ.* X. 431 f.); (4) Heywood's *English Traveller*, II. 1, no doubt from Athenaeus, and (5) Cowley's *Naufragium Joculare*, from Heywood.

[2] E.g. Nash again, in *Pierce Penniless:* 'thus the Ship of Fools is arrived in the haven of felicitie;' Decker in *Gul's Horn-booke:* 'longing to make a voyage in the Ship of Fools;' in the *Whore of Babylon* (Decker's Works, II. 214): 'your ordinarie is your Isle of Guls, your Ship of Fooles;' and in *Patient Grissel*, III. 1.: 'Here's a ship of fooles ready to hoist sail; they stay but for a good wind and your company.' Even the grave R. Scot (*Disc. of Witchcraft*, x. 6): 'Such should be embarked in the ship of fools.'

them had achieved the free outlook, the intellectual disengagement of the universal satirist. Not one of them approached either the tragic pessimism or the cynical scorn for humanity at large which seriously adopts as its motto the '*plena stultorum sunt omnia.*'

As the century drew to its close however, this provincialism sensibly lost ground. For the first time in our literature, a distinct literary class had begun to emerge, who, themselves neither citizens nor courtiers, parsons nor politicians as such, stood, as no other class did, in a sort of neutral relation to the rest of society. In their hands the stage, the focus of Elizabethan literary life, was becoming instinctively in some degree what Jonson consciously and in set terms strove to make it altogether, an arena for the exhibition of every man's humour,— a mirror, as his greater contemporary, echoing the thought of the old *Ship of Fools*, put it, in which all the world might see the bodily image of its own qualities. And it was in close neighbourhood to the stage that the Brandtian satire of society at large under the scheme of a collection of Fools, was for the first time taken up. The delightful *Jigge*[1] of Tarlton naturally makes no pretension whatever to the seriousness of Brandt. The favourite jester of Elizabeth does not pose as a moral reformer. He rejects even Brandt's suggestive imagery, and instead of summoning his Fools with solemn irony to embark on a mysterious and ill-omened voyage, trots them merrily through Fleet Street in a pony-cart to be exhibited in a puppet-show[2]:

Tarlton: A Horse-load of Fools.

> Ime an excellent workeman, and these are my tooles ;
> Is not this a fine merrie familie?

[1] 'A Horse-load of Fools,' printed from Collier's MS. by Mr Halliwell in *Tarlton's Jests* (Shakspeare Soc.), p. xx. f.

[2] It would be tempting to find the origin of this figure in

One by one the Fools are displayed; first Tarlton himself, as the 'player fool,' and the 'converted player' Gosson, as the 'Puritan fool;' then a series of typical figures,—the Fool of State, who 'being born verie little would faine be verie great;' the poet-fool, starving and pastoral-writing; the physician-fool, 'who killeth us all I weene with such skille and arte......he makes dying quite a pleasure;' the lover-fool, 'with ragged hair and band untied;' the citizen-fool, that 'hates all kindes of wisdome, but most of all in playes;' the country-fool, anxious to be made a gentleman,—with many other fools not specially described,—'lawyer fooles, Sir John fooles, fooles of the court,—a large and loving familie.' 'But *noverint universi*,' he concludes, 'good neighbours I have done; you have seen my horse load of fooles.'

Such was the pleasant use to which the best of Elizabethan jesters put the conception of the austere doctor of Strassburg. The buoyant humour with which the genus Fool is distributed into species, each attached to a particular calling, is only a heightened reflexion of the grim irony of the *Ship of Fools*. No doubt Tarlton confined himself to professional types, and those for the most part unknown to Brandt; but a *Jigge* was not the occasion for moral satire, and it was only in so far as it was a satire of manners that he could in any sort adopt or imitate the *Ship of Fools*.

Brandt's first woodcut (preceding the prologue), where a cart loaded with fools is drawn by a pair of horses tandem, the leader being however only visible on a close inspection. But precisely this woodcut was omitted by Locher, and naturally by Barclay also; and that Tarlton had seen the original is not to be assumed. His neologisms 'Player-fool,' 'courtier-fool,' &c., are also a curious parallel to Brandt's *Büchernarr* and the like, which nothing in Barclay could well suggest.

Exactly the opposite method was followed, twenty R. Armin:
years later, by Tarlton's 'adopted son,' Robert Armin. *'Nest of Ninnies,'*
The well-known *Nest of Ninnies* is one of the earliest 1608.
illustrations of the combination of two distinct literary
genres which in the first half of the seventeenth century
were often blended,—the jesting anecdote and the satirical *character*. Its substance is a string of anecdotes
about six well-known court-fools of recent history, which
he had published three years earlier independently under
the title of *Foole upon Foole*. In so far, it belonged to
the class of jest-books devoted specially to the sayings
of professional 'fools,' combining the plan of connected
histories of a single Fool, like the Jests of Skelton,
Scogin, or Tarlton, or the German *Claus Narr* (the
Duke of Saxony's Fool), and *Clawert*, with histories of
a series of 'Fools,' such as the slightly earlier *Jack of
Dover*[1]. This somewhat crude and unpretending collection of anecdotes Armin now provided with an ambitious allegorical framework, in which the feats of the
six simpletons and buffoons are laboriously made to
symbolise as many human failings. The World, 'wanton
sick as one surfetting on sinne,' is shown the images

---

[1] I see that Dr Grosart has also made this comparison, *Works of
Armin*, p. xi. At the same time the fools whom Jack of Dover
reviews in his quest for the 'Foole of all Fooles,' are rarely professional, like Armin's; most frequently they are either the local
'character' or the local prodigy,—'a certain simple fellow......that
could not well remember his owne name yet would many times
give......good admonitions,' or 'a plaine country farmer, but none of
the wisest,' or the 'marvellous boy' of Windsor; but in many cases
the stories merely relate casual witticisms, and are indistinguishable
from those, for instance, of the *C. Mery Tales*. Thus the 'Foole
of Lincoln' is an adaptation of Socrates and Xantippe, and the
'Foole of Northampton's jest might be that of 'any husband with
any wife.' *Jack of Dover* is reprinted in Percy Soc. vol. 7.

of the fools in the 'prospective glass' of the cynic
Sotto, who briefly moralises them in turn.   Thus the
wasteful fool Jack Oates is found to represent the
prodigals, the 'fat fool' Camber, the wanton and gluttonous, the 'lean' and envious 'Leanard,' the grasping
landlords, and the 'mirth without mischiefe' of Will
Sommers is made by a violent effort of cynicism to stand
for 'saucie adventure in follie.'   The 'clean fool' is
ingeniously interpreted of the sort of people who fall
into the ditch in their anxiety to avoid the mire, and the
last, 'the Very Foole,' of the worldly religious, 'who
come to church to meet acquaintance more than for
piety.'

The *Nest of Ninnies* was thus a somewhat clumsy[1]
attempt to turn a book of personal anecdotes into a uni
versal satire on the age.   'Stultorum plena sunt omnia,'
he wrote on the title-page, thus voluntarily associating
his book with the older Fool-literature, rapidly passing
into oblivion, of which this was the fundamental maxim[2].
And there was some ground for the association.   The starting-point of Fool-literature was also the court-fool, and the
existence of this ludicrous and universally familiar sy-
nonym for folly was the source of most of its success
and not a little of its piquancy.   To that starting-point,
still recalled as it was by the wood-cuts of the *Ship of
Fools* if not by its text, Armin returned, when he

[1] Necessarily clumsy, because the six court-fools were originally
chosen for so wholly different a purpose.   For moral allegory Oates
and Camber were too much alike, while Sommers is drawn with an
undisguised partiality which proved awkward when he had to pass
for a type of folly.

[2] A little later (1609) Decker prefixed the same motto to a work
which as we shall see in the next chapter was also, by a somewhat
longer route, descended from the *Narrenschiff*,—the *Gul's Horn-
booke.*

derived his satire of contemporary folly from the history of the contemporary court-fool. No doubt it was not in his case a felicitous idea; the intractable realism of his subject maimed and harassed his satire, where Brandt's only gained effect from the motley and bells which his *Narren* alone retained of the fools of history.

The epoch of almost unparalleled fertility in satire, *Later* which may be said to open with the *Nest of Ninnies*, *Satirists.* could still find a relish in motives more or less kindred to his, but the *Ship of Fools*, still faintly discernible there, sinks definitely below the horizon. Samuel Rowlands, the prolific and genial ' Martin Marke-all ' of Jonson and Decker's London, could still amuse the fashionable world with endless literary processions of Knaves and Fools, in which satire, anecdote, fable and epigram, were heaped in confusion together[1]; and it is easy to detect, say in his 'Sixteen Knaves, marching in order[2],' and cleverly tricked out with humorous and highly-coloured detail, the apotheosis of the ' Quartern ' of the honest bookseller of sixty years ago. But we have in fact moved into a new phase; the old form and method linger, but their work is done. They had furnished a mould in which the early efforts of social satire slowly took shape. New influences and better models were now at hand, and the old were gradually disused. Above all we must count two forces; that of the drama, which tended by its intrinsic variety of type to make the old plan of a *row* of 'knaves' or 'fools' hopelessly insipid; and that of Theophrastus' Characters, newly edited by Casaubon,

---

[1] For example, the collection called *A Fooles bolt is some shot*, contains stories headed 'A flattering Fooles bolt,' 'A shifter's bolt,' 'A clownes bolt,' 'A Spaniard's Foolish bolt,' 'A Merry Fooles bolt,' &c.

[2] In the *Knave of Harts*, 1609.

which showed how this variety might be indefinitely increased by patient study of character, and drew satire into the subtle psychological way, from which the old formal classifications were as much beyond recovery as the Seven Deadly Sins, or the Fifteen Signs of Doom[1].

[1] Another result, which it would be interesting to work out at length, was the transition from the satirical to the purely analytical disposition which is obvious from the first in these English Theophrastians. They try to appeal to admiration as well as to contempt. Hall, the earliest, has his picture of 'A good magistrate,' Overbury his 'Good Woman,' 'a Wise Man,' 'a Noble Spirit,' &c., Breton his 'good,' 'wise,' 'honest' men, Earle his 'grave divine' and his exquisite if slightly unreal picture of 'a child.' So, the astounding prodigals and gluttons, &c., who consult the *Man in the Moone* are followed by an equally astounding 'Virgin.' Breton's title-page 'where the Best may see their Graces, and the Worst discerne their Basenesse' almost literally echoes Hamlet's well-known prescription for the stage.

CHAPTER VII.

GROBIANUS AND GROBIANISM.

AMONG the various satiric currents which were excited
by the passage of the 'Ship of Fools,' the most remarkable and lasting by far remains to be mentioned. Murner's Gilds of Fools and Assemblies of Gowks, vivid as
they were, were not remembered beyond the century, the
Ship of the *Bundschuh* lost its significance with the social
crisis which brought it forth. But the 'order of Grobians'
or 'School of Slovens,'—a mere parenthetic sarcasm of
Brandt's in the midst of his abuse of the *Grobe Leute*,
ripened in the hands of two gifted successors, a young
student at Wittenberg and a schoolmaster at Worms,
into a satiric creation the point of which was not blunted
a hundred and eighty years after, and which found eager
imitators in the London of Jonson and the Oxford of
Selden. As a pregnant type of sixteenth-century Germany its hero stands beside Faustus[1]. What Faustus is
to its intellect, Grobianus is to its manners. As Faustus
stands for the Titanic aspiration of Humanism which
repudiates divine law for the sake of infinite power, so
Grobianus represents the meaner presumption which
defies every precept of civil decorum and suave usage in
the name of appetite and indolence. 'Faustus' is a

---

[1] Scherer in *Allg. D. Biog.* : 'Dedekind.'

tragedy of the scholar's chamber, of the magician's cell;
'Grobianus' is the drastic comedy of back-parlour sym-
posia where unseemly manners hob-nobbed with gross
living and with foul dress.

For such satire German town life offered material of
extraordinary variety as well as amount. The 'new
saint' whom Brandt by a careless stroke had brought
into existence, had his busy votaries everywhere and in
almost all ranks of society. The taunts which refined
Europe directed against the gross and drunken being
whom it assumed to typify the country of Goethe, were
the commonest of international amenities. Erasmus,
who could be severe upon the filthiness of the English
streets, upon the house floors with their twenty-year old
carpeting of indescribable abominations[1], mourned the
change from the obsequious hospitality of an English inn
to the rough fashions of its German counterpart[2]. 'Porco
tedesco,' 'inebriaco,' 'Thudesque yvrongne[3],' 'Come-
dones,' 'Bibones,'—were phrases as familiar as the later
'drunken Dutchman,' 'butter-box,' &c., of the English
stage. In Germany itself these taunts were industriously
turned to account by satirist and reformer. 'We must
indeed be well-pleased,' wrote Kaspar Scheidt, 'with these
aristocratic and courtly titles of ours, since we hold so
fast to that which procured them for us[4]'.

But Grobianism was not to be so lightly put to shame.
It was not merely the blundering improprieties of ill-breeding, but an aggressive and militant grossness, trampling on

[1] Erasmus, Epp. 432, C.
[2] Id. Colloquia: *Deversoria.*
[3] Du Bellay's sonnet (No. 68 of the *Regrets*).
[4] Letter to Dedekind prefixed to his translation of the *Grobianus*
(1551). Cf. the chapter: 'Germanis Ebrietas ab Italis objicitur' in
the *De generibus Ebriosorum* (1515), and Hutten's *Inspicientes.*

refinement, and glorifying its own excesses,—not ἀγροικία, but βδελυρία and ἀναισχυντία,—which the satirist had to meet; and he attacked it with every variety of resource. Here it was a plain speaking 'elegy' on drunkenness[1]; there a polemical dialogue, where, in all seriousness, Bacchus and Silenus defend the art of drinking from the attacks of a temperate Pittacus[2]; or a romance where the ruin of a gross-living prodigal is held up as a warning to gross-livers in general[3]; or a drama where, still more solemnly, the typical German reveller is startled in the midst of his excesses, like the heroes of *Everyman* and *Hecastus*, by the summons of Death[4]. But far oftener the satire was ironical. And here it fell in with a fashion which found extraordinary favour with Humanists, small and great, from Erasmus and Scaliger and Heinsius and Pirckheimer to Martin Schook and Conrad Goddaeus,— the fashion of burlesque *encomia*. Often no doubt these were little more than *jeux d'esprit*; but satire insinuated itself in details if it was excluded from the general intention, and it is hard to draw an absolute line between harmless laudations of Smoke and Shadow, Blindness and Deafness, Gout and Ague[5], and the scathing satires in which

[1] N. Frischlin's *Elegia in ebrietatem.*

[2] Leonhart Schertlin: *Künstlich trincken;...den dollen, vollen weinsäuffern und Bachi dienern wird für die augen gstelt, der gross mercklich, erschröcklich, onaussprechlich schad...so aus dem... vihischen...volsauffen herkumpt.* Strassburg, 1538.

[3] Wickram's *Junger Knaben Spiegel.* Wickram also translated the *De arte bibendi.*

[4] Stricerius: *De düdesche Schlömer,...ein geistlick Spil,* &c., Lübeck, 1584.

[5] Schook's *Encomium Fumi,* Dousa's *E. umbrae*; Guther's *E. caecitatis,* Schook's *E. surditatis,* Menapius' *E. febris quartanae,* Pirckheimer's *Laus Podagrae,* the last an often repeated subject. A useful collection of nearly the whole of this curious literature is the Nymwegen *Pallas,* 1666.

Bebel 'praised' Venus and Erasmus eulogised Folly.   It
was a fashion easily adopted, and before the century was
over the learned world was deluged with the sonorous
praise not merely of negations or vacuities such as these,
but of ridiculous or loathsome things, asses, owls, geese,
vermin and dung.   No modern literature has showed
so keen and unaffected a relish for the comic qualities of
the disgusting.   Greek and Italian had found heroes for
their burlesque epics in the denizens of the warm
summer air; the typical German humourist selected them
from an old mattress.   It was reserved for Fischart in
modern literature to 'create' the flea, in the extraordinary work which celebrates its 'eternal war with
women.'

Both these current qualities of German satire, the
love of irony, and the humorous relish for foul things,
help to explain the course assumed by the special satire
of Grobianism.   Towards the end of the fifteenth century it struck a vein which in its precise form had never
been worked before,—the *inverted precept*, a code of
rules framed upon the principle of Hamlet's answer to
his mother : 'What shall I do?'—'*Not this by no means
that I bid you do.*'   To the plain man, Ovid's 'art of gal-
lantry' had all the air of such a code, and Obsopoeus'
'art of drinking' suggested the same by its title, though
the one was a perfectly serious exposition, and the other
an equally serious exposure.   The new Cato on the other
hand was an ironical re-writing of the most famous of
mediaeval prescriptions of etiquette, the Catonian coup-
lets in which 'a master teaches his son[1].'

---

[1] Hans Krug's ironical '*Wie der meister seinen sun lert*' is
printed in Zarncke's *Cato*, p. 144 f.   It deals chiefly with bad
manners in church (Vv. 50—71) and in the tavern (72—143).

A few years later appeared the *Narrenschiff*, with its
notable chapter on the *Grobe Narren*. The 'new Saint'
was speedily installed among the standing figures of
satire. Grobian became the Cato of inverted etiquette[1].
A slight and obvious improvement on this hint gathered
round him the society in which the inverted etiquette
was to be observed, made him, in short, the eponymous
founder of a polity of gross livers.

This combination was first made in the little tract of *Grobianus'*
seven pages called 'Grobianus' Tischzucht[2].' It consists *Tisch-*
of sixteen articles for the regulation of 'a new brother- 1538.
hood,' or 'order of swine,' with Grobianus as 'abbot' at
its head, and open to every sincere repudiator of good
manners, virtue and honesty. The obedient Brother is
required, for instance, to go out to dine where he is not
bidden, after carefully inquiring where the best dinner is
to be had; boldly to take the best seat at the table; to
dip first into the dish and secure the best portion at all
hazards; not to put down his last glass except under the
three conditions, that his eyes run, that his breath is
short, and his glass is empty[3]. When the meal is over
he is to sleep an hour, then to rush out and riot in
the streets. For the rest, it is concluded, the discipline
of the Order may be learnt without teaching; but the
timid novice may consult the Abbot, or his subordi-
nates—Doctors Full-man, Wine-love, Spithardus, &c.,
who will teach him effectually 'how never to come to

---

[1] Sachs wrote a '*verkehrte Tischzucht Grobiani*,' which is quoted
in full in Zarncke's *Narrenschiff*, Einl.

[2] *Grobianus' Tischzucht bin ich genant, Den Brüdern im Sew-
orden wolbekant.* [Von W. S.] Wilkefüge, 1538. It is dated
ominously at 1 A.M., on the Carneval night, 'so Dhoren und Gecken
gemeiniglich yhr grösstes Regiment halten.'

[3] So Dedekind, *Grobianus*, Bk. II. ch. 3.

honour, but to lie all his days with the sow upon the dung-hill, to suffer shame, poverty and contempt, and miserably die,—and may God the Lord,' adds the writer, his serious purpose suddenly breaking through his ironical mask, 'punish such and more sins Here, and spare them There. Amen.'

This *jeu d'esprit* is chiefly remarkable as a precursor of the more famous book of Dedekind. Its humour lies in the grave and legal precision with which, like the author of the famous *Quodlibets* of the previous generation, it tabulates indecencies and classifies improprieties. Its dry and formal irony nowhere expands into dramatic life, nowhere recalls, for instance, the vivid pictures of society in which Swift, the great master of this literary *genre*, sarcastically taught his contemporaries how *not* to speak[1].

F. Dedekind : *Grobianus*, 1549.

Far inferior in this respect to Swift was likewise, no doubt, the imposing structure which, eleven years after the *Tischzucht*, Frederick Dedekind reared on its foundation. Yet it was crowded with suggestive material, which at more than one point needs only to be released from the formal outlines imposed by the plan to become the literary equivalent of Hogarth or Jan Steen. It carries us through all the stages of the Grobian's day ; his midday rising, his simple toilette ;—the hands and face scrupulously unwashed, the hair uncut, 'for so they wore it in the golden age[2].' And so we pass rapidly to the central institution of Grobianism,—the table, every phase and vicissitude of which is exhaustively reviewed. The very servant who waits has two chapters of instruction,

---

[1] Swift: *A Complete Collection of Genteel and ingenious conversation, according to the most polite mode and method, now used at Court and in the best companies of England.*

[2] Book I. ch. I.

in which he learns how to appear in rags, to catch flies
when he should be handing dishes, to spill all he carries,
and devour all he can get, and defy soap and water[1].
But it is the guests and their host on whom the keenest
and most constant satire is focussed.   When invited
out, for instance, the true Grobian is to take every
precaution against an unsatisfactory dinner.   Before
giving his consent, he demands a list of the dishes
and a programme of the music, makes sure that the
pies will be excellent and the ladies fair, and, when
quite satisfied on these heads, says 'well, I will come.'
When the day arrives, he takes a copy of the bill of
fare with him; he is then able to check the dishes as
they appear, to make his choice before they are un-
covered, and above all to secure that none is kept
back.   If this should happen, he is still equal to the
occasion, and, storming and fuming at the treachery
of his host, commands that the defaulter be instantly
fetched in[2].   'We are in no mind to have our dinner
docked of a dish; bring the pasties, bring the cakes!
—Do ye serve your guests with crab-apples?'   Whereat
the host greatly abashed, is fain to go forth and bring
out his whole store himself[3].   If a Grobian, however,
he has his turn.   It is for him to greet any less welcome guest at the outset with the assurance that any
invitation which *he* had received was sent in a drunken
fit and meant nothing[4].   'If the guests are not complete
when the hour for dinner strikes, he takes his seat nevertheless, orders in the dishes, and relegates late-comers to
a trencher of dry bread by the stove, or better still, he
has his gates bolted and barred, and if the guests have to

---

[1] Book I. capp. 3, 8.   [3] ib. Scheidt only.
[2] Bk. II. cap. I.   [4] Bk. II. cap. 9.

go empty away it will not hurt his wine. Even if they
are punctual, he is by no means to bid them welcome,
but to talk loudly of his expensive dishes,—'a splendid
eel, but it cost me dear,'—and what stores of spice,
saffron and sugar have been used and lavished on them,
and how his wife has cooked them in her own incomparable way[1].

C. Scheidt: Dedekind is one of the half-dozen figures in literature
Grobianus,   who have been outshone by their translators, and one of
1551[2].   the two or three who have been unaffectedly grateful for
it. Kaspar Scheidt, a scholar of high talent at Worms,
hailed the Latin Grobianus with delight, and after pro-
ducing a German version, teeming with new additions,
mostly admirable, of his own, dedicated it to the young
student in a letter of enthusiastic admiration, which
might have disarmed a more captious vanity than Dedekind's. 'For even as musicians, he writes, do oft times
interpose a flourish of their own in the score set down
for them, yet alway fall again into the measure, so have
I touched nothing of your meaning and intention.' A
year later Dedekind published an enlarged second edition
of his own book, in which, like Schiller in a parallel
case, he adopted a large number of his translator's suggestions.

By far the most important of Scheidt's contributions
is a prologue, which serves both as introduction and as
setting to the mock-code. 'Master Grobianus,' a 'cunning
carver of spoons and bearer of blocks' is, in other words,
the master of a Grobian school. But the labour of

---

[1] Bk. II. cap. 9. I adopt here the more graphic version of
Scheidt.

[2] *Grobianus, Von groben sitten und unhöflichen geberden,...*
Worms. The capital edition with introduction, by G. Milchsack,
among Niemayer's *Neudrücke* has been of great use.

teaching has told upon his advancing years; he has no heir; and as Grobians mostly pass betimes out of this Vale of Boors (*Grobenthal*), the art which he professes 'of unseemly, riotous and filthy behaviour' is in danger of being utterly lost. He appeals for aid to his patrons Bacchus and Ceres, and finally, on the advice of his 'tender and virtuous housewife Grobiana, chosen mistress of sluts and slatterns,' resolves to obviate that calamity by compiling a systematic treatise on it. Dedekind's code naturally follows. Scheidt thus added two figures to literature, the one hinted, but only hinted before, the other wholly new. The 'Saint' Grobianus was a name, the 'abbot' was a shadow; but the 'schoolmaster' (who alone of the three, speaks in person), is a living character, with his airs of tenderness for his 'grobe kindlin,' his ejaculations of Grobian piety, his apprehensions of premature dismissal by the 'slut Atropos,' his curtain lectures from the amiable housewife. To the author of the *Ship of Fools*, however, Scheidt owed more definite hints than this. Like Brandt he poses as a universal satirist; the world teems with Grobians as with Fools,—'*Grobianorum infinitus est numerus!*' He calls in his scattered recruits to the school, as Brandt in his famous *Clamor* had rallied them to the Ship; and, most characteristic touch of all, he reckons himself among them. Brandt in sober humility had professed to be only the chief of Fools[1]; Scheidt ironically assumes to be not only a Grobian but the 'meanest of the order,'— honoured with permission to serve as 'Porter and Bedell at the gate'[2].

[1] *Narrenschiff*, Prologue *ad fin.*, and cap. 111, 76.

[2] *Grobianus* &c., 'Beschluss,' where Brandt's precedent is referred to.

Such strokes betray Scheidt's evident wish to make the *Grobianus* a rival to the *Narrenschiff* in his own field of slovenry, which he significantly treats, not, like Brandt, as a subdivision of Folly, but as a coordinate genus[1]. And they were adopted, in substance, into the new and final revision of the poem which Dedekind published a year later. The alteration of most importance however for the literary future of the book was a new chapter, suggested by Scheidt's picture of Grobiana, for the regulation of 'Sluts and slatterns.' The female Grobian[2] is however immodest as well as slovenly,—a trait of some moment for her future history;—she not only 'walks the streets with draggled stockings, munching fruit, not greeting acquaintance,' &c., but frequents theatres and taverns, blushes at nothing she hears there, and permits her drunken lover the extremest familiarities as he sits at her side. The rest of the prologue, on the other hand, survived, at most, in a vague suggestion of the 'school' of slovenry,—a suggestion however which, as we shall see, was not allowed to drop. With these, and hundreds of minor additions, the *Grobianus et Grobiana* took its place among the best-read books of that hybrid literature of refined grossness and learned buffoonery which amused the later sixteenth century. The first fifty years saw twenty editions of the original and fifteen of two different translations[3]; and the seventeenth century brought not only eleven more editions of these, but three new translations which went through five

Dedekind: *Grobianus,* [*et Grobiana*] 1552.

[1] Cf. e.g. *Grobianus* II. 7, where the *Narr* and the *Grobian* are compared : 'Ein Narr macht zehen, ein Grobian macht zwanzig.'

[2] Book III. c. 8.

[3] Scheidt's and Valentin Helbach's. The latter, after Scheidt's death in 1567, was called in to translate the revised *Grobianus et Grobiana.*

more[1]. Abroad too its reputation extended. To France Grobianus, like the Kalenberger and Ulenspiegel, contributed a new word[2]. To England it brought, in addition, a new method, and to some extent a new subject, of social satire.

I.

The satire of bad manners was still an essentially, and the satire by ironical precept a wholly, unworked vein when in 1605, the English version of Dedekind gave an example of both[3]. The irony of a religious order of fools or rogues was faded and familiar; but there was still piquancy in the device of a text-book of etiquette for their peculiar use. Brandt's 'Saint Grobian' had indeed already appeared in Barclay, who represents him, in even fuller detail, as the new 'Saint' to whose 'vile temple renneth yonge and olde, men, women, mayden, and with them many a childe, worshipping his festis with theyr langage defylde'; but the idea was not in the manner of English satire, and had remained barren. Awdeley, the first English satirist to deal with manners rather than morals, came near the Grobian type in one or two of his 'knaves,' such as 'Unthrift' the careless and 'Green

[margin: GROBI-ANUS IN ENGLAND. The Gul's Horn-booke.]

---

[1] For the detailed bibliography see Milchsack's edition of Scheidt.

[2] *Grobianisme* occurs, for instance, in Cotgrave (1611),—rendered by 'grobianism, slovenliness, unmannerly parts or beastliness.'

[3] *The Schoole of Slovenrie: Cato turned wrong side outward...* By R. S. Gent. Milchsack (Grobianus p. xxxii) quotes this title with no less than four errors, and transforms the author, 'R. S., Gent.' into 'R. J. Sent.' 'Sents Uebersetzung' of Dedekind may be classified with the works of 'Dr Ebenda.'

Winchard' the slovenly; but of 'Grobianism' either as a word or as a single specific vice he knows nothing. And it cannot be said that fifty years later, what Dedekind meant by Grobianism was a more obvious and natural subject for English satire. The combination of brutal manners and slovenly habits was scarcely normal in the England of James I. *Grobianorum infinitus est numerus* would hardly have summed up the daily observation of a Jonson and a Decker. Whatever might be the case among the poorer classes,—whom it would have been as pointless to ridicule for their bad clothes or rough ways as for their poverty,—the middle and upper classes were not generally liable to the charge which they themselves habitually brought against the countrymen of Dedekind. It was only in sections and fragments that English society adopted Grobianus; and then not so much from any stubborn remnant of unsubdued barbarism as from some whim of fashion or of philosophy, an affectation of courtly *hauteur*, an enthusiasm for Arcadian simplicity. The Grobian with overbearing manners is of irreproachable dress; the ill-dressed Grobian is some 'mere scholar' who despises forms, but who is neither a glutton nor a ribald; the Grobian who offends in all these ways belongs to some brotherhood of *dilettanti* misanthropes sworn to pursue unalloyed nature by eliminating civilisation. The fop, the rusty scholar, the misanthrope, were the most available equivalents, in terms not of English language but of English society, for the exotic and unfamiliar creation of Dedekind; and they were in fact substituted, more or less explicitly, for it in the two remarkable English satires which I proceed to notice.

Decker: *The Gul's Horn-booke*, 1609.   Decker's *Gul's Horn-booke*, the best known and most vivid satire of the popular school which immediately preceded the Theophrastians, was the result of a com-

promise which would be glaringly obvious even if the
author had not candidly pointed it out. The book was
begun, he tells us, long before upon the lines of Dedekind. 'This tree of guls was planted long since; but
not taking root, could never bear till now.... It hath a
relish of Grobianism, and tastes very strongly of it in the
beginning; the reason thereof is, that having translated
many books of that into English verse, and not greatly
liking the subject, I altered the shape, and of a Dutchman fashioned a mere Englishman.' And this English
version of the 'Dutch' Grobian is, purely and simply,
what Earle would have called the 'mere common' Fop,
the empty and frivolous 'Town-gul' with whom the
Grobian shares a certain cynical egoism of manner,
without in the least sharing the subtle, half instinctive
deference to fashion by which it is at once sustained and
balanced. Between the two characters the whole book
fluctuates, awkwardly enough. The opening chapter, as
Decker says, 'tastes very strongly' of the Grobian. The
'saints' whom he appeals to for aid are those of mere
grossness and brutality;—'Sylvanus—father of ancient
customs...and most beastly horse-tricks,' 'Comus, the
clerk of gluttony's kitchen,' and 'homely but harmless
Rusticity,' 'midwife of unmannerliness[1].' The old world
is ironically contrasted with the new, the plain and
homely ways of the Saturnian age, when all men were
Grobians, with the luxurious refinement of London. In
the second and third chapters the Grobian is still prominent; the 'young gallant' is advised, as in Dedekind, to
sleep late, to wear his hair long, and to dress on cold
mornings before the hall-fire *sans gêne*. In the fourth,
however, the portrait begins decisively to change character, and a new subject emerges, of totally unlike habits

[1] *Proœmium.*

and ideas, no regretter of the primitive age 'when all men were 'Grobians,' but the most fanatical devotee of the latest fashion. 'He that would strive to fashion his legs to his silk stockings, and his proud gait to his broad garters, let him whiff down these observations, for if he once get to walk by the book—Paul's may be proud of him.' The fashionable promenade is the subject of a series of regulations. Decker warns his gallant at what hour to walk in the middle aisle, 'wherein the pictures of all the true fashionate and complemental gulls are,' frequently to 'make his tailor attend him there to note the new suits,' ...and to 'greet none unless his hat-band be of newer fashion than yours, and three degrees quainter'; to stay there not above four turns; then to pass to the book-seller's, 'where if you cannot read you can smoke, and inquire who has writ against the divine weed;' to appear again after dinner, but (unlike the true Grobian) in a changed suit, 'then to correct your teeth with some quill or silver instrument,—it skills not whether you have dined or no,'—another trait impossible to the complete candour of Grobianism. In the fifth chapter ('At the ordinary') and the sixth ('At the play'), the common link between the two characters at length comes clearly into view. After riding to the dearest ordinary at the most fashionable hour (11.30), he is above all 'to eat impu-dently, for that is most gentlemanlike; when your knight is upon his stewed mutton, be you presently, though you be but a captain, in the bosom of your goose,' &c. Then at the play, follows the familiar picture, so often drawn, of the loungers on the stage, ostentatiously late in arriv-ing, laughing at the most pathetic moment of a tragedy, trifling over their tobacco, jesting with their neighbours; no doubt the best illustration of Grobianism which the society of Jacobean London afforded.

Wholly different was the Grobianism of Jacobean
Oxford, as it appears, caricatured by a contemporary
Oxford hand, in the MS. drama of *Grobiana's Nuptials.*

II.

This piece, hitherto known chiefly from a brief and *Grobiana's*
contemptuous notice in Dr Nott's edition of the *Gul's* *Nuptials.*
Hornbooke, is nothing more than a one-act interlude. Its
plot is of the slightest. 'Old Grobian' is the head of an
Oxford[1] club of slovens, rusty pedants, and Mohocks,
sworn enemies of good manners, from among whom he
desires to choose a husband for his daughter, Grobiana.
His Prologue gives a graphic description of the composition of the club :—

'I am he that hate manners worse than Timon hated men ; and
what did he hate them for? marry for their foolish, apish, compliments, niceties, lispings, cringes....I'll tell you, fellow Grobians,
what our sport is to-night; you shall see the true shapes of men,
not in the visor and shadow of garbs and postures, but very pure
pate men, such as nature made 'em, such as ne'er swath'd their feet
in stocks, for fear of the grain of their own bodies, whose beards
and hair never impoverish'd the wearers, that banish wisely a
barber as a superfluous member for the commonwealth....Here's
true and honest friendship, no slight god speeds, but a how do you,
so well set on you shall remember the salute a week after. We
doff our heads sooner than our hats, and a nod includes all
ceremony. Our scholars are right too, such as if you did but
see them, you would swear they did look to nothing but their
books, very plodalls of Art, not a leaf turn'd o'er but ye have
his hand he hath read it. Libertines you may judge them by the

[1] This inference, suggested by the locality of the MS, confirmed both by the sketch of 'our Scholars,' quoted below, and
by the evidently local allusion to the game of 'Banbury cockles'
in the 'rules' (Sc. 3).

clothes, and Nazarites by the hair: the gown is like a dun at your
backs which they would shake off.   Then for the matter, no grand
sallets and kickshaws of learning, but the very bruise of divinity....
These are the men old Grobian loves; out of these pickt models of
humanity shall I seek out a son-in-law.[1]'

The occasion is naturally chosen with reference to
the true centre of the Grobian cult—the table.   The
society is met, 'according to our annual custom,' to dine.
Three typical members,—Pamphages, the glutton by
profession, Vanscop, the representative of the 'Dutch'
founders of the order, and Tantoblin, a passed master in
the entire range of Grobian accomplishments,—take the
leading part, appropriately enough, in a plot of which
the incidents are the changing phases of an entertainment, the tragic suspense that of deferred dinner.   Successive scenes introduce us to the before-dinner conversation, in which Pamphages thus records his experiences
by the way :

'I saw a gentleman, handsomely in my conceit, tying up his
torn stockings with a blue point.
Vans.   Did you invite him to dinner?
Pamph.   He told me he would not fail.
Tant.   He shall be welcome.'

to the rules of the society :

'Here Pamphage, read the orders concerning the games that
shall be used among the grobian.
Pamph.   It is edicted that every grobian shall play at Bambery
hot cockles at the four festivals,...
Tant.   Indeed a very useful sport but lately much neglected
to the mollifying of the flesh.

---

[1] The spelling in this and the following extracts is modernised.
They were made some years since, and though I should now prefer
to print them exactly as they stand, I have had no more recent
opportunity of consulting the MS.

Pamph. Every apprentice is tied to leave his business whatso-
ever to go to foot-ball (if any be in the street), or if they hear the
bag-pipes,...'

and, finally, to the dinner itself, with its gross fare and
grosser manners.   'Hands were made before knives'
is the significant apophthegm of a devotee of the more
venerable method.   Grobiana here plays a part little
inferior to that of her namesake in Dedekind, the fre-
quenter of masculine drinking-parties[1].   She shares the
men's manners as well as their company, and is worthily
adjudged at the close to the accomplished Tantoblin.

A piece of work so slight as the *Grobiana's Nuptials*
would hardly deserve notice if it were not one of the
most curious productions of international satire, and also
one of the most direct of the series of literary links which
connect Wittenberg and Oxford.   If Greene borrowed
any traits from the university of Faustus, it was only to
colour the purely English and Oxford story of Bacon;
but the Wittenberg satire of slovenry has supplied the
whole conception of the Oxford satire; *Grobiana's
Nuptials* is entirely due to the *Grobianus.*

Grobiana's Nuptials is nevertheless as distinctly of
Oxford as *Grobianus* is of Wittenberg, and as distinctly
of the seventeenth century as this of the sixteenth.
Its rough unpolished prose may show little literary advance upon Dedekind's fluent elegiacs; but it reflects a
far more advanced society, a more pregnant and stirring
intellectual atmosphere.   It is no accident that Old
Grobian is made at the very outset to associate his creed
with the philosophicaɩ misanthropy of Timon, while the
earlier Grobian was a mere clown, who defied social

---

[1] *Grob. et Grobiana* III. 8, 8 f. :

  Nec tibi displiceant hilares convivia coetus
  Quae celebrant iuvenes quae celebrantque viri, &c.

amenities simply because he found them inconvenient, to the newer variety it is an affectation, an eccentric or fashionable humour.   If he is unpleasant he can give reasons for it.   He dwells on the sincerity of bad manners as well as on their practical utility.   Grobianus, the legislator for the slovens, is a shrewd egoist, who can doubtless defend his unpleasantness, but who only affects to defend it by its ultimate utility to himself.   Old Grobian belongs to a more polished and plausible school.   He can give slovenry an air of morality as well as of prudence. He lays more stress on the insincerity of bad manners than on their impolicy.   His bluntness is a weapon against flatterers, his egoism a protest against hollow obsequiousness.   If he is uncivil it is because, like Timon and Rousseau, he abhors civilisation ; if he will not affect the 'foolish, apish compliments, niceties, lispings, cringes' of mankind, it is in order to present society stripped of its mask,—'the true shapes of men, not in the visor and shaddow of garbes and postures, but verie pure pate men, such as nature made 'em'; 'true and honest friendship' divested of affectation and ceremony; scholarship recalled from pretentious trifling to concern itself with the weightiest of all matters.   The old-style Grobian let his hair grow out of laziness or at most out of regard to the fashion of the golden age ; the new is a social theorist and regards the barber as 'a superfluous member of the commonwealth.'   The old had an unaffected disdain for literature, the new might be a bookish man whom absorbing study had first beguiled into Grobianism, and then supplied with arguments in its defence ; the old was a savage in civilised life, the new had read Montaigne's essay on Cannibals, and defied conventions in the honourable disguise of a worshipper of nature.

Such satire could hardly have attached itself to that
of Grobianism in the Germany of Dedekind.   It could
hardly have arisen except in a society artificial enough
to affect simplicity.   Dedekind addressed himself to a
society too intolerably natural to even affect refinement.
The day of Pastorals and Arcadias was still two generations away.   In England, on the contrary, the sentimental regret for lost simplicity which is at the root of
all Arcadian poetry, was already vigorous thirty years
after Dedekind ; and having, as usual, powerful patrons,
it became also a fashion, and left its mark in the literature of convention, as well as, here and there, in the
cardinal creations of the age.   The language of such
regret, become an intellectual common-place of English
society, was caught up and somewhat happily applied
by the author of *Grobiana's Nuptials;* and the contrast
which Dedekind found in the German society of his day
between the 'respectable' burgher and the wilfully offensive boor, was qualified by the finer contrast of which
English society afforded suggestions, between the de-
votees of social convention and of the 'simplicity of
nature.'

Here for the present the literature of Grobianism
closes.   In the next century, however, Dedekind was a
still unforgotten name. His book, or the German versions
of it, had gone through an unbroken series of editions in
Germany up to 1708. His ironical method suited the
taste of the contemporaries of Pope and Swift.   The
author of the '*Genteel and ingenious Conversation*' can
hardly have been unacquainted with the classic of inverted etiquette ; and to him, as one 'who first Intro-
duc'd into these kingdoms...an *Ironical Manner* of

Writing' was dedicated, some ten years after the appearance of the *Dunciad*, a new translation of the
Grobianus[1]. Thus the most artificial in manner, the
most prosaic in subject, of the German satires of the
16th century, was the last to be forgotten in an age
peculiarly disposed to appreciate these forms of literary
distinction.

But its time was at length come. Some forty years
after the translation of *Grobianus*, polite England was
weeping over the translated *Werther*. The typical German
figure of the later eighteenth century follows hard upon
the last traces of the typical figure of the sixteenth; the
master of callous brutality and phlegmatic ill-breeding
leaves the stage as the classical victim of sentimental
passion enters it. With Grobianus, the old epoch of
literary intercourse with Germany—which the present
volume is an attempt to describe—draws to its lingering
close; Werther is the vehement opening of a new and
profoundly different one, in which the two countries
assume in a measure inverted parts, and Germany, at
length emancipated from the old alternatives of satiric
humour and drastic prose, becomes for England, slowly
groping towards the renewal of her old imaginative
glories, the herald of the poetic Romanticism of the
nineteenth century.

[1] Grobianus, or the Compleat Booby. An Ironical Poem...
Done into English by Roger Bull, Esq. London, 1739.

APPENDIX I.

The Date of Coverdale's Hymns.

It seemed best to reserve for an Appendix the question of the date of Coverdale's books. The only existing copy has no indication of either place or date ; and the earliest definite notice of it occurs in the 1546 list of prohibited books[1]. It was evidently written at a time when Coverdale had access to a considerable amount of German hymnal literature ; and we may assume therefore that it belongs to one of his two earlier exiles in Germany,—viz. that from 1529—1535, when he was at work upon his translation of the Bible, probably at Zurich[2] ; or the later and better known years 1540—48, when he lived as pastor of the church at Bergzabern.

Dr Mitchell, who has discussed this question apropos of the similar work of his countryman, John Wedderburn, which was certainly produced between 1540 and 1546, decides for the later, and even urges that Wedderburn's book preceded Coverdale's, and that four hymns, almost identical in the two, were adapted from his by Coverdale.

For the earlier period is the fact already stated that the whole of his originals were published by 1531. The latest hymn that, in my opinion, he can be shown to have used, is Johann Agricola's 'Ich ruff zu dir' (*Geistliche Lieder*, Er-

---

[1] In the first edition of Foxe it was inserted in the previous list of 1539; but all subsequent editions struck it out, and Townsend testifies its absence in Bonner's Registers.

[2] On this period cf. Dr Ginsburg in Kitto's *Dict. of the Bible*, art. 'Coverdale.'

furt, 1531). The production of the years which followed, only less vigorous than that of the previous years, is wholly neglected.   Luther himself, it is true, wrote little after 1530, but among his later hymns are two of such importance as the 'Vom himel hoch da kom ich her' (1535), and his version of the Lord's Prayer ('das deutsche Patrem') 1539. As Coverdale has omitted several of Luther's hymns which must have been known to him, nothing can be inferred from his omission of the child's Christmas hymn ; but it is un-likely that if a Lutheran version of so important a part of the ritual as the Lord's Prayer had lain before him, he would have used inferior versions by obscure writers, like Moibanus and the anonymous poet of Erfurt, when he has carefully adopted Luther's rendering of the Creed and both his ren-derings of the Ten Commandments[1].   It is also remarkable that Coverdale's correspondence during the years 1540—8 with the hymn writer Conrad Huber, who later edited the Strassburg Gesangbuch of 1560, should contain no allusion to the hymns, on which Coverdale must, on the second theory, at that very time have been engaged.

The same conclusion is suggested by a comparison with him of his Scottish rival in this field, Wedderburn. John Wedderburn, Coverdale's junior by some twenty years, probably fled from Scotland in 1540, when Coverdale was already old in exile and hardened in persecution.   His 'Compendius buik of godly and spiritual sangis[2]' is certainly superior in every way to his English rival's ; it is equally certain that it reflects a later epoch of German Hymnology. Luther is represented by his later as well as his earlier work[3], and while he is still the most important contributor, his predominance is much less decided than is Coverdale's.

---

[1] The 'Deutsche Patrem' was subsequently translated, according to Prof. Mitchell, by Coxe.

[2] This was accessible to me only in the edition of 1600 (Edin-burgh).

[3] His *Pater noster* of 1539 is the basis of the third, his 'Vom himel kom ich her' of the twelfth, of Wedderburn's hymns.

The old associates of 1525—30 are reinforced by new writers of 1535—40,—Hermann Bonn, Nicolaus Boie, Georg Gruenewald, Heinrich Witzstadt[1].

Finally, there is the evidence of the four pieces which, as noticed by Prof. Mitchell, are 'almost identical' in the English and the Scottish poet[2]. Prof. Mitchell decides that they belong to his own countryman, on the ground that he was, as everyone admits, the better poet, and that the common versions are, as he thinks, superior to the usual level of Coverdale. There is here no external evidence whatever ; and, with so narrow a field for comparison, internal evidence is almost necessarily inconclusive. The divergences in phrase and even in metre of the two versions are tolerably numerous,—more so than Dr Mitchell's language would suggest ; but they offer little ground for deciding whether it was the capable Wedderburn who deliberately improved upon the plodding Coverdale, or the plodding Coverdale who perversely deviated from the capable Wedderburn. On the other hand, their coincidences offer one or two slight points of vantage. Wedderburn's rapid style has caught up, I think, certain Coverdalisms and Anglicisms, of which Coverdale's version would be the natural source. It would be hard to discover in his undisputed work so genuine an example of the Coverdalian 'tag' as occurs in his version of the Magnificat :

> For he has seen the low degree
> Of mee his hand-maiden *trewlie*—

---

[1] I take these identifications from Prof. Mitchell's book, but have verified them in each case with Wackernagel: N. Boie's '*O Gott wir danken deiner güt*' (Magdeb. 1541, not 1543 as M. says); H. Bonn's '*O wir armen Sünder*' (Magdeb. 1542, not 1543 as M. says); the '*Nun hörend zu ir Christen leut*' of Heinrich Witzstadt (in Magdeb. book of 1541 according to M.); Gruenewald '*Komt her zu mir*' in 'der ganze Psalter' 1537.

[2] These are: (1) The version of the *Magnificat*; (2) Agricola's 'Ich ruff zu dir'; (3) Creuziger's 'Herr Christ der eynig Gotteszohn'; (4) Psalms, 'Deus misereatur nostri.'

where Coverdale's rendering verbally corresponds[1]. And, lastly, we have an instance of the most trustworthy of all kinds of evidence in cases of disputed priority, that of rhymes. The following stanza of the northern poet's *Magnificat*

> And helped his servants ane and all
> Even Israel hee has *promesit,*
> And to our fathers perpetuall
> Abraham and his *seid*—

is easily explained if he had before him Coverdale's version, in a Southern dialect, in which *sede* can rhyme unimpeachably with *promysed.*

---

[1] For similar otiose uses of 'truly' in Coverdale, cf. e.g. his first *Creed* (twice), and second *Creed* (thrice). It is of course, a lineal descendant of the *trewlie* and *verrament* of the rhymed romances.

APPENDIX II.

THE sacred drama of Chilianus Millerstatinus on the *Dorothea* story, which occupies a somewhat obscure place among the beginnings of the modern Latin drama (cf. p. 79 f.), remained, with one exception, wholly unnoticed abroad. It is however associated with the first germs of dramatic art in Denmark, where it was translated by Chr. Hansen the first Dane of whom anything in the shape of drama survives. The translation exists in MS. only, and the work to which I owe my knowledge of it is so little accessible to English readers that a brief extract and paraphrase may not be unwelcome here. I quote from Nyerup's *Bidrag til den danske Digtekunsts Historie* I. p. 147 ff., part of the critical scene in which Dorothea is brought before Fabricius. ' I will make thee my wife,' says the prefect ; 'a great honour for thee!' 'I am plighted to a gentle Bridegroom,' she replies, 'whose glory is over earth and heaven, and I have promised him to be true while I live. I take no other husband, I tell thee on my faith.'—' In that, 'tis clear, thou followest the Christians.'—Dorothea reproaches him with his unbelief in Christ who died for him.—' He was a liar,' retorts Fabricius, ' as any to be found in Judæa.' Dorothea breaks into indignant protest. She is threatened with torture. ' My body ye may torment, but my soul ye cannot harm':

> *Fab.* Jeg vil dig have til min Husfru kjære
> det skal dig blive til mögil [megen] Ære.
> *Dor.* Jeg haver lovet en Brudgom fin,
> Som over Verden og Himmelen skin',

Og lovet hannem Kydskhed at bære,
imedens jeg i Verden mon være.
Jeg lover mig aldrig anden Mand.
Det siger jeg dig paa min sandt.

Fab.   I det du följer christne Klerke,
dermed lader du dig meget mærke.

Dor.   Hvi forsmaar du Jesum Christ,
Gud og Menneske alt for vist.
Han taalde og Pine for dig og mig
paa Korsets Træ, det siger jeg dig.

Fab.   Det var en Lögner og utro Mand
Som han kunde findes i Jödeland.
....

Dor.   Skamme dig din fule Hund,
at tale telige [deslige] med din Mund.

Orest. O du Skjöge, ti nu quær,
för ikke for Herren slig Blær [Larmen].
Vilt du ikke vore Guder ære,
vi ville dig med Kjeppe og Ris lære.

Dor.   Mit Legem kunne I pine og brænde,
min Sjæl kunne I dog intet skjænde.
&c.

It will be seen that style and metre were equally in an elementary condition in Denmark when Hansen applied them to render his not very powerful or stimulating original.

APPENDIX III.

The English Prose Versions of Fortunatus[1].

THE first known versions of the romance of Fortunatus in English fall in the latter half of the seventeenth century. The earliest of known date was printed in London in 1676; and a second, identical, edition of it appeared in 1683. Another version, without date, is placed by the British Museum Catalogue conjecturally in 1650. Both versions, though differing considerably, are ultimately derived from the Frankfurt edition of 1550. The earlier or Augsburg editions, with their ungermanised names and their slightly more copious incident, have had no influence. Nor, on the other hand, has the more recent translation in Dutch. The *Fortunatus* was translated at a time when Dutch was no longer the usual intermediary between English and German. The Dutch version diverges from the Frankfurt editions on which it was ultimately based, (1) in omitting numerous comments on unessential incidents usually at the ends of chapters, (2) in several new woodcuts, (3) in altering various proper names. Thus, the Dutch omits sentences at the ends of chapters II, IV, V, XIV, where the English (1676), like the German, version retains them. Or the Dutch version is simply less verbose, the English as before agreeing

---

[1] Mr Halliwell has briefly discussed these in his *Descriptive notices of English popular Histories*, Percy Society, Vol. 29, but apparently with no knowledge of the originals.

with the German.　Thus the description of Fortunatus' early
success is given thus in the three versions :—

'Nun, wie viel der Fürsten und Herren edler knecht oder
sonst diener, mit ihn auff der Hochzeit gebracht hetten, so was
doch keiner under ihn, des dienst und wesen gemeinlich Frauen
und Mannen basz gefiel den F.'

'Onder hem allen was niemans dienst en manieren den Vrouwen
en Mannen aangenamer dan F.'

'Although there were assembled at the wedding no small number
of proper and comely servitors attending on the chief estates; yet
there was none of them all, whose service and behaviour was more
commended than the service of F.'

The English woodcuts, though fewer and poorer than the
German, most frequently agree with them and differ from
the Dutch.　Cf. e.g. cuts of Lady Fortune giving Fortunatus
the purse (p. 43 of English version) and that of Fortunatus'
escape with the Hat (p. 108).　Lastly, the following divergences in proper names appear decisive.　The town to which
Fortunatus seeks to escape is called in the German (1650)
Lauffen, in the Dutch, *Löwen*.　Only the former can have
produced the English *Lausan*.　The town at which he arrives
on his way to the Purgatory is called *Waldrick*, *Maldric*,
Waldrink respectively ; the town at the Purgatory *Wernicks*,
Vernies and *Vernecks*.　The Dutch names are here from the
French version which has *Maldric* and *Vernieu* for these
two towns.

Of the two English versions that of 1676 is a tolerably
faithful rendering, with a strong religious bias ; that of 1650 (?)
a free and conventional paraphrase by a man of letters and
of the world.　The former qualifies the bold mythology of
the story in the interest of Christian piety, (substituting *e.g.*
God for Fortune as the ruler of the universe) ; the latter
freely curtails it in the interest of enlightened common sense.
'I found much childish and superfluous inventions, he says
in the preface, intermingled also with some sparks of profane superstition (according to the manner of penning used
in that barbarous age) ;... I thought it most convenient, by

rejecting what was unseemly, rather to collect an abstract of the substance thereof in a plain and English phrase, than to have respect to the literal translation.'

A short specimen, from the opening of the chapter in which Fortunatus receives the purse, will illustrate their difference of manner. Here is the 1676 version :—

'As soon as he awaked, he saw standing before him a Fair and Beautiful Woman, muffled over her eyes. Wherefore he praised and thanked God devoutly, that yet he beheld some man-kind before his Death. And to the woman he said, I beseech thee sweet Virgin for the love of God to assist me, that I may come out of the wood, for this is the third day that I have here irksomely wandered without any meat, and herewith declared to her also what had chanced concerning the Bear. Then demanded she of him saying, Of what country art thou, and what moved thee to come hither? He answered I am of the Isle of Cyprus, and poverty hath constrained me to wander, I force not greatly whither, until such time as God (when it pleaseth him) shall provide for me a competent living.'

And this is the version of 1650 (?):—

'Fortunatus, being got out of the city of Orleance took his way towards Paris, when travelling through a huge forest, he on his right hand perceived a beautiful creature in female Habit, sitting under a broad-spreading Beech-tree with a Vail over her Eyes, who as he came near, arose and crossed him in his way, at which he rejoiced not a little, for he had thought there had been nought but Bears and wild Beasts in that place, but looking steadfastly upon her he began to ponder whether she might not be a Fairy or bodily shape composed by delusion. But whilst he was in this doubt, she taking him by the hand, gently asked him whither he was going, upon which he told her, desiring she would accompany him out of the wood.'

INDEX.